D1480889

DISASTER PLANNING AND RECOVERY

DISASTER PLANNING AND RECOVERY

A Guide for Facility Professionals

ALAN M. LEVITT

John Wiley & Sons, Inc.

New York ■ Chichester ■ Weinheim ■ Brisbane ■ Singapore ■ Toronto

This text is printed on acid-free paper.

Library of Congress Cataloging-in-Publication Data:

Levitt, Alan M., 1931–
    Disaster planning and recovery : a guide for facility professionals /
Alan M. Levitt.
        p.   cm.
    ISBN 0-471-14205-0 (cloth : alk. paper)
    1. Crisis management.   2. Emergency management.   3. Risk
management.   4. Facility management.   I. Title.
HD49.L49   1997
658.4'--dc20   96-35914

Printed in the United States of America

10 9 8 7 6 5 4 3 2 1

CONTENTS

v

PREFACE

A "disaster," it is often stated, can bring about the demise of a business. Unfortunately, and unnecessarily, that is too frequently the case. That process of becoming extinct may be immediate upon the impact of the "disaster," or a process lengthy in extent and painful in affect. Statistics and examples illustrative of the inherent causes and results abound, although many of these have mellowed with time. Yet the potential advantages that can derive from *managing* and *planning* techniques to better the ability to survive or endure an out-of-course event remain unexplored by management or, at best, underutilized.

An integrated, comprehensive strategy for disaster planning and recovery is undoubtedly of greater import in assuring the continuance and ultimate survival of any enterprise or organization than any other single factor. A reorganization or re-engineering, a centralization or decentralization, concentration on a core business or diversification, compartmentalization of functions, or the expanded utilization of and reliance upon computing and communication technologies may help the organization prosper and succeed, but none of these will assure its survival. In reality, these management techniques, by their nature and their dependence on increasingly complex technology, serve to broaden the need for a disaster planning and recovery strategy. That there is a lack of an integrated, comprehensive focus on the ability of any enterprise to continue and to recover cries for a remedy.

The need for a proper disaster planning and recovery strategy increases in many ways: as the size and complexity of organizations grow; as their use and reliance upon increasingly elaborate technology expands; as competitiveness increases and profit margins shrink; as the buildings that house the organizations and the civic infrastructure that support them increasingly suffer from neglect and ail because of deferred maintenance; as liabilities and the penalties imposed for neglect or omission or oversight multiply. Yet managements fail to recognize that "disasters" are more than severe weather conditions or earthquakes. Little—if anything—is undertaken to determine where and how the organization is at risk, the degree of risk present, and what can be done to reduce that risk. Much is done to save the computer and the telecommunications network, but efforts to "save the business" remain sorely neglected. To "save the business" must encompass not only the business processes themselves, but with equal importance, must encompass the people associated with organization, and the place where the organization functions. This guide considers the people, the place, and the processes inherent in the organization's creation and delivery of products and services.

When I was asked if I would like to think about writing a guide to creating a strategy for disaster planning and recovery, my personal interest was immediately aroused. I have long felt that many opportunities that can be embraced to increase an organization's chance of survival when impacted by an out-of-course event were omitted or neglected, underutilized, or, at best, misdirected. I have long perceived that the ultimate responsibility for assuring the creation of a disaster planning and recovery strategy was vested in the wrong slots in organization charts. I hold that any organization can best prepare for a "disaster" (read, the *consequences* arising from the *impact* of an *out-of-course event*) by determining the risks present, measuring them, reducing these risks to a level as low as reasonably practicable, and then, devising the necessary means to deal with the unavoidable or uncontrollable so that the organization *can continue* to function and to find the opportunity for *recovery*. The correct balance of these preparatory steps becomes the organization's plan or disaster planning and recovery strategy.

I have, over the years, been in quest of sensible guidance for "disaster planning" that extends beyond the pale of the computer room. I have searched the available literature seeking wisdom and direction in the creation of comprehensive and integrated "disaster planning" for an organization as a dynamic entity engaged in activities above and beyond computing and telecommunicating. I have sought information on means to *address the causes* (and to get rid of them, or at least mollify them!) of things that are unwanted or undesirable, yet that will inevitably occur. This—management of risk—is the keystone or foundation of "disaster planning." Management of risk is pertinent to the *entire* organization, and to *all* its activities. Any consideration of "disaster planning" should be so grounded. Sadly, I have found little to mine with profit. There is a pressing need for proper guidance in the creation of a disaster planning and recovery strategy that will—simply put—*work*! This guide is intended not only to put the situation right and to help save organizations, but more importantly, to help save lives and to avoid casualties.

In addition to this "what can be done?" to help save the organization and to help save lives and avoid casualties, is the question of who is best placed—both within an organization or as an advisor to it—to determine the risks present, to measure them, to reduce them where possible, and to plan compensation for what risk remains. That person is, undoubtedly, the facility professional. Whether the facility professional is an architect, a designer, or an engineer giving counsel to an organization, or a facility professional responsible for the operation of a multitenanted property, or a facility professional within a specific organization, that person undoubtedly has the most appropriate vistas for creating the disaster planning and recovery strategy.

But my enthusiasm was tempered by uncertainty about available materials. Most of the literature is parochial in nature, focusing only on the computer or the telecommunications network. There is much coverage of "disasters" in the press, but emphasis is on "headline grabbers" and "catastrophes." "Disaster" publications focus on high-visibility "natural" disasters; communications and computer "technical" publications focus on "downtime" rather than on maintaining as-intended functioning. Many major "disasters" and their consequences simply do not reach the printed page or television image, purposefully or otherwise omitted. I have tried to present an even spread in coverage; any imbalance reflects the amount and type of material available. Any errors or omissions are entirely mine. Expressions of opinion are personal. Much of that cited relating to risk management reflects the work done by railways. This is not coincidental, for the railways have themselves have devoted substantial resources to risk management from the very first turnings of their wheels in the 1830s, and provide us with many valuable insights and lessons. Railways are not inherently free of risk; their managements and prescriptors strove—and well succeeded—in making themselves that way. Their historical development into the most complex of any type of organization or enterprise evidences that complexity of the business need not be a deterrent to planning. Additionally, the railways' management of risk has been the subject of diverse prescriptives, as well as the objective of the efforts of professional institutes and organizations. When out-of-course events have occurred, these have been subject to deep investigation and analysis by regulatory bodies.[1, 2] All of this has been extremely well-documented and recorded, and fully analyzed and deeply interpreted in the professional literature. This latter fact is important when consid-

---

[1] This can be traced back at least as far as to the establishment of Britain's Board of Trade in the Regulations of Railways Act of 1840 (3 & 4 Vict., cap. 97, sects. 3, 5).

[2] In 1871, a Board of Trade inspecting officer would officially report, "Nothing can more plainly exhibit the entire absence of responsibility that exists on the part of [the] directors, their officers and servants, for the occurrence of preventable disasterous accidents . . . [and] it appears to me that the company's management is wholly to blame."

ering what—if anything at all—other businesses have told us about their "disaster planning." These principles, the lessons taught, and the lessons learned by the railways, can be beneficially studied and adopted by organizations of all types.

This guide is based on my own experiences, and the lessons I have learned through research, practical applications, and from the experiences and expertise of others, over the course of several decades. My firm, Levitt, Conford & Associates, has for well over a decade, assisted numerous organizations in creating integrated, comprehensive strategies for their risk management and disaster survival and recovery. Some of the sections in this guide may be more applicable to your interests and the needs and nature of your organization. You can read—or skim—accordingly. But extract the approach, or an approach, that will enable you to create a disaster planning and recovery strategy that will *work*.

Creating a proper plan is paramount to the survival of your organization; having the plan in place is tantamount to good management. Yet the creation of such a plan and the strategy supporting it is not a simple process, for the organization itself is a complex and dynamic family of relationships and interrelationships, rivalries, dependencies, and diverse and varying goals and objectives, all attempting to operate successfully, using, perhaps, a vast array of belief systems, while competing for scarce resources. Nor is the process of creating your plan—a comprehensive, cost-effective plan that will *work* for your organization—a simple matter. A plan cannot be purchased, prepackaged, off-the-shelf, in the same manner as household remedies or prepared meals. Despite such encumbrances, it is vital that an organization create, install, and continually test, re-evaluate, and update a plan designed to enable survival when the inevitable out-of-course events strike home. *Sun-Beams may be extracted from Cucumbers, but the process is tedious.*[3]

There are many important lessons in this guide, important because the actual survival of the organization may be dependent upon what is learned and what is accomplished based on these lessons. There are important lessons for you, no matter what the extent of your responsibility, the scope of your authority, the breath of your interests, the enormity of the challenges you face, or the character of the facility. The lessons are important, and can be of far-reaching value for the people, the place, and the processes. The lessons are applicable whether you are a facility

---

[3] David Daggett, *An Oration, Pronounced on the Fourth of July, 1799. At the Request of the Citizens of New-Haven [Connecticut]* (New-Haven: Thomas Green and Son, 1799).

professional providing counsel, or a facility professional implementing counsel.

This guide, although addressed by title to facility professionals, is written to assist, benefit, and encourage every person, whether on the staff of an organization or providing counsel to it, in their efforts to create a cost-effective strategy that will to enable the impacts and consequences of out-of-course events to be dealt with efficiently and effectively, so that the normal day-to-day activities can continue, or be restored, with the least possible expenditures of money, time, and effort. Of equal importance in its focus, this guide is written to create an understanding—both on the part of those who are on the staff of an organization, as well as those who provide counsel to the organization—of the importance of creating a cost-effective strategy that may provide a return on investment, minimize the expenditures of money, time, and effort, and reduce exposure to liability. This guide illuminates the path leading to the protection of an organization's vital resources: people, place, and processes.

The question of text references—how many and where—is always perplexing, especially in a book which it is hoped will have both a general and a specialized appeal. I have compromised by restricting references mainly to materials deemed to potential value to planners addressing specific challenges, or who seek parallels between the experiences of others and latent circumstances within their own organizations.

Consider the risks of out-of-course events, of their potential impacts, and of the possible consequences, that your organization faces. Measure them, and—where possible—reduce them as low as reasonably practicable. Compensate for residual effect with contingency and recovery planning. This is risk management or (as some prefer to state) management of risk; it is done with profit.

ΣΗΜΑ ΦΕΡΩ ΤΗΛΑΥΓΕΣ
I bear a far-shining signal

INTRODUCTION

The title of this book, *Disaster Planning and Recovery: A Guide for Facility Professionals*, might also be expressed as *A Guide to Disaster Planning and Recovery*, or *A Guide to Disaster Recovery Assurance*. The purpose of this guide is to provide you—whether you are a "facility professional" or not—with insight into both the principles and precepts inherent in the planning processes, and the goals and objectives of the plan you ultimately create. Disaster planning is about *people*, *place*, and *processes*. These are individually and collectively at-risk to the impact, consequences and affects of any out-of-course event. Not only are there vast potentials to reduce these risks, but there are, additionally, opportunities to reduce both the impacts and their consequences and affects. The planning processes themselves often identify conditions where savings in money, time, and effort can be achieved.

At the outset, just what "disaster planning" is, as well as what "recovery" is, need be defined, as these frequently used terms have numerous—and, sometimes, conflicting—definitions that confront the facility professionals and others concerned with the continued existence and operations of their organizations. In this guide, a "disaster" is not a hurricane or a flood or a terrorist bombing. A *disaster* occurs when the organization cannot function on an as-intended basis. It is a *disaster* when products cannot be produced, or when services to customers or internal users cannot be provided. An organization does not plan to have a disaster! Planning is undertaken to prevent a disaster from occurring when an out-of-course event strikes the organization. "Contingency plans" provide the continuity of operations between the impact of the strike, and the return to as-intended functioning. "Recovery" is not provisions to restart the production of products or provision of services, but the planned activities necessary for repair, rectification, and restoration of the loss, damage, and harm resultant from the impact and its consequences.

I

Thus, the ideal disaster planning results in *not having any disasters*, or in a more practical sense, in *reducing the risk of having a disaster as low as reasonably practicable*.

There are, in the planning process, five inherent steps: First, determine, recognize, and appreciate *all* of the potential out-of-course events that could strike the people, the place, or the processes. It is essential for you to identify and understand *each* of the potential events; the event you fail to consider may well be the organization's undoing. Second, determine the level of risk of those events occurring. Impressions about quantifiable risk are no substitute for measurement. Third, reduce the level of risks as low as is reasonably practicable (ALARP), or to an acceptable level. Here, the investment of money, time, and effort can be—but need not be—excessive. Determining "ALARP" or an "acceptable level" of risk is as significant as the reduction in risk itself. Fourth, ascertain where and how each out-of-course event can impact the people, the place, and the processes, and the consequences of such impacts. The consideration of "when" is as crucial as "where" and a time line must be developed. Finally, fifth, countervailance—establish the means and mechanisms by which the consequences can be counterbalanced in a manner acceptable to the business requirements of the organization, or to the regulatory agencies that govern the organization and its functioning. It might be said that the key to planning is *awareness*.

Whatever your own personal authority, responsibility, or interests—as a facility professional or other staff member—are, there are indispensable contributions that you should provide in each of the five steps.

The focus of this guide is to assist you in planning all the vital considerations essential in enhancing the likelihood of your organization's continuity and survival when impacted by an out-of-course event: planning to prevent disasters, planning to reduce the likelihood of disasters, planning to deal with disasters, and planning to recover after a disaster has affected the organization. *Disasters*, as they will be considered, are not events, but the consequences of events. A disaster results when the as-intended functioning of the organization, or any part of it, is interrupted for a time span that impacts revenue. *Planning* comprises all the actions embarked upon both to (1) study the means that enable the reduction in risk of occurrences, impacts, and consequences; and (2) undertake steps to actually minimize the levels of risks, the impacts, and the consequences. *Planning* also provides for the activities that will be embarked upon to enable to organization to "carry on" during the time span of interruption, as well as to correct, repair, restore, or replace anything that may have been hurt by the impacts or consequences and affects of the impacts. This planning can be termed "managing risk" or "risk management".[1]

Risk can be equated to "probability" or "chance" and, for the most part, can be measured on a quantitative or mathematical scale. *Risk* is not an event or an occurrence; risk is the degree of certainty with which we can predict that a particular event will occur. Determination or measuring of risk is based on experience.[2] It is important to remember that "risk"—although more frequently associated with "bad" events—is also the measurement for "good" or "desirable" events. Throughout this guide it is emphasized that impressions about the quantifiable are no substitute for measurement. Using actual measurements of risk—a process sometimes tedious—rather than impressions about the degree of risk not only serves to conserve valuable resources and assets, but can also be the ultimate deciding factor in whether or not the planning will work when put to the test. In the measurement of risk, it is important to remember that the level of any risk cannot be equal to zero; some level of risk is always present (>0), albeit in certain instances, the level of risk can be extremely low.

Measuring risks and then managing the risks deemed significant is really what disaster planning and recovery—and this guide—is all about.

Disaster planning and recovery is a science and an art. Arguably, it might also be considered an art and a science. Whether you, as a facility professional, place *science* or *art* as the focus of primary importance reflects a number of considerations: your educational training and background; your professional practice; the organization you work for, and its culture; the position you hold, and your responsibilities and authority; and, your own personal beliefs. In addressing the challenges of disaster planning and recovery, it is actually of little consequence whether you personally place *art* or *science* first. The vital factor is to address all the challenges in a comprehensive, fully encompassing manner, providing for each and every type of "problem" the organization might encounter.

In your real world it may not be possible—or practicable—to plan for *all* possible disasters, or for recovery in each and every potential circumstance. What must be considered is the likelihood of each of the potential "problems" occurring, the impact that would be created, and the

---

[1] "Risk management," in some contexts, refers to, or is concerned with, potential legal and insurance liabilities. These specific matters are not addressed in this guide.

[2] As an example, we can project from information available (weather records spanning over a century), with an acceptable level of mathematical certainty, that a particular river will flood its banks by over 15 feet every 7 years. We can also project the likelihoods such as whether 5-foot floods might occur in two consecutive years.

consequences and affects that would touch upon the operations of the organization. These concepts, and the terms used to identify them, will be carefully explained as this guide takes you through the steps and processes of creating a strategy—a plan—for disaster planning and recovery.

The facility professional—and the other professionals and practitioners within an organization who might be called upon to contribute to and support the planning efforts—can encounter, in the literature and in educational sessions, various definitions or meanings ascribed to core words and concepts. At times, the same key words or concepts are given different, often contradictory, meanings within the same publication or session. The appellation "facility professional" itself can be defined in a number of ways. The term "disaster"—core to our considerations—bears a legion of different meanings within the "disaster preparedness" literature, and for the professionals and others endeavoring to aid you in being prepared! To assist you in using this guide, words and concepts inherent to the subject matter will be defined and used throughout on a standardized basis. Definitions of these words, and explanations of concepts, while perhaps at variance with the usage of others, will undoubtedly be acceptable to them. The disaster planning and recovery terminology used in this guide is incorporated in the Glossary. While publishing tradition places the Glossary at the back of a book, it can be valuable to begin your reading there.

This book will not attempt to provide simple solutions or easy answers to the challenges of disaster planning and recovery. The reason itself is quite evident: There are no simple solutions or easy answers to these challenges! This book *will* help you achieve the most effective disaster planning and recovery scheme resources and ingenuity can provide. Defined management solutions for the goals of disaster planning and recovery *do* exist; you, the facility professional, will discover methods through which you can attain these goals, efficiently and cost-effectively. These solutions are referred to in this guide as the plan.

It is frequently said, and said sometimes with a bit of facetiousness, that the purpose of disaster planning is to save the business, not just the computer. In the real world of disaster planning too much—if not all—planning and resources are often focused solely on the computer operations of the organization, and while at that, fail to take desktop and portable computing into account! As a result of this approach, tens of millions, if not hundreds of millions of disaster planning and recovery dollars go down the drain simply because of failure to ask the right question: How do you save the *organization*? The questions about the means to save the computer alone will not lead to saving the organization. This book is concerned with what the facility professional can do to prevent to organization from being placed at-risk or in jeopardy, and, if such unavoidably occurs, to provide the organization with the flexibility and elasticity to be able to bounce back with minimal effect on operational continuity. The organization needs to be prepared to deal with any fault or failure that might occur and result in an interruption of the organization's as-intended functioning. While not a simple process, it is "doable" and "doable" in a practical, cost-effective manner. There are a number of discrete steps in the process; each will be explained and explored.

This book is a facility professional's guide to disaster planning and recovery. It applies to all types of organizations—large, medium-sized, or small—in the private sector or in the public sector. The guidance applies to organization with one, a few, or with many locations. It applies to domestic organizations and to multinational organizations. This guide is a primer for a most vital, and too often neglected, aspect of strategic business planning: establishing a viable plan to assure that the organization has the necessary contingency arrangements in place to enable the desired level of continuity of operations. It is a primer for establishing the continuity plans, as well as launching them when necessary, with minimal expenditures in terms of money, time, and effort.

Disaster planning and recovery is a comprehensive mixture of planning to reflect the unique needs of *each business function* and the requirements for ongoing business operations established by the organization's principal decision makers. Although this might appear complex, the reader should remember that, first, that disaster planning must provide for the needs of the entire organization, not just some business functions which might be "more visible" or perceived as "especially critical"; and, second, such planning is best orchestrated by a person with both the responsibility and authority to coordinate planning among the several business functions, and who is vested with "what it takes" to get it done. In the practical day-to-day business sense, the person who is most appropriately suited—both from an organizational point of view, and from the aspect of their competencies—is the facility professional.

The approach to establishing a comprehensive business strategy for disaster planning and recovery that will be explored can be described as management of risk. The approach, the underlying philosophy, and the operational activities and functions are based on the premise that the organization (1) faces a finite number of definable risks; (2) each of these risks can be measured in terms of likelihood of occurrence; (3) there are substantial opportunities to reduce these inherent levels of risk; (4) the impact of any of the risks, when occurring, on each business function can be determined or predicted before it occurs; and, (5) each risk, and its impact on any business function, can be managed in a manner consistent with the needs of the organization.

The term "management" connotes the ability to establish control through the expenditure of money, time, and effort. To manage risk, there need be an accurate awareness of risks present—the events and happenings that can occur—which can strike the organization. Such events include those natural, those resulting from human intervention, those resulting from use of technology, and those that occur because of events taking place outside the organization itself. "Risk" deals with the relatively likelihood of the event taking place. With rare exception, the risk of an event occurring can be quantified although such quantification might require significant research or calculation. Yet risk must be quantified: Impressions about the quantifiable are no substitute for measurement.[3] (If someone in your insurance department or in your pension department suggests that your newfound concerns about risk management are an incursion upon their "turf," you might allay their fears by noting that the risks with which they deal are rather specialized and narrow [you might wish to say "different"] in context. You will be concerned with risks to people, but in a different sense.)

Management of risk will focus on three areas: the people, the place, and the processes of your organization. The place is the totality of your building or buildings, and adjacent spaces such as parking facilities or picnic areas, lawns or wooded areas—in all, the entire site which "is yours" through ownership, rental, lease, or right-of-access. The people include your staff: all employees, executive, managerial, and support. The people also include those "outsiders" who might be in your place on a routine basis, occasionally, or casually there at the time of any out-of-course event. The "outsiders" include visitors, letter carriers, passersby, service-providers, contractor's staff, and the like.

The processes are your business activities; what your organization does. Your organization may not be a "business" as such; it might be a governmental unit or agency, a not-for-profit organization, or an educational or cultural institution. Thus, processes can be assessment and collection of real estate taxes; processing of requests for aid or grants; an art exhibit; a recital or concert performance; or the testing of student qualifications and recording of performance. The processes will be considered in both a "macro" sense as well as in a "micro" sense.

---

[3] The significance of this phrase in your planning strategy will be underscored by its repetition in several sections of this guide!

As a "business" example, "sales" is a "macro" process which encompasses a number of component processes such as actually selling the product or service, sales performance reporting or catalogue page distribution, and after-sale customer support. Considering process continuity, the organization could easily falter if the "sales" activity was interrupted for three consecutive days; on the other hand, while the sales force can be making sales recorded by order entry on an uninterrupted basis, it may be acceptable to suspend sales performance reporting for four weeks or until the interruption to that activity has ended.

It is not only a question of whether there is danger that the organization might suffer severe financial loss as the result of a disaster, but also a question of the amount or level of risk of loss present. In managing this risk, standards (1) of reliability—the protection against significant business-processing-impacting faults occurring; (2) of availability—the time line response for recovery-to-as-intended functioning of the fault- or failure-impacted business processes; and (3) of maintainability—acceptable cost and adaptability of the plan to changes in people, place, and processes must be established. The aim is simple: to create the means for continuity in the delivery of the organization's products and services at minimum cost consistent with these standards, while obtaining the best value from any necessary investment of capital. The philosophy behind the planning must be based on management of risk to maintain the organization's processes, rather than to restore them after fault or failure. However, *maintaining* is not always possible. Therefore, equally crucial to efforts to *maintain* are the planning and efforts to *restore*. It is the facility professionals who, well-suited and advantageously situated in their organization, are in an ideal capacity to undertake the responsibility for disaster planning and recovery in their organization.

This guide is not made up of technical theories hiding in a jungle of scientific or other mumbo jumbo. Yet the solution to some disaster planning and recovery challenges are best based on the application of scientific principles, rather than on a seat-of-the-pants approach. For this reason, some "technical matters" are introduced into this guide. Explanations of the terms used, as well as the theories applied, will be explained in layperson's terminology, and in the Glossary at the back of this guide.

A number of the examples of disaster planning cited in this guide are theories and practices applied by railways—major mainline companies, commuter railroads, subways and metros, and street car lines. These examples have been chosen for several reasons. Railways have undertaken, since their inception over 150 years ago, concerted, serious efforts to lower the levels of risk of problems—out-of-course events that could harm their people, place, or processes—occurring, and of the impact, consequences and affects of any problem that might occur. It is significant that "The railway is not . . . inherently safe—it is safe because we use our long experience to make it so."[4] (Your organization's people, place, and process are likewise not inherently safe; they can, however, be made safe— or, at least, considerably safer!) Railways are undoubtedly the most complex organizations we have, both in terms of engineering technology and in structure, and have been the subject of risk reduction mandates from regulatory and supervisory agencies, their own managements, and from owning governments and investors. Safety-related prescriptives and mandates were enacted by Parliament as early as 1845 in the Railways Clauses Act, and were also issued by the (U.K.) Railway Clearing House (beginning in 1842), the Board of Trade (beginning in 1844), and by the Railway Inspectorate (1840).[5] Techniques for risk reduction are continually being developed and undertaken, within the railway organizations themselves, by suppliers, and by trade organizations; some of these may be appropriate for your planning. The author has not found any other type of organization that has done, and continues to do, more research and development in the realm of risk, impact, and consequence reduction and mitigation.

As you ponder the possibility of a disaster striking your organization, and its consequences, do not lose sight of the all-important truism of disaster planning: It is not a question of *if* a disaster will strike, but a question of *when* and *where*. It is at that time and in that place that we will be judged; such judgment will be based upon what we have finished— not upon what we have started.

This guide will be of particular relevance to facility professionals, and others, who are involved in the formation and development of a disaster planning and recovery strategy, and those concerned with the needs for continuity in the functioning of an organization's business processes.

This guide is written to enable you to ask the right questions concerning the needs for a disaster planning and recovery strategy; to determine which responses are important and correct; and then, to be able to act in a manner which will result in suitable planning for the organization.

---

[4] "Accidents on B[ritish] R[ail]," *Journal of the Stephenson Locomotive Society,* Vol. 65, No. 737, (May/June 1989), 82.

[5] The nature of the prescriptives to which your organization is subject will be discussed later on.

The prime objective in this guide is to create an environment wherein you can build the proper foundation upon which to consider and to weigh the totality of all of the elements and all the factors inherent in establishing a viable strategy for disaster planning and recovery to support your organization—its people, place, and processes—during times of need. This guide is designed to create a frame of reference for you in which you *think* in terms of levels of risks and *act* in terms of management of these risks. The guide is meant to help you recognize what the right questions are in creating a strategy for disaster planning and recovery, as well as determining the means to obtain the answers to them. This is of far greater importance and value to you than providing a finite list of tasks to be accomplished. *If* you opt to provide for the risk of a rising tide of potential problems it will be because you *recognize and are aware* of that risk, and have *determined* the most appropriate means to deal with it.

This guide is concerned with three components of your organization or enterprise: the people, the place, and the processes. There is a common thread linking this triad, no matter what the organization or enterprise does or conducts. Whether it be an *enterprise* established to manufacture or assemble a product or to render a service as a profit-making venture, or an *organization* providing some service—such as a governmental body or agency or a not-for-profit cultural or educational group— the *problems* and the *risks* that are faced are the identical. In this sense, the strategy for disaster planning and recovery that you evolve is transparent to the nature of the organization. The term "organization" is used in this guide to include both enterprises and organizations.

The concern for the people focuses on *reducing the level of risk* of death or injury that might befall them as the result of an out-of-course event. Concern for the place deals with *reducing the level of risk* that your site, office, space, equipment, and information will not be usable or available to conduct or perform the processes—the various inherent activities which the organization performs—as well as *increasing the level of risk* that alternatives will be available if and when needed.

The guide is not concerned with people from the perspective associated with human resources or personnel activities of an organization, although their morale may be enhanced through their knowledge of the existence of the plan. *Safety*—undertaken to reduce the risk of death or injury in the workplace or from workplace activities—is not a focus, as such, in creating a disaster planning and recovery strategy but is a part of the strategy. Lapses in safety can be revealed, however, in the vulnerability search that is a part of the planning process.

A cautionary bit of advice: Any treatise (or computer disk!) on this subject or on a topic of this nature cannot serve as a "kit" or simple "fill-in-the-blanks" outline that will be, when completed, a plan workable for all organizations under any circumstance. At the end of any attempt to shortcut the planning process lies a vast abyss, filled with a highly probable inherent danger and potential pitfall: The plan is likely not to function at the time and in the manner for which it is intended. In another age, in other terms, it was said that, "A machine, called an *automaton* [which] was, not long since, constructed. This was designed to transport from place to place, by land, any load without the aid of horses, oxen, or any other animal. The master was to sit at helm, and guide it up hill and down, and over every kind of road. This machine was completed, and proved demonstrably capable of performing the duties assigned to it, and the only difficulty which attended it, and which hath hitherto prevented its universal use, was, *that it would not go.*"[6]

In *your* planning, you must take all steps necessary to assure that your plan will *go*, and will be able to carry its load wherever and whenever necessary!

Some disaster planning literature assigns meanings to certain terms that are different from those that are used in this guide. You might have found, in some literature, more than one—often contradictory—definition given for the same term. The facility professional, in harvesting diverse sources, need be wary of such variances. You, and others with whom you will share ideas, may have become accustomed to such at-variance meanings. This can lead both to complications in planning, and to confusion in discussions. Disaster planning and recovery is a science and art; an art and science. It cries for a standardized vocabulary. All concerned with the survival of people, place, and processes would profit from such a standardization.

The Glossary, in addition to providing a more detailed explanation of the language of disaster planning and recovery used in this guide, can also provide the reader with a "frame of reference" for a plan when read as an additional—perhaps preferably the first—chapter of the text.

There are, within the realm of disaster planning and recovery, several specialized, technical areas of focus that this guide addresses only in a general manner. These include:

---

[6] David Daggett, *An Oration, Pronounced on the Fourth of July, 1799. At the Request of the Citizens of New-Haven [Connecticut]* (New-Haven: Thomas Green and Son, 1799).

1. Computer security administration, including communications/network security; computer access control; virus protection; encryption; physical security; and, media protection.
2. Records and archives—both hard copy and magnetic media—management.
3. Health and safety.
4. Premises and building security and protection.
5. Telecommunications systems security—including telephone, facsimile, radio, telex, Teletype—and computer networking (via LANs or WANs, either hard-wired or radio, transmission-based).
6. Unauthorized access, use, copying, or alteration of files, either hard copy or magnetic media.
7. Financial risks and ventures.
8. Legal liability.
9. Insurance.
10. Industrial or business espionage.

Importantly, however, your vulnerability search/vulnerability analysis process may well uncover circumstances where risks to, or impacts or consequences and affects on these can be detected. The opportunities of vulnerability rectification, when taken, will reduce the risk of consequences that might impede, interrupt, or halt the intended functioning of business process cells (BPCs).

This guide presents a disaster planning and recovery philosophy based on management of potential faults and failures to retain the ability to provide the organization's products or services rather than to restore them after a break in continuity.[7]

What can you learn from this book?

First, that you must be concerned, in creating your disaster planning and recovery strategy, not only with the physical place, but—perhaps even more importantly—with the people, and with the processes the people conduct within the place.

Second, how to determine *where* or *in what ways* the people, the place, and the processes under your care face the risks and vulnerabilities of death or injury, of fault or failure, or of damage or destruction.

---

[7] Brian Mellitt, "Value-for-money policies transform engineering procurement," *Railway Gazette International,* May 1995, 275.

Third, how to determine the *level of risk*, or—put another way—the *relative likelihood* of something bad or undesirable occurring.

Fourth, how to *eliminate*, *reduce*, or *compensate* for these risks and vulnerabilities, as well as to *recover* from any occurrences.

You can also gain the vital awareness that for the survival and well-being of the people, place, and processes—the organization—it is of substantially greater importance that you plan to *eliminate*, *reduce*, or *compensate* for the risks and vulnerabilities than to focus solely on *recovery* from impacts, consequences and affects.

Let us all finish a disaster planning and recovery strategy for our organizations, for we will be judged by what we finish, not by what we start.

CHAPTER

1

THE FACILITY PROFESSIONAL

THE PROFESSION AND THE INDIVIDUAL: THEIR ROLES AND OBLIGATIONS IN DISASTER PLANNING AND RECOVERY

The Facility Professional

This book is written for the facility professional. Some who are facility professionals might not deem themselves as "professionals" but rather as "practitioners" in that science and art (or, perhaps, art and science!) of concern for an organization's people, place, and processes. Here we shall consider them collectively as "facility professionals." This book is a guide to disaster planning and recovery for the facility professional. It can be said that *everything* the facility professional is responsible for, or concerned with, is at risk, and that such risks can—with rare exception—be reduced to an acceptable minimum. This book is about all the things a facility professional can do—and *should* do—to reduce the risk that something will either impede the organization's ability to function, or completely prevent the organization from functioning at all. The facility professional needs to know what a "disaster" is; conversely, what a "disaster" is not; what causes a disaster to occur; how to identify causes that could impact the facility with which he or she is concerned; how to reduce the likelihood that any cause will be manifest; how—when the cause occurs—to reduce its impact, and the consequences and the affects of the impact; and, how to effectively and efficiently recover from the consequences and affects of that disaster. That's what this guide is all about!

The benefits the facility professionals can bring to their employers or clients through disaster planning and recovery are enormous. As a facility professional, you can reduce casualties, both injuries and deaths, that may occur as the result of an impact or its consequences. You can save the organization money, time, and effort. You can provide cost avoidances, and other "soft" benefits. You can, ultimately, save or help preserve the very existence of the organization. But these advances require understanding, dedication, and experience. A partnership is needed: between you, as a facility professional—a planner and/or a designer and/or a manager—and the organization for which you are planning, designing, or managing. It must be also a partnership embracing science and art, or as some might say with equal validity, between art and science. It will embrace technological expertise. It will require design, planning, installation, and testing. It will require after-installation review and updating. Effective and successful solutions to the challenges of disaster planning and recovery require allocation of resources and expertise. That, too, is what this guide is all about!

The Facility Professional: The Person

We need first examine who are "facility professionals." You might actually be a "facility professional" without that term appearing in your title or in your job description. You might actually be a "facility professional" without recognizing it! You may have the duties, responsibilities, or obligations that categorize you as a "facility professional" yet not realize that distinction or be recognized for it. The International Society of Facilities Executives (ISFE),[1] founded by the Massachusetts Institute of Technology, defines its "professional" membership to include those with direct or oversight responsibility for the architectural, engineering, or construction management of a facility; the asset-related administrative services; environmental, health, or safety compliance; property or building management; real estate; and, space accounting, allocation, or planning.

There are two distinct, separate groups of facility professionals: those who plan and design the facility to "house" an organization or organizations and their activities, and those who—on behalf of the organization—manage and operate the facility, or the activities that are conducted within the facility. There is also, arguably, a third group of facility professionals: those persons who administer, on a contractual basis, the performance of certain of the organization's functions that have been "outsourced."

Facility professionals are concerned with people, place, and processes. We can define "place" as the facility where an organization's

---

[1] International Society of Facilities Executives, 336 Main Street, Room E28-100, Cambridge, Mass. 02142-1014.

activities—its processes—are conducted by the organization's "people." "Organization" can be defined as the business, service-provider, governmental unit, or enterprise that occupies or uses the facility, and "processes" are the sum-total of all activities that the organization engages in order to create its product or to provide its service, and/or to make a profit. People, place, and process will be discussed in greater detail, further on.

Architects, designers, engineers (who may practice in civil, construction, mechanical, structural, electrical, or other disciplines), planners, and all those others who create the place are facility professionals and have a distinct and extremely critical role in disaster preparedness and recovery. These facility professionals may be independent of the organization or might be on the organization's staff. The architects and engineers who plan and design the place or the new interior for it are most likely are practitioners independent of the organization. Those who plan the seemingly never-ending changes to the layout of space, telecommunications and computing wiring and terminals, or landscaping are often on the organization's staff. The usual focus of this latter group of facility professionals is on the place—the site and building where particular activities take place. These professionals have a statutory duty to create a safe place in which the people perform the organization's processes. This "statutory duty" takes the form of local laws, ordinances, codes, prescriptives, and mandates. In addition, there are professional "practices and procedures" and "standards" established by professional organizations, to guide the facility professional in the design processes. Too often, the planning professionals do not look beyond their own patch of interest for solutions. These professionals have a responsibility—to their clients, to the clients' customers, and to their clients' employees—to go beyond the "statutory duty" and to carry out a risk assessment program covering all aspects of their work—and the nature and level of risk of consequences and affects of the work should something go amiss—to assure that all risks have been reduced to a level at least as low as is reasonably practicable (ALARP; more about this concept later on).

It is not sufficient for the "outside" professional to consider the risks to the place alone. The "outside" professionals also have an obligation and a responsibility to go beyond the place, as well as to go beyond the prescriptives, in their planning. Unfortunately, the potential risk-reduction role of these "outside" facility professions—as well as their obligation and responsibility—in contributing to the organization's disaster planning and recovery strategy is very often neglected or completely overlooked. They may consider the risks, but not reduce them to a level as low as reasonably practicable. To cite an example, in a place that was acclaimed for its architectural design and innovation, only limited over-head clearance was provided in vehicleways. When a fire broke out, firefighting equipment could not gain access to all (in the event, the necessary) parts of the site, and proper firefighting platforms could not be established. All the prescriptives had been complied with, but the prescriptives had not taken the design innovations into account!

The processes that occur in the place, and the people who conduct those processes, are sometimes not given proper consideration in terms of potential out-of-course events, or problems, that can occur. There need be an ongoing "disaster planning and recovery dialogue" between the "outside" facility professionals and the "insiders" to assure proper groundwork for minimizing risks has been established before mortar is committed to the bricks or before the cement dries.

The "outside" professional, in exploring this guide, should occasionally pause and glance over his or her shoulder to consider the disaster planning and recovery strategy (or lack of it!) within his or her own practice or firm. Although the cobbler's child often treks shoeless, it is as important to work in an environment that has a proper strategy as it is to contribute to a strategy for the client. The principles and precepts in this guide are as applicable to *your* people, place, and processes as they are to those of your client.

The second category of facility professional encompasses those—usually on the organization's own staff—who are responsible for specific functions and support services. These often include vital activities such as real estate, property or building management; space planning, outfitting, and accounting; mail and messenger services; building and site maintenance and cleaning; forms and records management; copying, printing, and reprographics; computing services; telecommunications; safety and security; travel planning; and other support services. These facility professionals might either be responsible for a specific function or functions, or oversee a group of them. These professionals might also be responsible for overall performance of some or all contracted or outsourced services. These "in-house" facility professions are responsible for implementing, or compling with, certain statutory and regulatory mandates within their scope of authority. They, too, must carry out risk assessment programs for all aspects of the people, the place, and the processes for which they are responsible.

A facility professional might be responsible for a building or group of buildings, some services provided to tenants, and, perhaps, if the professional's organization also occupies space in the building, for "in-house" services provided to his or her own organization. In the scenario where one or more organizations are tenants in the building, the facility professional should carry out periodic risk assessment programs (a vulnerability search, vulnerability assessment, and a vulnerability rectification process—more about this later) for all tenants in terms of any avoidable risks that might be present in the tenant's space or operations that could impact either the building, other tenants, or the facility professional's own organization. The facility professional would be concerned with the "disaster planning" of the tenant as it relates to the level of risk presented to other tenants and to the facility itself, but not necessarily with the tenant's provisions for "recovery." (One might be concerned with tenant recovery in terms of the tenant's ability to meet rent payments! If the tenant organizations cannot recover as a result of the disaster, there can be serious problems with lease obligations.) Examples of tenant-created risks—which may or may not be a risk to the tenant itself—include emissions of electromagnetic forces (EMFs); food service areas that could be the source of fire or water leakage into the computer or communications facility of another tenant; improper storage in wiring closets; improper use or storage of inflammable or toxic chemicals; blockage or disabling of fire and safety appliances; or failure to participate in fire and other emergency drills. Lease agreements should provide for inspection and assessment of risks present in the leased spaces (the vulnerability search and vulnerability analysis process) to be conducted by the facility professional or by other professionals, and for abatement of risks present (the vulnerability rectification component).

The facility professional has obligations—statutory, professional, ethical, and moral—to assure that disaster preparedness and recovery planning is optimized—that all risks are as low as reasonably practicable. The facility professional must be a "prudent person" taking all the reasonable precautions that any prudent and reasonable person would take under like circumstances. The facility professional must play an active role in this planning for disaster preparedness and recovery, rather than a reactive one.

As a definable group, the facility professionals have a most important and influential role in the disaster preparedness and recovery planning process. In this planning, the facility professional must correctly balance "facility" responsibilities and commitments with his or her task of creating or managing a disaster planning and recovery project. If a conflict exists here, it may be one of short-term priorities, or one of time allocation. A disaster planning and recovery project, properly researched and structured, can be extremely time consuming, in terms of both hours-per-day and total days required. Because of these time requirements, it can be advisable for the facility professional to be "detached" from usual day-to-day responsibilities, and thus be enabled to devote full time and effort to the project. As an alternative, an individual, whose sole responsibility it is to coordinate plan creation and implementation, can be appointed and report directly and independently to the facility professional. The question of "time" also enters here. How much time should be devoted to the creation and implementation process? (*Implementation* is stressed; too frequently plans—proper or otherwise—are created but never move beyond placement on someone's shelf as a dust-recipient and gathering place. Unless the plans are *implemented* or installed, they are useless in preventing a disaster beyond providing insight into predetermined impacts and consequences.)

The facility professional, responsible for creating a strategy for disaster planning and recovery, might find himself or herself in unfamiliar territory or foreign waters, or, at the least, engaging in information-gathering activities outside of usual activities and treading on new paths of authority and responsibility. The facility professional might be faced with a "cultural change" that brings some "cultural shock." To create a comfortable fit for this new realm, the creation of a strategy for disaster planning and recovery, it can be advisable and advantageous to work under a modified organizational structure. In addition to one's "facility professional" title and reporting structure, the role as "disaster (or contingency) planning and recovery manager" or "coordinator" can be established on an ad hoc basis, preferably with a reporting line directly to the president or CEO. Not only does the Plan itself derive stature and prestige for such structure, but also it gives the facility professional a "new hat" (or a slight recocking of their present hat!) that will facilitate the entire process of creating the plan. An independent, auditing-like or re-engineering-like access to the business processes is especially necessary in the "fact-finding" inherent in the steps in planning.

Some organizations realize their *own* creation of a plan would be feasible, but would consume time extending over an unacceptably lengthy period. Recognizing that, once having obtained commitment of resources for disaster planning and recovery, it is crucial to complete the creation and implementation of the plan in as short a time span as practical. This short-time-span completion reduces the risk of encountering a potential problem *before* there has been opportunity to complete and implement the plan. Often, organizations utilize outside expertise in plan completion, not only for the expertise, per se, but also because of the "additional eyes, hands, and minds" that will shorten the time span required to complete the task.

The facility professional can provide "competent stewardship" over others in creating and implementing the disaster planning and recovery strategy for the organization. Especially in an effort of this nature, and its coordinate responsibilities, the facility professional must guard against the tendency, on the part of several business processes sometimes in competition with each other, to provide excessive redundancy or to establish a plurality of disaster and recovery systems. Although properly planned redundancy can ensure failures are less frequent, the existence of an excessive number of systems can increase the level of risk of failure of the systems themselves when they are called upon.

In whatever role the facility professional takes in creation of the disaster preparedness and recovery project, it is essential that all aspects of design, coordination, and implementation of the project, and its ongoing maintenance, be analyzed for simplicity, reliability, costs, and savings. The facility professional must assure that the organization will achieve the most effective disaster planning and recovery plan that resources and ingenuity can provide.

Too often the facility professional is concerned with (or becomes channeled into preoccupation with) reprographics, signage, forms, HVAC, contracted work, graffiti, costs, budgeting and charge-back, user interfaces, lighting, and safety and security. These are all vital activities to assure that the organization can function; they relate to the care and maintenance of the facility and are structured to safeguard the property and the costs of operating it, and to avoid litigation that might result from oversight in operations, but they do not comprise its disaster planning and recovery strategy.

The facility professional, as a planner, designer, and counselor—and probably a member of a professional discipline—and the facility professional who operates, manages, or administers the facility on a day-to-day basis, must each, in their individual work, not rely on prescriptives alone to reduce risks as low as reasonably practicable. The facility professional must determine if the prescriptives applicable to each risk have reduced the level of that risk ALARP, or have minimized it to an acceptable level. If it is determined that such is not the case, he or she must go beyond the prescriptives in their disaster planning. The purpose of this guide is the illuminate the path to disaster planning, and to light the way to recovery from unavoidable consequences and affects.

The facility professional must work to overcome any fear of the unknown that the organization's management and staff, its customers and suppliers, and its shareholders (collectively, "stakeholders"), might have concerning what can happen to the organization which would impact them in any way. The facility professional must communicate to management and staff, and to the other stakeholders, the risks that the organization faces, and what has been undertaken to reduce the level of such risks ALARP. And, but of not the least import, the facility professional must minimize the potential of failures that could surprise either management and staff, or stakeholders.

What Are the Potential Roles of the Facility Professional in Creating and Implementing a Disaster Planning and Recovery Strategy?

The facility professional can best serve his or her organization—be it either an organization that is planning *for* the place, or an organization that is planning to *operate* and *administer* the place as well as the people and the processes within the place—by managing the disaster planning and recovery project.

We can define "project management" as the processes necessary to accomplish all the desired goals and objectives of the project while expending the least practical amounts of money, time, and effort. Accomplishing these goals and objectives will pose a considerable challenge to the facility professional, especially when the work has to be dovetailed with providing the existing level of services. Generally speaking, the facility professional will have to undertake the disaster planning and recovery strategy without the luxury of turning off other services, or hiving the responsibility for providing them to someone else. Therefore, great emphasis has to be placed on managing the project. A project team may be formed; this would be ideally comprised of representatives from the business processes most likely to be impacted by an out-of-course event, and whose recovery would need be given primary priority. This project management team would be given responsibility for the design of the project, and to analyze the plan for simplicity, reliability, costs, and savings.

As the leader of this team, or as a "sole practitioner" if the facility professional must himself or herself create the disaster planning and recovery strategy, the nature of the strategy that must be created requires certain leadership characteristics that may not come into play in carrying out other responsibilities. The leadership that is manifest can be pivotal in determining whether or not the project—thus, the strategy for disaster planning and recovery—will be successful. The success will be measured in the plan itself, and—most importantly—whether or not the plan will work as intended—when an out-of-course event occurs, impacts the organization, and results in one or more consequences and affects. If the plan does not work, or does not work as intended, it may simply be too late to do anything else!

In creating strategies for the organizations for which they are planning, or by which they are employed, the facility professionals should be, and act as, agents of change. "Change" from the way things have been planned or have been done in the past, as well as the manner in which things are currently planned and are currently being done, is inherent as well as vital—thus, perhaps a valid term for the process—in creating the organization's disaster planning and recovery strategy. This, however, should not be taken to infer that there should be change for the sake of change; serving as an "agent of change" is a role of potential action, not a role of *necessarily* acting. ("Change" is not a one-time affair. After a strategy is in place, periodic reviews can determine that additional "change" is necessary to keep the plan effective.)

The facility professionals must have the insight and capacity, as well as the strength, to be able to abandon outmoded assumptions (such as belief that prescriptives reduce risks ALARP), and be willing to employ innovative concepts (such as computer-based modeling and simulation). They should be able to mobilize people and resources necessary to initiate and implement innovations and change. They should involve their own people, as well as the people in the processes concerned, in planning and implementing change.

As an agent of change, the facility professionals must seek and accept the ideas of others, and be able to accept criticism of their own ideas. This is a part of team development—teams not only to plan the strategy, but also teams that will called upon to put the plan into action when an out-of-course event looms or impacts the organization.

The facility professionals must effectively communicate to the entire organization the purpose and benefits of the plan and strategy. (See Communication, further on.) They must generate the feeling that the change is a normal business development or advancement, rather than something being done because of some disastrous event seen on the horizon. The need for, and especially the values of, changes in individual activities and in business processes, as they impact each individual, should be clearly communicated to the affected members of the staff.

A project with the wide scope inherent in formulating a disaster planning and recovery strategy might place the facility professional in arenas and in forums not always heretofore, or usually, visited. As the leader in creating the strategy and the plan, it could be beneficial for the facility professional to undertake some introspection for this "new" leadership role. The basis for such introspection is not within the remit of this guide; however, prudent suggestions can be found elsewhere.[2]

Frequently, the facility professional does not take every available opportunity to reduce the level of the risks of casualties, damage, or interruption to business processes. This situation might be the result of failure of the place's owners or managers *to task* the facility professional (or anyone else!) with that responsibility. Yet some facility professionals, tasked with that responsibility, fail to recognize and appreciate *all that they can do* to reduce the risks. They may not be aware of all of the risks of out-of-course events, impacts, or consequences and affects, or they may not be aware of the actual levels of risk present. Facility professionals might not recognize that many of the risk levels can be reduced to a level that is as low as reasonably practicable, or to a level that is "acceptable." An important purpose of this guide is, in addition to re-establishing the facility professional's awareness of previously recognized types of risks and their levels, is to *create an awareness* of very real—but not always too apparent—*additional* or *other* risks that can strike people, place, and processes, and the potential relative level of such risks..

In some facilities, the facility professional—in devising a disaster planning and recovery strategy—might fail to look beyond the "facility" itself, and not provide for the management of risks present in the business processes and in the services that support these processes. While there is risk that the elevators or the heating, ventilation, and air-conditioning (HVAC) system might fail or falter, or a water main or water tower burst or the river flood, there is also risk that information or data might be unavailable, unaccessible, or unusable, or that the local area network (LAN) or wide area network (WAN) or telecommunications systems might fail or falter. In creating a proper disaster planning and recovery strategy—a strategy that will *work* in the manner in which it was intended—the facility professional must embrace a holistic approach: He or she must provide for the entire organization, all its people, the totality of place, and all of its processes.

At the end of the day, when all the planning has been completed, and the plan itself has been implemented, tested, and proven, the facility professional might feel like the Cinderella of the organization. He or she has done a lot of very hard work, and was often oppressed by the malevolent, and undeservedly forced into wretched tasks. And although he or she displayed unrecognized talents and ability, the facility professional

---

[2] William D. Hitt, *The Leadership Assessment Inventory* (Columbus, Ohio: Battelle Press, 1995), provides both suitable outlines for assessment, and additional sources.

probably will not be invited to the ball, and will not find a Prince (or Princess) Charming. But when an out-of-course event occurs, the facility professional who created the plan will be a hero or heroine.

The Facility Professionals: Their Facility

The terms "facility" can be, and is, applied to a very heterogeneous group of physical entities. The only thread common among these entities is the fact that they are all *places*. A "facility" may be a space or an office or suite of offices; a floor or group of floors within a building; a single building or a group of buildings or structures. These structures may be in an urban setting or freestanding in a suburban or rural setting. The structures or buildings may be a part of a complex or office park or campus. The *places* are delineated into one or more areas in which an activity, or a number of different activities, are conducted. The *place* may be a physical structure or an open space, or a combination of both. The "facility" is an arena: a place where people come together to engage in activities; the processes. In this book, we shall term that open space and/or its buildings and structures as the place, or place.

The place, in addition to being an office or group of offices or buildings, may be a factory, a warehouse or distribution center, a theater, a concert hall, a library, a museum, a hospital or healthcare facility, a railway station, a casino, a hotel, motel or resort, a restaurant, or a sports stadium. Whatever the function the place is used for, a structured disaster planning and recovery strategy is vital. The nature of the strategy will vary with the nature of the place. Without the place, or a place to conduct activities, the organization cannot function. This guide will enable you to tailor your own strategy to the nature of your place. Bespoke disaster planning and recovery!

The *activities* conducted within the place are, here, termed processes. These processes will be considered as "elements" or parts of the overall business activity. Thus, focus will not be on "banking" as an activity, but as all the individual activities that make up banking: receiving deposits, accepting loan applications, preparing statements, cashing payroll checks, ordering transaction tickets, answering telephone inquiries, stocking ATMs, wire-transferring of funds, filing federally mandated reports, locking the vaults, and so on and on. Each of these, and the many, many other things that are done, are processes—business processes. Some processes are freestanding; others, are linked to related processes to receive or provide information or physical items. Each process takes place within a predetermined time frame. A delay in completion of a process can have a domino effect, impacting other processes depending upon the former for information or for specific material. A "disaster" occurs when the processes cannot take place within a predetermined time frame, and an impact on revenue occurs.

The individuals who conduct or perform the processes, and those who oversee and manage the performance of the individuals and processes are the people. In many processes, the people are employees of the organization; in other processes, the customers, visitors, service-suppliers, and others, are also numbered among the people.

The aggregate of processes may be commerce, finance, consulting, manufacturing, warehousing and distribution, entertainment, transportation, education, healthcare, hospitality, or any other "industry." The specific aggregate of your organization's processes may be a casino and resort, an insurance company, a law firm, a department store, or a rapid transit railway. Dependent on this, the ratio of people between "yours"—management and staff—and "outsiders"—transients and visitors—varies. Your place may have very few, if any, visitors or outsiders—with the exception of the Postal Service, courier, utility, and other service personnel—who call at the place. Conversely, the ratio of clients or outsiders to staff may be very high. Just what this ratio is, and the nature of it, has considerable impact on some aspects of your disaster planning and recovery strategy.

Often, in the course of a day's work, someone will appreciatively remark, "Thanks! You've saved my life!" You may have solved their problem, provided some needed supplies or equipment, or had a flawed device set right. Disaster planning and recovery is about saving lives, albeit extending to a vastly broader plain: It is saving the lives of people who work in or who are visiting the place; it is saving the life of the place itself—the facility and its site; and it is saving the life of the business—the sum total of the processes that are a part of creating its products or its providing services. Creating a disaster planning and recovery strategy will not, at least ultimately, be a thankless chore!

The question sometimes arises concerning the level of risk that the facility professional might be held liable for if the organization fails to create a disaster planning and recovery strategy. The analogous question concerns the level of risk that the facility professional might be held liable for if the strategy he or she creates does not—simply put—work. The level of risk in either case would depend on a widely ranging group of factors but would rarely be at an "acceptable" level. A prudent alternative or countervailance would be protection under errors and omissions insurance coverage.

THE PEOPLE, THE PLACE, THE PROCESSES

A problem occurs: the problem results in one or more *impacts*; each impact creates a *consequence* and an *affect* or a sequence of *consequences* and *affects*. Disasters come about because of chain reactions, because of "domino affects." Disasters just don't "happen." We will look at the categories of problems or potential problems and will see that they manifest diverse characteristics. Potential problems are found in every possible part of our surroundings—in every nook and cranny of our circumstances. The potential problems range, in the likelihood—or level of risk—of occurrence, from the extremely rare to the fairly common.

There are, within some categories of potential out-of-course events, specific problems that because of their nature cannot occur within your particular venue. As examples, considering nature-based potential problems, if you are sited in Arizona you would not be subject to hurricanes as you would in New England coastal areas. This is because Arizona does not fit within the definition of what a hurricane is. If your building was one-story, you need not be concerned with elevator failure (as you probably do not have one!). *But whenever any potential problem becomes manifest*, it will have an impact on your people, and/or your place, and/or your processes. In the real world, *the impact* more-often-than-not strikes upon all three, simultaneously or successively, but in different ways: the people, *and* the place, *and* the processes. The impact itself, or the consequences of the impact, on the place can have consequence and affect on the people and on the processes, as well as on the place itself. The consequences of an impact on the people not only affects the people. Frequently, it also affects the processes, and can also affect the place. And when the processes bear one or more affects, there are ordinarily consequences (and other affects) that the place and the people endure.

In view of these interrelationships, the facility professional, in considering disaster planning and recovery, must focus on all three aspects of an enterprise: its people, its place, and its processes. If the facility professional's role is that of an architect, designer, or as a civil, structural, mechanical, or electrical engineer, the place he or she creates must necessarily be such that the character of the place itself, as well as the environment for the people within it, and the arena where the processes take place, will be of a nature that maximizes resistance to any impacts, consequences, and affects resulting from problems or out-of-course events. If the events are such that the place—or the processes—lack resistance to, or durability in the face of, the impact, it must be able to recover or be recovered ("bounce back") with minimal expenditures of money, time, and effort. Impacts on the people that take the form of casualties—deaths or injuries—provide less generous opportunities for recovery.

When the facility professional's role is one concerned with the functioning of the place, or the functioning of a process, the planning must provide for the ongoing functioning of the place and the processes, or for the restoration of them after the impact caused by a problem or out-of-course event.

Understanding the concept of people, place, and processes is vital in the creation of effective, comprehensive, and integrated disaster and recovery plans. You are the facility professional; you are tasked with the mission of disaster planning and recovery. Who are the people about whom you are concerned, and for whom you must plan and prepare? What—or where—is the place? What are the processes that transpire?

The People

It is often said that an organization's most important and valuable asset and resource is its people. This is quite true, especially in the perspective of disaster planning and recovery. As a facility professional, you might have little to do, directly, with the organization's personnel, other than those people who report directly to you in the functions you are responsible for. But as a facility professional concerned with disaster planning and recovery, the *people* are as vital a consideration as the place or the processes. In fact, few would dispute the fact that the people are even a more vital consideration.

The people within the scope of your concern include not only your the totality of your organization's staff or personnel, but also a goodly number of "outsiders." In terms of your organization's staff, your concern is for the staff who work at the place, and those who might visit the place. Thus, all executive staff, management personnel, operating personnel, and support staff who are assigned to the place, and those who come to the place must be provided for in disaster and recovery planning.

Your planning must also account for people who are not employees of the organization, but who perform some function at, or provide some service to, the place. Included in this group are service-providers, contractors' staffs, outsourced function staff, temporary staff, consultants, certain staff members of outside law and accounting firms, and independent contractors. The concern for these people in your planning is also related to their direct participation in, or direct contribution to the processes. Put another way, planning must consider these people as both persons present at the site and as persons engaged in the processes. As examples, the on-site representatives of your computer services or telecommunications services providers, or on-site elevator maintainers require consideration in your planning. Any transportation staff the organization uses on a regular basis might require consideration. The question here is, "How will the organization fare if any of these people can not provide their usual services?" If their services are inherent to the functioning of any process, then contingency plans for them need be a part of your overall planning. Your planning must also encompass provisos for those individuals or groups who are "casually" present at or in the place, or passing through or by it.

Some of the people for whom you must have concern are involved *directly* in the processes for which the organization exists; other people are engaged in activities that are "support" processes. *People* are considered in the plural; rarely, if in any instance, is an "organization" comprised of only one person. Even in terms of a "solo practitioner," the people directly concerned with the ongoing functioning-as-intended operations encompass more than that solo practitioner alone.

The Place

The place is the envelope within which the processes are conducted by the people. (The term *envelope* refers to the *total site*, and is distinguished from a *shell* or building. The *shell*, when fitted with elements of infrastructure, equipment, and furnishings, is where specific process activities take place. The *envelope* can include more than one *shell*, and may also contain other elements such as paved parking areas, landscaped and natural-growth areas, recreation and sports areas, and the like.) All of your processes might not be conducted within one place. In terms of crafting a disaster planning and recovery strategy, *all* processes are created equal, and must be so-treated. (Differences arise when viewing the consequences. Some consequences have greater affects on the as-intended functioning of the organization.) As many organizations have, or operate from, more than one place, we shall consider "the place" in a collective sense, although *each place must have its own bespoke disaster planning and recovery strategy*.

In terms of place, disaster planning and recovery cannot be restricted only to the individual office or offices or suite within a building. (As buildings themselves are becoming increasingly large and complicated structures, they are—especially in view of the "technology" being utilized to "manage" and "operate" them—at increasingly higher levels of risk to out-of-course events, their impacts and the ensuing consequences and affects). It is not sufficient to consider only the working spaces, and the planning—such as provision of fire detection and suppression devices—

for them. Nor can only the building itself be considered the entity of place. The place extends beyond the *space* where the organization operates or conducts its processes or business. The place encompasses not only the work areas as such, but also support areas, as well as the corridors, hallways, lobbies, and all other "spaces" within the confines of the building shell. Thus, if your organization occupies but part of the space within a building, the facility professional who has governance for the building as a whole plays a vital role in your organization's disaster planning.

The place also encompasses the *site* upon which the building stands. In an urban environment, there may be little, if any, apparent site beyond the walls of the building itself, but sidewalks, driveways, easements, and other like spaces—*and what is beneath or over them*—must be considered when one considers the place.

In an suburban environment, the building might be located on a campus-like site, alone, or with other buildings. Landscaped areas, parking lots, access roadways, and paths—*and what is beneath or over them*—are all parts of the place. This land area, or the land occupied by an urban building, can be considered the place in terms of control: The organization or enterprise has some degree of control over this aspect of the place in that many conditions or circumstances are subject to negotiation in purchase, lease, or rental agreements. There are other aspects of the place in which the organization has little or no control of conditions or circumstances, and beyond the option to reject that place as one where the organization can function. In some considerations of a particular place as the potential site whereon the enterprise will function or can continue to function, the facility professional, having conducted a study for disaster planning and recovery, might validly conclude that the organization should not occupy the site, or should move! The existence of many relatively high levels of risk of potential problems can prompt the alternatives of *move*, or, if that is not feasible, to *pray a lot*! However, prayer is not considered as an alternative in disaster planning and recovery in the context we are considering. The fact that the potential problems at so many places or sites present such relatively high levels of risk underscore—very, very boldly—the criticality of studying risk levels for all potential problems before committing the organization to a site or building.

When examining the place—the total envelope in which the organization operates—there are many areas for consideration in addition to the office or offices, the suites, the floor or floors whereon the organization will be situated, and the building itself. The site itself must be examined for potential problems. In addition to the "surface" of the particular site—the land—and what is present, close examination must be made of where the site is in relation to what can occur on *adjacent* sites and on nearby sites, and what can occur *under* the site. If there is highway nearby, what is the risk of a truck crash resulting in explosion, fire, or leakage of dangerous chemicals or gases? If there is a railway line nearby, what is the risk of collision or derailment that can result in fire, explosion, or leakage of dangerous chemicals or gases, or an evacuation because of potential dangers? There might be an abandoned or underutilized railway line nearby that is under consideration for use as a commuter rail path. Such usage would probably entail electrification; possibly at 600 Volts dc, or at 25,000 or 50,000 Volts ac. Any of these could be the source of electrical interference (EMFs) with consequences or affects on your people, computers, or telecommunications devices.

Consideration need also be given to what is *under* the site, as well as what is *under* adjacent and nearby sites. Had there been mining at any of the sites which could trigger subsidence or spontaneous combustion or emergence of fire? Are there any hazardous materials buried? Is there a gas or petroleum pipeline that might explode or be ruptured? Is there is a water main that could burst and cause flooding, or a wastewater main that could cause an undermining? What are the soil conditions, especially important if the area is prone to earth movements? The presence of these factors must be searched for, detected, and their potential—the level of risk—for causing a problem measured.

The facility professional cannot neglect examining what is *over* or *above* the site, as well as what is over or above adjacent and nearby sites. An array of potential problems lurks over the site! Very often there are high-voltage or very-high-voltage electric power lines passing over the site or over an adjacent site. These power lines can be the source of emanations of electromagnetic forces (EMFs). Concerns about the effect of EMFs on the people nearby not withstanding, the EMFs can cause considerable interference or disruption to computer operations, wireless local area networks, and on other forms of telecommunications. High-voltage power lines also tend to attract lightning strikes which, in turn, can impact your building, or the equipment you are using. Too frequently, measurements for the presence of EMFs, or for lightning-strike potential is neglected; in some instances where measurement is made, the time span of measurement is too short to determine exacting characteristics and an accurate level of risk.

Another aspect of *above* concerns the proximity of the site to airport approach patterns. The facility professional should consider the place not only in relation to present-day patterns, but also to changed, planned, or proposed patterns that can emerge from community noise abatement programs, airport expansion, or changes brought about by different aircraft.

The Processes

The *processes* are the things your organization—the enterprise or business (which we shall call "organization" for simplicity)—does, and the manner in which these things are done. Quite obviously, the nature of the organization, its size, scope, and extent, and the degree of automation are just a few of the factors which govern the nature of the processes. In reality, two organizations, identical in size and nature, might utilize significantly different processes to accomplish their goals.

The basic objective of disaster planning and recovery is to enable each process to continue or to be restarted if interrupted. Thus, it is critical to identify each of the processes and what each is intended (or presumed) to accomplish; what each of the processes actually does; and, what is the relationship of each individual process with each of the other processes in the organization. In your examination of the processes, it might be noted that one or more process plays no role of value in accomplishing the organization's goals and objectives (the production of product in a manner that maximizes profit, or the delivery of services in a maximum profit or least-cost manner). This examination of the roles of each process within an organization—and changes that emerge therefrom—is frequently called *re-engineering*. Re-engineering of the organization is essentially outside of the scope of disaster planning and recovery; however, in examining each process, opportunities for re-engineering—and cost savings and cost avoidances—can arise.

In "isolating" each process, it is important to focus on the function of the process. The *function* might be order entry, invoicing, payroll preparation, accounts payable, commission calculation, widget painting, quality assurance, shipping, purchasing, marketing, promotional mailing, tax accounting, training, or any of the myriad of other activities present in organizations. In considering these functions, it arises that certain functions are "more vital" in a particular organization than others. Put another way, the organization might be able to defer the performance of certain functions for different lengths of time. Under pressing circumstances, promotional mailings might be deferred to several weeks. Marketing activities can sometimes be postponed, but a delay in payroll calculation, preparation, and distribution can have catastrophic consequences taking the form of disgruntled employees, labor stoppages, or undue hardships for employees.

Interrelationships between functions have an impact on time lines. As an example, if there is a process flow from order entry to manufacturing to shipping to invoicing to accounts receivable, the order entry function could be "acceptably down" for a week if the manufacturing function had a two-week backlog of orders. But if manufacturing was completely current, an interruption in order entries would bring manufacturing to a halt. Thus, interrelations between functions have a time-line factor; this factor can vary with business volume or season.

THE DISASTER PLANNING AND RECOVERY STRATEGY

Disaster planning and recovery is concerned with people, place, and processes: The objective is to protect, preserve, and safeguard these, and to shield them against harm and danger. Determining the *business processes* that are the dynamics or functioning of the organization is one of the most important phases in establishing a disaster planning and recovery strategy.[3] This determination is important whether your role, as a facility professional, is planning or designing the place, or is managing or administering the place, or is managing or administering one or more of the processes themselves that function in the place. In planning or designing the place, or in managing or administering it, there is an inherent necessity that the place "will work" in terms of being able to "accommodate" the processes, as well as to provide the means for each of the processes to take place in an optimal manner. In administering or managing any of the organization's processes, you have to provide all the means (including people, place, infrastructure, equipment, facilities, furnishings, information, and data) that will enable the processes to function optimally. A vital part of your design or planning considerations, or your management or administration, must be an obligation for the well-being of the people. Your objective in formulating and crafting a disaster planning and recovery strategy is to assure that the organization (the sum of all of the processes) will be able to continue in a predetermined, as-intended manner (although not necessarily the "usual" manner)—or will be able to recommence "acceptable" functioning in a predetermined manner within a predetermined time frame—whenever the organization

---

[3] In the approach to "disaster planning" utilizing the "business impact analysis" (BIA) formula, the "business" that may impacted, an thus subjected to analysis, should be the BPC. The BIA—as a methodology—is discussed in Chapter 2.

is impacted by, and affected by, the consequences of an out-of-course event that impairs, impedes, interrupts, or halts one or more of its processes. Put broadly, "acceptable continuity in the faces of adversity." (The plural, "faces," is by intent.)

All organizations, no matter what they do or what their size, structure themselves in some functionally related manner akin to their processes. The structure may be formal or informal; it may be rigid or flexible. Whatever form the structure assumes, it can be generalized that the larger the organization, the more formal and complex, and more rigid the structure becomes. This "structure" usually appears on organization charts (if there are any in the organization!) as operating and support units or departments. These are often typified as "sales administration," "human resources," "payroll," "production control," "shipping," "mailroom," "information sciences," and other "tasks." Dependent upon the size and complexity of the organization, and upon what it does, the chart or charts will vary in intricacy and detail. One or more individuals may be assigned to each of the "tasks"—a task may be his or her only responsibility, or one of many; the task may be a full-time duty or only part-time work; individuals may perform the task only occasionally or all the time.

These "tasks" are of fundamental concern to the facility professions whether they are in the role of planner, designer, or administrator. The effectiveness of the ultimate plan, its workability when called upon, as well as the costs of designing, implementing, and maintaining the plan, are directly related to the correct identification of the "tasks" within the organization or business, what each task performs or accomplishes, its interrelationships with other tasks, and its relative necessity for and importance in the as-intended functioning of the organization. The concern here is not *how* the organization is structured, but with what each bit and piece of the structure does. (The planning process itself, because of the inherent requirement to view the tasks in terms of the functioning of the organization, can reveal unexpected, beneficial opportunities for change—or re-engineering—of the structure.)

In creating your plan (in addition to endeavoring to reduce the level of risk of casualties to the people, and of damage or harm to the place),[4] you are striving to provide protection against interruption or impairment of the needed performance of these "tasks," or conversely, striving to enable continuity in their functioning, or to restore or reinstate their function-

---

[4] In the reality of the "real world," much disaster planning and recovery is focused solely on, and justified by, "saving the computer" or (in rare instances!) "saving the business." That the plan can also save people as well as save the place can then be taken as an unexpected—albeit, not insignificant—benefit or advantage!

ing.[5] To accomplish this in the arena of disaster preparedness and recovery strategy, it is necessary to identify and segregate each of these "tasks." Each task can be termed "business process centers" or "business process cells"—BPCs.[6] The BPCs are typically smaller than a "department," but are not always the minimally reducible unit. "Payroll" is often a BPC within an organization, especially when actual payroll checks are prepared elsewhere. However, if these checks are prepared in-house, the check-preparation activity would be a BPC. Product information fulfillment would probably be a BPC, as would advertising. In a manufacturing environment, packing and shipping might be a single, or two separate, BPCs. Quality assurance and final inspection, likewise, might be separate, or a single BPC. The facility professional responsible for the operation of a place for tenants or clients would consider specific services or functions as BPCs: provision of electrical power, HVAC, elevator service, cleaning, maintenance, water supply, catering facility, and the like.

It is essential that *each* BPC be correctly segregated, properly identified, and accurately linked to other BPCs when developing a workable, comprehensive disaster planning and recovery strategy.

A facility professional designing, planning, equipping, or furnishing the place for a tenant or client would have to view each of the tenant's or client's BPCs in terms of where it will function within the organization as well as within the place, and what it uses. In creating a disaster planning and recovery strategy, it is necessary to view that smallest individual unit—a BPC—without which the organization cannot function on an as-intended basis. It is important to define, unambiguously and completely, each BPC, *what it does*—its intended purpose as well as its actual purpose—and *what it requires* (in terms of information and data input from other BPCs, equipment and furnishings, HVAC, electrical power, communications media, personnel, etc., as well as the time-line tolerances for the nonavailability, nonaccessibility, or nonusability of any of these) to accomplish its task or tasks. Put another way, each BPC has to be examined in terms of what will *knock it out* (impede, impair, interrupt or halt its as-intended functioning), and when knocked out, how much time will elapse before the knockout's effects will cascade down to

---

[5] In some "disaster plans" the sole purpose—or the dominant objective—is to "recover" from the inability of one or more "tasks" to operate.

[6] The BPCs might be thought of as "atoms" (borrowing a mathematician's analogy). As is the case with "physical" atoms, BPCs are constantly in motion, linked to other BPCs, and are inherent to the [business] whole. The motion or nature of atoms can be changed or destroyed by an outside force (the amount of force necessary being predictable based on the nature of the particular atom), and such change can alter the nature of the whole.

other BPCs, and how much time will pass before the latter BPCs will be knocked out.

Each BPC is presumed to perform a *vital* function within the organization! If not, why would or does it exist? The establishment of your plan provides interesting opportunities to uncover, identify, and isolate BPCs that may not be necessary, or may no longer be necessary in the organization. This process—in which BPCs of questionable value to the organization are identified—can provide some important groundwork for what is frequently termed "business process re-engineering." While a business process re-engineering undertaking involves work substantially different in scope than that undertaken in creating a plan, the planning process of identifying the BPCs, their function in, and their value to, the organization can provide the springboard for often quite-significant cost savings and cost avoidances. The cost savings and cost avoidances that result from the information discovered in the course of the creation of a plan might actually pay for a goodly portion of plan.

The basic consideration, here, is to define the above-mentioned *vital*. As an example, in identifying BPCs in a brokerage firm, a moderately sized room, filled with seemingly countless file cabinets each containing thousands of 3 × 5-inch file cards was observed. These cards, containing details of each past and current customer's transactions, dated back many, many decades to the founding of the firm, were updated and keep current by several staff members. Much of the information was purely historical; a substantial amount was available from computer-based data. However, since the maintenance and preservation of these records was of very significant interest (ergo, importance) to the firm's founder and owner, there was absolutely no question *whether this BPC was vital*. A planning concern was—in addition to whether these records were sufficiently protected—how long an interruption in updating process would be acceptable!

Thus, the consideration that follows is: How long can the organization function in its as-intended manner after the as-intended functioning of *any* particular (read, vital) BPC is impaired, impeded, impaired, interrupted, or halted? The answers to these questions are something the management of the BPC in question, as well as the managements of the BPCs on the input and output sides, must determine. Finding the answers should be accomplished outside of the political arena of departmental self-importance! In the real world of departmental introspection, most managements will tend to grossly overstate the importance of their particular BPC, its relations with other BPCs, and especially, the importance of the BPC in its function-time relationships with other BPCs. The "how long" is actually the maximum interval of nonfunctioning that can be tolerated. Planning must provide for some alternative site or means or procedure to takeover before the expiration of the interval.

Each of the BPCs has to be examined in terms of the affects of consequences, their durations, or the product of affects *and* duration that will impede, impair, interrupt, or halt that BPC's as-intended functioning, as well as the manner in which impediment, impairment, interruption, or stoppage will occur. In a practical consideration of this, a hierarchical approach can be used: If it is determined that an outage of the power system feeding the computer local area network will cause that network to cease functioning after 1.7 minutes, the cascading effect of such an outage would impact all terminals in the BPCs connected to that network. It would then not be necessary to consider the impact of that outage on each individual terminal or BPCs where they are situated, but only to consider whether the BPC can function without the terminals.

The answers to the core-critical question (How long can the organization continue to function *without* a particular BPCs being able to perform?) provide the basis upon which the plan is founded. While *some* interruption in functioning of particular BPCs may be tolerable, the vital question is: *How long* can the organization live without that particular BPC functioning? What is the time tolerance? How long is management (here, "management" equates to the consensus of both the managements of the particular BPC and the BPCs related to it, as well as various levels of management "all the way to the top") willing to "live" without that discrete BPC functioning? What is the resiliency? The goals and objectives of the plan, put in terms of BPCs, is to do what is possible to reduce the level of risk that the out-of-course event will occur; to limit the intensity of the out-of-course event; and to limit the duration of that out-of-course event, so that the problem will not impact the BPC. We need also determine what can be done to mitigate or to counteract the intensity (that is, the impact and ensuing consequences and affects) of the out-of-course event (if the out-of-course event cannot be avoided), and—when the intensity has been mitigated—to lessen the duration of the "residual effects" out-of-course event, and to do what is possible and what is practicable to accomplish each. Doing "what is possible" and "what is practicable" invariably introduces the issues of what will be necessary in terms of cost: the money, time, and effort that will be required. The "what is practicable" concept is an especially important planning consideration because it encompasses the totality of the costs of money, time, and effort. As an example, you may, through proper planning, be able to reduce the level of risk of a particular event occurring *at an intensity* sufficient to totally disrupt your wireless telecommunication network to once in 25 years, with a duration of 120 minutes. Spending the incremental costs of reducing that duration even 5 minutes would undoubtedly be deemed "not practicable" because the level of risk of the event itself occurring is—at once in 25 years—acceptably low. (The concept of "what is practicable" is further explored in consideration of reducing risks as low as reasonably practicable—ALARP.)

Certain vital aspects in determining a time-line index of importance of a BPC's ability to function, and establishing the inherent value of each BPC to the organization, has been termed by some planners as a "business impact analysis" (BIA). In investigating the present-day "BIA methodologies"—either as a computer-based prepackaged product (usually presented in multiple-choice or limited-selection formats), or as a questionnaire-and-interview technique, this writer has not been able to find any technique so-termed a BIA that embodies sufficient analysis of the intensity or duration of the out-of-course event, or that provides for business process segmentation to justify its use as the sole foundation for the survival of an organization.

Business Process Centers

The reason—apparent or otherwise—that you are creating a disaster planning and recovery strategy is to enable the organization to be able to function following the impact of any out-of-course event, its consequences, and the affects that ensue. This does not necessarily infer (or suggest the necessity for) *continuity* in functioning or *uninterrupted* functioning, but means that the out-of-course event will not ultimately result in the demise of the organization. From the perspective of the structure of the organization, provision must be made for affected (by either the impact or the problem, or the consequences and affects of the problem) business process centers (BPCs) to either (1) be able to continue functioning "normally" after the impact of an out-of-course event and its consequences and affects (a "problem"); (2) be able to function in an "alternative" mode after suffering the affects; or (3) be able return to "normal" functioning after the affects have dissipated or have been mitigated. Thus, we must consider, initially, the organization's BPCs.

The BPC is a center of activity. It may be a department or a part of a department. In some organizations, it may be several departments. The size, and the activities, of BPCs are generally related to the size and the nature of the organization. Just *what* a BPC is or does matters little; the essential characteristic is that it performs a specific task or tasks. When the BPC—after a specific lapse of time—is unable to perform its task or tasks, the "normal" functioning of the entire organization ceases. When the cessation of "normal" functioning halts or precludes the delivery of products or of services, or impacts "the bottom line," it is—by definition— *a disaster*. (Ah! This is the "disaster" in "Disaster Planning.") Planning and recovery must, therefore, be concerned with—and structured specifically for—each BPC.

It is necessary to delineate the organization's various BPCs, what they do, and what time span of interruption in functioning can transpire before they affect other BPCs, and ultimately, before the organization's overall functioning is impacted. It is absolutely vital to consider *each and every* BPC functioning in the organization. The BPCs may be "owned and operated" or may be a contracted—or "outsourced"—function or service. The "ownership" of the BPC is not of concern; it is the functioning of the BPC that has to be considered.[7]

It would be most unusual to find that an organization has a listing of its BPCs. It is necessary in creating a disaster planning and recovery strategy—just as it is in creating a re-engineering strategy—to determine the organization's BPCs. This is not a simple task; the facility professional may well need the assistance of various managers and administrative personnel who are well-versed in the organization's functioning and processes to properly demarcate the overall structure of, and inter-relationships between, the BPCs.

The demarcation of BPCs is the foundation of the strategy under development, and should not be done casually. Often, management might overlook or forget some functions, especially those rarely or nonroutinely performed. It becomes incumbent upon the planner who is to "demarcate" to discuss a unit's activities not only with its management or supervisors, but with the people themselves. If this seems a tedious endeavor, regard it as a keystone in your planning efforts.

---

[7] There are some specific aspects of outsourced BPC-functioning that need be considered in creating a disaster planning and recovery strategy. These include the level of risk associated with the provider furnishing a continuity in services, the levels of risks associated with equipment supplied by the provider either on-site or used at the provider's site, and the level of risk associated with as-intended performance of out-sourced tasks. The decision to outsource any function (read, BPC) is, in part, an analysis of all of the risks involved. This analysis process must encompass the analysis of risks associated with out-of-course events, their impact, and the ensuing consequences and affects as well as of the levels of risks associated with the outsourcing itself.

As the BPCs are related to the size and nature of the organization, you might determine that *a particular* BPC is your accounting function, or payroll, of payroll check preparation, or salaried payroll check preparation, or head office salaried payroll check preparation, or something within the latter.

In determining the roles of individual BPCs in the organization, the relationships between BPCs, and what consequences and affects each BPC might be susceptible or sensitive to, you must investigate the following considerations:

1. What is the role of the BPC within the organization?
2. Where is the physical location (with in the place) of the BPC?
3. What space, infrastructure, equipment, facilities, and furnishings does the BPC require ordinarily? What are the minimal requirements of each? What space, infrastructure, equipment, facilities, and furnishings does the BPC use exclusively? What is shared with other BPCs? Which BPCs? What are the minimal requirements of each of the sharers?
4. Which people are engaged in the BPC? What *knowledge* do they require?
5. What elements of the organizational memory (information and data records and files) are vital in the functioning of the BPC? Where (plural!) are these elements maintained and stored?
6. What would be the impact on the BPC if some of its on-site stored memory or work-in-progress memory was unaccessible, unavailable, or unusable?
7. What organizational memory (information and data) does the BPC use exclusively? What is *shared* (in contrast to *exchanged*) with other BPCs? Which BPCs?
8. What computing and communications resources are normally required to collect, process, store, and forward this organizational memory?
9. What is the relationship of the particular BPC with other BPCs? What organizational memory is input? Output? Exchanged?
10. What is the time-span tolerance of each *other* BPC in terms of lack of memory sharing, input, or exchange?
11. Is the BPC's role vital (an actual necessity in the as-intended functioning of the organization)? *Always* vital? If not, when?
12. What specific out-of-course events can strike the BPC?
13. What *impacts* can result?
14. What *consequences* can occur?

15. What specific *affects* of the consequences will give rise to the BPCs as-intended functioning becoming impeded, impaired, interrupted, or halted? How much time would ordinarily elapse between the *affect* and the impairment, impediment, interruption, or halt?

This determination of the organization's BPCs (both "owned and operated" as well as those out-sourced), their roles and the vitalness of these roles, their inter-relationships with other BPCs, as well as their susceptibility or immunity to the consequences and affects of the impacts of out-of-course events is a (if not "the") foundation in the creation of a disaster planning and recovery strategy. (See Steps in Planning in Chapter 2)

The individual BPC must be considered not only as a *function* or *operation* or *process* that is a part of the organization "doing its thing." In addition to being considered as a process, each BPC must be considered as a portion or segment of the place ("space") where people engage in or conduct the organization's activities ("work"). You must examine, first, the place that each BPC occupies; second, the people it utilizes; and third, the processes that it performs. You must determine what can happen to each of this triad. Which of the out-of-course events (see Disaster Defined) that can strike the organization *can impact the BPC?* What is the level of risk that such *strikes* will occur? That *impacts* will occur? That the impacts will cause *consequences and affects* to befall the BPC?

These consequences and affects have to be considered in terms both of their *intensity* and their *duration* to determine whether they will affect the as-intended functioning of a BPC. A power overvoltage or undervoltage of 10% would not affect a typing pool using electric typewriters, but could be disastrous to one fitted with desktop computers. A 2-second interruption in voice telecommunications would be little more than annoying, but a microsecond interruption to data transmission could result in corrupt data. "Duration" is not always measured in seconds: In some BPCs, a lack of HVAC for several days or weeks may not have any affect on role-performance (albeit, the people might despair).

Planning strategy regarding each BPC must consider several factors:

1. The reduction in the levels of risk that the consequences and affects of the impact of an out-of-course event will impede, impair, interrupt, or halt the as-intended functioning of that BPC to a level ALARP.

2. The means to increase the fault-tolerance level of the BPC so that the processes it conducts, the people it employs, and the place it occupies have greater resistance to, or immunity from, the consequences and their affects.

3. The means that will enable the BPC to function in an alternate mode if as-intended functioning is impeded, impaired, interrupted, or halted as a result of the consequences and their affects.

4. The provision to restore the BPC to its as-intended mode after the cause of the impediment, impairment, interruption, or halt has sufficiently ebbed, or has ended.

Thus, the plan you create may be considered as having two parts: First, <u>disaster planning</u>, and second, the shaping of provisions for <u>recovery</u> or restoration. The disaster planning segment is designed to reduce the level of risk (ALARP!) of an event occurring and impacting as-intended functioning of the BPC's people, place, or processes. The recovery segment is vital because the level of risk that consequences and their affects will occur cannot be reduced to zero (it's not a question of *if*, but one of *where and when* . . .). There will always be events of sufficient duration and intensity to affect the as-intended functioning of the BPCs.

DISASTER DEFINED

Understanding What a "Disaster" Is

The Tangle of Terminology　　Like many disciplines, *disaster planning and recovery* lacks both a standard or a universally agreed-upon vocabulary and agreed-upon definitions for all the various terms used by different practitioners in the field. Considering that disaster planning and recovery is both a science and an art (or, in the minds of many, both an art and a science) and the simple fact that this is a facility professional's guide to disaster planning and recovery, it is vital that a syllabus of terminology—fitting for those professionals—be established and explained. We need an acceptable, agreed-upon vocabulary so that, when we speak with each other, or present information to our managements or associates, the terms related to disaster planning and recovery that we use will conjure up but a single meaning or definition. This guide will not attempt to overcome various applications of language as used by other practitioners in the field. However, by establishing a definition for, say, <u>disaster</u>, whenever *you* use that term, the same meaning should always be conveyed and understood by the various constituencies with whom you are communicating. Conversely, when you or a member of your constituencies encounter a word in the literature or in a discussion, say *disaster*, you will be able, from the context in which the word is used, to "translate" it into something meaningful in *your* vocabulary.

Undoubtedly, the most "problematic" word is *disaster*.[8] Frequently mentioned in the news media, the word "disaster" may create an image quite remote from the facility wherein our concerns lie. The various news media—newspapers, radio, television, news magazines—apply the term "disaster" to events that result in considerable physical damage, usually accompanied with substantial numbers of casualties, both injuries and deaths, such as earthquakes, hurricane land-falls, tornadoes, aircraft crashes, explosions, and major bombings. It is unlikely that one would find the term "disaster" applied to an earthquake that completely destroyed an uninhabited, remote island in the Pacific Ocean. Likewise, a letterbomb injuring two or three people would not be considered a "disaster," nor would a battle in a civil war that resulted in vast casualties. The breaking of a truce that reignited that war might be termed a "disaster," but that would be a "political disaster."

Business-oriented publications, both those which focus on business news events, and those which focus on business operations, use the term "disaster" to describe something catastrophic that has interrupted as-intended functioning of computer operations. This event could be the result of a "news media" type of disaster, or the result of something inherent in computer operations, such as a disk crash. Computer-oriented publications apply the term "disaster" to an event that has caused an interruption in the functioning of the computer facility or of computer functioning, or a failure to correctly back up data, or a failure in the backup system. Another cadre of business publications—those concerned with telecommunications—apply "disaster" to an event that severs or reduces intersite linkages. Business publications of another ilk term significant losses (either in balance sheet reckoning, in market share, or of top executives) as "disasters." Product performance failures or less-than-anticipated acceptance of the product are also often identified as "disasters." Seminars and other educational sessions—presented for business leaders, or for technical specialists—present "disasters" wearing various hats; their styles and sizes seem without limit.

We see references to "disasters" in the variety of publications that appear in our mail: "The evolution of Bank of Boston's telecommunications disaster prevention/business resumption plan,"[9] or, "Find out if wars, natural disasters, industrial disputes or other unexpected events are

---

[8] Words that are perhaps less "problematic" are defined in the Glossary.

[9] "Fifth Annual Conference & Trade Show—Disaster Recovery, Contingency Planning & Business Continuation Using Telecommunications"—Boston, Mass., March 12–15, 1995.

affecting or restricting mail delivery,"[10] or, "Disaster Recovery for Local Area Networks,"[11] or "Since 1989, there have been six disasters that generated at least $1 billion apiece in insured losses" [1983, wind, snow, and freezing rain—$880 million; 1989, Hurricane Hugo—$4.2 billion; 1889, San Francisco earthquake—$960 million; 1991 and 1993, fires in California—$1.7 billion and $950 million, respectively; 1992, looting and riots in Los Angeles—$775 million; 1992, Hurricane Andrew—$15.5 billion; 1992, Hurricane Iniki—$1.6 billion; 1993, "storm of the century"—$1.625 billion; 1994, earthquake in southern California—$6.5 billion; 1994, snow and ice storm in Washington, D.C., and along East Coast—$1.7 billion].[12] In the latter examples, "disasters" are not what impact businesses, but rather the amount of insurance claims that result from the impact and its consequences (a "disaster" for insurance company profitability!). The dollar amount of the consequences were undoubtedly much greater, for not all losses were insurable or were insured. Yet, one cannot engage in disaster planning and recovery until establishing firmly just what a *disaster* is or what a *disaster* entails.

Disaster planning is <u>not</u>—as some wags might suggest—planning <u>to have</u> a disaster, or planning <u>for</u> a disaster, but it is the planning undertaken to *prevent* a disaster from occurring, or to reduce the level of risk that a disaster will occur. Why not, then, "disaster prevention"? That term is frequently used in the literature and in tutorials and educational sessions, but is not preferred here since disasters are not easily or simply prevented: It requires substantial, comprehensive, coordinated planning to prevent a disaster from occurring in an organization. *Disaster prevention* <u>can be</u> defined as planning steps taken, individually or in concert, to prevent an out-of-course event escalating *into* a disaster. This concept is well-expressed in a description of Hiroshima's Astram metro line: "The disaster prevention module (of the Central Control Office) monitors the fire detectors at each station, and collates related data such as earthquake and wind-velocity warnings [and] and special overflow circuits are provided at the three underground stations to indicate when the deep-level water effluent tanks exceed their rated capacity".[13]

[10] "Incident bulletin" in "The Royal Mail" published by Royal Mail, London EC1, Summer 1995.

[11] The subject of a two-day workshop, presented by the Data-Tech Institute, Clifton, N.J., in eight cities, summer and fall, 1995.

[12] John S. McDermott, "Battening Down the Hatches," *CFO*, September 1994, 74–86.

[13] Kazunari Hayashi, "Astram Line Is the Winner at Asian Games," *Developing Metros 1995*, 1995, 55–57.

It is important that the facility professional, when reading of, and considering, such "disasters" and the solution paths taken to deal with them, to think of the *actual* cause of the event described, and the means that might have been taken to reduce the likelihood of that event occurring, and its impact, consequences and affects ensuing.

The questions, "What is a facility professional?" and "Who are facility professionals?" have been explored. In the arena of disaster planning and recovery, some professionals prefer to use the term "facility"; others, "facilities." In this guide, the term "place" is used to describe the "facility" or "facilities." *Place*, then, includes "facility" in its collective sense: a single facility, or more than one facility. That facility may be a single building or a group of them. The group may be on one site, or on several sites. "Facility," in this sense, refers to a physical entity: a site, its buildings, the infrastructure, as well as the equipment, and the furnishings a part of it; *the place*. "Facility" (or more often, "facilities")—in another sense—is often encountered in reference to the activities—likely to be support activities—that are vital to the place and inherent within the organization or processes. Such activities under the aegis of a facility [facilities?] professional frequently include, among others; security, cleaning, and maintenance; forms management and records management; mail and messenger services; telephone and telecommunications services; catering services, purchasing and office furnishings; and provision of lighting, repair, heating, ventilation, and air conditioning. The strategy for disaster planning and recovery, as will be considered here, will encompass "facility" in both of these senses.

The title *Disaster Planning and Recovery* includes four separate planning elements:

1. The plans established to reduce the likelihood that an out-of-course event, or that a fault or failure, will strike either people, place, or processes.[14]
2. The procedures established to prevent any impact occurring as a result of the out-of-course event, or to minimize that impact.
3. The prestructured actions designed to countervail or mitigate the consequences and affects that ensue from the impact, so as to preclude escalation into a disaster.
4. The plans established for recovery, and for restoration of as-intended functioning of the affected people, place, or processes.

---

[14] An out-of-course event may have its root cause "outside" of the place, or be something emanating "inside." When emanating from something "inside" the place, particularly when rooted in the infrastructure or equipment, the designation "fault" or "failure" is sometimes applied.

The result of this four-pronged planning will be referred to as "the plan" or "a plan." Thus, the facility professional will, following this guide, be able to create a plan.

A *fault* occurs when some element of the people, place, or processes does not function as is intended, although some functioning is present. ("As-intended" functioning can be equated to "normal functioning." The former refers to the preferred or ideal; the later, to what is usually taking place. There can be a gap between "as-intended" and "normal" without a fault occurring.) A *failure* occurs when functioning of the people, the place, or a process has stopped or has been stopped. As an example, a *fault* in the HVAC might result in the inability to cool below 82° F or to heat above 55° F. A *failure* of the HVAC would result in no cooling and/or no heating. The plan is established to prevent, or to minimize if not preventable, the revenue loss that can result from a fault or a failure. In all probability, this revenue loss drops to the bottom line.

A "disaster" does not occur; a "disaster" *results*. A "disaster" strikes the *entire organization*, not just one or several operating functions within the organization. A "disaster" is not the inability of a support service or activity—be it computer operations, telecommunications, or elevators—to function in an as-intended manner, but the *inability of the organization to function in its as-intended manner*. The inability of the organization to function *may* result from the mal- or misfunctioning of a support service or activity—possibly a fault or failure—but just because there is a fault or failure does not mean that the entire organization may or might not be able to function. Because of this aforementioned reality, we undertake disaster planning. We <u>plan</u> so that when the out-of-course event occurs (or when a fault or failure takes place), the level of risk that its impact, consequences and affects *will escalate into a disaster* will have been reduced as low as reasonably practicable.

In this guide the term "disaster" is or represents the <u>result</u>—rather than the <u>cause</u>—of an event. A *disaster occurs* or *it is a disaster* when the organization is unable to continue to function in a predetermined manner, or is unable to recommence such functioning after the lapse of a predetermined, tolerable, time lapse. As an example, it would be a *disaster* if the organization's offices were unable to reopen after five business days have elapsed following a shutdown resulting from flooding *if it has been determined*, in the process of establishing a strategy for disaster planning and recovery, that a tolerable closure would be up to a maximum of two business days. In another perspective, it would be a *disaster* if the cost of a closure or of impeded business activities exceeded a predetermined amount, say $1 million. In this circumstance, a loss of business in excess of $1 million due to closure of the entire business process, or of particular processes, would be a *disaster*, regardless of the time period through which the closure extended. The *cause*, in either example, could be rooted in any "problem" out-of-course event: a hurricane, a work stoppage, a fire.

"Disaster" is also *relative* term. It means different things to different people. It can also mean different things to the same person. As the "person" with whom we are concerned is the facility professional, we must create and establish a suitable, working definition for "disaster" for him or her. We need a term applicable to the facility professional's entire organization, as well as to the individual units or functions within the organization. Ultimately in the search for funding and support to enable proper planning to prevent or avoid disasters, and for planning to recover from disasters when they occur, acceptable attributes—a definition—for the D-word are necessary. Just what is a "disaster?"

If we were to ask someone, "What is a 'disaster'?" the response could well be in the nature of "A disaster is something horrible . . . terrible . . . horrific . . . *a disaster*!" Such explanations provide little guidance when we undertake to plan for the prevention of disasters, for our responses while they are impacting us, and for our response to them when we are amid the consequences and affects that ensue.

We appreciate that a "disaster" is equated to something bad, something that usually results in destruction, injuries, deaths, and other losses. Articles in various newspapers, magazines, and journals usually characterize "disasters" as hurricanes, earthquakes, floods, droughts, riots, blizzards, wildfires, lightning, tornadoes, and typhoons. The news media caption stories about bombings, major explosions, aircraft crashes, ship sinkings, railway derailments and collisions, and the like, as "disasters." Often, there were a number of casualties (deaths or injuries) that occurred—or *might* have occurred—during, and following, such "disasters." The "might" enters the scenario because such events usually have the potential to place large numbers of people at risk. This latter group of "disasters"—perhaps better-termed as "accidents"—receive much media attention because of an overwhelming public fascination with accidents and their causes. This is due not so much to a sense of morbidity, but because of an interest to learn the lessons necessary to—hopefully—prevent such tragedies from ever happening again.[15] These accidents prove our increasingly technological society has no guarantee of a fail-safe manner of operation. "Accidents are a fact of life: they have always hap-

---

[15] Nick Pigott, "Disaster!" *Railway Magazine*, July 1995, ii.

pened and will always happen. As long as man's inventive mind drives him to venture into the unknown and reach ever higher, so such accidents acquire the potential to grow in scale. A simple misunderstanding; a momentary lapse of concentration; a small matter overlooked; a weakness in materials or design—even a straightforward act of God—can bring numbingly horrific consequences."[16] Add to these potential causes a lack of maintenance, or disregard of procedures, and the potential mayhem and devastation can be readily seen, whether within your place or exterior to it. Despite humankind's achievements—great or small—fallibility is omnipresent. It is for the potential impact and consequences of this fallibility, too, that the facility professional must plan and prepare.

Dictionaries tell us that a "disaster" is a sudden and extraordinary misfortune; a calamitous event, especially one occurring suddenly and causing great damage or hardship. Catastrophes, cataclysms, mischances, misfortunes, misadventures, mishaps, adversities . . . , all are synonyms.

If we look at some of the materials that are being written and advertised about "disasters" and their scope, we can become more addled rather than enabled to frame a definition. Advertisements in leading computer-user oriented publications tout "disaster prevention kits" priced at less that $1400 for the "basic" and less than $2900 for the "professional" kit! (Is the distinction between *basic disasters* and *professional disasters*?) Another publication equates "computer downtime" to disaster. Other publications, featuring articles on "disaster recovery" illustrate earthquakes, hurricanes, floods, and major fires (individually or together) on their covers. Some consider outages of power or telecommunications or the local area computer network as "disasters." Another publication considered only five major hotel fires. Bombings, such as those in New York's World Trade Center or the Oklahoma City's Alfred Murrah Federal Office Building, are clearly "disasters."

Is a "disaster" an event or the result of an event? In this guide, for planning purposes, a "disaster" is considered the *result* or *consequence* of the impact of an event—an out-of-course event. Events occur; events have consequences. Some events are predictable; others, not. Some events are avoidable; others, not. When an event occurs, it has an impact. As an example, weather-related events can result in lightning, wind, rain, snow, sleet, and other precipitation, and the like. These "events" can be normal or routine, or can be out-of-course. Generally speaking, it is the out-of-course event that has significant consequences: lightning strikes that cause fires, rains intensive enough to cause flooding, or winds fierce

---

[16] John Slater, "Historic Railway Disasters," *Railway Magazine,* April 1993, Supplement, ii.

enough to cause damage or destruction of buildings. If the resultant damage impacts to a sufficient degree, there are consequences resultant from the out-of-course event. Roads may become impassable, parts of a building blown apart, or a destructive fire started.

The occurrence of out-of-course events, their impacts, and the consequences that ensue, are not random happenings. There is a pattern of probability or likelihood behind each such incident. This pattern, a time-based phenomena, is called *risk*.

Risk—a word that frequently appears in the literature, and that is often encountered in seminars and other tutorials—can also be found carrying several, distinctly different connotations. *Risk* can be used as a noun, or as a verb; too frequently the usage is indiscriminately interchanged, and there is considerable risk[!] that the intended meaning behind the user's voice may not be apparent from the context in which the word is used. It is important to recognize some of the different meanings attributed to *risk* so that you can realize what different people may be describing, as well as the meaning ascribed in this guide. The word "risk" can be used to mean *exposure to*, or *chance of*, injury, hazard, or peril; it can be used to mean *hazard* or *peril*. "Risk" is also used to convey *degree of probability of loss* or *hazard or chance of loss*. "Risk" can also mean the *amount or value subject to loss* or *that can be lost*. As a verb, "risk" means *to expose to the hazard or peril*, or *to the chance of hazard or peril or loss*.

In this guide, the word "risk" is used to mean the relative likelihood, or relative probability, that a particular event—be it a good event or a bad event—will occur. For the most part, concerned with disaster planning and recovery, we will confine use of the word to the likelihood of bad or undesired events! "Risk" connotes the relatively likelihood that an event will occur—a statement of the relative probability of occurrence. Such likelihood or probability is often expressed in general terms: "It will probably rain tonight." The same risks can, with rare exception, be quantified: "There is little (better, a 10% chance) of rain tonight." (Impressions about the quantifiable are no substitute for measurement!) The term "risk analysis" refers to a process. It is the determination of the relative likelihood of an occurrence of a particular event in a particular place at a particular time.

For the facility professional, when considering disaster planning and recovery, it is a *disaster* when the organization cannot function as intended. The disaster is the *result*, not the cause. Here, too, we are in the arena of semantics when speaking of "as intended." "As intended" might not be equated to "normal" functioning, for an organization might not be atypical if its day-to-day activities were not optimized. The sought-after number of widgets may not pass quality acceptance, or the blue color may not be to desired specification. If there is a gap between "as-intended" functioning and "normal" functioning, then an impact can widen that breech.

When an event occurs that impacts the as-intended functioning of the organization to a degree that—after a specified time lapse—the bottom line begins to erode, then there is a *disaster*. Put another way, a disaster occurs when the ultimate consequence and affects of an event's impact erodes the organization's bottom line. As a simplified example, an area is hit by torrential rains. Flooding results. An organization's otherwise empty basement is flooded, necessitating shutoff of all electrical power late Friday afternoon. (In the simplification, consideration of what happened to computer-stored data will not enter the arena.) The building is normally closed from 4:00 PM Friday until 7:00 AM Monday. During that interval, the organization could not function, but since it normally does not then function, there is no impact on business functions. (Does a tree that falls in a forest where there is no one to listen make noise?) Because the organization did not have contingency plans in place in which pumps would be available for bailout immediately upon need, drying out could not commence until late Tuesday afternoon. The organization could not resume functioning until Thursday at 7:00 AM. The three-day closure resulted in loss of sales and production, while overhead and personnel costs continued. These factors combined to result in loss of revenue, and of profits.

In the case of a governmental unit or agency, or non-for-profit or educational organization, when the delivery of service commitments—the response of a fire department, the opening of a museum display, an artistic performance, or the provision of information—cannot be met when required or when scheduled as the result of the impact, consequences and affects of an out-of-course event, an *erosion of services*—equatable to an erosion of revenue in the case of a enterprise—occurs. This is a "disaster."

There are four elements in "a disaster": (1) the out-of-course event, or the problem; (2) the impact caused by the event; (3) the consequences and affects of the impact; and (4) the erosion of the bottom line resultant from the consequences and affects.

Disasters, in and of themselves, do not occur: they *result* from out-of-course events (which might be called <u>problems</u> or <u>potential problems</u>) taking place, causing impact and resultant consequences and affects. Neither the impacts nor their consequences and affects will themselves occur or take place. The impacts and the ensuing consequences and affects "cause" the disaster; the intensity of each impact and its consequences being a factor of precautions established in the disaster planning process.

The underlined word problems or potential problems that can occur in any business environment are many, and may be manifest in widely divergent forms. To exemplify planning in view of this—and of the potential for loss of life, for casualties, and for loss of place—more effort and investment has been directed at discovering all potential problems present in the building and operation of Eurotunnel (the English Channel Tunnel) than—without question—any other undertaking in history. The searches for potential problems were in the realms of social, political, and economic considerations, technology, and contemporary and future business operations and policies. The independent intergovernmental group responsible for discovering the potential problems, the Safety Authority, sought to eliminate any risk or combination of risks which could be identified, even if the calculated probability of occurrence was extremely low.[17]

The aim was (and remains) to reduce the level of every risk to passengers and to staff, as well as to the infrastructure and equipment, as low as reasonably practicable (ALARP) or to an acceptable level. The safety case approach used by the Safety Authority offers many important lessons to the facility professional. As we shall see, the approach has two important elements: quantified risk assessment, and the concept of reducing the level of each risk to a level that is "reasonably practicable." This latter concept is considered reduction of the risk to a level "as low as reasonably practicable." The work of the Safety Authority can be categorized as focusing on nine areas of potential problems: flood; railway accidents; train breakdown; fire; suffocation; rabies; tunnel collapse; explosions; and power failure.[18] (Do not too readily dismiss the sixth concern, the potential problem of rabies carried by animals traveling or "escaping" from France to Britain! This was an extremely important political consideration; such considerations are an area that will come into focus later in the facility professional's planning processes.[19])

Concerns about the risks of tunnel collapse were, as can easily be appreciated, were among the most numerous. Although the English Channel does not come to mind when thinking of earthquakes, research was

---

[17] In this context, the word "eliminate" was used to describe the undertakings of the Safety Authority to reduce the risks "as low as possible"—a risk level lower than "as low as *reasonably* practicable" (ALARP).

[18] Richard Morris, "Safety in Depth," *Railway Gazette International,* May 1994, Supplement, 14+.

[19] "The Government was so worried [that rabid Continental animals would use the Channel Tunnel to slip unnoticed into Britain] that it threatened to scuttle the tunnel unless ways of deflecting the disease were introduced." See "The Travelers' Pet Peeve: Britain's 'Jailing' of Animals," *New York Times,* October 2, 1996, A4.

undertaken to determine when the last significant shock occurred in the area (1531). Considerable research and effort was required to estimate its magnitude. Although the tunnels themselves were especially designed to be resistant to earthquakes, steps were taken to minimize possible damage to equipment installed in them, and to ensure that entrances could not be blocked by landslips or local collapse.[20] (Unfortunately, the designers failed to consider the potential of EMFs leaking *through* the tunnel walls. The postconstruction determination that the EMFs may effect the navigation of both ships and jellyfish may require modification in the optimized running patterns of trains.)

In disaster planning, the facility professional must focus on several areas of out-of-course events that can be potential problems. We will examine these potential problems in terms of *the people*, *the place*, and *the processes*. First, let us consider the areas of potential problems. In considering out-of-course events, it is important to recognize that not *each and every* one of them can loom as a potential "problem" that can strike your place. The measured level of risk that certain out-of-course events might strike your place may be acceptably low, thus precluding the necessity of providing for that particular event in your plan. When the measured level of risk of individual out-of-course events is not acceptably low, such events are problems (or may be considered as *potential* problems) and thus must be provided for in your plan and planning.

When considering the problem events that can impact a business process center or business process cell (the BPC, described elsewhere), it is important to recognize that some problems are *latent* and some are *kinetic*. A hurricane or the loss of vital business records or sabotage are latent problems: they *can* occur. *Kinetic* problems, or "conditions"—such as electromagnetic forces (EMFs), improper or inadequate wayfinding signage, or insufficiency of emergency lighting—are *present* on or at the place. The basic difference between potential and kinetic problems is that impacts, consequences and affects of the former probably has less-than a 100% risk of occurrence, while the latter's level of risk *can be* 100%. Needless to say, both the *latent* and the *kinetic* problems must be dealt with!

Among the most vital steps in formulating a disaster planning and recovery strategy is to recognize and appreciate each of the potential out-of-course events that you need be prepared to deal with.

---

[20] Richard Morris, "Safety in Depth," *Railway Gazette International,* Supplement, May 1994, 14–17.

This vast array of potential out-of-course events—your latent problems—lend themselves to arrangement into convenient groups, albeit, this can be an arbitrary process. As the foundation of your planning strategy and processes will undoubtedly be based on what you ultimately consider to be the needs and the possible approaches for addressing them, the following groupings are suggested as logical and advantageous. These categories are arranged in alphabetical order, not in hierarchy of potentiality or problematicality. When considering each category, it is essential to remember that any out-of-course event, no matter how low its probability of occurrence (risk), *may* strike your place, and have impact, consequences and affects on the place, and on your people, and on your processes. As you consider each of these in terms of your people, place, or processes, do not fail to ponder both those which are "obvious" and those which might appear to be "rare." The facility professional *is* responsible, and must act in a responsible manner!

The categories are being considered *here* as the potential out-of-course events, or as the *root cause* of an out-of-course event, or of a fault or failure. Several of the categories can also be the target (or "the impact zone") of an out-of-course event's strike, or where the resultant *consequences* and the latter's *affects* are borne. These same several categories will be later discussed in terms of *impacts upon them* and the resultant *consequences* and *affects* arising from an out-of-course event.

Out-of-Course Events

Business Process-Rooted   These potential problems are related to whether or not your business processes or business functions are organized, systematized, or engineered or re-engineered in a manner that provides for continuity.

Business processes embrace the totality of just how each individual business process center or cell, and the aggregation of these, are established and operated. They are your systems and procedures—whether formally documented or conducted and performed according to "lore"—which form the foundation upon which the organization functions. In formulating your disaster planning and recovery strategy, each business system or procedure or process has to be considered as the root of a potential *cause* of an out-of-course event—or a place of fault or failure—that *can impact* the functioning of the organization. (Business processes themselves are obligatory considerations in formulating your strategy because they are where the *impact* of other out-of-course events are felt, or where the *consequences and affects* of the impact ensue.)

A frequent fault in the manner in which a business process functions is the failure to have necessary business information, data, and records of these available, accessible, and usable whenever and wherever needed. Without a proper records management program, the organization may fail simply because provision was not made to save and protect necessary business information and data. Information later *needed* may not have been saved, or it may not be *protected* against the impact or consequences and affects of other risks, or it may not be *accessible* or *usable* simply because of neglect to also preserve the software codes, or computer hardware, or other equipment necessary to convert magnetically stored data into eye-readable information. An area that is very frequently neglected is the need to systematically archive *and* properly (in terms of both site and situation) store data on PC disks.

As important as *saving* and *preserving* business information and data is the judicious *destruction* of information and data for which there are no legal or sound business reasons for saving and preserving. The potential consequences of preserving information or data you do not need are as dangerous as not having that which you should have preserved. The *risks* involved increase dramatically as the amount of information and data created and received mushrooms! (Historical materials—sometimes referred to as archival materials—should be saved, preserved, and protected. However, the existence of such information can result in an increased level of risk of liability or penalty simply because the organization has the information.)

Another common business process fault is lack of communication between two or more BPCs, or among BPCs. "B" may not know what "A" is doing, and why, with a potential impact, say, on sales or customer service. The ultimate consequence and affect can be loss of sales and revenue.

Civic and Governmental-Based These potential problems arise when a governmental body—international, national, state, or local—*does* something, or *omits* doing something. Besides the obvious "big bangs"—wars, military actions, and trade embargoes—actions or inactions of your government, and the governments of others, can impact your people, your place, and your processes, resulting in consequences that interrupt, impede, or halt your business processes.

These governmental-based events are diverse, and include (in addition to the "big bangs") curfews and imposed closings (whether a specific area or a specific function), activation of the National Guard (which can absent key personnel), export and import regulations, and the imposition of prescriptives. Your place might be "commandeered" for use as a firefighting platform, limiting your access, interrupting your processes, and possibly harming the infrastructure, equipment, or furnishings. Your place may be commandeered or designated as an area of refuge during an government-declared emergency, preventing or impeding its as-intended use. Civic events include riots, civic disorders, and insurrections which themselves may interrupt or impede your conduct of business, or may be the basis for curfews or imposed closings, or result in damage or destruction.

Work stoppage by a governmental or quasigovernmental agency—such as the Postal Service—or the lack of an approved budget (federal, state, or local) can result in a shutdown of specific governmental services, which can impact BPC's as-intended functioning.

On the "omission" side, a governmental body may fail to contain or control rioting, fires, or prevent the escape of prisoners.

Construction and Materials Problems, within these realms, are concerned with whether the place (again, site, building, space, and infrastructure) has been built in a manner that will suit its intended purpose. Of particular concern can be historic or old buildings that have been "recycled" for new uses.

Landslips—as distinct from earthquakes, earth movements, and other seismic events—can result from the impact of out-of-course events that result from faults and failures or oversights and omissions in the engineering, construction, or materials that *formed* the land that slipped. Landslips can also result from that which surrounds the land that slipped, and which should have prevented the landslip.

As in the design-based potential problems, the onus for creating the place with risks as low as reasonably practicable is with the civil, mechanical, and electrical engineers. The prescriptives must be considered; modeling and simulation should be utilized to determine the advantages of going beyond the prescriptives.

Design- and Engineering-Based These potential problems are related to the integrity of the place: your site, building, your space within the building, and its infrastructure, equipment, and facilities. These problems focus on, as examples, how proof against earthquake or earth movement the building is, how great a snow accumulation the roof will bear, how proof against fire, and evacuation safety navigation paths. Design- and engineering-based potential problems are generally within the aegis of the engineering professionals: the civil engineer, the mechanical engineer, and the electrical engineer.

The germane question here is, "Should design considerations only reflect the applicable prescriptives, of should they go beyond them?" There is no simple answer; however, before *any* conclusion is reached, all elements of design should be judged in the light of prescriptives (discussed elsewhere) and in terms of the potential advantages and benefits gained through computer-based modelling and simulation (also discussed elsewhere). The modeling and simulation can, as examples, point up design alternatives that can reduce the risks that a fault or failure might emanate from design of the place, and optimize emergency evacuation path design.

In that the prevention of casualties (both deaths and injuries) is a prime motivation in justifying the creation of a strategy for disaster planning and recovery, the design of evacuation paths and their physical characteristics should be considered not only in the light of prescriptives, but also in the light of what computer-based modeling and simulation can indicate in terms of alternative (yet complying) designs that can reduce, or reduce ALARP, the level of risk of casualties—both injuries and deaths—in an evacuation.

Human-Intervention or People-Rooted　There is a wide range of potential problems rooted in people, whether these people are a part of the organization, or whether they are "outsiders." These potential problems include error, oversight or omission (probably the most common forms), theft, malicious mischief, arson, vandalism, terrorist attacks, assassination, sabotage, kidnapping, hostage-taking, bomb- (explosive and smoke or chemical) placement or mailing, and espionage. Manifestation of the problems may emanate from a variety of causes: political or religious fanaticism, incompetence or lack of sufficient training, social or cultural or psychological "problems," substance abuse, or from interpersonal relationships between employees, between the employee (or former employee) and "the organization," or between an employee and an "outsider."

Bombings—such as those of the World Trade Center in New York (1994) and the Alfred Murrah Federal Office Building in Oklahoma City (1995)—represent high-profile targets selected by the terrorists responsible. The planner cannot assume, however, that only such "high-profile" places will be the exclusive venue for future attacks. The nature of the place, and its processes—in addition to its people—must be considered in determining risk; however, the irrationality of terrorism can target a relatively "anonymous" place.

Some of these potential problems—as well as problems stemming from staff shortages or labor stoppages—and the task of reducing the risks of "internal" human-intervention and people-rooted causes of impacts may be more appropriately within the province of human resources or labor relations departments, and of safety and security departments. The effectiveness of these undertakings can have a direct relation to the level of risk that any of these causes will become manifest and impact as-intended functioning. The risk that any of those causes that are initiated by persons "external" to the organization can be reduced by the organization's security department.

Illness—usually not purposeful—can have potent impact on one or more BPCs. This risk of such impact can be reduced by providing cross training for the appropriate people. The Greater Manchester [England] Passenger Transport Executive, operators of Metrolink, which provides light rail services covering 31 km from Bury to Altrincham, including the Manchester city center, chose to provide a pool of skills to significantly reduce the risk that illness or other emergencies faced by staff might reduce the level of services provided. All operational staff from the operations director downwards—nearly 300 staff members—are trained as tram [street car] drivers. This means that they understand the equipment they are dealing with. This training also provides a pool of skills to safety operate the equipment for emergencies or epidemics that may deplete the team of full-time drivers.[21] This risk-reduction provision is especially significant in England, where staff illness frequently results in the cancellation of British Rail, London Underground, and other public transport services.

Shift patterns—the system of work organization where one employee or team takes over from another in order to maintain continuous working—and the error and accidents that result from fatigue resulting from the inherent decrements in sleep, performance, and the mood of workers—can result in errors and accidents that are the root cause of people-based out-of-course events.[22] These biological, social, and health effects

---

[21] Eric A. Block, OBE, TD, FCIT, "Unique Funding Formula Pioneers Britain's Light Rail Rebirth," *Railway Gazette International,* November 1991, 759+.

[22] The health and—especially—the performance of people engaged in shiftwork are impacted by physiological factors which include circadian rhythms, ultradian rhythms, elapsed time since last sleep, duration of last sleep, quality of last sleep, and a number of other equally effecting factors. The operational aspects of these factors, and their implications, are being increasingly recognized by businesses, and are being considered in work scheduling and in creating work environments. The implications of these factors in the reduction of levels of risk of out-of-course events are a vital consideration in a disaster planning strategy. See, for further discussion, Martin Moore-Ede, "When Things Go Bump in the Night," *ABA Journal,* January 1995, 56+; "Fatigue: The Hidden Culprit," *USA Weekend,* January, 29–31, 1993, 14+; and "Virtual Reality," *Technology Review,* October 1993, 52+.

not only impact the processes, but also are important factors when people respond to emergency scenarios, and impairment may have serious consequences for safety.

People-rooted problems also include those that are ergonomics-related, such as cumulative trauma disorders (CTDs), carpal tunnel syndrome (CTS), and seven others listed by OSHA.

Error, oversight, or omission arise when people who are entrusted with responsibilities do not act responsibly. This can be exemplified by the failure of New York City Transit safety officials to notify subway train operators that the signaling system does not (and did not for several decades) provide sufficient room for trains traveling at acceptable speeds to stop before a crash. These same safety officials failed to consider whether the braking characteristics of recently built trains would enable the trains to stop within the assumed distance when emergency brakes were activated.[23]

"Workplace violence" is not a new phenomenon, but now appears to be receiving greater media play rather than increasing in and of itself. What distinguishes "workplace violence" from sabotage, rascality, and roguism is that the former is directed against an individual—usually a specific person—while the latter three are directed against the organization or against "random" individuals.

Espionage can take several forms: It can be deliberate, or it might be inadvertent. It can encompass "hard copy information" that is stolen, copied, or "remembered," or it can take place through unauthorized computer access, tapping of telephone lines, or interception of wireless computer networks. Papers not shredded properly can be reconstructed; cellular telephone conversations can be monitored; and proprietary information left behind on copying machines can be lost.

Financial losses from computer breakins and other security breaches, including the losses resulting from the impact and consequences of hackers, viruses, sabotage, corporate spies, and incompetent employees, are frequently classified as "computer-" or "technology losses" while these—and actual theft of computing equipment and supplies—are, essentially, human-intervention or people-rooted events. *Risk reduction* in connection with these losses should first address the human-intervention aspects, and then technology-based aspects. *Countervailance* should address the business process, the information-based risks, and then the human ele-

---

[23] Richard Pérez-Peña, "Motormen Not Warned On Signals," *New York Times,* 22 June 1995, B3, and testimony given at special Metropolitan Transportation Authority safety hearing, July 19, 1995.

ments and the people who have any manner of access to the computer system.

Information-Based These potential problems encompass the availability, accessibility, and usability of information and data necessary to conduct business functions. "Information," here, is used in the connotation of "corporate memory," or "knowledge," or "learning" which, when recorded, is either "information" or eye-readable or "data" or electronic-based. Has the requisite business information (business records) been gathered and saved where necessary, and stored and protected as appropriate, as a part of business processes? Will this information (perhaps created in a digital-based data format) be available when needed, accessible as required, and be in a (or convertible into a) usable format? Do procedure and instruction manuals exist? Are they up-to-date?

Information-based potential problems also include the provision of adequate wayfinding, and evacuation navigation path signage, as well as instructional signage providing guidance for emergency equipment shut-off, alarm transmittal, as well as warning signage for hazardous or potentially hazardous circumstances.

Infrastructure The infrastructure of a building has many potential problems, including the proper functioning of the over-all heating, ventilation and air conditioning, the elevator and escalator systems, fire detection, alarm and suppression systems, as well as the "specialty" systems intended to protect computer and telecommunications equipment, the cafeteria, vaults, and other specific areas requiring special concern. Burst or leaking supply and waste pipeage, mains, sprinkler systems and standpipes, blocked drainage, and elevator and escalator failure or malfunctioning can be at the root of problems.

Infrastructure external to the building or site can also be the root of potential problems: water-, gas-, and steam-main breaks or leakage, severed electrical and telecommunications lines, road collapses, damage to adjacent buildings.

Maintenance Improper maintenance, or lack of maintenance, can be a potential problem area. "Maintenance" is concerned with the site, building, infrastructure, equipment, and facilities of the place. In addition to maintenance of the place and of the processes (*and* of the people!) in terms of safety in the workplace, there must be proper maintenance of the disaster preparedness and recovery plan. This includes periodic drills and practice sessions, review of the scope of the plan, review for changes in the people, the place, and the processes, and review for changes in the technology utilized in the processes. "Maintenance" also encompasses the "sick office syndrome" wherein the presence of microbials (air-borne bacteria, fungi, dust, and chemical particles)—usually associated with the HVAC system—and gaseous elements (often carcinogens)—usually emanations from furnishings—can impact the people's health and well-being.

Nature-Based Nature-based problems encompass the "acts of God," and include seismic events such as earthquakes and earth movements, hurricanes, tornadoes, typhoons, floods, tidal waves, lightning strikes, precipitation—rain, hail, snow, sleet, and fog—winds, sun spots (electromagnetic storms), volcanic activity, water shortages and droughts, and other similar events we usually attribute to, or blame on, Mother (or Father) Nature. Another group of Nature-based events involve animals. Animals—in response to instinct—can be the root cause of a variety of out-of-course events. Some examples of disasters rooted in the instinctive actions of animals are described in following pages.

Lightning strikes and their transients, in addition to damaging power lines and possibly impacting switch gear causing interruptions, can also cause power line and telecommunications line surges that damage or destroy equipment connected to them. Lightning arrestors associated with telephone lines prevent damage only in 95% of strike instances. Lightning strikes can be characterized as causing unexpected and unexplained damages.[24]

Place-Related Place-related problems emerge from circumstances that can be described as being "in the wrong place at the wrong time." The out-of-course event or the problem *does not* strike your organization's people, place, or processes directly, but strikes another's people, place, or processes. The "impact" on your organization occurs as a consequence of the impact on another organization, but only because you are relatively near to that other organization's place. A flood (a nature-based event) can be anticipated and planned for, but if the flood waters can become contaminated with hazardous chemicals or other substances leaking into the flood waters from an up-water site that might flow into your place, you are faced with another dimension in planning and recovery.

Other place-related event include an aircraft—or falling piece of equipment from an aircraft—that crashes onto your place or building; a

---

[24] Application Note 109, "Testing ITE and Telecommunications Equipment for Immunity to Lightning Transients," *Compliance Engineering*, 1992, 7.

railway derailment, or highway or waterway accident that releases (or might release) toxic or inflammable chemicals or gasses near your place; or the grounding or sinking or a ship or barge carrying essential staff or materials. (Highway accidents that cause leakage of hazardous substances or that cause significant fires are becoming increasingly common and a growing concern of federal regulatory agencies. The increasing number of fires resulting from propane tanker-truck accidents—exemplified by a massive explosion and fire that resulted from a crash because the driver had fallen asleep at the wheel after working more hours without rest than permitted by law—has prompted the National Transportation Safety Board to recommend that the "Jersey wall" highway dividers be redesigned to resist the impact of trucks.) You can—through site selection—reduce the risk of such out-of-course events impacting *your* place.

Place-related out-of-course events can also be rooted in subsurface gas mains, or petroleum pipelines on or proximate to your site.

Technology-Based Here we have a vast range of potential problems, many of which related to the continuity of supply of proper electrical power, both *to* the place (for which the utility is responsible), and *within* the place (for which the facility is responsible). Power-related problems include failures, outages (blackouts) or shortages of electric power; sags or voltage drops (brownouts); spikes or transients; surges or over voltages; and "electrical noise" (harmonics, electromagnetic interference or radio frequency interference *in* the power lines). Other technology-based potential problems include communication (whatever the medium) failures or delays, failures in computing systems, whether hardware or software, and failures in intercomputer linkages. Technology-based problems also include electromagnetic forces (sometimes termed "fields") (EMFs), electromagnetic interference (EMI), electrostatic discharge (ESD), and other electromagnetic radiation phenomenon that may emanate from various sources, such as medical treatment devices, vapor disposition systems, packaging systems, industrial processes, testing equipment, personal computers and their (and television) screens, fluorescent lighting fixtures, microwave devices, high-voltage power lines and transformers, radio (and other broadcast) and television transmitters (including cellular telephones), copiers, and laser printers. "New" sources of EMFs are magnetic levitation high-speed transport systems, and can be a concern if proposed or planned lines are proximate to your place. EMFs that radiate from airport (and other) security X-ray probes, and from refrigerators and loudspeakers, *may* cause laptop computers to lose information. In this guide, "EMF" will be used as the all-inclusive term.

EMFs can be, or may be, at the root of a number of significant problems. In terms of impact on BPCs, the EMFs can contaminate or disrupt magnetic data. That means—simply put—that EMFs can destroy the data stored on computer disks, drives, and tapes. EMFs can also corrupt data being transmitted on both hard-wired and wireless connections and networks. EMFs can cause interference on FM, AM, and cellular radios (themselves emitters of EMFs!). It is strongly suspected, by some authorities, that EMFs—based on epidemiological studies—may cause, or increase, the incidences of leukemia, birth defects, breast cancer, and other diseases, although the evidence in this regard is far from conclusive.[25]

Problems related to the supply of electric power can cascade into several related technology-based problems. It is common to use an "uninterruptable power supply" (UPS) device in conjunction with personal and enterprise computers. However, "UPS" is a generic term used to describe power-conditioning or power-condition-correcting devices rather than devices used to assure an uninterrupted continuity in proper power. Often, power-protection devices are installed without knowledge of what actually should be protected against. Many devices do not provide the "popular concept of protection" associated with them. Some battery devices provide only limited (limited to a period much briefer than thought!) power continuity. Power "conditioning" and power "continuity" have to consider sags and undervoltage, surges and overvoltages, transients or spikes, outages, and "noise." There are widely differing rates of occurrence of these anomalies, reflecting times of the day, days of the week, period of the year, and the geographic location of the place.[26]

A technology-based event, say, an outage in the supply of electricity, can actually itself be caused by human intervention (perhaps sabotage or rascality at the power generating plant). Technology itself tends to convey the implication of less involvement of, or reliance on, people. The utilization of "technology" places increased dependence—as well as different types of dependence—on people (although the actual number of people conducting the processes may be reduced as a result of the technology). While there is strong evidence indicating that people are becoming increasingly less reliable in risk-related environments, little understanding of the cause has emerged. The root cause of this phenomenon has eluded considerable investigation, both in university studies and work

[25] See Chapter 6.

[26] National Power Laboratory Power Quality Study: "Power Quality: Yesterday, Today, Tomorrow" paper presented at First International Disaster Avoidance & Recovery Conference, Chicago, June 29, 1992.

by specialists. The problem has been seen in railway operations (increasing numbers of signals passed at danger, and conscious overriding of safety warning devices[27]); in shipping (audible warning devices silenced); in buildings (warning devices disconnected); and in telecommunications switching centers (low-battery indicators muffled). In the latter instance, emergency generators at an AT&T facility could not switch in because the starter-batteries were drained. One of the more-serious long-distance telephone interruptions ever occurred as a result. Disaster planning strategy must compensate for potential failure of people during the impact of a problem, and in dealing with the consequences of the impact.

Transport Transport delays or shortages, include traffic jams, road closures, delays or interruptions in public transport systems, fuel shortages, and the like, which impact the ability of your staff to arrive at work on a timely basis, as well as delays to people in other organizations with whom you must deal. Shortages or delays in transportation of materials and goods (including food for your company cafeteria, and your mail!) can also be potential problem areas.

Another aspect of potential problems related to transport are the out-of-course events which can befall a transport mode and which result in impacts on and consequences for your organization, such as an aircraft crash that causes the death or severe injuries to key members of your organization. Your disaster planning and recovery strategy should incorporate—as an element of corporate succession planning—limitations on the specific individuals within the organization who are permitted to travel (by aircraft and otherwise) together.

The organization of this—as any—list of potential problems can be mooted. Fire is not included on the list although it is a major cause of casualties, business process interruptions, damage, and monetary losses. A "fire" does not simply occur by itself; it is the result of some other out-of-course event. It can be the result of a nature-based event (lightning), human intervention (arson), or technology based (electrical short circuit or over-heated wiring), or the result of improper maintenance (spontaneous combustion in improperly stored waste), transportation (a truck crashing into a power line pylon), or infrastructure (inadequate or improper wiring in your place), as well as other out-of-course events.

The occurrence of any of the above-mentioned out-of-course events *may* or *may not* impact your people, place, or processes when it strikes.

[27] *Some* instances of these problems have been attributed to shiftwork. See footnote 22, above.

When an event impacts people or processes and the consequence and affects of the impact impedes, interrupts, or halts the as-intended functioning of one or more BPCs, the processes of business continuation and of reinstatement of as-intended functioning can be termed "recovery." When the place is impacted, the repair, replacement, or rebuilding of parts or the whole can be termed "restoration."

In creating your disaster planning and recovery strategy, you should—in addition to being concerned with the *root cause*—be concerned with the *potential problem* as it affects your organization. Thus, as an example, in terms of outage or shortage in the supply of electricity, you should determine the impact or consequences of this on your processes, and then focus on the means with which *you* can prevent or counter the shortage or outage (such as by having your own generating capability) rather than focusing on the "problems" of the electric company.

CHAPTER

2

WHY A DISASTER PLANNING AND RECOVERY STRATEGY?

The process of creating a disaster planning and recovery strategy is, in reality, the result of determining the organization's goals and objectives for business continuation—the ability to deliver its goods and services in the as-intended manner, utilizing its as-intended processes, methods, and procedures—whenever any out-of-course event might impair, impact, impede, interrupt, or halt the as-intended workings and operations. *A disaster planning and recovery strategy* is not a method; it is a medium to sustain—a medium that sustains—the organization.

There are several, discrete, steps in creating the disaster planning and recovery strategy for your organization. We will call this strategy "The Plan" or, "Your Plan." These steps, all of which should be undertaken, are not lineal: the first need not be completed before commencing work on the second, and so on. The important consideration is that *all* the steps must be completed before you attempt to create (or put together) your plan. It is the sum total of these steps which provide the foundation upon which your plan is created; any shortcutting in these steps, or the avoidance of one or more of them, can be the cause of a shaky foundation, or one that might crumble and fail.

In formulation of a disaster planning and recovery strategy, the questions facing the facility professional—whether a designer or planner who is creating a place, or an executive or an administrator who is managing the place or one or more of the processes therein conducted—are simple and to the point. First, what can hit or impact the people, the place, or the processes? Second, how strong or intense or extensive does any spe-

63

cific hit have to be? Third, how long does that specific intensity have to last before it becomes a problem? Thus, the elements of *event*, *intensity*, and *duration*. The *types* of events might be seen to be almost limitless in number; they can, however, sit comfortably in 12 categories.[1] What any impact might occasion is the product of its intensity and its duration. As an example, a 50% voltage drop in electricity supply lasting 20 microseconds will have little or no affect whatsoever, while a 20% voltage drop lasting 50 seconds can be extremely harmful to both the devices connected to the supply as well as to the BPCs dependent upon those devices.

The key element in successful planning is *awareness*. Awareness of what can happen. Awareness of the likelihood of it happening (the level of risk). Awareness of the means available to reduce those levels of risks, or to countervail them. Only when you, the facility professional, are aware of these circumstances can you take the steps appropriate and necessary to assure that a "disaster" will not befall the people, or the place, or the processes.

You must first determine *what can occur*. This is the sum-total of all of the *out-of-course* events that can take place. These are the elsewhere-discussed categories of out-of-course events that originate in or from your business processes; civil or governmental actions (or in-actions); the design and engineering, and the construction and materials used for your place (the site, building and infrastructure, and equipment); human-intervention or people-related activities; the availability, accessibility, and usability of your information and data; the civic infrastructure; maintenance of your place and its infrastructure, equipment, and facilities; nature-related occurrences; place-related events; technology; and transport.

The next planning step is to classify each of the out-of-course events that are likely to occur into "*intensity*" categories. As an example, one of the technology-based out-of-course events can be an interruption in telephone service. The "intensity" would apply to the scope of interruption: service to part of your facility, your facility's PBX, the exchange serving your site, all exchanges in your area, your long-distance carrier, or several long-distance carriers. In a nature-based event, abnormally strong winds can affect your place. The effect will undoubtedly increase with the intensity (both literally and figuratively) of the winds: 50 mph, 60 mph, 80 mph, or possibly greater.

Next to be considered is the "*duration*" of the out-of-course event, or how long it lasts. In terms of technology-based out-of-course events, a

[1] The twelve *categories* of out-of-course events are described in Chapter 1, "Disaster Defined."

split-second interruption or lightning surge in the power supply can be disastrous to certain power uses. A computer crash could result, or an unintentional automatic transmission of an alarm of fire, or a flicker in corridor lights. In terms of human-intervention events, or torrential rains, either an "industrial action" or a downpour lasting 45 minutes would probably have little impact in an office environment (although it might dampen the annual picnic), but could effect a manufacturing activity.

The *intensity* of an event determines whether or not that event *is* a "problem." The *duration* of an event determines whether or not that event *can become* a "problem." As a facility professional, you are concerned with events that become problems. As a facility professional, you should be equally concerned with steps that can prevent events from being, or escalating into, problems. These are the integral elements in planning, and will be dealt with in due course.

Intensity and duration need be considered together: An event of substantial intensity lasting but a micromoment may or may not be of consequence, while that same event extending over time can have a substantial impact on the organization. Conversely, an event of little or small intensity, such as a telephone installers strike, can have considerable consequence when it extends over a long period. A brief 60-mph gust of wind may do little damage to the site; but these same winds lasting for hours, or days, on end, will result in drastically different results.

The plan you create will, in actuality, have two separate, distinct parts: first, the "disaster planning," and second, the planning for "recovery" or restoration of as-intended functioning of the affected BPCs[2] when or after a disaster strikes. The "disaster planning"[3] segment is created to reduce the likelihood of something undesirable or something bad occurring and impacting and affecting the as-intended functioning of the organization, and resulting in a problem. This planning is based on reduction in the risks of out-of-course events occurring, of their impact striking the organization's activities, and of the consequences and affects of the impact on as-intended functioning, to a level as low as reasonably practical. The planning is structured in reflection of the nature and the level of the risks, and their potential affects, coupled with sound business judgments, and the required investments of probably scarce money, time, and people resources.

---

[2] BPCs—units of function within an organization - are explained in the guide's section on business processes in Chapter 1.

[3] "Disaster planning"—within quotation marks—is so-styled because, although this term is frequently encountered, planning for a disaster is not the goal and objective. Planning so that a disaster *will not* occur is what this strategy is all about!

The recovery aspect takes into account two considerations. First *some* problems cannot be avoided, and the likelihood of *other* problems occurring cannot be reduced to zero; thus, problems of an intensity and duration sufficient to impact as-intended functioning will occur.[4] Second, the investment necessary to reduce the likelihood of some problems occurring may not be an acceptable business expenditure. Recovery is the preplanning undertaken to assure that the functioning of the interrupted BPCs is restored to the as-intended manner as quickly as is practical. Recovery also encompasses the preplanning that enables impacted BPCs to function in an alternative manner or through the use of alternative processes, in an alternative place, and possibly, with alternative people. Recovery planning considers the mitigation of damage that might occur to the site, building, infrastructure, equipment, facilities, and furnishings, as well as the repair, restoration, or replacement of these assets. "Insurance" is *not* equated to recovery, nor can it replace recovery planning. All that insurance can do is to reimburse the organization with a predetermined maximum amount of money to offset insured-value losses. Thus, part of the planning takes into account the activities and steps— including compliance with provisions of the insurance policy, and proper claim substantiation and submission when a loss occurs—that will be necessary to assure that all insured values are recovered.

THE STEPS IN PLANNING

An organization without a disaster planning and recovery strategy is abdicating its responsibilities to its people, its customers and other constituencies, its investors and other stakeholders, and to its community. You cannot find HELP in the Yellow Pages—a disaster planning and recovery strategy must be *created*.

The process of "creation" embraces several considerations. As a planner, it is absolutely vital to define the requirements of the plan you are creating. What can occur or happen that will affect the people, place, and processes? What is to be saved? How is that to be accomplished? What continuities in operations are necessary, both in terms of tolerable interruption intervals, and of people, place, and process resources required? It is both impractical and wasteful to define such requirements "as you

---

[4] "Problems" are those out-of-course events for which the risk of occurrence (even after the level of risk has been reduced to a level ALARP or an "acceptable" level) is deemed sufficiently high so as to be a concern in formulating the disaster planning and recovery strategy.

go along," although necessary *changes* or *modifications* can (and often do) emerge in the planning process. You must conceptualize the essential methodology or systems or procedures that will have to be designed and be put into place to enable the requirements to be met. Next, you must decide the resources necessary for the methodology and systems and procedures to function effectively under the worst possible conditions. These resources encompass people, place, and processes and the infrastructure, equipment, facilities, furnishings, information, data, and all else used by or for the resources. In addition to your "internal" resources, it is also (usually) indispensable to establish contracts and arrangements with "outside" providers (to "outsource") for the provision of specific people, place, processes, as well as what these will need or use.

You need to consider, additionally, the events, the consequences and affects, and the countervailance systems and resources in terms of (1) the worst possible scenario, and (2) the possibility that more than one event will occur at the same time. You need not only, as an example, prepare for the impact, consequences and affects of *a* hurricane, but for a hurricane of the highest possible intensity likely to strike your place. You need not only prepare for such a hurricane, but also for the (obvious) other out-of-course events such as electrical power and wire-based communications outages (hurricanes can interrupt microwave communication, too, so alternate communication paths have to be carefully selected), flooding, and the like, as well as for (the perhaps less obvious) possible road damage isolating your place—presenting a requirement for catering and lodging for staff—or contamination of the public or private water supplies. (How much bottled drinking water will be required in the place? First-aid supplies? Toilet tissue?) You also have to consider that your alternate sites might be at the same time impacted by the same, or a different, out-of-course event!

It is also essential to consider human behavior, and what the reactions of your people (as well as you customers, suppliers, and other stakeholders) will be during short-term consequences and affects, as well as during long-lasting interruptions to as-intended functioning.

The "creation" entails not only the "creation" as such, but also the testing, practices sessions, reviews, and updating of what you have put into place.

The first, and most important, *step* in disaster preparedness and recovery planning is to create and install a plan *before* your organization (or the place) suffers from the impact and consequences of an out-of-course event! Unfortunately, some organizations do not find the time, or the resources (necessary funding, staff or outside expertise, or asset commitment), or the motivation, or the understanding of the urgency to create a disaster preparedness and recovery strategy until *after* they—or some other organization suddenly thrust into the limelight—suffers an impact and its consequences! It can be said, with certainty, that it is not a question of *if* there will be an out-of-course event, with its impact and consequences striking your organization, but a question of *when* and *where*! The door to the barn must be locked *before* the horse runs away!

In your approach to creating a plan, there are six broad "steps" that you must undertake. Before embarking upon a consideration of these steps, a word or two must be said about the planning process itself. If these seem "complex" or "involved" and, perhaps, unnecessarily so, keep in mind that the place that you are responsible for is itself very complex, with many interacting and interrelated systems that have developed and emerged over a long period of time. The organization, too, is a complex structure that developed over a period of time. Neither the place nor the processes arose overnight. It would be unrealistic to think that either of these, or the people who are a part of them, can be satisfactorily protected and preserved through a simple process. There is no easy road to creating a strategy for disaster planning and recovery that *will work* when called upon. The disaster planning and recovery strategy you adopt and the manner in which it is implemented will make the difference in the organization's ability to continue to provide products or to deliver services when a problem occurs and its consequences and affects impairs, impedes, interrupts, or halts as-intended functioning. This strategy will also make the difference in the organization's capacity to survive. Your disaster planning and recovery strategy will be a strategy for survival!

There are no hard-and-fast rules governing either the exact contents of each of these steps; you may find it convenient to undertake elements of more than one "step" simultaneously. You may also find it appropriate, in your organization, to somewhat modify the sequence in which they are addressed. The governance is based on the "culture" of your organization, and additionally, its size, the nature and scope of its processes, and the existence of any current "plan," as well as on the priorities that are established. The manner in which you would structure your approach, as a facility professional—whether you are an architect, designer, or engineer creating the place, or are responsible for the management, administration, or operation of the place and/or the processes—is fundamentally the same. The several learned fields of interest and domains of responsibility or influence of the "facility professionals," are discussed in Chapter 1.

It is a primary necessity to obtain the endorsement and commitment from top executive management of the organization, or of the owners of the place, both to *undertake* and to *support* the creation (which includes its installation and implementation) of the plan. In many instances, the requirement for the preceding—often burdensome—task is preempted by a mandate that you *will* create a plan. It is also an obvious necessity to obtain commitment for the expenditure of the necessary money, time, and effort for the plan. It is difficult—if not unrealistic—to create a planning budget until you have determined (1) just *how much* plan you will need; (2) the *net* cost (planning expenditures less savings resultant from the plan); and (3) the personnel time and costs that will be required in the planning, installation, and implementation activities. A prudent alternative to seeking an up-front budget is to seek initial funding only to survey needs (a "needs assessment") and to establish costs. (Again, this process is a factor of the "culture" of the organization.) Considerations inherent in gaining the management support are discussed later on in this chapter.

Your initial step in creating the plan *itself* (which, for convenience, will be termed step 1) is to determine which out-of-course events can befall the people, or the place, or the processes that your are concerned about, and are creating a disaster planning and recovery strategy to protect.[5]

In theory, *any* of the out-of-course events *can* occur! Therefore, you need determine which of the out-of-course events are *likely* to occur in regard to where your place is located, where the organization's processes take place, and what people are present. In this procedure, you calculate the likelihood (the level of risk) of each out-of-course event occurring. In your reckonings (the plural is intended, for you need calculate the risk of *each* out-of-course event; there are no shortcuts), there are two extremely vital points to remember: first, that impressions about the quantifiable are no substitute for measurement, and, second, that the level of risk is never *zero*, although the level may be *low enough* or *close enough to zero* to be disregarded. In some instances, you may be able to *reduce* the level of risk to a level as low as reasonably practicable (ALARP), or to an "acceptable" level, or to a level low enough to be disregarded.

Quite obviously, as the number of out-of-course events that can be disregarded increases, the complexity and number of planning burdens

---

[5] Out-of-course events—disaster defined, and people, place, and processes are described in Chapter 1.

decreases. Obviously, too, the greater the number of ALARP risks, and the greater the number of relatively low risks, the simpler the planning burdens become. Put another way, the processes that lead to and effectuate risk management and risk reduction contribute to overall plan simplicity. This process—in effect, not worrying about and not providing for things you really don't have to worry about—provides two important benefits: first, reduced planning costs, and second, a less-complicated (thus, less costly to implement and more reliable in its accomplishments) plan.

Each of the out-of-course events has the *potential* (that is to say, there is some level of risk present) to affect people, to affect the place, and to affect the processes. In your determination of levels of risk, the fact that any particular out-of-course event may be relatively "low" in terms of, say, its effect on the people does not mean that its effect on place or processes will be of a like low level.

The out-of-course events *that are likely to occur* (the events that have not been discounted) may be termed "problems." It is these problems that your planning must take into consideration. Determining which out-of-course events are potential "problems" is a measurement-based process, and is expressed in terms of the measurements themselves. As an example, you may determine, with 95% certainty, that your place is likely to be impacted by a hurricane every 3 years, or by flooding every 7 years, or by an interruption in mains-supplied electricity 15 times a year. Or, you may determine, with 30% certainty, that your place is likely to be impacted by an earthquake or other seismic event every 250 years, or, with 99% certainty, that your place is unlikely to be impacted by volcanic activity for the next 500 years. Geographic location precludes some considerations: Tidal waves simply do not occur in Kansas, while tornadoes *do*! Tornadoes—more characteristic of Kansas—also occur in what-some-times-might-be-thought-of-as-unlikely-places such as Connecticut and Massachusetts, albeit rarely. The relative rarity or low risk (which can be quantified) of tornadoes in those two states should not preclude consideration of them in planning.[6] Just because a particular risk is relatively low should not prompt you to disregard that risk; you must consider it in your overall strategy, albeit in a somewhat manner different than something with a greater risk. The consideration you give the level of risk inherent in any out-of-course is a judgment factor in your planning, and reflects how prepared you wish to be for the potential strike or impact or consequences and affects of that event.

---

[6] Although the level of risk of a tornado *occurring* may be low, the level of risk of *consequences and affects* stemming from the always-inherent *intensity* impacting the as-intended functioning of the organization is high.

The out-of-course events that have been determined *with a degree of certainty acceptable to you* as unlikely to occur *within a period acceptable to you* may can be dismissed as potential "problems." This process is, admittedly, extremely vexatious, but if you travel on a "Eurostar" train through the English Channel tunnel, you can find comfort in the fact that—in addition to the myriad of safety precautions taken for the trains and the tunnels—the engineers and designers, while finding that the last significant earth shock occurred in that area in 1531, found it prudent to build separate running tunnels for each direction, and to incorporate entrance designs that will prevent any blockage caused by landslips or local collapse.[7]

The second step in creating your plan is to determine *how* each of the problems could impact people, place, or processes when it occurs. The processes have to be examined on an individual basis, determining what (if any) impact there will be on each of the business process cells (BPCs). BPCs are described below. As an example of the out-of-course events listed in Chapter 1 that you may have determined to be potential problems, a hurricane could severely damage your building, bringing all processes conducted there to a halt. That hurricane might not damage your building, but might bring down electrical pylons and wires, interrupting the supply of electricity to your place; again, processes conducted there would be brought to a halt. Even thought your place might escape damage, and have an auxiliary electric source, your people might not be able to reach the place because of severe wind and rain, or flooding, or because of a civil emergency declaration restricting travel.

Insufficient air conditioning (an infrastructure problem) can cause shutdown of your computer system, bringing to a halt a large number of processes, but the BPCs not related to the computer system could (or might) continue. The inability to locate vital business information (the organization's "memory" or "records") as the result of not saving the information (which could be a business-process problem, or a information-based problem) could shut down one or more BPCs.

In examining the *impact* of each problem, you can discern what actions can be taken to either eliminate the impact, or reduce the extent of the impact ALARP. Knowing what the impacts are, you can determine

---

[7] In pondering how deep one's considerations should delve, there was litigation concerning trade name protection afforded "Eurostar." It appears that the railway's nomenclature planners failed to do all their sums, for a French court held that "Eurostar" infringed upon the trademark protection given a Paris-based courier firm trading under the name "Eurostart" (the French pronunciation of which—typically dropping the final letter—is *Eurostar*).

what will be the *consequences and affects* of each impact on people, place, and processes. The *consequences and their affects* can be reduced to a level ALARP. This is the third step.

In the fourth planning step, the *consequences and affects* on people, place, and processes of each impact—having been reduced ALARP—must be compensated for. "Compensation" is—wrongly—the sole substance of many "disaster plans." The proper approach (and the approach used in this guide!) is to reduce, ALARP, where feasible, the risk of a problem arising; to reduce, ALARP, the extent of the impacts; and, to reduce, ALARP, the consequences and affects of the impacts. The task is a tedious one.

"Compensation" or "countervailance" can often be equated with "alternate" or "contingency": an alternate source of power in the event of an interruption in the supply of electricity; a contingency computer site ("hot," "warm," or "cold") at which operations can continue; an alternate manual paperwork system to replace a "down" computer-based system. A factor in establishing "compensation" is the determination of time-line requirements for uninterrupted continuity of the particular process. Certain processes can be suspended for a finite period without serious repercussions; others, only on specific days; some cannot be interrupted for more than seconds or minutes or hours without causing disruption to the organization. This time-line determination requires a meeting of the minds, usually the facility professional's and those responsible for processes. The thinking tends to focus on the "indispensability" of *my* processes, and without the needed intervention, here, of the facility professional, can result in unnecessary yet quite extensive expenditures for "compensation" or "contingency" or "alternate" plans!

Step five deals with planning for, selection of, and contracting with, on-call impact and damage mitigation, and damage restoration resources and services that may be required—indispensable!—in dealing with the impacts and their consequences and affects whenever they occur. In addition to the organization's own people, representatives of contracted resource providers can prove advantageous as members of the contingency management team.[8]

The sixth step includes the mechanics of incorporating all aspects of the plan into a *plan manual* and a *primer for survival*[9] (both of which

---

[8] Representatives, appropriately selected, of the damage mitigation and restoration resources providers can, with profit, be included on the CMT. Their participation, and contributions—from their specialized perspectives—to the planning and review processes, can provide important value-added factors to the plan.

[9] The *plan manual* and *primer for survival* are described, in detail, in Chapter 10.

must be periodically reviewed and updated to accommodate changes in staff, use of technology, and of space), as well as the commissioning of the plan, testing of the plan, and a trial period for the plan.[10]

An ongoing aspect of the sixth step is the vital practice sessions. Practice sessions—"drills"—must be conducted on a periodic basis to assure that the plan will work when called upon, and that the contingency manager (CM), the CMT, and the people are familiar with their particular roles—whether active as in the case of the CM and CMT, or responsive, as in the case of the rest of the people—in plan implementation and operation.

In the course of each and every stage of planning activity, it must be remembered that the plan you are creating must have *sustainable development*. This means that in addition to meeting the disaster planning and recovery needs of the organization *here and now*, these needs must be met without limiting the options for *future* disaster planning and recovery needs. The people, the place, and the processes considered in terms of today's requirements must also be considered in terms of all reasonable potential changes in the future. The people—in terms of who they are, the number of staff, their competencies, and so forth—can (and probably will!) change. The place—in terms of amount of space occupied, where it is situate, the equipment and furnishings provided—can change (and possibly might!). The processes—the products produces or services provided, how business is conducted, the technology used, etc.—can change (and likely will!). Planning must incorporate the flexibility necessary to be able to accommodate any required modification when change to people, place, or processes takes place. A signal example of lack of flexibility for change that could have been anticipated is the inability of a frighteningly vast number of computer-based applications wherein dates beyond December 31, 1999 cannot be accommodated or recognized. The cost of correcting this oversight will be measured in millions, if not billions, of dollars *if* the particular applications can be modified; the consequences where corrections are deemed impractical might be total demise of the organizations so-impacted.[11]

In the process of creating a disaster planning and recovery strategy, the first plateau is a determination of what *planning steps* or *planning*

---

[10] In the *commissioning* phase, individual parts or systems of the plan are proven; *testing* is the period of adjustment and tweaking, and a demonstration that all the parts or systems can work together; during the *trial period*, the ability of the plan to deal with normal as well as emergency conditions is proven.

[11] John Xenakis, "The Fin de Siecle Computer Virus," *CFO,* July 1995, 67–68. Also see Chapter 6 for further discussion of this topic.

elements are to be taken. (The second is to take or implement the chosen steps!) In order to make sound business decisions as to what planning steps should be taken, the financial penalties of *not* taking the particular steps must be determined and examined. Thus, the planning decisions need be judged *not* on what the elements or provisions in the plan will cost, but on the potential costs, or the potential liabilities, that will be incurred if the elements or provisions of a plan are not undertaken. Put another way, it is not what the plan will cost, but what can the costs be if there is no proper plan in place to counter the impacts, consequences and affects of out-of-course events. Thus, the costs of not having a plan can be equal to the sum of (1) the *costs of the casualties suffered by the people* (including the value of human lives lost, and the value of human injuries incurred including and the value of lost time because of the injuries, as well as the added costs of salary guarantees or allowances for lost time, benefit payments, and the like), plus (2) the *costs of the damage and harm to the place, its infrastructure, equipment, and furnishings* (including writeoff of assets, damage mitigation, repair, replacement, and restoration costs), plus (3) the *costs of impaired, impeded, interrupted or halted processes* (including the costs of lost sales, of lost customers, the penalties for unfulfilled contracts and delays in delivery of products and services, unproductive equipment, and spoiled or damaged products and materials). If it appears that many costs may be incurred as a result of "a disaster," there are! If all of this appears to sound macabre, it is because of the nature of out-of-course events, their impacts, and their consequences and affects: there are macabre impacts and macabre costs.

The costs of the disaster you need calculate include costs of place and of processes, plus the costs in terms of people (deaths and injuries). In establishing *costs of place*, site, building, infrastructure, equipment and furnishings, and lease or rental values should be considered. In the extreme case, there can be total loss at the site and to the buildings and all they contain. At the opposite end of the spectrum, there can be a small fire damaging but one or two rooms in a suite. A price tag must be affixed to each of these circumstances. If you own the property, and lease or rent space to others, your calculations of costs of place must include cost responsibilities to the leasee that you can incur, such as temporary relocation expenses, responsibility for equipment and furnishings, and other liabilities the lease agreement specifies. Iteration of insured values simply won't do: you may be underinsured! And, you cannot exclude these costs of place simply "because we have insurance." The insurance you *do* have may not cover the particular loss, or all of it.

The costs of processes are the costs—or the penalties—that will be incurred when one or more departments or functions cannot operate. These costs are wide ranging and include, for example, additional costs for products or services you must now buy because you cannot produce them; the costs for activating and operating your computer "hot site"; the value of lost cash flow because receivables cannot process customer payments, or because accounting cannot invoice; the interest lost on overnight investment of capital your treasury undertakes when it can function; and the costs of renting temporary space, equipment, and services. These *costs of processes* typically increase as the time line of interruption extends: the greater the length of interruption, greater the numbers of processes are affected because of the interdependency of processes, generating additional costs. (The business process centers or cells—BPCs—of the processes, and their interdependencies are discussed in Chapter 1.)

The costs of people is an extremely important consideration. The value of each life that does not become a death resulting from the impact or consequences of an out-of-course event might be taken to be $1 million; if the modeling and simulation of your place indicates that a particular out-of-course event that could occur once every 10 years, and result in three deaths and 25 injuries, your potential costs of deaths (using the probably-way-too-conservative figure of $1 million) is $300,000 annually (to this must be added the potential *costs of injuries*.)[12]

Attributing a cost to any injury is difficult; to some degree it is dependent on whether the injured person is willing to accept an insurance, or other, settlement, or will litigate for personal damages.[13] A wide range of statistics are available describing "costs of injuries." (An attorney, when considering a $80,000 investment in computer modeling and simulation for evacuation safety management, remarked, "That's less than the cost for a sprained ankle!")

The *costs of people* calculation should also include costs that would be incurred, incrementally, for overtime, temporary staff, transportation, lodging, and catering whenever as-intended operations are not possible.

These are not simple mathematical calculations. In addition to the mathematical computations involved, a good number of subjective cost

---

[12] For a discussion of the associated costs, see "Value of a human life" and "Value of a human injury" in the Glossary.

[13] Your costs of defense in a litigation—discussed in the consideration of EMFs—can themselves be exceedingly high.

assessments must be integrated into your determination of total costs. As an example, what are the costs associated with the loss of a *specific* customer? A *typical* customer (if such exists)? What are the costs of landing a new customer? Chances are that the organization does not have an accurate reckoning of these amounts. But the importance of the process cannot be stressed too strongly. You will be making a substantial investment in terms of money, time, and effort in the establishment of a plan to deal with disasters and the ability of the organization to recover from such. You will want your plan to work. You would not wish it to fail for lack of full investigation, or for lack of basic investment. You would wish the organization to benefit from incremental investment where additional monies would equate to ALARP reduction in levels of risk. "For the want of a nail . . ." is an inherent danger in forming any strategy for disaster planning and recovery. As has been stated, there is no fairy godmother to undertake disaster planning and recovery strategies! Impressions about the quantifiable are no substitute for measurement!

In some planning "aids" (instructions or advice or "tools"), the determination of "costs of the disaster" is imprecisely referred to as the "business impact analysis" (BIA). The BIA "techniques" that exist in the marketplace (usually a part of a "packaged planning aid") characteristically rely on "high/medium/low" categorizations of both an unrealistically narrow range of potential out-of-course events and their impact targets, and the areas where business consequences could occur. BIAs—as a planning methodology—often falter or are deficient because they fail to ask the right questions. As a result, thousands if not tens or hundreds of thousands of planning dollars go right down the drain![14]

The shortcomings of the typical BIA approach or concept are several in number (here, not arranged in order of importance):

1. The typical BIA-focus is on recovery, rather than prevention or avoidance. There is nothing about quantified risk assessment or quantified risk measurement, or on risk management that promotes reductions in the levels of risk to an ALARP level, or to an "acceptable" level.

2. It is really not "impact" that should be the focus of concern of a disaster planning and recovery strategy—as in the typical BIA's vista—but "consequences and affects" of any impact.

---

[14] The several BIA "products" reviewed by this author can be described as an unsatisfactory (or, at best, an imperfect) methodology. None of those found have been judged suitable for recommendation to clients, or for use in conjunction with projects for clients.

3. The typical BIA customarily provides for a determination of monetary values only, not for a measurement of possible deaths or injuries to people, or of damage or harm to the place.

4. In its consideration of monetary impact, the typical BIA does not gauge the affects on service to customers, relations with investors and other stakeholders, potential harm to the organization's image, or on other obligations, legal, ethical, and moral.

5. The typical BIA is structured around "affordability"—the maximum affordable or tolerable downtimes or out-of-service periods for so-called mission-critical business processes. *All* business processes are, arguably, mission-critical. The perhaps fallacious notion of "affordable" downtime can be equated to "affordable" defects in products or services. An organization cannot "afford" downtime; some, predetermined span of downtime can be *tolerated*, but the span of toleration is a factor of out-of-course events. The goal of "zero downtime" should be as important a goal as "zero defects" in both as-intended functioning, and when something is amiss. Neither downtime nor defects—in any amount or quantity—are "affordable," but under specific conditions have to be "tolerated."

6. As the BIA typically determines what is "affordable," and thus, the resources requisite to achieve those parameters, the implication inherent is that unless the resources are obtained, the planning and recovery strategy will be unworkable. Proper strategy formulation must strike a balance between the resources available (or acquired) for commitment to the strategy and what has been determined as the "ideal" "tolerable" downtimes or out-of-service periods.

7. The typical BIA does not consider the type of disaster, but only how the loss of process will affect the business. Here, both the potential for reduction in level of risk, and consequences on people and on place not affecting the business do not enter the arena of consideration.

8. The BIA typically takes into account only the *actual* damage to the business, and does not attempt to sketch a picture of the *potential* enormity of losses.

9. The typical BIA process is founded on questionnaires (themselves often faulty in structure, or subject to misinterpretation by respondents) or on a limited number of interviews (wherein the interviewer and interviewees often have opposed vested interests), creating appreciably skewed[15] disaster planning and requirements. Participa-

---

[15] Possibly "skewered" too!

tion by questionnaire respondents or interviewees in the BIA process is not necessarily a advantage, nor does it assure they will ultimately "buy into" or participate in the planning.[16]

10. Although the typical BIA's focus on "mission critical" has worthiness, respondents and interviewees will ordinarily overly reckon the "criticalness" of their own business function.

In researching and measuring the factors inherent in creating a plan, some facility professionals may have to engage in activities, or tread in waters, outside their usual scope or realms of responsibility. Considerable merit rests in a organizational restructuring (perhaps, of temporary duration during the creation of the plan) that will enable the facility professional to work comfortably (and effectively!) in this unaccustomed environment of determining BPCs and their interdependencies. As discussed in Chapter 1, a new, or modified, facility professional's hat can be fitted on a "pro tem" or "ad hoc" basis, and the appropriate hat rack provided in the president's or CEO's office.

The Strategy Focus: Business Process Cells

The reason—apparent or otherwise—that you are creating a disaster planning and recovery strategy is to enable the organization to be able to function following the impact of any out-of-course event. This does not necessarily infer *continuity* in functioning or *uninterrupted* functioning, but means that the out-of-course event will not ultimately result in the demise of the organization. From the perspective of the structure of the organization, provision must be made for affected (by either the impact or the problem, or the consequences of the problem) business process cells (BPCs) to either (1) be able to continue functioning "normally" after the impact of an out-of-course event (a "problem"); (2) be able to function in an "alternative" mode after the impact; or, (3) be able return to "normal" functioning after the impact. Thus, we must consider, initially, the organization's BPCs.

The BPC is a center of activity. It may be a department or a part of a department. In some organizations, it may be several "departments." The size, and the activities, of BPCs are related to the size and the nature of the organization. Just *what* a BPC is or does matters little; the essential characteristic is that it performs a specific task or tasks. When

---

[16] One could surmise that the goals and objectives behind the design of many BIA-related products were to either enable the capture of some readily available bits and pieces of planning information on a desktop computer disk, and/or to create a do-it-yourself planning environment using such bits and pieces.

the BPC—after a specific lapse of time—is unable to perform the task or tasks, the "normal" functioning of the entire organization ceases. When the cessation of "normal" functioning of the BPC affects the delivery of products or services, or "the bottom line," it is—by definition—a "disaster." When the functioning of a BPC is an enabling factor of other BPCs (the reality for nearly all BPCs, and likewise a reality in nearly all organizations) and the *latter* BPCs create products or deliver services, the cascading effect of the consequences upon a BPC carried to other BPCs results in a "disaster" rather quickly. This really means that there is a relatively short "tolerable" downtime for the affected BPC before a "disaster" arises.

If the affected BPC (as an example, advertisement enquiry fulfillment) is relatively "distant" from the BPCs which create products or deliver services, the downtime tolerance is relatively long before the emergence of a "disaster." Planning and recovery must, therefore, be concerned with each BPC, and its role in the overall functioning of the organization.

In creating the disaster planning and recovery strategy, it is necessary to delineate the organization's various BPCs, what they do, and what time span of interruption in functioning can transpire before the organization's overall functioning is impacted. It would be most unusual to find that an organization has a listing of its BPCs. It is necessary in creating a disaster planning and recovery strategy—just as it is in creating a re-engineering strategy—to determine the organization's BPCs. This is not a simple task; the facility professional may well need the assistance of various executives and administrative personnel who are well-versed in the organization's functioning and processes to properly demarcate the overall structure's BPCs.

The demarcation of BPCs is the foundation of the strategy under development, and should not be done casually. Often, management might overlook or forget some functions, especially those rarely or not routinely performed. It becomes incumbent upon the "demarcator" to discuss a unit's activities not only with its management or supervisors, but with the people themselves. If this seems a tedious endeavor, regard it as a keystone in your planning efforts.

As the BPCs are related to the size and nature of the organization, you might determine that *a particular* BPC is your accounting function, or payroll, of payroll check preparation, or salaried payroll check preparation, or head office salaried payroll check preparation, or something within the latter.

When the BPCs have been demarcated, your next planning step is to determine *how much time* can elapse before there is some affect on the organization or on other BPCs. Put another way, how much time can pass before something "starts to hurt"? Not only can this time span vary with the calendar (tax return preparation, for example, is seasonal, as are monthly "closings"), but also with the days of the week (payroll checks may be "cut" on Wednesday, mailed on Thursday, with Friday a relatively quite day for the BPC). If your cafeteria or in-house catering (a BPC!) serves food on Mondays through Friday, a interruption in power supply to the kitchen ovens on Tuesday will have some consequence, while a similar interruption on Saturday will probably have no consequence, and possibly be unnoticed. (A power interruption to refrigeration equipment on Saturday could have consequences, and should not go unnoticed!)

A potential pitfall in the planner's time determination is the tendency of a BPC's management or staff to *decrease* the time span they perceive (or aver!) can transpire before there will be any consequence or affect on other BPCs, or before any consequence to, or affects on, the organization occurs. This phenomenon is characteristic of a "my department is the most important, and you can't do without us!" rationale, and must be dealt with cautiously. In formulating the disaster planning and recovery strategy, the facility professional should sidestep "internal" value judging of any BPC, its function, or its importance. Equally vital, however, is the fact that the ultimate costs of the plan, and putting it into action when necessary, are related to the lengths of the time spans. As an example, if the nonfunctioning of a specific BPC can be tolerated for over 12 hours, there is little, if any, necessity to accommodate that BPC's power requirements in determining total emergency generating capacity requirements if the level of risk of a power outage extending over 3 hours is once in 10 years. Put another way, as the length of time that the organization can function without a particular BPC operating increases, the amount of investment necessary for alternative or remedial provisions decreases. Investment in factual determinations is vital; here, too, impressions about the quantifiable are no substitute for measurement. (The aforementioned "no necessity" has an additional aspect: If the noted BPC uses relatively little power, and if its power needs can be accommodated by a planned generator without creating the requirement for incremental capacity, it would undoubtedly be prudent to wire-in that BPC. But after so-doing, if additional capacity is required for other BPCs at some later date, a re-evaluation of *all* power requirements should be undertaken before committing to a new, larger—or additional—generator. The re-evaluation would point-out the "gratuitous" provision for the considered BPC, and it might be appropriate to then dewire it.)

Out-of-Course Events: The Why of
Disaster Planning and Recovery Strategy

The business process cells have been identified. The time-line importance of each BPC has been determined. The next step in creating a plan is to ascertain which out-of-course events *can impact* or *are impacting* individual BPCs. As has been noted (Chapter 1), you are likely to find not only problems that *can* occur, but also problems that *are* occurring. The *risk* of the former can be, by definition, less than 100%; of the latter, 100%. However, that a problem can occur, or is occurring, has no relation whatsoever to its impact or the consequences and affects of that impact on the BPC. In formulating the plan, you must consider, first, the level of risk of each specific out-of-course event occurring; second, the level of risk of each of its potential impacts occurring; and, third, the level of risk that consequences and affects that might ensue from each impact. Each of the consequences and affects, then, must be viewed in terms of the as-intended functioning of each individual BPC will occur.

Distinction has been made between the impact(s) and the consequence(s) and affect(s) of a problem. Impact is the "hit" that the problem has on a BPC. A flood (the impact that resulted from the nature-based out-of-course event, a hurricane) in the records storage basement may make the information stored there inaccessible during the flood period (a consequence); additionally, it may damage the records to a degree that renders them useless (a consequence). The organization's legal department cannot, therefore, access the information contained in the damaged records (a consequence), and may lose a legal suit (an affect). An interruption in the supply of electricity (the impact that resulted from a technology-based out-of-course event, a step-down transformer explosion) may shut down computers in the customer care center (a consequence). Some customers might seek an alternate source of the product or service (a consequence), resulting in lost income (an affect) and lost profit (an affect) for the impacted organization. An emergency posthurricane road repair project several miles from the place can accidentally sever telephone cables (the impact, probably human-intervention or people-caused) and interrupt telephone service (a consequence). Lacking telephone service, the payroll-preparing BPC may not be able to obtain payroll data (an affect), and thus not be able to prepare payroll checks (an affect). Unpaid, employees may walk off the job (another affect). There are several messages: First, an impact, whether internal to the place or external to it, can have consequences both internal and external to the organization. Second, not only can the impact create a cascading of consequences, but many of the consequences (or their affects) may not be, initially, obvious. It is incumbent upon the planner to consider *all* potential consequences of an impact, and the likely costs that might be incurred.

As an example, when records *are* stored in a below-grade facility, the ultimate consequence and affect may be the fiscal penalty of lost litigation. The planner cannot escape consideration of such potential penalty when weighing the cost of remedial action that reduces the risk of ultimate loss of records (say, by utilizing a proper off-site storage facility for replications of the records). It is important to recognize that, as an example, below-grade records storage can be susceptible to more relatively high-risk problems than apparent. Vital records have been inaccessible, damaged, or destroyed in the sub-basement of a major office building in New York City because of failure to consider sufficient historic flood levels of a river; in a sub-basement adjacent to a railway tunnel; in a basement directly over a now-underground stream that still tends to "flood its banks"; in a basement records center in an area subject to far-above-average water main breaks; and where the municipal archives of a moderately sized city are stored in a building on the summit of one of the highest points in the city, albeit over an underground stream!

The strategy you formulate should function optimally to (1) prevent; (2) enable you to cope with; (3) survive; and (4) recover from out-of-course events and emergencies that can impact your business processes, and have undesired consequences on your people, place, and processes. In this formulation process, you must recognize that your organization is unique, and its needs are unique; thus, there are no easy approaches, shortcuts, or off-the-shelf solutions. Your site is unique; your building and the space you occupy is unique; the infrastructure is unique; your business processes are unique; the equipment and facilities you use to accomplish these business processes are unique; your people are unique; and, your management's goals and objectives *for* and *in* a planning and recovery strategy are unique. It is difficult to envision a series of fill-in checklists, or a computer disk or two than can "accommodate" such sorts of uniqueness!

Formulating a strategy is a "scary" process": "scary" because of the almost-infinite variety of things that can occur, and of all the potential impacts they can cause, and because of all the consequences and affects possible from the impacts; "scary" because of the frequent failure of some planners to consider so many of the possible out-of-course events, and their impacts, and their consequences; "scary" because it's not a case of *if* but rather a case of *when and where*.

A comprehensive, detailed analysis of the levels of risks of potential out-of-course events, the levels of risks and the nature of their impacts, and the levels of risks of possible consequences and affects, backed by sound management judgment is the basis for a workable disaster planning and recovery strategy. In creating this strategy, it is more prudent to first focus upon the relative low-risk/high-consequence problems than the high-risk/low-consequence problems.

Most executive managements, standing in front of a mirror and asking themselves if their organization's disaster planning and recovery strategy—*if, indeed, they had one*—was still in the 1970s or 1980s, would be embarrassed by the result. Unfortunately, these managers spend too much time on day-to-day matters and not enough on strategic thinking about *survival of the organization*! It is no longer enough to solve the technical problems of the organization—greater attention has to be paid to disaster planning and recovery.

MANAGEMENT SUPPORT

The very fact that many organizations lack any disaster planning and recovery strategy—whether it be a comprehensive, integrated plan, or simply a plan providing solely for the computer system or for the telecommunication network—suggests, to many, that such lack is based solely on the want of management support.[17] To many others, the lack of a plan stems from the nonexistence of any regulatory requirement that the particular organization *must have* a plan. Although between one-quarter and one-third of the "stimulus" for establishing a plan has been attributed to what can be broadly termed "regulatory requirements," such "requirements" focus on the need for, and the ability of, an organization to *recover* from the consequences and affects of an out-of-course event, rather

---

[17] See, as an example, "Fortune 1000 Companies Commit to Crisis Management," *Contingency Planning & Management,* May 1996, 1+. The article, citing several sources, including surveys by the Corporate Response Group of Washington, D.C., and The George Washington University Institute for Crisis and Disaster Management, Research, and Education, and *Management Review,* August 1995, indicates "less than 60 percent" and "95%" (based on stated 10% and 20% responses) have made a "commitment." The respondents included, among their "major types of hazards, risks, and vulnerabilities" "stock price drop or market share loss," "whistleblowing and scandal," "hostile takeovers," "mergers and acquisitions, downsizing, facility closure, union troubles," "product tampering," "copyright and patent infringement, trade secret leaks, counterfeiting, rumors," and "media and press crisis." [There *may* be a high level of risk that the survey methodology and the sampling techniques may be wanting.—*Ed.*]

than on the reduction of the levels of risk of out-of-course events, their impacts, and the ensuing consequences and affects. Such "recovery" very frequently finds its foundation in the back-up of specified data, and in the off-site facility to use the backup.[18]

It is frequently stated that demonstrating tangible, measurable results that will emanate from a disaster plan will turn the heads of management and move their pens. Quantification and demonstration of a cost:benefit ratio are often taken as key reasons in creating a plan, although some sources state only 20% of respondents indicated their company have a way of measuring that ratio.[19]

In many instances, the facility professional will be assigned the responsibility for creating a disaster planning and recovery strategy, and will be spared the effort of convincing management of the needs. "Management" might also provide a sufficient budget, sparing one the ordeal of calculating a "financial impact estimate!" It is undoubtedly impossible to create such an "estimate" that is even remotely accurate (although some have stated an average hourly financial impact down to the dollar!) or that would be applicable to any of the ultimate range of consequences and affects that can occur in your organization. "Average" aside, how does one determine which "hour?"

Here, *impressions* will have to suffice or you may be spending more money, time, and effort in an attempt to determine what the strategy might save (and this would only be in questionable dollars) than you would in creating and implementing the strategy itself.

How do you reach top management and convince them of the potential impact and consequences of an out-of-course event on the ability of the organization to survive? How do you obtain management commitment, involvement, endorsement, backing and support, and the necessary budget for creating the disaster planning and recovery strategy? Unlike many "disaster planning tools" one can encounter, this guide is

---

[18] Determining *why* an organization establishes a disaster plan can be a risky business! Some "statistics" appear to be based only on organizations (or perhaps only on the clients of the compiler) that have established "hot-sites." Categorized "reasons" are not always mutually exclusive: was the reason "management requirement" or "auditor pressure" or "legal obligations" or "regulatory requirements"? Did management "require" a plan on its own initiative or because of "regulatory requirements" or "legal obligations" (and do the "statistics" precisely distinguish between the latter two categories?).

[19] The presentation of "statistics" in some contingency planning publications fall short of accepted protocols, often making verifications impossible and comparisons impractical, while raising questions about the methodology employed. Such "statistics"—often, the only source for anything "quantitative"—should be employed with great circumspection!

not the forum to explain how to deliver presentations to management or how to create flip charts or which colors should be used with overhead projectors.[20] If for no other reason, each management and each organization is unique in how they are "sold." Yet there is another reason: you are a *professional* and are studying these pages to find and explore guidance in creating a strategy for disaster planning and recovery, rather than seeking the recipe and ingredients for shaping a facility professional.

Often—too often—directors, boards, and executive or top managements are perceived as having interest only in projects that generate significant bottom-line, hard-dollar profits. (In the case of not-for-profit, cultural, educational, and like organizations, substitute *exhibits*, *concerts*, *displays*, *scholarship*, and *enlightenment* for "hard-dollar profits"!) This interest exists because it is their obligation to their various constituencies that such significant bottom-line whatever be generated. A disaster planning and recovery strategy is not a profit-making endeavor. Forming and implementing the strategy can result in cost savings, and cost avoidances. The strategic benefits obtained are, surely, of greater importance. It is when the out-of-course events strikes, its impact felt, and when consequences and affects ensue, that the costs of *not having* a disaster planning and recovery strategy—in comparison with the costs that would have been incurred in creating a strategy—become a reality. This reality arises when it is too late! The costs, on both sides of the equation, include money, time, and effort as well as the strategic benefits or costs. Thus, to obtain the resources necessary to create, implement, and maintain the organization's strategy, the facility professional—unless already given the authorization and allocation—must demonstrate that the costs of not having a strategy greatly exceed the costs of creating one. This process might be termed lighting the fires of enlightenment under management!

The process of creating a disaster planning and recovery strategy *is about* earning a return on investment. That "earning a return" is not earnings in the sense of dollars that drop to the bottom line. The "return" derived *is*, first, reduced levels of risk of harm or injury to people, place, and processes. Second, the "return" is a lessening of the likelihood that such injury or harm will impede, impair, interrupt, or halt the intended functioning of the people, place, or processes. Third, the "return" is the readiness of alternate means of or for the people, place, and processes to function acceptably and to produce product or deliver services during the period of impediment, impairment, interruption, or stoppage. Lastly—

---

[20] One might be wary of "disaster planning products" that emphasize presentations rather than saving the organization!

but of equal importance—the "return" is an enabling of the people, place, and processes to return, in a timely manner, to the intended manner of functioning. The process of creating an integrated, workable disaster planning and recovery strategy *is not about* finding the means of minimizing the costs of the plan.

Factors key to the success in the creation of any disaster planning and recovery strategy are (1) top management commitment, involvement, and support; (2) participation of front line managers and staff teams to plan and implement the strategy; and, (3) an ongoing communication with the organization's staff and constituencies about what is being done, and what it means to them collectively and as individuals.

The organization's executive management must formulate and approve an investment strategy based on value-for-money criteria applied to a rigorous analysis of the risks of out-of-course events occurring, the risks of impacts, and the risks of their consequences and affects. This strategy should be viewed as investment to save and sustain the organization rather than as an investment in disaster planning and recovery.

One of the gravest oversights in business planning is the failure to recognize that an organization both *requires* and would *benefit from* a disaster planning and recovery strategy. Facility professionals may be, at times, guilty of such oversight. The organization's management is frequently also a party to such guilt. One of the gravest errors in business planning is the conviction that *some* disaster planning and recovery strategy will compensate for *any* or *all* out-of-course events, their impact, and the ultimate consequences and affects. The "some" is often equitable to planning to save the computer! Here again, the facility professional or management may be guilty, or they may share in the guilt. Too often— and often too tragically—the facility professional or "management" believes that only the computer or telecommunications system is vulnerable, and vulnerable only to "catastrophic" events, and any disaster planning and strategy need provide only for those two business tools and for "catastrophic" events. It is often only when the realities of events, impacts, and consequences and affects become apparent, and the price and penalties must be paid, that such oversights and errors become evident. Such need not be the case.

How do you establish the need for your disaster planning and recovery undertaking, and obtain top-level support and sponsorship? It might be said, "With great difficulty!" Although disaster planning and recovery should be a top-priority strategic planning activity, managements too often look the other way, and defer allocation of necessary resources. It is frequently believed that either (1) It won't happen to us, or if it does, (2) We have insurance. These myths are challenged elsewhere in this guide.[21]

What starts a disaster planning and recovery program rolling in any organization? The initiation—or, perhaps, inspiration for a program or plan—can come from one or more of several directions. The impetus and stimulus can emerge from any of the organization's stakeholders. At times—often prompted by toll wrought on another organization from the impact and consequences of an out-of-course event that was well-publicized by the media—you may find motivation for creating a plan emerging from more than one sector of stakeholders.

One form of motivation emerges from *recognition of risks and potential losses*. "It's probably a good idea! Let's do something!" suggests that there is, somewhere among stakeholders, that recognition. The other type of motivation emerges from *mandated regulations and rules*, and from the provisions incorporated in *codes* promulgated by professional societies and organizations. These mandates and codes can be collectively referred to as "prescriptives." A governmental or regulatory agency or quasiregulatory body, or a code-establishing or professional group, recognizing the risks and potential losses, stipulates "You shall do such and such!." (It is interesting to note that many mandates speak in the voice of "shall" rather than—perhaps, correctly—"will," but lawyers will—shall?— be lawyers!) The various governmental and regulatory agencies—federal, state, and local—as well as the other professional organizations and standards-setting bodies, that issue rules and regulations impacting or "guiding" the organization are legion; the numbers of such rules and regulations seem to be without number!

The realm of prescriptives and their incorporation into the site, building, infrastructure, equipment, facilities, furnishings, *and* procedures applies to the facility professionals who are architects, designers, engineers in various disciplines, and planners who provide professional services, counsel, and advice to the organization. Prescriptives also enter in to the arena of the facility professionals who are on the organization's staff. While the very nature of prescriptives provides little element of choice, the process of incorporating or implementing prescriptives should be integral to your disaster planning and recovery strategy.

Generally speaking, you have little option but to comply with prescriptives, whether the prescriptive is promulgated by law or regula-

---

[21] The belief that "It won't happen to us" is often based on the conviction that, by following all the prescriptives, all will be well.

tion or ruling, or by a code-establishing organization. The prescriptive rule or provision is established and the organization must conform with within a specified, allowable period of time. Generally speaking, the budget necessary for compliance is forthcoming if only because the organization does not have any option but to comply. The issuance of a prescriptive can be the basis of other important elements in the organization's disaster planning and recovery strategy.

It is most important to recognize that compliance with prescriptives *is not* a disaster planning and recovery strategy. Such compliance is only *a part* of the strategy of a plan.

The primary question concerning any specific prescriptive is, "Does that prescriptive reduce the risk, the impact, and the consequences and affects—upon *our* people, place, or processes—at all, or as low as reasonably practicable (ALARP)?" It is very often possible to go beyond the requirements of a prescriptive and further reduce the risk, and/or the impact, and/or the consequences and affects, with little or any additional commitment of resources.

The related secondary but equally vital question is whether the organization will benefit from the prescriptive. Here, the role of computer modeling and simulation enters the strategy-forming arena. Computer modeling and simulation can be—and *has been*—successfully used to demonstrate to regulatory bodies that implementation of the prescriptives in all instances will not reduce the risk, and/or the impact, and/or the consequences and affects. Put another way, the simulation and modeling indicated that there would be no worthwhile return on the substantial investment required to implement the prescriptives. The governmental body accepted the results of the particular modeling and simulation (discussed in greater detail elsewhere) and exempted the organization from the prescriptives and what would have been the necessary investment.

There are two vital aspects of these "prescriptives" that must be kept in the foreground of planning considerations: First, that "prescriptives" cover specific aspects of the organization, not the entire organization. As an example, the Internal Revenue Service stipulates (in Procedure 86-19) certain requirements for computer records containing tax information. But the I.R.S. is not concerned with computer records relating to other vital business matters such as human resources, customer lists, and accounts receivables. The prescriptives of the Clinical Laboratory Information Act of 1988 require protection of specific laboratory data, but do not provide for the survival of the laboratory itself. Following all the prescriptives applicable to your organization (and even those that do not directly apply) *does not* a disaster planning and recovery strategy make, but is only one bit of a comprehensive, integrated plan.

Second, following "prescriptives"—both in letter and in spirit—will not always serve to reduce the level of risks as low as reasonably practicable (ALARP). An important goal in disaster planning is to reduce all levels of risk ALARP after having determined the incremental costs and benefits of reducing risk levels. As an example, prescriptives relating to evacuation path lighting in your building (that might cost $250,000 to install) might reduce the level of risk of injuries during an evacuation resultant from a power outage to 1 in 1000. Installing additional and/or different evacuation path lighting—at an incremental additional cost of $10,000—may reduce the level of that risk to 1 in 10,000. Unquestionably a prudent investment, especially if you have 3,000 people in the place! "Prescriptives" and the concept of ALARP are discussed, in greater detail, elsewhere.

In terms of *recognition of risks and potential losses*, you, the facility professional, with a likely overview of the entire organization, can determine what is at risk, and how the organization could be impacted, and what the consequences would be on day-to-day functioning. You can see the need for a plan, and set into motion the steps—perhaps unique to your organization—inherent in obtaining the approval and necessary funding and commitment of resources necessary to create a plan.

The impetus for establishing a disaster planning and recovery strategy may emanate from the board room or from the executive suite. Seeing what has happened to another organization, or realizing what can happen to his or her own organization, or to themselves as individuals, an executive, may wisely set the wheels into motion for the creation of the necessary strategy. The board of directors,[22] in recognition of the potential consequences of a disaster, can provide the impetus for the creation of a plan. American law requires a board of directors to act on behalf of the company's investors, not its management. This mandated concern for the investors—their equity in the company, and the value of shares—can prompt (and should!) the organization's most powerful decision-making body, the board of directors, into assuring that the organization has a proper disaster planning and recovery strategy in place.[23]

---

[22] In some venues the term "board of direction" is employed. This suggests a focus on achieving a particular objective, and, in the case of a disaster planning and recovery strategy, a proper, clear-cut "direction" would be invaluable!

[23] Thus, "stock price drop or market share loss" among "major types of hazards, risks, and vulnerabilities" [see above] may not be ill-founded.

"A growing fraternity of CEOs are facing the fact that business continuity planning cannot be delegated" and that the "process must begin and end with them." Yet, "many chief executives consider business continuity planning a data issue, rather than a business issue."[24] Thus, too often the board's or the CEO's setting-into-motion memo (if there is one!), "Shouldn't we have some sort of plan for *computer* disasters and recovery?" is dictated without appreciation that a plan should *focus on saving the business*. Often, too, there is little appreciation of what is entailed, in terms of resource commitment, in establishing a plan. Involvement—on the part of the board or of management—in the form of awareness of some of the needs—is there; the commitment of resources and the full domain of the needs has yet to come.

Your investors may be the source of impetus and inspiration! Investors, individually or as a group, aware of loss of share value of other companies that have suffered the impact and consequences of a disaster, may provide the impetus for the board or for management to set into motion actions leading to the creation of a strategy for the yet "untouched" company. Too often, consideration of impact and consequences is limited to the organization's computer operations, network, and telecommunication system, without any thought given to the potential consequences on the value of the company's shares. Yet one need look no further than Bophol, India or Danbury, Connecticut to appreciate the ultimate effect on share values in an instance where disaster preparedness did not properly consider the potential impact on processes and consequences the community could suffer.

A manager or executive-in-charge of a business process or group of processes perceived as at a particularly high level of risk might be the initiator of the progression of steps in establishing a plan, and spur on management action and support. This is frequently the case in information- or data-related processes: the computer center, the computer networks, the telecommunications network, and the data storage systems. There is considerable focus on these fiefdoms: by vendors, technical groups, and trade media, and the disaster planning and recovery programs of many organizations take into account only the risks and potential losses related to these "technologies." The other areas within an organization that are at-risk, and where potential losses can have devastating affect on the organization's ability to function, will be discussed in the consideration of vulnerabilities. The motivation for establishing a disaster planning and recovery strategy might come from the management of a unit or department itself—such as the organization's

---

[24] John Kador, "Protecting the Business is Your Business," *Beyond Computing,* March 1996, 20+.

records management department, the human resources department, or the safety and security operations, or from the management of another unit or department dependent on a function wherein vulnerabilities are apparent or sensed.

In many instances, consultants, retained for the specific purpose, or as a by-product of other work, will focus your attention on the risks and potential losses. Your insurance carrier can also be the source of impetus. Insurance carriers often identify risks (many of these safety-related), and can work with you to reduce the risks, their impacts, and the consequences. In many instances, the fact *that you have a plan* can be the basis of reduced premiums, something surely of interest to top management.

Top-level involvement is critical because of the strategic importance of the disaster planning and recovery project. It is a project that is a part of both short-term and long-term planning: Without a strategy for disaster planning and recovery, there may quite likely not be an organization to which to apply the short or long-term plans. While an organization plans for the future in terms of products manufactured or services provided or market share, there are certain decision makers and opinion formers who consider disaster planning and recovery to be of no significance and to bring no particular benefits. These people hold that there is no strong link between disaster and recovery planning and the future of the organization, and whatever planning that might be undertaken can be done without seeking specialized guidance, and that such planning can be purchased in the same way as most common office supplies or temporary cold remedies. Put another way, without a proper disaster planning and recovery strategy, the organization may be lost as the result of the impact of a potential problem, and its consequences.

Top-level sponsorship is necessary because your disaster planning and recovery strategy will be both a time-consuming and perhaps costly series of activities. It will be necessary for you, as a facility professional with myriad other duties and responsibilities, to balance the planning and strategy with your other commitments.

In some organizations, the "corporate culture" must be modified in order to achieve the goals established for a proper disaster and recovery plan. Creation and implementation of the plan must be put before operational convenience or tradition, and "cultural artifacts"—ranging from rivalries to decentralized forums of authority—must be placed aside during the creation and implementation processes so that all departments— all processes—can row in unison.

There is no fairy godmother of disaster planning and recovery! There *are* disaster planning and recovery goals for which defined management solutions exist. In managing or guiding a disaster planning and recovery project, involvement and support of top management—ideally that of the CEO or chairman—for both the project itself, and for the facility professional as the facilitator can be crucial. With the CEO or chairman participating in the project, if only on a nominal basis, the possible tendency toward economies of fact and of findings are prevented. So-called "sector leaders"—information or computer managers, sales managers, manufacturing managers, and the like—have a tendency to focus their findings and the facts revealed exclusively in their arena of responsibility (BPCs), to the exclusion of other areas (BPCs). When the CEO or chairman is involved, "economies" which can ultimately impact the effectiveness of the disaster planning and recovery project, as well as impact the costs of it, are averted.

It quite likely will be necessary to overcome resistance, inertia, and preconceived notions held by your organization's executive leadership, top management, staff- and line management, and the front-line workers.

How do you gain top-level support? Some suggest that experiencing a disaster within your own organization will prompt strong and immediate efforts to create a disaster plan and recovery strategy. Too often, this is far from the case. It is often perceived that once an organization experiences a "disaster" they have "had their share" and another "disaster" will not occur within the life-span of current management. Others suggest that when a disaster strikes another organization—especially an organization close to hand or well-known—planning will be immediately undertaken. This is sometimes the case, but it is as likely for the planning, or the enthusiasm for planning, to fizzle out within a quite short time.

Top-level managements will undoubtedly require an understanding of the potential consequences of the impact of the event before committing the required resources of money, time, and effort, and justifiably so. But the problem rests with the fact that with rare exceptions, it is not possible to determine the consequences without a rather detailed study of the consequences in and of themselves. Often termed a "business impact analysis," this process—unlike many of them conducted in good faith—must be based on the premise that impressions about the quantifiable are no substitute for measurement![25]

There are several crucial factors in obtaining project support and resource commitment that are undoubtedly applicable to most organiza-

---

[25] In this guide, the concept of "consequence analysis" is preferred to "business impact analysis."

tions. Your disaster planning and recovery project should have top-level management endorsement and "sponsorship." The reasons are several in number: First, top executives or top echelons of management are being held responsible, by both stakeholders, and by regulatory agencies and courts, for their failure to be a "prudent persons" in instances where a "prudent person" would have had foresight to institute measures that would have avoided or prevented, or lessened the impact of a "catastrophe." A executive or a manager *might* be held personally responsible if he or she failed to assure that the organization had proper disaster and recovery plans in place.

Second, the process of determining needs, creating the plan, and installing and maintaining the plan, often requires substantial investment commitment in terms of money, time, and effort. The investment necessary may well require approval of top management within your particular organization.

Third, the need-determining process may require diversion of personnel from their usual activities. This commitment of time—often substantial—and "temporary duty" may need the endorsement of management levels above the individuals' function or department. As an example, an information management person may have to devote a significant amount of time to determine the adequacy of documentation, file backup and archiving, and coding structures.

Fourth, the need-determining process may give rise to interfunctional rivalries which can be adjudicated by executive management. One function may over- or underrate their importance or realistic timeline needs. As an example, the sales literature fulfillment function may themselves determine that an interruption of their service in excess of 24 hours would be detrimental to sales, while in reality, an interval of 10 business days might be a realistically acceptable interval.

And, fifth, because of the organization-wide nature of the disaster planning and recovery plan undertaking, it may be deemed prudent for the facility professional to report directly to a chief executive, or to an "independent" executive—such as a chief internal auditor—during the course of planning and installation activities. This structural arrangement would probably require endorsement by top management.

The disaster planning and recovery strategy may not be tactile; executive management may not be able to "touch" or otherwise "sense" it, thus making it a hard sell. The often-asked questions, "What will it cost me?" "What will it save me?" may not easily be answered in executive suite specifics. The costs may not be relatively great, and what might be saved is the organization itself. This notwithstanding, the commitment to disaster planning and recovery is a sale that must be made! The sufferings of the people, place, and processes of other organizations—in both terms of experiences and of statistics—can serve in lieu of "touch" and "sense" in gaining management's approval for creating a disaster planning and recovery strategy.

A word of caution concerning the citing of "statistics" in seeking management approval and support is appropriate. As indicated elsewhere in this guide where "statistics" are quoted, some variances occur in the reporting of the same "original" studies (which, themselves, might be open to question as to statistical techniques and methodology upon which they are based). In citing "statistics," it should be emphasized that these are, perhaps, more *indicative* than *exacting* so that approval and support of your planning proposal will not fall victim to the inexacting practices of others! In pursuing support for a plan, it is prudent to select with great care any numbers that you present in seeking management support. Percentages variously cited by different "authorities" can be a sitting duck for someone hunting for an excuse to shoot down a proposal!

"Problems . . . Impacts . . . Consequences . . . ," further on, presents a synopsis of what organizations have experienced. These misfortunes can well create an awareness of the need and value for a disaster planning and recovery strategy for your organization. In "Problems . . . Impacts . . . Consequences . . . ," some "costs" are indicative of the price paid for the lack of planning or preparedness. However, the "costs" *avoided by planning and preparedness* rarely, if ever, find voice in print.

The basic question, "How to gain top-level sponsorship for a disaster planning and recovery project?" lacks simple answers. Awareness of need is predicated on whether or not any of several events have occurred. If your organization has suffered a disaster—or a "near-miss"—this *should*, but often does not, since the "it won't happen to us again" syndrome enters the arena, create a recognition of need. Such recognition can also be heightened by a disaster striking a nearby organization, or by the occurrence of a headline-grabbing disaster. Enthusiasm for creating a disaster planning and recovery strategy seems to quickly wither.

The facility professional, recognizing the need for a strategy, has as his or her first task convincing high-level management that they must balance disaster planning responsibility with other commitments. This task will require less effort as investors, and the courts, hold boards of directors and managements responsible for failure to provide an adequate (or any) disaster planning and recovery strategy.

In some enlightened venues, high-level managements decree that a strategy be created (hopefully, to encompass a realm greater than just the computer, and hopefully, too, to be created by the facility professional as the individual best positioned to accomplish the task).

Even within such enlightened venues, there is need to overcome resistance and inertia from managers and front-line workers.

The role of "top management" in the creation of a disaster planning and recovery strategy is only a one-third aspect of the necessary "triple alliance" necessary for the strategy—and its resultant plan—to work, and to work in the manner intended, when an out-of-course events strikes. The business supremo or the executive suite can provide the impetus as well as "clear the path" for the planning process. These leaders of the organization need do so because of their responsibilities and obligations: to investors, to trading constituencies, to staff, and to the community. There are also clearcut (as well as some not-yet-so-clear-cut) legal obligations pressing on these leaders' shoulders that can be eased by an effective plan. Staff management—facility executives and managers, as well as departmental and function managers—have an imperative role in establishing the organization's plan.

Staff management—either collectively on an enterprise-wide basis, or on a departmental, modular basis—provide indispensable guidance in discovering potential risks of out-of-course events occurring, their likely impact, and the resultant consequences. These managers are additionally the most likely source of advice on the affects of the consequences on the normal, as-intended functioning of business processes. Staff management, for their individual arenas of responsibility, can provide the necessary damage-mitigation and restoration information of what to save, what to save first, how to save it, and where it is located within the place.

The planners, designers, and owners of the place, as well as the management of tenanted places, have profound responsibilities in the creation of an environment wherein the levels of risk of out-of-course events striking, impacting, and resulting in function-affecting consequences are as low as reasonably practicable. In too many instances— often, instances where the end results are or will be casualties that might have be avoidable, harm to the place that may be circumvented, and interruption to processes that could be precluded—the vulnerability search process will reveal aspects of the place with inherently unnecessarily high levels of risk. Revealed are instances where prescriptives do *not* result in levels of risk that are as low as reasonably practicable. Because the bricks are in place and the mortar and concrete have dried, reductions in levels of risk cannot be as low as reasonably practicable only because the place is finished. The costs of change or modification impact "reasonably" and "practicable" and place risk reduction considerations outside of the arena of possibilities. Had aspects of the place, and their connective relation with levels of risk, been considered from a level-of-risk aspect in the planning and design stages then, cost-effective attainment of levels of risk that *are ALARP* would be more likely. It is here, in striving to achieve levels of risk that are ALARP, that modeling and simulation can be an indispensably valuable tool.

You—the facility professional—have been tasked, chosen, designated, selected, assigned, or in some other way commissioned to create, implement, and maintain a disaster planning and recovery strategy for an organization, its people, its place, and its processes. You—possibly alone—may have recognized the need for such a strategy and have brought into action the processes and procedures for action necessary in your organization. Your undertakings in relation to the people, place, or processes may be as a planner, a designer, a leader, or as an administrator. An ultimate achievement of your efforts can be change: You can lower the risk of casualties, damage, and business interruptions. You have the opportunity to institute such change—seize it. Combine management backing with your ability and institute change.

THE PLANNING PROCESS:
BEFORE, DURING, AND AFTER

The creation of a proper, integrated, and comprehensive *strategy* to secure the survival of an organization's people, place, and processes when an out-of-course strikes is divided into three phases separate and distinct planning phases:

1. The Before Phase, or the planning and activities that *prepare* the organization (the aggregate of its people, place, and processes) for the out-of-course event, its impact, and the consequences and affects.
2. The During Phase, or the implementation of processes (in the manner preplanned in the Before Phase) under contingency conditions because the impact and ensuing consequences and affects of the out-of-course event preclude the functioning of the people, and/or place, and/or processes in the normal or as-intended manner.
3. The After Phase, or the activities (again, as preplanned in the Before Phase)—including restoration and repair—that enable the organization to reestablish as-intended functioning.

There are several elements within each phase. The facility professional—dependent upon whether he or she is designing or planning a place or processes, or is responsible for the administration of the place, or for the conduct of processes, or for the services that support the place or processes—must take into consideration some or all of the elements. Each phase, and the elements within it, will be briefly explained below; the fuller explanation—and the means and manner in which the facility professional effectuates them—is what this guide is all about.

In creating your plan strategy, each of the three phases—Before, During, and After—while of equal significance and importance in accomplishing the goals and objectives of your plan, do not require equal (or even similar) investments and commitments of your money, time, and effort resources. Your *planning* activities and efforts, as well as the resources required for them, might be distributed among Before, During, and After on a 6:3:1 ratio. That is to say, for every $10 of resource expenditure for your planning, 60% might be devoted to the Before-planning phase, 30% to the During-planning phase, and 10% to the After-planning phase. It is important to note that these percentages represent *planning investments for each phase*; they do not represent the costs of each phase in the event of an out-of-course event occurring.

Phase 1: Before

Before one embarks on planning to protect and save the organization, the planner must have management's authorization and its support in terms of committal of money, time, and other resources, as well as in terms of endorsement and advocacy.[26] While this *sine qua non* is self-apparent, some planning aids devote too many words (many of which may be inappropriate) to an approval processes that would be inappropriate or unsuitable because of the uniqueness of your organization and its culture. Other than pointing up the obvious necessity for management approval *and* support (there can be a vast and distinct difference between the two) for the creation of a disaster planning and recovery strategy, the means utilized to achieve this in or for your organization are best based on your personal knowledge and experience in (what might be termed) the project authorization or approval process. Important tools for the substantiation of the case made for creating the strategy can be found in three areas.

---

[26] There are some organizations wherein the "approval to proceed" process resides within the structure of the project itself. Thus, the first step *within* any project is "project approval." This approach seems to hold less logic than the necessity of project approval prior to project commencement or to embarking upon the project.

The first is the experience of others. The statistics showing the out-of-course events that have struck other organizations, their impacts, and the ensuing consequences is an excellent resource (but as noted elsewhere—because of some methodologies and sampling techniques used to amass some "statistics"—should be used with caution). These can be assembled with relatively little effort and expenditure; some examples are given in *Problems . . . Impacts . . . Consequences . . .* later on. An important aspect of presenting such supportive statistics is that they be representative of a variety of "disasters" and that they include instances with resultant costs that are measurable and documented.

Second is a presentation to management of representative levels of risk of out-of-course events, their impacts, and their consequences that could impair, impact, impede, interrupt, or halt *your* business processing functions. Gathering and documenting this is more resource-consuming than the gathering of statistics, but the fact that the process "brings home" the realities of being at-risk can be a vital factor in project approval. Third—but of no lesser importance—(and something we at times undertake in marketing disaster planning consulting services) is to conduct a representative Vulnerability Search/Vulnerability Analysis/Vulnerability Rectification. This can demonstrate not only the vulnerabilities present, but importantly, the often relative ease in reducing the levels of risk associated with each. The "mini" VS/VA/VR is an awareness-arousing process that can well serve to "break the news" to the executive suite that all may be far from "love and roses" in terms of the organization's current state and its ability to cope with, and recover from, out-of-course events. The "mini" VS/VA/VR can lead, with benefits, to some reduction in levels of risks even though the approval or planning process does not move beyond this step.

It is reasonable to presume that when your management becomes fully aware that the people, place, and processes *are* at risk, approval will be granted to undertake, and to move forward, with the creation of a disaster planning and recovery strategy custom-tailored for your organization. (If their awareness of *risk*, per se, fails to launch approval, add to this in the boiling cauldron the *levels of risk*, the *melange of risks*, the likely *impacts*, as well as their potential *consequences and affects*!) Management, as well as the approval hierarchy, need, at this planning juncture, to also be aware that bespoke tailoring of a plan is an extremely important consideration: many of the risks that are present in *your* organization, the levels of such risks, and the impacts, consequences and affects that each can have, are undoubtedly unique because of the very character of your organization, and its people, place, and processes. A "one-size-fits-all" or "off-the-shelf" plan might result in considerable disappointment. That disappointment can be the failure of such a plan to rescue or save the organization!

The initial step in the Before Phase is to identify *each and every risk* that could strike the people, place, or processes. These risks include the occurrence of *out-of-course events* (examples of some types of out-of-course events are listed in Disaster Defined, Chapter 1); the occurrence of *impacts* (that result from out-of-course events) upon the people, place, or processes; and the occurrence of one or more *consequence and affect* (that ensue from that impact) that (1) can cause casualties (injuries to, or deaths of people); (2) bring damage or harm to the place, or impair, impact, impede, interrupt, or halt the as-intended functioning of the place; or (3) that can impair, impact, impede, interrupt, or halt as-intended functioning of one or more business process cells. This is an identification of the *can occur* events, not the relative likelihood (level of risk) that they will occur.

An out-of-course event *can* strike without creating any impact on either people, place, or processes. An example would be a hurricane that does not (even without any contingency planning in place!) cause any damage to your building or site, and that does not interrupt electrical or communications services, and does not cause any delay or inconvenience to your staff. That same hurricane could strike on a Saturday (when the organization and facility are closed) and impact (read, sever) telephone service. But if this service was restored prior to Monday morning's opening, there would not be any consequence.

Then, *each* of the risks in *each* category (there are three categories of risk: the risk of the event occurring, of it causing impact, and of consequences and affects resulting or ensuing) has to be measured or quantified. This is the process of determining the likelihood of its occurrence. The fundamental consideration here is that *impressions about the quantifiable are no substitute for measurement*. Although *measurement,* as such, might be impossible or impractical, good *statistical determination* can be undertaken, and can well suffice. Here, it is important to base the "measurement" on as much empirical material as is available (although it may not be *readily* available), and to apply the accepted statistical techniques and methodology to establish the validity of the derived figures. As an example, in utilizing historic information, the planner should derive little comfort from the use, as an example, of the usual 75-year historical weather information for the basis of planning if a greater time span of information is available. The 75-year retrospect is commonly used, but if 90- or 100- or 112-year-old records exist, they surely should be brought into the arena of consideration of risk.

With the level of each risk determined, the next planning step is to reduce (where reduction is possible) the level of risk as low as reasonably practicable (ALARP). Obviously, levels of risk associated with many potential out-of-course events cannot be reduced. Nor can the levels of many potential impacts, or consequences and affects, be reduced. But the levels of risk that *can* be reduced should be reduced to a ALARP level. The "reasonably practicable" element is subjective: In the case of out-of-course events, it is somewhat dependent upon the possible impact; for impacts, upon the consequences; and for consequences, upon the affects on business process cells. In some instances, an "acceptable level of risk"—which might be higher or lower than the ALARP level—is established.

Risks cannot be "eliminated" or "removed." (Vulnerabilities, on the other hand, can be "eliminated" or "removed.") There are, however, some risks, that by reducing their level ALARP, can be "eliminated" in the practical sense, or in the sense of being a consideration in planning.[27] The vast majority of the risks in each of the three categories will, nevertheless, remain, albeit at lower levels. Planning must then provide the means to compensate for the effects of such risks when they are manifest. The compensatory put-into-place arrangements are your contingency plans: an emergency generator, a "hot site" for computing operations, archived copies of information and data, alternate telephone lines, basement pumps, manual systems for interim use, and the like.

Inherent in these considerations, and in the consideration of "support services," below, is the ultimate effect of the impacts and consequences of the out-of-course event on the ability of each business process cell—ergo, each business process, and the organization as a whole—to function. This is the often-called "business impact" that considers which of the business processes will be impaired, impacted, impeded, interrupted, or halted and the time span of such interval that can elapse (sometimes characterized as "be tolerated") before the ability of the organization to deliver its products or services (in the short-, medium-, and long terms) is affected. The nature of the so-called "compensatory arrangements" is

---

[27] This is an area in which the planner must tread cautiously and lightly. That the levels of risk of certain occurrences have been reduced ALARP does not denote that the risk of such occurrences can be ignored in your planning. The "residual" risk is capable of presenting a significant menace to your people, place, and processes.

based on some type of intervention that precludes the expiry of the time span by providing whatever had been predetermined necessary to assure continuity in terms of requisite people, place, and processes. These alternatives are, in many ways, a partial replication of the organization itself: the backup information and data; the necessary computing resources and other procedures to process them; the people to use them; the place where they can be used; and, the power generating, communication, and other services to support them.

Planning the before phase also embraces the prearrangement of a diverse group of "support services" for contingency operations, including "hot sites;" damage mitigation; restoration and repair of damage to the site and building, to equipment, and to furnishings; cleaning; equipment replacement or interim leasing; transport, lodging, and catering; arrangements for temporary staff; and the like. Important here are the considerations (1) that these services be precontracted (the demand for such services may greatly exceed availability because of wide-spread impact—in terms of either area or scope or intensity of impact, or of all three—of the out-of-course event), and (2) that the precontracted service providers know what to save (or provide) first, where it is located (or to be located), and how to save it (or to put it into operation).

Then, all of your plans and procedures are incorporated into a plan manual and a primer for survival. These are the plan documents that provide your people with counsel, on an ongoing basis, concerning the approach and procedures to keep at-risk levels ALARP, and to guide your people in the event that and out-of-course event occurs.

With this accomplished, your plan is ready to be tested and evaluated. Any necessary adjustments or modifications are then made and incorporated into the manual and the primer. It remains, then, for the plan to be both tested and reviewed on a periodic basis, with appropriate changes and modifications made.

The before phase encompasses the preparatory steps inherent in creating a state of readiness: readiness for out-of-course events, their impact, and the consequences and affects.

There is a different perspective from which the before phase can be viewed. The building blocks or modules a part of this perspective are the same as those described above, as is the end result: preparedness. Faced with the responsibilities *in* or *for* or *to* the organization that you, the facility professional, have, you might wish to view, with advantage, a disaster planning and recovery strategy based on the following six building blocks or modules.

Building Block 1   Determine the *goals and objectives* for business continuation—in terms of delivery of products and services, and in terms of the time frame in which this delivery (on both an interim basis, and on an as-intended basis) will recommence—whenever an out-of-course event strikes the people, place, or process and its impacts and consequences impairs, impacts, impedes, interrupts, or halts that as-intended functioning (the delivery of products or services).

Building Block 2   Determine the *resources* (people, place, and *both computing and noncomputing* processes) required to achieve the goals and objectives of building block 1. In addition, determine which resources are now in place or now available, and those which need to be added or obtained.

Building Block 3   Identify the *vulnerabilities* inherent to the people, place, and processes, and the level of risk of each such vulnerability being struck by an out-of-course event. Then, determine the actions necessary to eliminate or remove the vulnerability, or to reduce the risk of a strike to an ALARP level, or to an "acceptable" level.

Building Block 4   Identify both the *impact* and the *consequences and affects* that would ensue on the people, place, and processes whenever any vulnerability is struck by an out-of-course event. Then, determine the actions necessary to eliminate the impacts and the consequences and affects, or to reduce the risk of their affecting the people, place, and processes to an ALARP level, or to an "acceptable" level.

Building Block 5   Review and evaluate the organization's present contingency and business planning (if there is any) to determine the changes necessary to accomplish the ends determined in building blocks 1–4 (i.e., the plan or the disaster planning and recovery strategy).

Building Block 6   Incorporate the logistics and activities necessary to achieve and implement the strategy (the plan) in appropriate documents and manuals (e.g., a plan manual and a primer for survival). Thoroughly test the plan, adjust it where necessary, and update it on an ongoing basis.

An important element in the before phase is to read your insurance policies. Although insurance is not a substitute for creating a disaster planning and recovery strategy, there are aspects of that strategy—recovery of certain monies—that depend on your insurance coverage. First, you should carefully determine that you are covered for all the occurrences that you believe you are covered for. Although this might be taken as simplistic, the coverage you have, and conversely, the exclusions that apply, might not reflect your impressions. Coverage, as a general rule, is inversely related to the level of risk while *need for coverage* is directly related to level of risk. The exclusions applicable to coverage are related to the level of risk! (Insurance companies are in business to make money, not to pay claims. You are interested in a plan to enable you, too, to stay in business and to make money!) Second—if you determined that you are not covered for all the risks you had believed you have coverage for, or if you believe there are risks for which you should have coverage—change your policy! Third, determine if the amounts of coverage are adequate. If not, increase your coverage! Fourth, you must determine whether or not the organization is in compliance with each and every provision of the policy. Failure to so comply can result in disapproval of claims. As an example, many organizations rely on valuable document insurance wherein compensation is provided for reconstruction of lost or damaged paper and magnetic media documents. Such policies usually state the *specific* safeguarding to be afforded the insured documents (rather than *that* safeguarding be afforded)—but frequently organizations fail to provide such protection.[28] Failure to "protect" in the specified manner can result in claim rejection.

It is important to identify items of equipment and furnishings, information and data, and other articles of value that should be protected, or removed from the place, when out-of-course events occur. In addition to their identification, as such, their location and how they are to be protected (by designated members of the CMT or by service providers if the latter are not included in the CMT) should be specified in the plan manual. If the items are to be removed from the place (and this can be safely accomplished), those designated or authorized to remove them should be specified in the plan manual. While these removals to places of safety should not be encumbered by the usual "parcel exit pass" procedures, there must be security provisions specified in the manual to prevent looting or the "liberation" of the organization's property.

Detailed inventories and records of asset values should be prepared "before" and maintained, on an ongoing basis, of equipment and furnishings covered by insurance to facilitate substantiation of loss claims. Policy-specified loss documentation requirements and processes should be a part of the CMT responsibilities, and should be incorporated into the plan manual.

---

[28] The quest for lack of properly safeguarded documents is a part of the Vulnerability Search.

Phase 2: During

As it is *not a question of if a disaster will occur, but a question of when and where*, an important element in your strategy is planning to assure continuity of business processes during the period in which as-intended functioning is impeded, impaired, interrupted, or halted.

The transition from the Before Phase to the During Phase, and the During Phase itself, is initiated by the contingency manager (or by an alternate CM or by a designated member of the contingency management team) who—in the plan manual and the primer for survival—is vested with the appropriate authority and responsibility for the declaration of an "emergency" (including announcements of "warnings," "alerts," and the raising of alarms), and to initiate the plan to prevent a "crisis" or "disaster" from occurring when an out-of-course event is imminent or has struck. (In some plans, the contingency manager is titled the "Disaster Manager." This is perhaps a mis-nomer, since the role of the contingency manager is to *avoid* the occurrence of a "disaster"—the inability of the organization to function—rather than to "manage" it.)

In the During Phase, the preplanned, tested, and practiced processes of countering the consequences and affects of the impact are put into use and action so that the number of casualties (both injuries and deaths) will be as few as possible, the harm or damage to the place kept at a minimal level, and any interruptions to business functioning be as brief as possible. Put another way, the During Phase is *management* that minimizes or eliminates casualties, damage, and business interruptions.

The During Phase *management* is usually conducted from the contingency management center, a designated place(s) where activities related to a declared (or about-to-be-declared) "emergency" are coordinated, directed, and managed in order to prevent (or with the aim to prevent) the occurrence from escalating into a "crisis" or "disaster." The contingency management team—the contingency manager, evacuation aides, searchers, the place's fire brigade, the organization's medical staff, and all others who have been assigned a role in the plan manual or primer for survival—carry out their assigned duties and responsibilities *to reduce the level of risk ALARP*[!] that the event will escalate into a "crisis" or "disaster."

The important functions in the During Phase are to eliminate or minimize casualties (reduce the risk of casualties ALARP), to provide for the continuity of business processes (reduce the risk of impairments, impediments, interruptions, or stoppages ALARP), and to mitigate damage (reduce the risk of damage to or loss of property and matériel ALARP).

Collectively, this is *impact management*. In the course of the During Phase, work toward recovery and restoration commences.

A crucial activity of the During Phase is to record and document *all events* and *all activities* as they occur. The plan manual should include appropriate forms for the log keeping, and designate the CMT member(s) responsible for the recordings.[29] An operative word here is *all*: The time and initiator of each and every action should be logged, for example, sounding of building alarms; notification of emergency services; start and completion of evacuation; "hot-site" activated; emergency generator started; computer shutdown; as well as all other actions taken. Where outside services respond, their arrival times should be logged. Expenditures made should be logged and early dismissal times noted. All in all, the logging process might appear tedious, but in retrospect, *precise* information will be indispensable, or extremely valuable not only for the debriefing and plan review processes, but also for substantiation of insurance claims.

Photographic records (still photos, videos or motion pictures), plus any other documentation specified in your insurance policies, should be made—primarily by a designated member(s) of the CMT—of casualties and of damaged property, and—if it can be safely accomplished—the casualties and damage as they are occurring. The time and location of photodocumentation should be recorded at the time the images were taken. A photographic chronicle of records (hard-copy, magnetic-, and optical media), as well as other matériel and property being removed from the place for protection, conservation, or restoration should also be made. The CM *and* specified member(s) of the CMT should have authority to authorize removal of property from the place for protection, conservation, or restoration; site and building security personnel—as well as the local police department—should be aware of in-place procedures authorizing such removal. (In an actual infrastructure-based out-of-course event, a watermain break caused (inter alia!) substantial flooding in a historic building at a major university. In consequence, there was severe water damage to priceless antiques, and to irreplaceable records. Because the *only* person empowered to authorize removal of this property from

---

[29] Although perhaps technologically passé, provision for and reliance upon logging on paper forms is more prudent than use of a desktop or portable computer. The conditions prevalent might not be a suitable milieu for using a computer! All logging forms provided for the CMT should be printed on "waterproof" paper and furnished with appropriate waterproof markers.

the building was out of town when the break occurred (and was not aware of it), substantial otherwise-avoidable, irreversible damage, and unnecessary deterioration ensued.)

Phase 3: After

The After Phase does not start when the out-of-course event ceases or disappears, but when the affects of its impact and its consequences are no longer interfering with as-intended functioning of the business process cells. A hurricane or flood or power interruption might itself be over, but if structural or water damage remains, or if activities that moved to the "hot-site" because of the power interruption continue there, the organization is still in its During Phase.

The photographic recording begun in the During Phase should continue into the After Phase, documenting all damage that might have befallen the place, its infrastructure, furnishings, equipment, and all else that might require repair, refinishing, or replacement. Photographic documentation of activities being conducted in the "hot-site" should also be made. Photographic documentation (of events both in the During and After Phases) can be essential in substantiating insurance and other claims.

The process of returning to as-intended functioning includes recovery and restoration of the place and the processes. Often, various types of cleanup assistance are required; these should have been prearranged as a part of activities in the Before Phase.

An important part of the After Phase is the "debriefing." The debriefing process should include the CM, CMT members, service providers—including alternate site managements, damage and impact mitigation, restoration, and recovery providers—who are not a part of the CMT, and emergency response officials and personnel, as well as other people who were "touched" by the out-of-course event. The latter group should include both those who were directly affected by the out-of-course event, and those who were spared. The debriefing process is a review and evaluation of the disaster planning and recovery strategy and its effectiveness in minimizing the impact, consequences and affects of the out-of-course event. The knowledge and insight gained directly in actually experiencing the happenings and incidents, coupled with the knowledge and insight gathered in the debriefings, can prompt modifications to the plan. Any modifications deemed necessary should be undertaken without delay.

A checklist of some items that should be considered in the Before, During, and After Phases are listed in Appendix I.

THE "SAFETY CASE" APPROACH

The "safety case" can be used—with noteworthy benefits—to replace, or to go beyond, "prescriptives" as the basis of your disaster planning and recovery strategy. The safety case approach, as such, is the determination of what levels of risk that any particular out-of-course event will occur, or will strike, or will impact, or will result in consequences and affects that impact, impede, interrupt or halt the as-intended functioning of any specific business process cell, and thus, the as-intended circumstances of your people, place, or processes *are acceptable to the organization*. The operative word is *acceptable*.

As the facility professional creating a disaster planning and recovery strategy, you would determine, and then propose, the *acceptable* level (which might actually be greater than, or lesser than, the ALARP level) of *each* risk to people, place, and processes. Such proposed acceptable levels might be greater than, or lesser than, the level of risk resultant from prescriptives or other planning tactics. Often, as described elsewhere, with the advantages of the application of computer-based modeling and simulation techniques, as well as other approaches, applied to the establishment of a safety case, the actual levels of risk can be significantly reduced below that which results from the prescriptives with little or no additional investment (or, in some instances, actually at substantially lesser costs).

The safety case[30] is, thus, the sum-total of all endeavors to reduce the levels of risk that the planner and his or her organization deem appropriate. ("Appropriate" is, here, distinct from "can accomplish.") In application of the safety case approach or methodology, suitable levels of risk would first be proposed, as applicable, to the BPCs, then, with acceptance, to the other hierarchical levels in the organization's structure. The safety case can then be (and often, should be) presented for acceptance—with marked benefit to the organization itself—to mandating bodies outside the organization. These latter groups would include the organization's insurance carrier, code-issuing groups, and government bodies responsible for the issuance of prescriptives. The safety case, demonstrably effectuating lower levels of risk, can stand as the basis for exemption from prescriptives, thus not only accruing savings in money, time, and effort, but also accomplishing these in conjunction with lower levels of risk.

---

[30] "Safety case" is the internationally used and accepted nomenclature for this concept. "Safety" (capital "S") as used in this term conveys a meaning much distinct from—should not be confused with—that of "safety" as the avoidance of accidents and injuries in an office or industrial environment.

You, or your organization, may chose the increasingly practiced "safety case" approach because of an experienced judgment or a belief that the prescriptives themselves simply do not result in sufficiently low levels of risk, or do not lower levels of risk at all, or—at worst—actually increase the levels of risk. The "safety case" (*your* proposed means of achieving ALARP—or acceptable—levels of risk of out-of-course events, impacts, consequences and affects) is formulated, substantiated (often through modeling and simulation), and then presented—for comment, concurrence, and approval—to the rule-making bodies that promulgate the prescriptives that would otherwise be applicable to your own organization, and to any other interested parties (e.g., your insurance carriers). As an example, you might determine (through modeling and simulation techniques) that the prescribed building evacuation path design does not reduce the level of risk of casualties in an evacuation ALARP, or, that newly adopted prescriptives, when applied to your people, place, or processes (usually at great cost!), would not lower the level of the particular risk (but might possibly raise it). The presentation, to a statutory or regulatory body, of your substantiated safety case—taking into consideration *all the risks* present, their potential and possible interactions, and the measures to be provided that would contain these risks—can serve as the basis as an exemption from the prescriptives.

Also inherent in the safety case approach is identifying the organization's dominant concern (the dominant safety case issue). This means identifying *the risk* that would result in the most significant consequences and affects on the as-intended functioning of the organization. *"The risk"* is a factor of what the organization does, how it does it, and the nature of the desired continuity of doing it. Your planning processes and determinations must select "the risk" that is most essential to its indispensable as-intended functioning. In a somewhat subjective process, telephone enquiry response or shipping or accounts receivable or litigation or the well-being of its people or anything else at-risk might be deemed *the risk* upon which planning focuses. *The risk* about which your safety case planning is structured might be that nature-based hurricane, or an interruption in electric power supply (that is a result of the impact of the hurricane, or technology-based), or a computer crash (that is people-rooted, information-based, technology-based, or is a result of a nature-based or technology-based interruption in electric power supply), or whatever might be important to your organization's management.

The primary focus on *that* particular risk, and then focus on the other risks, is necessary to assure—when the out-of-course event occurs—that faults are corrected in correct sequence, to prevent other risks and costs arising from the precautions (the reduction in risks achieved) themselves, and to provide systems and procedures (the countervailances and alternative methods) that have the ability to handle all that which they are likely to be presented under the most adverse conditions.

Traditionally, an organization's disaster planning strategy has been founded on a groundwork of prescriptives coupled with one or more preplanned "responses" or "compensatory provisions" that would be called into action whenever something goes wrong. Essentially, the levels of risk accomplished (or achieved) by the prescriptives are taken to be "acceptable" or, at least, are levels presumed to be "as low are reasonably practicable." In reality, neither of these circumstances might be true! There are two inherent problems—perhaps dangers—in following this traditional methodology: First, there is the very real potential, as a result of "downsizing" in both governmental and private-sector regulatory bodies, coupled with governmental "deregulation," that the effectiveness of prescriptives may become diluted, or may lag behind the "state of the art" in maintaining coverage and applicability to changes in technology and techniques. Technology is advancing while techniques are becoming more reflective of cost-containment and cost-reduction. As a result of changes of this nature, prescriptives may not provide the "protection" usually associated with them, or that they at one time did. An example of this is the lack of prescriptives addressing numerous aspects of electromagnetic forces (EMFs) and the many problems believed to be associated with, or resulting from, them.

Secondly, there is a very real potential that you, as a facility professional, will not judge it prudent to accept the levels of risk attained by compliance with the prescriptives. Put another way, you may conclude that one or more of the levels of risk of specific out-of-course events occurring, or of their having an impact, or their resulting in consequences that affect as-intended functioning of one or more business processes, are not as low as reasonably practicable (ALARP) or are not "acceptable." You will seize the opportunity to reduce (or to examine the opportunities to reduce) the levels of risk. This is risk management.

In the "safety case" approach—utilized today in an increasing number of venues—the *organization* itself proposes to take the responsibility for establishing the compliance standards (that otherwise would be based on the laws, mandates, administrative orders, prescriptives, codes, and associated practices) *away from* the jurisdictional bodies (governmental agencies, code-establishing groups, and standards- and practices-establishing organizations). Then, the organization assumes the responsibility for *creating* the standards (as well as complying with the standards they have created). A governmental agency (but not necessarily the same agency that had previously promulgated the prescriptives) retains responsibility and authority to (1) pass on the *acceptability* of the levels of risk proposed for implementation (their standards and practices) by the particular organization, and (2) appropriately assure that the organization *internally enforces* their standards and practices, and *complies* with them. In this approach, the organization (rather than the outside regulatory groups) first writes the sermon (which the groups may edit before it is delivered), and then promises to practice what it preaches.

As radical as this might appear, the safety case approach is gaining wider acceptance, particularly in Europe. Rather than the regulatory body *setting* the standards (based on compliance with prescriptives), that body approves (or disapproves) the standards acceptable to—and proposed by—the organization concerned, be it in the private or public sector.

The safety case presents—to regulatory groups—a proposed, validated, alternative methodology to achieve levels of risk as low or lower than those obtained through compliance with applicable prescriptions. The safety case is used as justification for the organization's exemption from the prescriptives, and for approval of the substitution of the alternative methodology. The safety case is also used in the absence of prescriptives, where applicable legislation requires the organization to create, and to verify the effectiveness of, their own means to reduce the risk of casualties and of damage to a level ALARP.

The word "safety" is used in reference to the reduction in risk to a level ALARP or "acceptable" or lower; "case" is the method of demonstration and justification, by the organization, of the specific levels of risk, and the means and methods employed to achieve the levels. The "safety case" considers the entire inclusive process of risk management (determination and measurement), "business impact" determination, reduction in levels of risk, and the provisions and processes of countervailance, alternative sites and procedures, as well as damage mitigation, restoration, recovery, and return to as-intended functioning.

For the facility professional—whether planning or designing a facility, or managing or administering one—the safety case approach can function as a valuable resource in two distinct manners. First—and of most useful importance to the professional engaged in planning and design—is the presentation of a safety case to a governmental or regulatory body in seeking exemption from one or more provisions of a prescriptive. The safety case is utilized to demonstrate to the prescriptive-issuing body or agency that the *proposed* method or means for reduction in the level of risk will result in a level of risk *lower than* or *better than* that attained by following the prescriptives.

In presenting a safety case demonstrating a reduction in the level of risk of casualties (injuries and deaths), or of harm or damage, that would be predicted to occur as the result of the impact, consequences and affects of a specific out-of-course event, substantiation based on modelling and simulation (described elsewhere in this guide) would be indispensable. As a (simplified) example, the fire and building codes applicable to a specific building might specify that the emergency evacuation paths be a specific width (say, 3 meters) and be located in four specific areas within that building. The creation of a computer model of that building and the mandated evacuation path configurations, taken in conjunction with simulation of evacuations under the "worst case" scenarios, would indicate a probable number of resultant injuries and deaths. Then, through the modeling of other evacuation path configurations, the simulation of like-conditions evacuations might indicate a very significant reduction in the number of casualties. In other simulations, in addition to varying the evacuation path configurations, the potentially present conditions—such as smoke, heat, lack of light, noxious gasses, as well as the construction materials and techniques used—can be introduced into the simulation scenarios enabling determination of the affects of each variable, and of the variables in combination with one another. This means of reducing the level of risk of casualties ALARP through substitution of an optimal, alternate configuration—a safety case approach—can serve as the basis of exemption from the prescriptive. The alternate configuration can have extremely important values: the reduction in the number of casualties, and—possibly—a reduction in the construction costs of the facility.

Second, but of no lesser importance and value, is the utilization of the safety case approach in seeking executive management support—including the necessary money, time, and effort—for the overall creation, implementation, and ongoing maintenance of the organization's strategy for disaster planning and recovery. It is frequently mentioned, in the disaster preparedness literature, with some such mention probably well-founded, that upper-level managements are frequently loathe to commit the inherently necessary resources for an integrated, comprehensive strategy. One might suspect that the board room is shrouded in clouds of incorrect perceptions and of myths; the safety case will demonstrate both what you get, and what you will have to pay for it!

In this application, the safety case approach provides the means to demonstrate to management, on a comparative basis, the implications that the impact and consequences of an out-of-course event will have on one or more of the organization's business processes. On the one hand, the impact and consequences that will occur with a "No Action" (or No Plan) can be compared with those resulting from a "Quasi-No-Action Plan" (or Quasi-No-Plan) and those of the proposed "Action Plan" (the creation of a plan) can be established, documented, and demonstrated. This, in actuality, becomes a "What if we don't . . ." in contrast to a "What if . . ." approach, and is important in considering disaster planning because of its focus and emphasis on the *impact, consequences and affects* rather than on the possible *event* itself.

The safety case, when established, can also be presented, with benefit, to the organization's insurance carrier. As insurance rates are predicated on "typical" conditions and circumstances, your demonstration of going beyond prescriptives to reduce the levels of risks may result in a decrease in insurance premiums.

Your organization's safety case—the means by which you are *prepared* for an out-of-course event, and the manner in which you will *deal with* the out-of-course event—is also something that might be beneficially presented to the financial community as well as to other stakeholders, especially to your customers and suppliers. That you can present them with evidence that you have established prudent means to assure continuity in the delivery of products and the provision of services can serve to place your organization in a competitively advantageous position.

SAFETY AND SECURITY

The concepts of "safety" and "security" are possibly more familiar to the facility professional than the concept of "risk management." "Safety" can be considered as the absence of unacceptable risk of physical injury (absence of "consequence") from furnishings, equipment, maintenance and cleaning processes, or machinery in the place, or from the place itself.[31] "Safety" is a means to reduce the risk of casualties (both injuries and deaths) that might occur to people (both staff and visitors) present at the place. "Safety" in its traditional sense does not reduce the level of risk ALARP.

"Security" is a means to discern potential out-of-course events, their impacts, and the consequences that (with the exception of detection de-

---

[31] "Safety," as discussed here, differs from the concept of "safety case" discussed elsewhere.

vices that monitor ambient conditions to reveal presence of smoke, heat, fire, gases, or water) result from human-intervention out-of-course events. "Security" practices and procedures may not reduce to levels of risk of human-intervention events, or of anomalies, ALARP. "Security" encompasses or provides the physical means, and the systems and procedures related to them, employed to reduce the level of risk associated with certain human-intervention out-of-course events, and to reduce the risk of impact from fire (whatever its root-cause out-of-course event may be). There is often no clearcut distinction between "safety" and "security"— nor does there need be one—in terms of disaster planning and recovery.

"Security" most usually includes the realms of *access control* (that, itself, includes gates, sign-in and sign-out logs, badging and identification, personnel—such as guards, receptionists, and others responsible for establishing validity of reason for access to the place); *surveillance* equipment and devices (such as closed-circuit cameras, and mirrors to observe activities and events within the place); *intrusion monitoring* devices (to detect unauthorized intrusion or "break-in"); *screening* devices (to detect whether individuals entering the place may be carrying certain antisocial items such as bombs, explosives, guns, and certain metal objects, or whether in-coming mail, packages or parcels, or other deliveries may contain bombs or explosives); *detection* devices (to monitor ambient conditions to reveal presence of smoke, heat, fire, gases, or water); *theft prevention and detection* systems and equipment; and *alarms* or annunciators to convey information about the "security breach," and *event-recording devices* to document any anomalies that occur. "Security," additionally in some places, includes the fire extinguishers, automatic and semiautomatic fire suppression systems, and fire counteraction devices and equipment.

Many organizations, especially those engaged in manufacturing or processing, have long had some "safety" program in place, whether at their own initiation, or as the result of some prescriptives such as OSHA regulations. Frequently, an insurance carrier will provide guidance in establishing a "safety program." In terms of creating a disaster planning and recovery strategy, "safety" focuses on reducing the risk of casualties (both injuries and deaths) in the as-intended work environment. Likewise, many organizations of all types have some sort—ranging from the quite simple to the sophisticated and all-inclusive—of "security" in place.

The facility professional must have an understanding of both the "safety culture" and the "security culture" as they apply to the day-to-day workings of the organization. The "safety culture" is the foundation for placement of handrails, and guardrails, preventing—or alerting people to—wet or slippery floors, provision of evacuation path signage, clearing snow from paths and drives, salting or sanding icy pavements, as well as a myriad of other items. "Security culture" is at the root of the use—among others—of visitor screening practices, guards, perimeter cameras, in-coming mail and parcels scanners, and theft-deterrent practices.

Neither the "safety culture" nor the "security culture" applicable to either the people, place, or processes—in place when the disaster planning and recovery strategy is undertaken—can be allowed to substitute for risk management. *Potentially* dangerous practices or instructions—although such might be (mistakenly) held to be "safe" or "secure"—may be followed rather than a determination made as to whether these have reduced the level of associated risks ALARP. Prudent means to reduce the risk of out-of-course events, their impact, and consequences can increase the effectiveness of "safety" and "security" practices and hardware in achieving risk levels that are ALARP. There must be, on the part of all staff members, a real understanding of not only the organization's safety culture, but also its security culture, as both are a part of the organization's disaster planning and recovery culture.

It has been observed and remarked that "An evolutionary safety culture is [being] replaced by a quantitative analytical culture" and "few of those involved understand either the technical or the cultural implications of what is being attempted."[32] An example of what this means to the facility professional, in striving to maintain a historic low staff injury level through integrating standing practices into the disaster planning and recovery strategy, is that—simply put—just because no one has slipped on a wet lobby floor in over 25 years (ah! the level of risk of someone slipping is *very* low) don't remove the cautionary signs and barriers at the suggestion of the statistics-examining advisor. The level of risk may be as low as it is because the signs and barriers are in place!

Both the "safety culture" and the "security culture" have evolved to reduce the level of risk that something undesirable will happen. Thus, the guardrails or cautionary signage or staff badging are risk-reducing or risk management techniques or devices. The in-place and in-use (the latter, a determinant of their effectiveness, per se!) "safety" and "security" techniques and devices should be scrutinized and evaluated to determine whether they reduce the intended levels of risk ALARP. The

---

[32] Roger Kemp quoted in "Help Us Build Trains That Work," *Railway Gazette International,* June 1995, 391.

organization's "safety" and "security" should be integrated, with benefit, into a single responsibility, and coordinated with its disaster planning and recovery strategy. The organization might consider the value of placing both activities under the ægis of the facility professional.

These "safety" and "security" endeavors can prevent or deter human-intervention or people-rooted out-of-course events (by limiting access to the place, or by noting aberrant behavior), infrastructure-based and maintenance-rooted events (through inspection patrols, and observation of faults), and information-based events (through vigilant implementation of exiting procedures), as well as providing additional "eyes" alert for any irregular conditions that might be present or arise.

The security or guard force itself can both aid in providing evacuation guidance, and in emergencies if the force is trained in fire-fighting, first-aid, or CPR. You might wish to consider whether to have the security force as members of the CMT. There are, however, two inherent dangers: First, some security personnel might lack the qualities and qualifications necessary to advantageously function as members of the CMT. Second, there can be a tendency on the part of safety or security personnel (as well as on the part of other personnel!) to become "heros" by attempting to counter the impact or consequences of an out-of-course event without sounding the appropriate alarm, or delay sounding the alarm until the impact or consequences "gets out of hand."

The *Vulnerability Search* (described elsewhere) includes, in part, an examination of the organization's safety and security program. What that program has put in place to reduce the risk of casualties has to be viewed in terms of the overall disaster planning strategy; many of the risk levels achieved by the safety program will not be ALARP in terms of the disaster planning and recovery strategy. As an example, the banister configuration that reduces the risk of injuries from falls on stairs in the course of ordinary usage ("safety") may not reduce that risk ALARP in evacuation conditions because of possible limited lighting levels, presence of smoke, increased number of people, and stress conditions among the evacuees. Practices related to screening of both visitors to the site, and of in-coming mail and packages tend to fade into the background after other bomb- or explosive-related events quickly fade from the news media. Mail room and lobby screening and detection devices do not, themselves, reduce the risk of human-intervention out-of-course events; it is the *use* of the screening and detection devices that does!

The *Vulnerability Search,* and the *Analysis* of vulnerabilities detected, must examine the risks that the safety program or the security program have presumably "eliminated." It cannot be assumed that either "safety" or "security" has removed (as often they are assumed to do!) risks, or even reduced the level of risk ALARP or to an acceptable level. What "safety" and "security" encompass within your organization should be subjected to the scrutiny of the VS/VA/VR process, and to all other considerations.

CHAPTER

3

PROBLEMS AND PERFORMANCE

PROBLEMS

"Problems"—in the context of a disaster planning and recovery strategy—emanate from "potential problems." The "potential problems" that you need provide for in formulating a disaster planning and recovery strategy are those out-of-course events that have a risk of occurrence (even after the level of risk has been reduced to a level ALARP or an "acceptable" level) that is deemed sufficiently high so as to be a concern. The "potential problem" becomes a "problem" when it occurs. The problem may or may not escalate—depending upon your disaster planning and recovery strategy and the effectiveness of it—into a disaster.

The focus of this guide is on out-of-course events, their impacts, the consequences that emerge from such impacts, and the affects that the consequences have on people, place, and on the as-intended functioning of business processes. It is not the out-of-course event, as such, nor its impact or consequences that serves as basis for creating a disaster planning and recovery strategy, but its potential *affects* upon the people, the place, and on one or more business processes cells. As a facility professional, your concern is with an organization: specific people, in a specific place or perhaps places, engaged in specific processes. Your concern should encompass the *now* as well as the *future* tranches of time.

There are a lot of potential problems lurking out there! Most fortunately, not all of these, nor all possible impacts of each of them, nor all of the likely (or even probable) consequences of each impact may be felt by, or affect, your people, place, or processes. From another perspective, different potential problems can result in the same impact, and different impacts can create the same consequences. As an example, out-of-course events such as severe rains, tidal flooding, a watermain break, or an interruption in the supply of electricity to a basement sump pump can each result in more water in subgrade spaces than you wish to be the case.

In creating your disaster planing and recovery strategy, it is prudent to devote and commit resources only to reducing the level of risk of occurrence for those out-of-course events, impacts, and consequences which could *adversely* effect your people, place, or processes. Obviously, if a level of risk of occurrence is sufficiently low to begin with, use of resources to further reduce the level is simply imprudent.[1]

Although levels of risks of potential problems have been reduced ALARP, or to an "acceptable" level, the "potential" can *still* become manifest and place in jeopardy the as-intended functioning of the people, place, or processes. Your contingency planning strategy, in its various manifestations, is established because a problem may change from being "potential" to being "manifest" or being "active" or "real."

An important premise in planning that is recurring in this guide is that *impressions about the quantifiable are no substitute for measurement*! Put another way, the risk ("likelihood") that any particular out-of-course event, or its impact, or the consequences and affects will occur—and thus, be a problem for your organization—can be quantified. That an out-of-course event might become a problem can also—with certain exceptions—be quantified. This likelihood *should be* quantified if a comprehensive, workable, cost-effective strategy for disaster planning and recovery is to be the end result of your efforts. The effect, and the duration of the effect, of the problem can—with rare exceptions—be quantified. This intensity and duration *should be* quantified for the same reasons. The BPCs that will experience the problem *should be* identified, and the affects of the consequences of the impact *should be* both identified and quantified in terms of severity and duration.

In the real world in which the facility professional is endeavoring to create a plan, some out-of-course events occur so rarely or are so unusual that an attempt to quantify the risk of their occurrence, while desirable, is extremely difficult or impractical: Is a specific potential out-of-course event a potential problem, or can it be ignored? Earthquakes or earth movements are a good example. Dependent upon the geographic location of the place, the likelihood of an earthquake or earth movement occur-

---

[1] If you have limitless resources in hand there might be some value in the further reduction of risk level. However, inherent in a proper disaster planning in recovery strategy is the correct determination of "ALARP" and then, attaining that level.

ring might be relatively high or near zero. If you were planning for a site near Olema, California, your concerns would be great; for a site near New London, Connecticut, concerns would be much less, perhaps, near zero. Put another way, a seismic event would not be considered a potential problem in New London, while it would be in Olema. (Whether hurricanes are potential problems is the reverse: yes in New London; no in Olema.) There are sections of California (and elsewhere) where the likelihood of an earthquake occurring is high, and can be quantified within a time frame, and quantified as to expected intensity. On this basis, it can be stated (and planning formulated accordingly) that for a specific place, an earthquake of a particular Richter intensity (say, R_x) might occur every so-many years (say, T_y), and last for a certain time period (say, D_z). But planning based on *when* the next earthquake or earth movement will occur, or its Richter-intensity, or its duration, will be, at best, shaky! Scientific prediction of that *when* and *how intense* and of *what duration* is proving fruitless.[2] Planning has to consider $R_?$, $Y_?$, and $D_?$ in a manner *measuring* and considering historic statistical data as much as is possible.

In terms of a hurricane striking at New London, Connecticut (a potential problem) we accept that a "hurricane season" exists, from July to October, if for no other reason than a like storm outside of that period is given a different nomenclature. Thus, we should not plan for "hurricanes" but for potential problems with particular wind intensities, type of precipitation, and duration. The "hurricanes" can be classified by the wind velocities. Flooding of the Thames River, which flows past New London, can be caused by storm-borne winds, abnormal tides, spring runoff, or a combination of two or more of these. The risks associated with higher-than-normal water levels must be determined on the basis of *all* of these out-of-course events, not just one alone (such as the consideration of what flooding might occur from *a hurricane with 80 mph* winds likely to occur once every 3 years). The *quantifiable* should include all elements that can be measured or gauged!

Other types of potential problems present substantially greater difficulties in quantification, and thus, manifest significant challenges in determining a level of risk of occurrence. Many of this ilk are potential problems are in the realm of human-intervention-based events, such as terrorist bombings and attacks, and workplace violence. The probability of violence in the place—workplace violence—including violent actions against the organization, against specific individuals within the organi-

---

[2] Sandra Blakeslee, "Hopes for Predicting Earthquakes, Once So Bright, Are Growing Dim," *New York Times,* August 8, 1995, C5.

zation, or against random individuals in the organization, or randomly against the organization or the place, can stem from staff members, or be caused by outsiders. It is difficult, if not impossible, to statistically predict these. The nature of the processes occurring at the place, the political stance or religious connections of the organization, and governmental affiliations of the organization or the place might be related to the probability. Thus, an abortion clinic or a federal office building is *possibly* a more likely target for terrorist bombings than a chiropractor's office or the offices of the Automobile Association. An office park housing the offices of a company making armaments or toxic chemicals is *possibly* a more likely to be the target of pacifists or environmentalists than one housing the corporate offices of a bakery conglomerate.

Terrorist attacks have, in past years, tended to be directed at high-visibility buildings. Today, these buildings appear not to be the only potential targets of present-day and future attacks. Not only are high-profile buildings at risk ("We've never had terrorists or bombers before. And, there's no guarantee they'll hit only high profile targets"[3]), but other facilities as well. The religio-socio-economic-political orientation of your organization may give some clue as to the likelihood of a terrorist attack on your place, but here—most unfortunately—we can measure little more than "low", "moderate" or "high" likelihood, if that. We will be little able to, in the case of terrorism, replace impressions with quantifications until we are able to understand the scope and rationale of the terrorist threat.[4, 5]

Discussion of problems should note that it is indeed rare that a specific potential problem looms on the horizon with a measurable risk of occurrence equal to 100%! That level of risk is made even more extraordinary because the time of its impact can be predicted to the exact second with 100% certainty! The consequences, for countless BPCs in thousands of specific organizations, can be determined with 100% assurance! This rare combination of circumstances is the facility professional's dream—or nightmare! Although a disproportionate amount of "disaster planning" has been focused on the computer-based and computer-related activities

[3] Prospectus for Disaster Prevention & Recovery Symposium, sponsored by the Association for Information Technology, September 13, 1995.

[4] Robert D. McFadden, "Out of the Shadows of the World Trade Center Plot," *New York Times,* August 7, 1995, B1, B2. (It may only be macabre coincidence that "Lottery Numbers" was inset into a corner of this article.)

[5] For some insight into this area, see Christine Menapace, "Workplace Violence," *Today's Facility Manager,* May 1996, 1+, M. D. Kelleher, "The Lethal Employee," *ibid.*, 1+, and Kenneth Wolf, "Spillover Violence," *ibid.*, 1+

of the organization, countless planners have neglected to consider a factor that is inevitable as death and taxes themselves: the millennium. The "millennium" is discussed elsewhere.

PERFORMANCE

The consideration of *performance* is inseparable from the consideration of the problems and the countervailence measures taken to counter them, or to compensate for them. Your disaster planning and recovery strategy should include reduction in the levels of risk of occurrence of out-of-course events ("potential problems"), of their causing an impact (as "problems"), of the impacts having consequences on people, place, and processes, as well as the level of risk of those consequences having affects on as-intended functioning. Investment has been made: money, time, and efforts. Resources have been utilized. How will the evolved strategy perform? Will it, in fact, effectually work?

Unless the plan and its contingency measures are actually put into use, neither the actual performance of the plan itself, nor its contingency or countervailence measures, can be determined. This is quite unfortunate, and in some ways reverts back to considerations in obtaining management's support and commitment of resources both for creating the plan and for maintaining it. The plan can—and *should be*—tested and reviewed on a periodic basis. Modifications to the plan should be made based on circumstances experienced in the test process, and on changes in the people, place, and processes of the organization. No matter how "realistic" the tests are—with "realism" ranging from so-called desktop reviews, to active utilization of contingency plans coupled with computer modeling and simulations of events, impacts, and consequences[6]—it is near impossible to determine the actual performance of the plan.

A key issue is how to achieve an accurate measurement of performance based on suitable criteria. The ultimate measure—or determination—of performance requires a balanced system that enables all gauges to be linked and aligned with the needs of the organization: short-term financial considerations should not be overemphasized. Teamwork and achievements, customer satisfaction, and the quality of product and services delivered during contingency operations must be metered. Actual times must be compared to estimated times. Actual functioning of out-

---

[6] This application of modeling and simulation is different than the application leading to the reduction in levels of risk described in Chapter 5.

side facilities and resources must be compared to what was expected. Once determined, the results of performance measures should serve as the foundation of changes to be implemented in the plan. Performance must be measured in a balanced manner that links the various needs of people, place, and processes, with the needs of the organization's constituencies; the planner must ensure that this procedure leads to improvements, where warranted, in the plan.

PROBLEMS . . . , IMPACTS . . . , CONSEQUENCES . . .

"Potential problems" have been defined, elsewhere in this guide, as those out-of-course events that have been determined (preferably measured) as presenting a sufficiently high enough risk of occurrence to warrant careful thought in the disaster planning and recovery strategy. Put another way, "potential problems" are the out-of-course events that the facility professional may (read, perhaps, "should' or "will") lose sleep over, or otherwise worry about, until the plan is finalized, tested, and implemented!

Various studies and surveys instruct us that most organizations have not established a comprehensive strategy for disaster planning and recovery. The percentage of organizations that lack any semblance of a plan is, simply put, frightening large. The organization of which you are a part, or to which you provide design and planning counsel, may well lack a proper plan or strategy. *If* a is plan is in place, it might be applicable only to certain specific business processes (put another way, it is designed only to rescue specific bits and pieces of the business, not to save the entire organization!). That plan may not have been reviewed or updated within memory, if at all. The plan may never been put to a realistic test or drill. The in-place plan may not work! If your organization—or the organization you counsel—has not yet created a proper disaster planning and recovery strategy, it may not be because there is lack of a perceived need, but because of one or more of the following typical "excuses":

- We don't have the time, or the money, or the personnel, or the expertise to invest.
- We have tried to create a plan, but have failed.
- We just haven't gotten around to it yet.
- We have insurance.
- It won't happen to us.
- We have excellent vendors who will help us if we have any troubles.

■ Decision making is too decentralized in our organization to allow for the creation of a plan.

One way to create an awareness of the need—as well as the justification for a planning strategy—is to consider what has befallen other organizations, in terms both of impact and of consequences and affects, as graphically depicted in various statistics. It is difficult—nay, impossible—to "justify" any of the above-mentioned "excuses" in terms of the experiences of other organizations. The problems, impacts, and consequences described below, and the statistics cited, are but representative of what has occurred to organizations in the United States within the past few years. These examples are, obviously, the "headline grabbers" and the list does not encompass other events that went unreported for whatever-the-reason, or did not receive media attention, or were relegated to the back pages.

The examples cited not only confirm the adage, "if something can go wrong, it will go wrong," but also illustrate the important lesson that things—perhaps otherwise not considered—can be prevented from going wrong in the arena of your planning. It is not only the Nature-based earthquake or hurricane or flood that can be at the roots of widespread impact and consequence; it can also be the maliciously muffled alarm bell or a burnt-out indicator bulb that fails to signal the impending disaster. (One must wonder, validly, why "protective systems" are still designed to have fragile lamp bulbs ON as the signal of an alarm condition when OFF would signal an aberrant condition as well as provide a self-check of system functioning and the bulb! We permit the future of the organization to depend on the quality assurance in, and life expectancy of, a 39 cent bulb!) The facility professional must not only prepare his or her organization for the impact and consequences of the events over which there is no control, but also prepare for the impact and consequences and ensuing affects brought about by the "faulty 39 cent bulbs" in other organizations and—most importantly—in their own organization. There are many lessons to be learned from these examples.

A word or two about the statistics often cited. The very term "statistics" suggests a compilation of numbers collected on a systematic, scientific basis. One purpose of "statistics" is to provide a inference of general truths. "Statistics" describing the incidents related to "disasters" abound. There are statistics describing the percentage of organizations that have or do not have "plans," or the "disasters" that will or will not strike your organization, or the costs in terms of money, time, and effort that will be expended for want of a plan or be saved because of a plan. With not too much searching, one can find statistical justification for whatever one proposes to do, or proposes not to do. There are several potential short-comings relating to the statistics you will encounter when reading about "disaster planning" and when listening to presentations and discussions. First, many of the statistics are based on a sample that is either too small, or on a population not representative of the universe. Reliable statistics cannot be based on 68 companies and then projected to American enter-prise as an entity! Likewise, you cannot apply the experiences of banks to bakers, or compare apples with oranges. Few, if any, organizations are likely to admit they have suffered from a disaster, or are unprepared for another one. Such an admission would indicate vulnerabilities, possibly to other sorts of disasters. Thus, there is much "underreporting" and "no comments" that the information gatherer encounters.

Why, then, consider statistics—the experiences of others—in plan-ning? The available statistics—no matter how deficient they might be—present you with *good indication* of the experiences, the preparedness, and the needs of others. This can be taken as a *good indication* of what is likely to be the circumstances within your own organization, and the pros-pect of undesirable outgrowths from them. It is not significant, as such, that 63% of companies have no formal backup policy relating to their local area networks. The actual statistic might be 30% or 10% or 82%; what *is* meaningful is that a lot of companies—and yours may be one—do not have a LAN backup policy, and that such a lack can be the basis of an information-based problem.

The examples of disasters experienced by what are undoubtedly typi-cal organizations are meant to be indicative, instructive, and to illus-trate, in a summary fashion, how important the creation of a comprehen-sive disaster planning and recovery strategy really is. Many of the disasters described were rooted in "unlikely" causes; these examples re-veal how wide one must cast nets in order to fully prepare for, and com-pensate for, *all* potential causes of disasters. These examples, and statis-tics that follow them, are grouped according to the problems which resulted in the described impacts and consequences.

Of what value is the consideration of out-of-course events that have struck others—others, perhaps, who did not recognize these as potential problems and did not plan accordingly—to the facility professional, and how can they be assessed critically? The experiences of others offer the facility professionals engaged in creating a disaster planning and recov-ery strategy a bone to worry at.

The sampling of out-of-course events listed below strongly evidences lack of planning to *reduce the level of risk* that the event would occur. In most of the instances, the investment necessary to reduce the level of risk ALARP would have been quite low in comparison with the ultimate damages. The tragedy lies not only in the ultimate deaths, injuries, and other losses, but—even more importantly—in the lack of foresight to reduce the level of risk, of impact, and of consequences and affects, as well as the lack of foresight to plan proper countervailence.

Examples of some notable "disasters"—and some not so notable—that occurred because potential out-of-course events *had not been recognized as potential problems* can be found among organizations of all types, and in all places. These "bones"—and the "sniffing" that should have taken place in the creation of a disaster planning and recovery strategy—can be most instructive for the facility professional.

EXAMPLES OF ACTUAL OUT-OF-COURSE EVENTS THAT SHOULD HAVE BEEN RECOGNIZED AS PROBLEMS

Civil and Government-Based

- The Chicago Tunnel Company flood (see below) may be classified into any of several different root-cause categories. Human-intervention or people-based is surely an excellent candidate, but the oversight by Chicago's Department of General Services in not spending the $10,000 that could have prevented the ultimate $2 billion loss surely illustrates a failure of government to carry out its responsibilities and obligations.

Design-Based

- Snow-laden roof collapsed in Clifton, New Jersey, bringing down 5,000 automated teller machines.[7]

Engineering-, Construction-, and Materials-Based

- Two overhead walkways in Kansas City, Missouri, broke free, killing 113 people, and injuring 200 (1981).[8]

Human-Intervention or People-Based

- World Trade Center was bombed, 350 companies were directly affected, and 150 went out of business within one year. One of the largest WTC tenants—1200 employees occupying 300,000

[7] Kathryn Jones, "Teller Machines Are a Casualty of the Blizzard," *New York Times*, 20 March 1993, 1.

[8] "Bouncing Back From Disaster," *Meetings & Conventions*, February 1995, 45.

square feet—moved after the bombing, making "substantial cash payment" to get out of their lease.[9] While terrorist attacks are difficult to predict, the level of risk of occurrence can be reduced by increased surveillance, and by the installation of protective barricades (often masquerading as out-sized pots of geraniums) and bollards.

■ What was termed as the greatest or worst disaster ever to befall businesses "began" at 5:57 A.M. on April 13, 1992, in Chicago, when an engineer at the Merchandise Mart telephoned the Chicago Fire Department to report that water was inexplicably pouring into a subbasement. (Notice the past tense used in that sentence. The "greatest" or "worst" aspects of that disaster—in terms of costs—will be paled by the costs of solving the Year 2000 Problem. Estimates for solving the latter have been placed at between $300 to $600 billion! See Chapter 6.)

Ultimately, within a 100-block downtown area, 250 million gallons of the Chicago River poured into the abandoned railway tunnels—currently used for electrical, telephone, and other cabling systems—of the Chicago Tunnel Company. The tunnel system, about 100 years old, had been built to provide freight and coal deliveries to downtown Chicago buildings, and to remove ashes and other refuse. The railway system was abandoned in the 1940s, and was essentially forgotten except by utility workers responsible for the cabling. Access from the tunnel system to some buildings had been bulkheaded; to others, it remained unchanged.

The flooding impacted over 250,000 workers and residents in 600 buildings in the Loop. Fifteen of these buildings, representing 5.27 million square feet of space, were closed for at least one week, and for up to three weeks. Economic losses were estimated at $1.8 billion; the cost of repairs, direct business losses, and cleanup costs, $337 million. The potential costs of judgments in class-action and other suits is unknown. An estimated 400 data centers were impacted[10] and 150 companies never opened their doors again.[11]

The flood was the direct result of protective pilings being driven at the Kinzie Street Bridge by the Great Lakes Dock and Dredge

[9] Claudia H. Deutsch, "Firm Is Leaving the Trade Center," *New York Times*, 19 June 1993.

[10] Joseph C. Panettieri with Chuck Appleby, "Survival of the Fittest," *Information-week*, 10 January 194, 22+.

[11] Lenny Liebmann, "Providing a Safety Net," *Communications Week*, 28 August, 1995, 42.

Company in September 1991, which fractured the tunnel lining. Unusual water conditions were observed and video-taped on January 14, 1992 by cable television company workers in the tunnel, and reported to Chicago's Department of General Services. City engineers observed the conditions on March 13 and April 2, but failed to recognize the seriousness of the situation, and that immediate repairs were required. The city engineers estimated the then-needed repairs to cost about $10,000. Two construction companies visited the site to prepared their own estimates. Before their bids were received, the wall ruptured, with the disastrous results.

The Great Lakes Dock and Dredge Company, in a suit against the city, contended Chicago was at fault. "If Great Lakes had known about the existence of the tunnel, it would not have submitted the bid . . . and would not have undertaken the pile driving work. . . ."[12]

There is little question that this disaster was not the result of design, or of engineering, construction and materials, or maintenance, or nature. The disaster was the result of people: "It was a failure of memory."[13] The Great Lakes Dock and Dredge Company should have realized the presence of the tunnels even though the city may have been lax in not forewarning them in the piling contract. The city's engineers should have realized the potential consequences of the report in January and authorized the expenditure of $10,000 to rectify the leak without going through the bid process. The Tunnel had been "forgotten" by many until it was breached.[14]

■ An accidentally severed cable caused power loss to 13,000 customers in Chicago Loop on December 1, 1992. (The forty-minute blackout darkened McCormick place during a convention of the Radiological Society of America, where "It wasn't really a problem. Radiologists are used to working in the dark.")[15]

■ A major disruption in telephone service occurred in New York City at about 10:10 A.M. on September 19, 1991 as the consequence

[12] "Company Blamed for Flood Files a Suit Faulting Chicago," *New York Times,* 11 October 1992. See also editions of 14, 15, 16, 17, 20 and 23 March; 31 May 1992.

[13] William Cronon, "Mud, Memory and the Loop," *New York Times,* 2 May 1992.

[14] Some relatively simple ways to research public works and utilities that comprise our technological infrastructure—such as the Chicago Tunnel Company—are contained in Ann Durkin Keating's *Invisible Networks: Exploring the History of Local Utilities and Public Works* (Melbourne, Fla.: Kreiger Publishing Co., 1994).

[15] *Informationweek,* 7 December 1992, 8. *Meetings and Conventions,* February 1993, 30.

of the failure of an alternate power system at an AT&T switching center. As a consequence, over 5 million calls were blocked; air traffic control communications systems were paralyzed in the New York region causing up to four-hour delays in flights, as well as other major flight diversions and cancellations; half of AT&T long-distance traffic into and out of New York City was cut off; telephone links with Europe were interrupted; and other major disruptions impacted communications. The AT&T switch failed because technicians did not notice visual and audible alarms indicating generators had stopped, and the switch was operating on backup batteries. AT&T had stopped using commercial power and started using their own generators because of high demands on the public grid.[16]

Shortly after the cut over to their own generators, a rectifier failed, switching the load to batteries. For the next six hours, the alarms indicating generator failure, and dependence on battery backup, went unnoticed. Because of either an inadequate system or improper maintenance or tampering, the audible alarms had been silenced or muffled, and visual alarms went unnoticed or were not functioning. Equipment inspection procedures were neglected. When the conditions were ultimately observed by technicians, it was impossible to restart the generators, and the backup batteries were nearly flat.[17]

■ In another incident, an AT&T fiber optic cable in Newark, N.J. was accidentally severed forcing all incoming and outgoing flights at the three New York City airports to stop, halting the ATM transactions of 23 banks, forcing the Commodity Exchange and the Mercantile Exchange to close, and blocking 60% of long-distance telephone traffic into and out of New York City.[18]

■ In a Philadelphia skyscraper fire that burned for almost 19 hours and which resulted in three deaths, guards had delayed, for several minutes, reporting the fire, allowing the fatal blaze to destroy the building's electrical emergency system. Pressure valves on the internal hydrant system had been set below the prescribed standard, hampering firefighting efforts.[19]

[16] Dave Powell, "When the Public Network Dies," *Networking Management,* November 1991, 29+.

[17] Edmund L. Andrews, "A. T.& T. Admits Failure to Notice Alarms," *New York Times,* 19 September 1991, A1+. See also editions of 18, 20, and 21 September, and 1 October 1991.

[18] Barton Crockett, "N.Y. Rocked by Big A. T.& T. Fiber Outage," *Network World,* 31 December 1990, 1+.

[19] "Delay Worsened High-Rise Fire," *New York Times,* 14 March 1991.

- Two dozen firefighters were injured or felled by smoke in a New York office building fire searching for 20 people who had left the building before the fire, but failed to *sign out*.[20]

- Contractors, in New Jersey, failing to identify the locations of underground utilities, struck over 2500 buried gas mains, electric, and telephone lines in 1994. These resulted in major explosions and deaths (Edison, March 23, 1995), in closure of Newark International Airport for over 24 hours, and in other service interruptions.[21, 22]

- A cruise ship carrying 1509 people went aground off Nantucket in June 1995 after a cable in the global positioning system had become disconnected. The default navigation system functioned properly, but its placement prevented the watch officers on the bridge both from hearing the audible alarm and from seeing the visual alarm.[23]

- Seven of the 10 major power failures—resulting in blacked-out radar screens and severed radio communications—that struck air traffic control centers (in the latter months of 1995), some of which resulted in hundreds of flight delays and thousands of travelers being delayed, were largely caused by technicians who did not fully understand the new power-supply equipment they were putting into use. In addition, some equipment was installed in rooms with roofs that leaked or were susceptible to groundwater intrusion. Other new installations violated local fire codes. Happily, the Federal Aviation Administration reported that "no accidents or close calls had occurred" though controllers said at times "the situations had been worrisome."

  The F.A.A. report noted that some centers "rely on the experience of employees to deal with emergencies, rather than counting on the written contingency plans." In fact, the investigatory team found many of the contingency plans to be not workable.[24]

- A B-25 bomber, whose pilot became lost in the fog while approaching La Guardia Airport in New York City, crashed into the 78th

---

[20] "Fire Alarm, False Alarms," *New York Times*, 4 February 1993.

[21] Robert Hanley, "Finger-Pointing Begins Over Severing of Airport Cables," *New York Times,* 11 January 1995, B7.

[22] Matthew L. Wald, "Tighter Standard Urged for Buried Gas Pipelines," *New York Times,* 19 January 1995, B7.

[23] Matthew L. Wald, "Safety Board Cites Robot Pilot In Grounding of Cruise Ship," *New York Times,* 11 August 1995.

[24] Matthew L. Wald, "Rash of Failures in Flight Control," *New York Times,* 20 January 1996, 1+.

and 79th floors of the Empire State Building—then the world's tallest structure—killing 14 people in the impact and ensuing fire. The building and several elevators suffered considerable damage (but maintained its structural integrity), and a number of offices were destroyed. The July 28, 1945, crash was attributed to pilot error.[25]

Information-Based

■ Federally funded research databases submitted to the National Archives are usually undecipherable. Only 10% of the data promised by federal agencies is actually received by the National Archives; most of this is either missing outdated computer software needed to run programs or lacks codebooks needed to explain researcher's shorthand. The NA had to destroy 200 spools of research data submitted by the National Institutes of Health (in 1990) because nobody could explain what the coded information meant.[26]

Infrastructure-Based

■ A 30-inch, 41-year-old watermain ruptured and burst, disrupting two major office buildings in New York City's financial district. Activities of the New York and American Stock Exchanges, several security firms, banks, and law firms were impacted.[27]

Maintenance-Based

■ A mixup in the maintenance and repair shutdown procedures for the Pentagon's water supply rendered the 280 toilets in the world's largest office building unworkable when the Arlington County water system failed to function as the alternate source. Officials were prompted to give 24,000 workers the afternoon off for "health and safety" reasons, although the Pentagon "did not shut down."[28]

[25] James Barron, "Flaming Horror on the 79th Floor," *New York Times,* July 27, 1995, 1+.

[26] "Is U.S. R&D Losing Its Memory?" *R&D Magazine,* February 1991, 5.

[27] Clifford J. Levy, "Burst Pipe Disrupts Wall Street," *New York Times,* 2 September 1992, B1+.

[28] "At the Pentagon, An Afternoon Off," *New York Times,* 2 December 1995, 10.

Nature-Based

- Flooding caused by a severe winter storm and high tides affected banks, security trading firms, and other organizations in the New York City's Wall Street district, including companies in the same buildings flooded by a watermain burst three months earlier![29]
- Storm-caused rains and high tide inundated the Port Authority Trans-Hudson railway, flooding tunnels and stations, interrupting power supply, and halting trains. Lack of recovery planning resulted in inadvertent flooding of another tunnel and station with water to a depth of 3½ feet, and pumping water *into* a station rather than out of it.[30]
- In September 1995, an enthusiastic squirrel, gathering nuts for the approaching winter, climbed onto the 11 kV 60 Hz overhead power supply of the Metro-North Railroad resulting in a power surge that weakened a catenary support which then failed, causing the pantograph of an approaching train to become entangled in the overhead wires and bringing them down. Some 47,000 New York commuters were stranded for three or four hours, and damage to the electrical infrastructure was in the millions of dollars. The squirrel came to a rapid and rather smoky end.[31] This was not the first time a rogue rodent was at the root of a major Metro-North (or predecessor company, the New York, New Haven & Hartford Railroad) electrical failure, or had gnawed into the operations of a major organization.

A bushy-tailed acorn-eater, in quest of more interesting foods, ventured into the fenced electrical transformer domain serving the NASDAQ computer center in Connecticut's Fairfield County to savor the cable insulation. The resultant short-circuiting caused a complete power outages, effecting a consequent suspension of trading for several hours. (Unfortunately, neither the local squirrels nor NASDAQ learned from the first—1987—experience and failed to muster both preventative and contingency plans for such events; an identical scenario way played out in 1994! On

[29] Michael Quint, "Wall Street Finds Ways of Muddling Through," *New York Times,* 15 December 1992.

[30] Iver Peterson, "PATH Takes Lesson from Storm's Close Calls," *New York Times,* 20 December 1992, 44.

[31] "Rogue Rodent," *Railway Gazette International,* November 1995, 721. George Judson, "New Haven Line Back in Action After a Failure," *New York Times,* 13 September 1995, B5.

each occasion, the backup generators failed to activate.)[32, 33] Squirrels do not confine their nibbling to the East Coast! A squirrel in Idaho caused a power outage to over 10,000 homes and businesses after venturing into an electrical substation and causing a short circuit.[34]

Railways (as do motorists driving through deer- and moose-populated areas) face a high risk of an animal being the root cause of a disaster, and have found means to reduce those nature-based risks. Concerned that moose might wander onto the tracks between Oslo and Lillehammer causing a train to derail with a risk of casualties or delays to visitors to the 1994 Winter Olympic games, the Norwegian State Railways adopted sundry remedies to reduce the level of risk that train services would be impaired, impeded, interrupted, or halted by errant moose. Forest logging roads were ploughed to make them easier for the moose to follow; fodder was strewn along them to keep the moose from wandering toward the railway. Because the well-fed moose still roamed, the railway, recognizing that moose fear wolves (as much as humans do), discovered that by stringing out sachets containing essence of wolf urine in lines about 15 to 20 m away from the track, most moose would be deterred from venturing too close. Sections most at risk were also monitored by regular surveillance flights using infrared cameras, and—as a last resort—a net-equipped helicopter could noose a moose and let it loose elsewhere![35] In Australia, there is considerable risk that kangaroos—seemingly oblivious to locomotive whistles and other warning devices—will stray onto the track and be struck by, and derail, a train. To reduce this risk, a company developed a warning device, mounted on the train locomotive, which emits a tone within the kangaroo audible zone. Hearing the sound from the device—called a "Shoo-Roo"—kangaroos run from the track area. In Montana, bears, consuming grain that fermented in the mild, humid climate after spilling from passing trains, became intoxicated and wandered onto the tracks, heedless of locomotive whistles. To reduce both the risk of striking and killing bears, and possible derailments, the Burlington Northern Railroad replaced the then in situ track with smoother-surfaced rails to reduce the likelihood that grain would be shaken from the passing trains.[36]

---

[32] "Squirrel Causes Crash At NASDAQ," *Informationweek,* 15 August 1994, 22.

[33] The Metro-North and NASDAQ incidents should not be taken as a new problem! In a page 1 article, the *Whitehall Evening-Post* [London] for 6 November 1725 reported on the plague of squirrels in Connecticut.

[34] United Press International dispatch, Boise, Idaho, August 20, 1992.

[35] "There's A Moose Loose," *Railway Gazette International,* April 1994, 207.

[36] "Beer Necessities," *Railway Gazette International,* May 1992, 309.

■ Severe disturbances of the Earth's magnetic field, resulting from temporary changes in solar activity, can damage electric utility equipment and interrupt electrical transmission, interfere with broadcast and radio communication systems, and pose health concerns, especially for pregnant women. Such disturbances are thought to be the root causes of transformer explosions at the Maine Yankee nuclear plant in Wiscasset, Maine, and the Salem nuclear plant in southern New Jersey.[37]

As a means to reduce the impact of these disturbances, some utilities propose monitoring solar activity to give advance warnings. If solar storm occurred when power lines were fully loaded and several lines were to fail, blackout could result. With warning, utilities could try to reduce demand, and send less power over long distances, relying more on local generators.

Place-Related

■ A smoky blaze forced 3000 from a building; 46 were injured in the fire and 13 stuck in elevators.[38]

Technology-Based

■ Trading on the New York Mercantile Exchange halted for 25 minutes after a power surge hampered two New York Telephone switches located in the World Trade Center.[39]
■ Flooding of only generators capable of producing 25 cycle alternating current—required for safety signal system—halt most of New York City subway system.[40]
■ An electrical fire in Las Vegas, Nevada, hotel trapped more than 3500 guests and staff, killing 83 (1980).[41]
■ A fire disrupted Los Angeles telephone service for 3 million southern Californians, and knocked out the area's emergency 911 system for several hours.[42]

---

[37] Matthew L. Wald, "Severe Sun Storm Threatens Utilities," *New York Times,* 6 June 1991.

[38] Robert D. McFadden, "Smoky Blaze Forces 3,000 from Building [605 Third Ave., New York, N.Y.]," *New York Times,* 9 September 1995, 21.

[39] *Informationweek,* 12 July 1993, 8.

[40] James Deo, "Failure of Two Outdated Generators Cited in Disruption of Subway's Safety Signals," *New York Times,* 13 December 1992, 55.

[41] "Bouncing Back From Disaster," *Meetings & Conventions,* February 1995, 45.

[42] *New York Times,* 16 March 1994.

- Computer failures in midwest delayed at least 200 airline flights.[43]
- A computer breakdown caused flight delays up to 90 minutes at three major airports in the New York region.[44]
- A computer malfunction disrupted local telephone service to 6 million customers in Washington, D.C., and in Maryland, Virginia, and West Virginia, for six hours.[45]
- A computer-based wide area network at U.S. Department of Health and Human Services in Washington, D.C. was subject to periodic failure because improperly shielded cabling installed in elevator shafts acted as receptors to EMFs from elevator motors.[46]
- A power substation fire resulted in an outage in New York City's financial district and disrupted service to 4150 customers, including more than 300 brokerage houses, financial institutions, and international banks. Some were without power for up to five days.[47] A year later "Many . . . now perform more live tests of their battery power systems and diesel generators or have contracted with outside firms to bring in temporary generators. . . . Others have redefined their disaster recovery procedures. . . ."[48]

Transport-Related

- A derailed subway train hit a utility company's underground transformer, causing power outage in major office building. Among the many business consequences was an interruption in a West Coast-headquartered investment banking company's communications links with its New York and Boston offices, as well a power loss in the New York office.[49]

---

[43] *New York Times,* 13 September 1995, A21.

[44] Dennis Hevesi, "Computer Breakdown Causes Delays at 3 Major Airports," *New York Times,* 17 October 1992.

[45] Edmund L. Andrews, "Computer Failure Disrupts Phones for 6 Hours in Washington Area," *New York Times,* 27 June 1991, 27.

[46] Jim Tyson, "The Wednesday the Network Crashed," *Network World,* 18 February 1991, 59.

[47] Tari Schreider, "Power Outage Wallops Wall Street," *Contingency Journal,* October/December 1990, 15+.

[48] Wayne Eckerson, "A Year After Outage, N.Y. Users Still Wary," *Network World,* 12 August 1991, 27+.

[49] Denise Pappalardo, "Building a Better Network," *CommunicationsWeek,* 16 October 1995, 24+.

Some Statistics Related to Out-of-Course Events

(The author—in submitting that you might view these as potential problems in terms of your people, place, or processes—shuns the risk of vouching for the accuracy—or the inaccuracy—of the statistics cited, as many are gathered from primary sources that may be subject to scrutiny regarding technique and methodology, and from secondary sources. Accuracy to an acceptable confidence interval aside, these examples *do illustrate* that conditions are far from "love and roses" in the garden of disaster preparedness!)

■ Fifty-two and one-half percent of direct property damage stems from fires occurring between 8 P.M. and 6 A.M. 63% of damage occurs on Saturday and Sunday.

■ Sixty-six percent of fire-caused damage to data-processing equipment occurs between 8 P.M. and 8 A.M.

■ In the United States, a building is broken into once every eight seconds.[50]

■ Over 42% of respondents in a survey of 1290 companies reported the "security problems" resulting in financial loss (1994) were caused by Human-intervention or people-based out-of-course events, while 35% were technology-based; 23% resulted from "other" causes.[51]

■ In fiscal 1992–93, 2.2 million U.S. workers were physically attacked on the job, 6.3 million were threatened with violence, and 16.1 million were harassed. More than $4 billion was lost in work and legal expenses.[52]

■ *Reported* instances of corporate espionage have increased three-fold between 1992 and 1995. Losses of trade secrets, including research and development information, and sales strategies and price quotations occurred most often, with in-house personnel responsible for 60% of the incidents.[53]

■ Sixty-three percent of companies have no formal backup policy for computer-based information. Data loss costs U.S. businesses $4 billion annually in lost productivity. Less than 10% of compa-

[50] Simplex Time Recorder Co. brochure B110-589/EXC, 12-90.

[51] Joseph C. Panettieri, "Security," *Informationweek,* 27 November 1995, 32+.

[52] James Baar, "Putting an End to Violence in the Office," *Access Control,* October 1995, 20+. Author cites Northwestern National Life Insurance Co., and The National Safe Workplace Institute.

[53] "Espionage on the Risk," *Infosecurity News,* January/February 1996, 12.

nies with LANs have any type of contingency plan for their LANs. Fewer than 5% have an organized off-site backup plan in place. Fewer than 5% of all LAN users ever test their backup tapes. The cost to replace 1 megabyte of data is at least $5000.[54]

- The Millennium Bug: A normal midsize company has 8000 legacy programs with 12 million lines of code. On the average, 1 in 50 lines will have a date reference. This means 240,000 lines must be modified at a cost of 30 to 40 cents per line. A large company could have tens of thousands of programs.[55]

- Large corporations lose a document every 12 seconds. Three percent of all documents are incorrectly filed and 7.5% of paper documents are lost forever. U.S. business managers spend an average of three hours a week (four weeks a year) on searching for misfiled, mislabeled, or lost documents.[56]

- In a survey of nearly 200 large U.S. businesses, two-thirds revealed that they have no disaster recovery plan with off-site data storage for their client-server applications . . . nearly eight of every 10 companies with no disaster plan intends to implement a recovery scheme this year (1994) . . . New York dominates in disaster (declarations) (26.0% of 2,436 [power] outages since 1982), followed by California (18.4%) . . . 65.6% of companies have no disaster recovery plan for client-server applications and data . . . 76.7% of companies without plan intend to implement one.[57]

- Share of users with disaster plans: data network users, 82%; data center users, 78%; voice network users, 68%; image network users, 6%.[58]

- At least 20 organizations (of 1290 surveyed) reported loss of information worth more than $1 million [1994].[59]

- Watermain breaks per 100 miles of pipe reported in 1994: Philadelphia, 16.8 breaks; Chicago, 10.2; Denver, 8.9; New York, 8.1 (equating to about 600 watermain breaks per year); and Boston, 3.1.[60]

---

[54] Jon W. Singleton, "Vault to a Data Recovery," *Infosecurity News,* September/October 1995, 36. Author cites Rimage Services, Minneapolis, Minnesota as source of statistics.

[55] Joe Mullich, "Squashing the Millennium Bug," *Open Computing,* October 1995, 42. (See further discussion in Chapter 6.)

[56] Cited in *The Corporate Memory and the Bottomline*, published by Cuadra Associates, Inc.

[57] Barbara DePompa, "Date with Disaster," *Informationweek,* 2 May 1994, 48+.

[58] *Communications News*, October 1994.

[59] Joseph C. Panettieri, "Security," *Informationweek,* 27 November 1995, 32+.

[60] "New York City Water Mains," *New York Times,* 28 August 1995, B1.

- Gas pipeline explosions between 1984 and 1996 have resulted in 47 people killed, and 199 injured.[61]
- The number of hurricanes that directly hit on the U.S. Atlantic and Gulf coasts between 1900–1995 (part year) in Category 1 hurricanes or winds from 74 to 95 mph, 68; Category 2 or winds from 96 to 110 mph, 35; Category 3 or winds from 111 to 130 mph, 44; Category 4 or winds from 131 to 155 mph, 15; and Category 5 or winds more than 155 mph, 2.
- "A hurricane makes landfall in the (New York City Metropolitan area) only about once every ten years."[62]
- The air within a typical office building is 100 times more polluted that the air surrounding the outside of the building. Office air contains about 4700 different chemical compounds, about 43% of which are carcinogenic.
- The costs of interrupted computing in 1994 was $4 billion.[63]
- American businesses lost as much as $1 billion a year to computer fraud.[64]
- Each year the typical U.S. computer location experiences 36 power spikes, 264 voltage sags, 128 voltage surges, and 15 power outages.

  Estimated annual costs that can be directly attributed to power quality anomalies may be as high as $26 billion. Power anomalies are the source of 50% of data loss for computer installations.[65]
- Over 46% of power anomalies start inside the facility.[66]
- Plant stoppages caused by power irregularities cost more than $12 billion annually in the U.S.[67]
- More than 120 disturbances caused by power abnormalities hit a typical computer in a typical month; some have imperceptible effects while others cause data loss and expensive repairs.[68]

---

[61] Joseph Berger, "Builder of Pipeline for Canadian Gas Said to Admit Guilt," *New York Times,* 17 May 1996, A1+.

[62] "Pulse: Hurricanes," *New York Times,* 11 September 1995, B1. *The Times* cites the Pennsylvania State University and the National Hurricane Center as sources.

[63] Cited by Advanced Systems Concepts, Inc.

[64] "How Safe Is Your System?" *Beyond Computing,* September 1995, 44.

[65] Cited by Deltec Electronics Corp. attributing information to the National Power Laboratory, the Power Electronics Applications Center, and to Contingency Planning Research, Inc.

[66] "Many Power Problems Start Inside Facilities," *CEE News,* September 1991.

[67] David Stipp, "Software Industry Emerges to Prevent Costly Downtime from Outages," *Wall Street Journal,* 18 May 1992.

[68] APC publication, citing IBM.

- Thirty-six and six-tenths percent of office fires start in or from telecommunications equipment. These fires account for 42.2% of office fire losses.
- Disruptions in telecommunications systems caused by watermain breaks, fires, fiber cable cuts, natural disasters [sic] and sabotage affect nearly 60 thousand customers every day.[69]
- Thirty percent of companies lack confidence in their own disaster-recovery plans; 37% were found to be without any formal plans at all.[70]
- According to one reportage, the "most common sources of [computer] downtime, in order of frequency of occurrence (expressed as percentage of total)" are power outage, 27.7%; storm damage, 11.7%; floods, 9.6%; computer hardware error, 7.7%; bombings, 7.2%; hurricanes, 6.3%; fires, 5.6%; software errors, 5.4%; power surges or spikes, 5.1%; earthquakes, 4.9%; network outages, 2.1%; human error, 2.0%; HVAC failure, 1.4%; burst pipes or water, 1.0%; employee sabotage, 0.8%; and, "other," 1.5%.[71]

  These percentages were based on 5320 outage incidents since 1982.[72] In a recitation of the "Most Common U.S. Disasters," identical percentages were cited "based on 6320 incidents reported from 1982 through April 1995."[73] "Other" includes "contamination, insects [presumably, the multi-legged sort, as distinct from 'software bugs'], riots, transportation, [and] accidents."

- In another statement of the "varieties of disaster," the "causes of data loss at U.S. computer installations" is given as (here, based on 2428 incidents since 1982) power failure, 35.2%; power surge or spike, 10.1%; storm damage, 9.4%; fire or explosion, 8.2%; hardware error, 6.7%; flood or water damage, 6.7%; earthquake, 5.5%; network outage, 3.2%; human error, 3.2%; HVAC failure,

---

[69] "New York City Uses Wireless for Disaster," *Communications News*, May 1996, 40.

[70] "Don't Panic. OK, Panic!" *Informationweek*, 20 February 1995, 8. Source cited as survey commissioned by Comdisco and Palindrome.

[71] The distinction between "storm damage" and "hurricanes" was presumably made by the compiler or by those reporting "downtime." Perhaps "hurricanes" refers to "downtime" as a consequence of closings because of impending hurricanes (that did not cause damage) as distinct from hurricane-caused damage included in "storm damage."

[72] Mickey Williamson, "Daring to Look Down," *CIO*, 1 June 1995, 49+. Stated source is Contingency Planning Research, Inc., January 30, 1995.

[73] Kelly Jackson Higgins, "How Vulnerable Is Your Network?" *Communications Week*, 4 March 1996, 43+. Stated source is Contingency Planning Research, Inc.

2.3%; software error, 1.5%; employee sabotage, 1.3%; and, other, 6.7%. Here, the "other" is stated to include contamination, insects, riots and transportation accidents.[74]

■ In yet another statement of the "most common disasters [undoubtedly, but not so-stated, affecting computing operations]" appear power outage, 15.1%; fire, 13.2%; earthquake, 12.8%; fraud/hacker, 10.7%; virus, 7.3%; burst pipe/flood, 7.1%; hardware error, 4.8%; hurricane, 3.8%; terrorism, 3.4%; network outage, 3.4%; software error, 3.3%; and, other, 2.3%. These percentages are based on 523 incidents in North America since 1982.[75]

■ In reportage of 185 "disasters requiring computer system recovery services" that occurred between 1980 and 1994, 22% were stated as caused by flooding; 19% by equipment outages; 18% by power outages; 12% by fire or explosion; 7% by earthquakes; 5% by hurricanes; and, 9% by other causes.[76] In another narrative of the same original source,[77] floods are mentioned as 22% of the causes of computer shutdowns; equipment outages, 19%; power failures, 18%; fire or explosion, 18%; and, earthquakes, 8%.

A subtle message dwells in these statistics: They are, perhaps, more *indicative* than *exacting*. In pursuing support for a plan, it is prudent to select with great care any numbers that you present in seeking management support. Percentages variously cited by different "authorities" can be a sitting duck for someone hunting for an excuse to shoot down a proposal!

There is also a tendency, in the presentations by the media, to base the measurement of "catastrophes" (read, out-of-course events) on the value of insurance claims that resulted. These values—although of worth as illustrations, to managements, of the importance of a disaster planning and recovery strategy—are at once an understatement and perhaps misleading. At worst, they are indicative of the importance of preparedness. Insurance claims, per se, represent only insured values and do not indicate amounts recovered. Obviously, not all organizations are insured

---

[74] Kristina B. Sullivan, "Disaster-recovery Planning: Pricey, But Worth It," *PC Week,* 26 July 1993, 119+. Stated source is Contingency Planning Research Inc.

[75] Alan Berman, "Keeping It On the Line," *UniReview,* September 1991, 18+. Stated source is Contingency Planning Research, Inc.

[76] "Build Your Ark: Then Call Us," *CIO,* 15 October 1994. There is no mention of the residual 8% pie-slice! Comdisco Disaster Recovery Services, Inc. is cited as the source.

[77] "Disaster Culprits," *CFO,* October 1994, 15.

against the costs of every consequence and affect, and not every consequence and affect is insurable from a practical point of view. Under the heading of "The 10 Most Costly Catastrophes In U.S. History" the Insurance Information Service reported that "insured losses" included $880 million in claims resulting from the snow, wind, and freezing rain that impacted 41 states in 1983; that Hurricane Hugo (1989) resulted in claims of $4.2 billion; the Bay Area earthquake in 1989 was the basis for $960 million in claims; fires, in California resulted in $1.7 billion in claims in 1991 and $950 million in 1993; looting and rioting in Los Angeles, in 1992, resulted in $775 million in claims; Hurricane Andrew, 1992, $15.5 billion; Hurricane Iniki, $1.6 billion; claims of $1.625 billion stemmed from the 1993 "storm of the century" impacting 24 eastern states; earthquake in southern California, 1994, $6.5 billion; and, 16 ice and snow storms on the East Coast in 1994 caused at least $1.7 billion in claims.[78]

The variance between the sets of statistics bears a very important message to the facility professional who might relay on "statistics" alone in differentiation between an potential out-of-course event and a potential problem. It appears that reportage varies with the individual counting, and when the count is made! For the planner, any reliance on the experiences of others might be wrought with quandaries. Providing for faults or failure in the HVAC system is a case in point: The 1.4% or "none" or something hidden within the 2.3% "other" *might* be considered an "acceptable" risk level, but as the underlying statistics themselves appear to invite question, plus the fact that the level of risk *in your place* could be extremely higher, broad-based "statistics" might be dismissed as a planning tool.

[78] John S. DeMott, "Battening Down the Hatches," *CFO,* September 1994, 74+.

CHAPTER

4

PRESCRIPTIVES

If you read but one sentence in this chapter let it be this: *Don't presume that—by following all the prescriptives applicable to the facility—you have reduced all the levels of risk as low as reasonably practicable.*

The planning, design, building, and—ultimately—the operation of any place is subject to compliance with a significant number of prescriptives. Prescriptives are imposed to govern the safety and well-being of the people—both staff and visitors—who are present at and in the place. Prescriptives also regulate many of the processes that are performed by the people working in the place. It might be said that the creation, management, and operation of any organization is *at the mercy of* the wide variety of prescriptives. "Prescriptives" (literally, a dictating or an ordering) take many forms: federal, state, and local laws, rules, regulations, mandates, codes, standards, rules, and practices, established and promulgated by specialized, independent professional organizations or societies, some with applicable compliance required by governmental mandate; and "recommended practices" issued by interested associations and trade, artisan, or craft groups.[1]

Prescriptives do much to reduce levels of risks. Without prescriptives, we would be at considerably greater risk of harm in most of the places we go to, and in many of the activities we engage in. But prescriptives, by their very nature, have to be broad-based and have general applicability.

---

[1] Some prescriptives owe their inceptions to a desire—on the part of an interest group—to avoid govenmental interference in, or regulation of, what they do or create. The underlying premise is that "if we do it, it won't be as bad, or as hard to comply with, or as restrictive as if a governmental body did it."

Prescriptives, also because of their very nature, cannot be either site-specific or circumstance-specific. We tend to assume that prescriptives have minimized each and every risk that the people face in the place or in the process to which the prescriptive is applicable. We have come to believe that the elevator or computer or toaster has been manufactured in a manner that makes its use safe because of the prescriptives applicable to their manufacture and use. We believe that the building we occupy or visit is safe because the prescriptives applicable to its design, construction, operation, and use make it safe. Safe, yes, but perhaps *not as safe as possible*.[2] That is why, when creating a strategy for disaster planning and recovery, the facility professional must determine whether or not each applicable prescriptive has mandated all that is possible to reduce risks as low as reasonably practicable (ALARP), and whether the prescriptive does, in fact, actually result in risk reduction, or in risk reduction value in terms of the cost:benefit ratio.

The prescriptives applicable to the specific places for which a facility professional has concern (read, responsibility, accountability, and obligation) most usually apply to the *engineering* aspects of the site, building, infrastructure, and equipment. This applicability is then to the exclusion of both *operation* and *management* (including *maintenance*). If something can be the cause of an out-of-course event (or a problem), or be impacted by an out-of-course event (or a problem), then the facility professional must also take the steps necessary that assure that "it" is operated, maintained, and managed in a manner that reduces the risk of "it" being the cause, or being impacted, to a level ALARP. As an example, several, separate codes and other prescriptives will specify the manner in which an emergency power generator is built, where and how it is installed, where its fuel tank is located, and how it is connected to the building's power supply. But rarely is anything stated in the prescriptives about testing, maintenance, prudent fuel supplies, or stocking of spare parts. These factors can be equally vital to the availability of an alternate source of electricity as having the generator itself! (See further in Vulnerability Search, Appendix II.)

The facility professional must consider that the individuals who work in, or visit, our increasingly complex buildings—office buildings, hospitals and health care facilities, hotels, department stores, airport termi-

---

[2] One might ponder—if a particular prescriptive, say one related to fire alarm pull-boxes—reduces associated levels of risk as low as reasonably practicable—why the prescriptives addressing the identical issue may be rather different in another jurisdiction.

nals, arts and sports venues—are exposed to a vast array of out-of-course events—such as fire, explosion, fierce weather, floods, bombs, and other forms of violence—and have limited means of escaping from them. The people can become casualties. The facility professional normally only analyzes the hazards, and the effectiveness of planned emergency provisos, in the light of the "rules" or "conventions" that are intended to prevent or reduce casualties.

Traditionally, organizations have followed these conventions—rigid codes, standards, and industry practices—with regard to the safety and well-being of the people in or around the places facility professionals design, construct, and manage. These "rules" or "conventions" are commonly called "prescriptives" and it is generally accepted that if the organization follows the prescriptives, it is largely absolved from considering safety[3] further. These prescriptives or "rules" are normally based on history and are only changed when it can be proved that they did not prevent what they were intended to prevent.[4] But recent disasters, together with advances in risk analysis techniques, have led to a worldwide move away from dependence on prescription alone to utilization of a "goal setting" approach in concert with the necessary embodiment of the prescriptives. It is increasingly recognized that, first, the prescriptives sometimes fail to reduce the level of risk of casualties ALARP. Put another way, there are often reasonable and practical cost-effective steps that can be taken, above and beyond the prescriptives, that will reduce the level of risk of casualties to a level *lower* than compliance with the applicable prescriptives alone will accomplish. Second—but by no means of lesser importance—is that fact that, under certain circumstances, *some* prescriptives *may not* reduce the level of risk of casualties. This, put another way, means that full compliance with a particular prescriptive will not result in a lower risk level than noncompliance with, or nonexistence of, the prescriptive. This also can be viewed in the perspective of costs: the costs for compliance with the prescriptive may be greater than the cost of the loss through injury or death.

---

[3] In the context of a disaster planning and recovery strategy, "safety" can be read as "risk management" or as "reduction in levels of risk as low as reasonably practicable."

[4] "Troubled by the failure of safety systems after the explosion at the World Trade Center, New York City officials said yesterday that they were considering new building codes to govern the placement of backup generators that power alarms, ventilation fans and emergency lights." Clifford J. Levy, "Explosion May Yield New Building Codes," *New York Times,* 4 March 1993, B4. (The World Trade Center is exempt from city codes, but officials noted ". . . they could not ignore the lessons from the disaster.")

Compliance with the prescriptives may provide psychological comfort for the facility professional, but they no longer provide—as was once thought—practical liability protection for the owner and managers of the place. This is worth repeating: *Compliance with prescriptives does not absolve the owners and managers of a place from liability.*

It is therefore vital when establishing a strategy for disaster planning and recovery, that the facility professional not become victim of the often-held conviction that, by following all the applicable prescriptives, the risks faced will be reduced as low as reasonably practical (ALARP) in all circumstances, and under all conditions. The reality is, simply put, that even by following all the applicable prescriptives, risks may not have been reduced to their reasonably practicable minimum. By investing the necessary money, time, and effort *only for compliance* with prescriptives as the sole basis for risk reduction, the facility professional fails to determine whether an additional investment (*if* any additional investment is, in fact, necessary) of money, time, or effort (or whether the amounts need be substantial) could further reduce the particular risks to a level that is ALARP or to a more "acceptable level."

It can be said that the basic aim of *having* prescriptives, *applying* them to the site or building or space within the building, and *enforcing* compliance with and adherence to the prescriptives is to reduce the risk of harm befalling the people, the place, and the processes. To accomplish this, several "families" of prescriptives relate to the design and to the construction (in terms of both where the place might be sited, and the materials used), and the practices and procedures used to erect and install not only those features and items prescribed, but also just about everything else.

Another "family" of prescriptives is intended to provide for the safety and well-being of the organization's people. This broad range of mandates describe occupancy levels, the conduct of fire drills, signage, nonsmoking requirements, prohibitions against alcohol and drug usage by certain groups of employees, hours of work, health testing, and sanitary requirements for food service, and an impressive array of other long-established regulations, as well as the more-recently mandated OSHA requirements.

Prescriptives related to the processes—another "family"—fall into two groups: safety and well-being (often in manufacturing or extractive environments) of people who are directly engaged in the processes; and, the "safety and well-being" of the interests of those people or constituencies for whom the organization provides services and products. This important segment of the prescriptives related to the processes is a vital consideration for the facility professional when creating the mechanisms for continuity of processes: what the regulatory agencies require!

Concern with place is based on the premise that if the place is safe, the people in it will be safe. Prescriptives are intended to prevent or to minimize such casualties. Expressed in terms of risk management, the purpose of prescriptives is the reduce the levels of risk of casualty to people, of damage or harm to the place, and, of the processes being impaired, impeded, interrupted, or halted. A most vital consideration in establishing a disaster planning and recovery strategy is, arguably, not only the elimination or minimization of any casualties—both deaths and injuries—whenever an out-of-course event strikes the facility *through compliance with the applicable prescriptives*, but also to go beyond those prescriptives in reducing—ALARP, or to an "acceptable" level—the risks of casualties.

First, look at the range of these prescriptives. "Prescriptives" is the term applied to the sum and substance of all the things you must do, or take into account, when planning and when operating a facility, and when operating the business. These are the laws, regulations, codes, and standards, established by law or by an accepted association or professional organization, that may be applicable to, and govern and regulate much of what you have to consider in the design and operation of the place—the site, the building, the infrastructure, its equipment and facilities, and in the conduct of the processes.[5] Many of these prescriptives—such as those promulgated by the local building code (perhaps based on the Uniform Building Code), or on local fire codes or local laws,[6] or in NFPA, NEC, ANSI, ASCE, or IEEE standards, or by OSHA or the EPA or under the ADA—may seemingly be more closely associated with your disaster planning and recovery strategy than, as examples, those issued by the SEC,

---

[5] Many prescriptives are promulgated by nonprofit organizations that enjoy a special status as private-sector guardians of a specific realm. Working with business and industry, these organizations set voluntary standards and practices in areas where governmental-based regulations do not exist, creating a form of self-regulation. The potential shortcomings of self-regulation—whether the prescriptives exist for the benefit of the business or industry, per se, or for those who receive or use the services or products of the business or industry as they are intended—is receiving increasing attention.

[6] Among the New York City local laws that impact the facility professional/disaster planning and recovery strategy equation apply to building facades [Local Law 10/80], elevator inspection [10/81], and fire safety (including building alarm systems, maintenance, emergency lighting, appointment of building fire safety directors, and of building evacuation supervisors) [5/73, 45/83, 16/84, 58/87].

FAA, FCC, IRS, or any of the myriad of other regulatory agencies or departments, regarding availability, accessibility, and usability of your organization's records.[7] Other groups which issue prescriptives that directly or indirectly govern what you can do, or the way in which it can be done, include Underwriters Laboratory, Inc. (UL), the Canadian Standards Association (CSA[8]), and—increasingly—the International Standards Organization (ISO) through the ISO-9000 Series of Standards (ISO-9001 through ISO-9004) it promulgates, and the Comptroller of the Currency's Circulars. An interesting characteristic of prescriptives is that the requirements of one of the organizations providing mandates may not be in agreement with the requirements of another. As an example, ADA requirements may differ from the requirements specified by the NFPA regarding the placement of alarm manual pull stations, and the standards of audible signalling devices. An "interesting" prescriptive in New York City is the fire department's standard firefighting protocols requiring the shutoff of electricity—from both the utility mains and any emergency generators—in "tall" buildings where there is a "working fire" when the firefighters arrive on the scene.[9]

Prescriptives impose restrictions on where a building may be erected, its size, and the uses to which it may be put. Prescriptives specify that certain materials be used (or not be used), that certain practices be followed and standards complied with, in terms not only of the physical structure, but the space within it, and the manner in which the space is subdivided, equipped, furnished, and supported. The prescriptives applicable to an organization vary with the governments having jurisdiction, the size of the organization, nature of the organization, the type of business conducted, the products produced, the services rendered, and so on. In reality, many organizations are not aware of some of the prescriptives

[7] NFPA—National Fire Protection Association; NEC—National Electrical Code; ANSI—American National Standards Institute; ASCE—American Society of Civil Engineers; IEEE—Institute of Electrical and Electronics Engineers; OSHA—Occupational Safety and Health Act (CFR Title 29); EPA—Environmental Protection Act (CFR Title 40); ADA—Americans With Disabilities Act; SEC—Securities and Exchange Commission; FAA—Federal Aviation Administration; FCC—Federal Communications Commission; IRS—Internal Revenue Service. Other federal, state or province, county, district, and local standards, guidelines, regulations, laws, and codes are referred to as AHJ—Authority Having Jurisdiction!

[8] Here, not to be confused with the Confederate States of America.

[9] John F. King, "World Trade Center Blast Triggers Design Debates," *IEEE Spectrum,* May 1993, 83+. The author comments that the quite-possibly-valid elucidation of this *carte blanche* has eluded his pursuits during the long course of his professional career.

applicable to them until they are cited for failing to observe a prescriptive! Many prescriptives relating to the design of, and safety planning for the facility vary greatly between local jurisdictions. One town, or county, as an example, might require substantially more in the realm of evacuation path signage and wayfinding lighting, or in the realm of roof characteristics, than its neighboring town or county. A particular city may require considerably more sophisticated fire alarm and emergency communication systems than the city or town adjacent to it. A facility that straddles a town line may face conflicting rules and regulations! Prescriptives applicable vary with the governmental jurisdiction (New York City's various codes are different from those of Marin County, California), the location of the place within the governmental jurisdiction (an urban versus a suburban or rural area), with the size of the building (one story or highrise or something in-between), the use to which the space is being put, who owns the building (some government or quasi-governmental ownership obtains exemption from some prescriptives as tenants in the World Trade Center were to learn *after* the bombing), the age of the structure, its status as a landmark, and numerous other categories.

As a facility professional concerned with creating a disaster planning and recovery strategy, your particular role in the planning, design, and creation of the place, or the operation of the place, or in the processes conducted, must be performed in consideration of the applicable prescriptives.

Thus, the facilities professional must first take into consideration the prescriptives pertaining to (1) the place, (2) the people, and (3) the processes. Often, only the prescriptives related to the place are placed in the limelight. The facility professional, concerned with disaster planning and recovery strategy (and vitally, in overseeing the day-to-day operations of an organization without such strategy or plans) need, initially, determine whether or not the people or place or processes are in full compliance with all the applicable prescriptives. These would encompass the building and electrical codes (to cite but two) applicable to a new building or one in place or being refitted; the various safety codes applicable to the people (such as provisos for fire drills and OSHA-mandated work-environment requirements); and prescriptives related to the conduct of the processes (such as compliance with SEC, ACID, AICPA, or FASO rules and practices).

Second, the facility professional should be concerned whether or not a particular prescriptive actually reduces the specific risk or risks to a level ALARP. This is extremely important: many prescriptives simply do not reduce the levels of risk ALARP. This often provides meaningful opportunities for the facility professional to establish lower levels of risk at little or no incremental costs (or possibly at an acceptable increase in cost)! The implementation of ALARP risk levels—lower than achieved through compliance with prescriptives—is a very vital part of creating a disaster planning and recovery strategy.

Third—and by no means of least importance—the facility profession should be aware of instances wherein a prescriptive *would not* serve to reduce the level of risk, or perhaps the prescriptive might actually increase the level of risk in the place under consideration. These prescriptives could be "in place" and apply to the planning and design stages for the place, or might be mandated for retrofitment of the place. Here, the facility professional can find very important opportunities to initiate the processes for *exemption* or *variance* from conformance with the prescriptive. Such exemption or variance can result in the important ultimate advantages of (1) achieving a lower lever of risk than the prescriptive would provide, or an acceptable lower level of risk in terms of cost:benefit, and/or (2) the substantial savings that would accrue through nonadaptation of the prescriptive.

Computer-based modeling and simulation, discussed elsewhere, can provide important information concerning whether a particular prescriptive—implemented or pending implementation—actually *will* achieve the intended risk level in the specific environment. This "promise-versus-performance" determination is especially important when a (what might be categorized as a "politically motivated") new prescriptive is placed on the table.

Some instances of "political motivation" might be found among the concerns for fire safety and evacuation safety management in London Underground's stations. The Fennel Report[10]—an investigation into the disastrous fire at King's Cross Underground Station, London, in 1987, which killed 31 people and caused many horrific injuries—recommended a range of changes, including requirement for extensive fire protection hardware improvements such as automatic fire detection and suppression equipment, to be made to underground railway stations to minimize the chance of repeat incidents. These recommendations became law in the United Kingdom. The complete range of recommendations needed large capital investments; however, it was perceived, by London Underground, that some mandated investments would not produce a signifi-

---

[10] D. Fennell, *Investigation into the King's Cross Underground Fire* (London: Her Majesty's Stationery Office, 1988).

cant risk reduction. This meant that there was a potential for spending limited funds for requirements that were impractical, or were of little or no level-of-risk-reduction or safety benefit. The estimated cost of total compliance for the hardware improvements alone was in excess of £500 million (over $775 million). To obtain prudent exemptions, a full quantified risk assessment (QRA) and cost:benefit analysis with and without the prescriptive improvements in place was undertaken, supported by computer simulation and modeling, for a number of Underground stations.

The simulation and modeling process revealed that in some situations the prescribed fire detection and protection provisions were not justifiable in terms of reduction in levels of risk to ALARP levels. In other situations, the prescriptives were found justifiable only in localized areas within some stations (rather than throughout that station) to meet the ALARP levels in risk reduction. The results of the analysis were presented to the responsible regulatory authorities who both accepted the simulation and modeling methodology and the study results. On this basis, extensive exemptions from the prescriptives were granted; these resulted in an immediate cost savings of £10 million (over $15.5 million) *without* compromising the effective risk reduction. Other and considerably larger costs savings were anticipated from more extensive application of simulation and modeling as a means for exemption from prescriptives. In the initial work, the cost of creating the computer model, the simulation techniques, and the studies themselves represented an expenditure that was less than 2% of the initial savings.

Often, designers, planners, and managers comply with a prescriptive because it is "simpler"—they do not wish to rock the boat. While this is not without merit, it is important for the facility professional—whatever his or her role may be in relation to the place—to look beyond the prescriptives and determine whether (1) compliance actually does reduce the level of risk ALARP, or that additional risk-reduction steps should be taken, and, (2) will compliance with particular prescriptives actually reduce the level of risk in the intended manner.

The (or at least, a) most vital goal in establishing a disaster planning and recovery strategy is, arguably, the elimination or minimization of any casualties—both deaths and injuries—whenever an out-of-course event strikes the facility. The people who work in, or visit, our increasingly complex buildings—office buildings, hospitals, hotels, department stores, airport terminals, arts and sports venues—are exposed to a vast array of hazards—such as fire, explosion, fierce weather, floods, bombs, and other forms of violence—and have limited means of escaping from them. They can become casualties. The facility professional must analyze these hazards and the effectiveness of planned emergency procedures intended to reduce casualties. Emergency procedures, too, are customarily based on what can be termed "tradition": Traditionally, organizations have followed rigid codes, standards, and industry practices with regard to the safety of the people in or around the places facility professionals design, construct, and manage.

The facility professional must now utilize "goal-setting" as an effective means to reduce risk. The goal-setting regime requires facility professionals to set and achieve safety goals acceptable to those who own, occupy, and operate the place. Risk levels must be as low as is reasonably practicable (ALARP), and supported, and justified, by quantitative risk assessment. This process enables everybody concerned with a facility—owners, designers, managers, and users—to demonstrate that they are getting the best value for their investment in safety. Risk management becomes people-specific, place-specific, and processes-specific. Your people, place, and processes are unique; the means employed to minimize the risks to them need be unique.[11]

In evaluating whether you should *go beyond* prescriptives, some scenarios can be "investigated" through a disciplined examination and investigation of vulnerabilities present in the place through the vulnerability search and analysis processes, described elsewhere.[12] It can become readily apparent that the application of, or use of, the prescriptive alone does not do all possible to reduce risk of casualties. Examples of this include (1) emergency evacuation path illumination where floor striplighting can provide a *better* wayfinding path, producing a more-visible guidance in a smoke-filled corridor, to an emergency exit, and (2) provision of audible and visual emergency alarms, emergency lighting, and exit wayfinding signage in restrooms to aid in evacuation from usually "blind" or "dark" areas. The prescriptives applicable to your venue may not require these, but the need—as revealed in a vulnerability search and assessment—and the advantages become readily apparent when consideration is given to the prescriptives and to the means and manner in which they can be complemented in terms of both the additional risk reduction as such, and the cost:benefit ratio of the additional provisions.

Another opportunity to reach, with advantage, beyond prescriptives in lowering the level of risk of casualties that might befall your people, or

---

[11] This concept is further explored in the Safety Case Approach, Chapter 2.
[12] See Chapter 7 and Appendix II.

harm or damage to the place and processes, resides in the testing of the facility's fire alarm system. Fire alarm systems are prescribed in local fire and building codes; specific aspects of the systems (including installation, testing, and maintenance) are prescribed in other places, *inter alia,* the NFPA National Fire Safety Code 72. Section 7-1.6 of the latter requires that reacceptance testing be performed after any changes are made to software-based systems (which underlie almost every fire alarm system being manufactured in the United States today). Whenever changes or modifications are made to the software of such an alarm system, reacceptance tests must be performed. The *software functions* affected by any change are to be 100% tested. In addition, 10% of the initiating devices not directly affected by the change are to be tested. However, Section 7-1.6 does not indicate or suggest either *which* 10% should be tested, or a statistical methodology that would assure a representative 10%.[13] Testing of *all* of the nonaffected initiating devices (100% rather than 10%) is a prudent means by which the level of risk of compromise to the integrity of the alarm system (put another way, the alarm system not functioning in its as-intended manner) can be reduced ALARP with only minimal expenditures of money, time, and effort. This is very important because there *is risk* that some "initiating devices not directly affected by the change" may not function in their as-intended manner after the software changes; there *is additional risk* that "a 10% sample" may not be a statistically representative sample (as the sample percentage or the confidence interval would vary with the total number of initiating devices); and, there *is additional risk* that any specific 10% selected for testing might not be random samples. A 100% test would go above and beyond the prescriptives and would be a cost-effective approach to reducing the level of risk of alarm system failure ALARP!

A most frequently found compliance with prescriptives is the placement of EXIT signs, designed and manufactured in reflection of a widely applied standard—NFPA Life Safety Code 101—and appropriately placed within buildings as required by local fire or building codes, or by the quasigovernmental agency responsible for the site. With rare exception, the placement of these 12 × 8 inch signs (usually above egress doors) is considered to be "doing enough" or "doing all that is possible." Consider these questions: Are the signs sufficiently visible across a large space? Are wayfinding or directional arrows, frequently incorporated into the

---

[13] Ron Kirby, "Steps to Assuring Quality in Software-Based Fire Alarm Systems," *CEE News,* March 1996, 19.

margin of a sign or placed as an extension of the middle horizontal of the "E," sufficiently visible, especially across a large space? Do "punch-out" arrows appear as a "false direction"? Would you know to look for the wayfinding guidance of an EXIT sign that is placed a foot or two below the ceiling, as required by applicable prescription, in a space with 30- or 40-foot high ceilings? What is the lessened value of an above-door sign, or a sign below ceiling height when the space is filled with smoke, and you are crawling on the floor (as recommended by life safety experts!) seeking egress?

In many instances would not large signs be helpful in wayfinding, and possibly reduce casualties? Would not the additional placement of signs at near-floor-level (as some local codes now prudently prescribe!) be helpful in wayfinding, and possibly reduce casualties? Would not more conspicuous directional arrows be helpful in wayfinding, and possibly reduce casualties? The all-encompassing question is clear: Does the following of prescriptives alone reduce your risk of casualties as low as reasonably practical? A cost:benefit analysis in this instance will provide some clearcut answers!

Determining whether or not you should go beyond *other* prescriptives to reduce the risk of casualties ALARP cannot be "investigated" in the same, relatively uncomplicated manner. Manifold considerations, the variety of alternatives available, cost:benefit considerations, and—especially—the impracticality or impossibility of "testing" results in a decision arena, result in an appropriate application for computer-based modeling and simulation. Some prescriptives make it obligatory to spend large amounts of money, time, and effort required for compliance, although the investment might not produce a significant risk reduction. This means required spending (undoubtedly limited) funds for little or no benefit. In instances such as these, the prescriptives *may not* further reduce the risks. The ALARP level can be achieved *without* application of the prescriptives. As will be discussed in the consideration of modeling and simulation (Chapter 5), it is not always necessary to invest in *all* the applicable prescriptives in order to achieve the lowest risk level; computer-based modeling and simulation has provided acceptable substantiation that prescriptives do not reduce the risk of casualties, or might actually increase that risk. The facility professional can apply modeling and simulation techniques to measure the application of specific prescriptives in risk reduction to a level ALARP.

Some prescriptives, additionally, infer that it is possible, by following the requirements of that prescriptive, to completely *eliminate* particular risks. This, from a practical point of view, is not true. The risks encountered in disaster planning always exist, albeit some of them are extremely low. But a level of risk of any event is always present, and thus is always greater than zero (>0)! In fairness, this is not the fault of the prescriptives, per se, but in the interpretation of them and their effects.

It is often assumed that, as an example, by following NFPA's Life Safety Code 101 describing requirement for emergency egress signage, the risk of casualties in the wayfinding process will be ALARP. However, this is not always true. It is also often assumed that by following NFPA 101, or the findings of Fruin,[14] the risk of casualties in an emergency evacuation will be reduced ALARP. However, this, too, is not always true. It is often assumed that by following the local or state building code or electrical code the risk of fire will be reduced ALARP. Likewise, this is not always true. The list continues.

As mentioned earlier, the (or at least, a) most vital goal in establishing a disaster planning and recovery strategy is, arguably, the elimination or minimization of any casualties. Although this discussion has focused on the relationships between prescriptives and people, counterpart relationships exist between prescriptives and place, and between prescriptives and processes.

Because any regulatory body—governmental, quasigovernmental, or code- or standards-setting group—promulgates its prescriptives on the basis that it is doing the best possible to assure the safety and well-being of people and property, coupled with the fact that different regulatory bodies have different interpretations of "the best possible," surely suggest that following applicable prescriptives alone will not minimize risks, or impacts, or consequences. Yet, all too many facility professionals stand confident in a belief that with code compliance and by following standards, they have reduced all risks as low as reasonably practicable, and will be absolved from any liability. The challenge that faces the facility professional—whether planning, designing, or operating and managing a facility—is to *actually reduce* all the risks ALARP. This frequently overlooked potential advantage is a critical element in creating a disaster planning and recovery strategy.

There also exist additional groups of rules or recommendations or guide lines that might be termed "quasiprescriptives." These "quasiprescriptives" can, in addition to "actual" prescriptives, be the dangerous root of the facility professional's—or the planner's—belief that risks have been reduced as low as reasonably practical, or eliminated (some

---

[14] J. J. Fruin, *Pedestrian Planning & Design* (New York: Metropolitan Association of Urban Designers & Environmental Planners, 1971).

"quasiprescriptive" infer risks *can be* eliminated), and thus provide a false sense of security coupled with the creation of potentially greater risks. These "quasiprescriptives" are usually published or presented by, or on behalf of, some specialized organization, association, or institute. Often, these publications or tutorials take on an aura of authoratitveness and unquestionable competency, or at the least carry the implication of having created a valid foundation and sound basis for the information they propagate. When an organization is prestigious, it is taken that its publications and educational presentations are in the same manner prestigious. More often than not, these "quasiprescriptives" are written or assembled or presented by people who, while probably well-qualified in their own fields (the fields represented by the organizations), have professional disaster planning credentials that are little more than a well-meaning desire to be helpful (or to be in print or behind a podium).

The present author has studied a number of such publications and presentations prepared for members of "organizations," "associations" and "institutes." Often offered at a high price (perhaps to give credibility) and presented under a broad-based disclaimer, many of these publications and presentations propound to iterate *all* the tasks and *all* the precautions necessary to prepare for, or to prevent, disasters from striking and emergencies from occurring. The intent here is not to critique these publications and presentations, but to underscore the importance of facility professional viewing such words of advice most warily.[15] In one publication, the facility manager is counseled that "how to plan for emergencies" and "developing an emergency procedures plan" can be accomplished through (in an actual list of 19 items) steps to (1) "post signs by wet floors, open holes, and defects in floors floor coverings", and (2) "avoid use of extension cords." This clearly raises quite serious questions about the publication itself, and the integrity of any "plan" that might result from following its "prescriptives" and advice.

In a continuing education course "developed and taught by practicing professionals" sponsored by a major university for design professionals, the syllabus recites, "Emphasis is on code compliance, including NFPA standards, the Life Safety Code, [and other] Rules and Regulations." Clearly implied is the sufficiency of following the codes. Nothing else is considered, unfortunately and possibly tragically, concerning the desirability and importance of going beyond prescriptives in striving to further reduce risks ALARP. Another group of 10 courses, developed by the

---

[15] Specific identification of items criticized is intentionally omitted.

same university, for professionals in the facility management, design, construction, property management, and maintenance disciplines, focuses on the compliance with local laws and codes and on the requirements for fire/life safety systems these prescriptives nominate. In these courses, too, the concept of risk reductions ALARP is completely wanting. Clearly, these courses suggest that only an abyss lies beyond the protective wall formed by prescriptives, and that the risk-reduction techniques so advantageously used in so many venues merely do not exist!

In an another instance, a specialized organization's guidelines for bomb threats, the importance of risk assessment *is* stressed. A number of (valid!) questions are raised, but nothing is presented as benchmarks against which the disaster planning undertaken by the facility can be judged. The first item mooted, "Is there a current and complete Emergency Action Plan (EAP)? Review it," fails to provide guidance as to the meanings of "current" or "complete" or even what an "Emergency Action Plan" is or should be! Even a "yes" answer would not provide the slightest hint whether or not the place in question has reduced their risks ALARP, or is prepared to deal with out-of-course events.

In terms of disaster planning, such guidelines, while well-intended, rarely go beyond what might be termed the "adage stage": the reader of such "quasiprescriptives" may be cautioned, by his or her professional association, to be sure the place has taken some steps in creating a disaster preparedness and recovery strategy. But this "quasiprescriptive" information rarely goes beyond the point, that, for example, one should be certain that there are adequate exits. Indeed this is true! But nothing is said of what comprises "adequate exits" or how this should be determined.

There can be a wide chasm—one that will be ultimately expressed in casualties—between the results that follow from compliance with "prescriptives" and/or "quasiprescriptives," and the disaster planning and recovery strategy that *should* and *could* result from a properly structured approach. Beware of just how the clear and present dangers are addressed, and especially of those that are *not* addressed. Beware of the "planning" that presents "checklists" without any clue as to how you should judge the adequacy of each "yes" determination.

The potential value—here, the reduction of the level of risk of casualties—in going beyond prescriptives to reduce that risk is exemplified by a fire in a home for the elderly, in southern New England, that occurred early in 1996. A fire that caused the deaths of three persons, and placed nine others in hospital, blazed in the top-floor hallway of a three-story wing of an assisted-care facility. The surviving residents who, followed instructions, and remained in their rooms, opening windows for air, were not harmed. The fire chief reported that ". . . we had no possibility of the fire extending into the [individual resident's] rooms as long as the [fire-proof] doors were [kept] closed." The 24-year-old wing where the fire occurred had only one sprinkler, placed at the end of the hallway where it connects to an addition built in 1988; this single sprinkler *did* help prevent the fire from spreading to other parts of the building. The state law does not require sprinklers in elderly-housing complexes of less than four stories, although—as the fire chief stated—sprinklers "absolutely would have helped."[16]

In retrospect, one wonders whether the building design was limited to three stories to avoid the necessity of prescriptive sprinkler installation. One wonders, too, what the cost of original installation, or retrofitment, of a complete sprinkler system would have cost. What part of this cost could have been passed on to the approximately 55 residents of the wing who pay up to $5600 per month? In terms of *value of a human life,* preventing the three deaths could have an ascribed investment value of between $12,000,000 (the lowest value found—see Glossary) and $3.6 billion (the highest value found). Surely, the investment for sprinkler installation beyond that required by prescriptives to reduce the risk of casualties from fires ALARP would have been substantially lower than the value of human lives lost!

There is another, important, facet of prescriptives. In addition to (1) the prescriptives that—while reducing the level of risk to some (often significant) degree—fall short of reducing the level ALARP, and to (2) the prescriptives that *do* reduce the level ALARP but that contain some requirements that contribute nothing to risk reduction, there are (3) the prescriptives that reduce the level of risk to an inappropriate level. In terms of the latter, an examination of prescriptives, their requirements, the incremental costs (which would be passed on to customers), and the ultimate delays caused reveals an interesting example of, perhaps, prescriptive "gone too far." As an example, the group (resultant from Britain's privatization of railways) that specifies the acceptability of locomotives (Railtrack's Electrical Engineering & Control Systems Safety Assessment Panel—EECSSAP (pronounced eek-zap!)) has demanded mathematical proof that certain conditions will not cause a wrong-side failure more than *once in a million years* (that is, a level of risk of occurrence of less than once in

---

[16] George Judson, "Fire at Home for Elderly Kills Three in Stamford," *New York Times,* 12 February 1996, B4.

a million years). Even if this level of risk were to be deemed reasonable and warranted, it could not be proved in the numerical sense because all the facts required are not available. Mathematics is only part of the determination; an intellectually rigorous analysis is also fundamental. Significantly, this sort of out-of-course event—a wrong-side failure—if occurring, *might not* have any casualty-causing or damage-causing consequences. In addition to the facts that no extant locomotives can pass the test, and that no serious accident has resulted from the conditions (a specific type of wrong-side failure) in almost a century, implementation of the prescriptive is estimated to add £3 million and £5 million (say, $4.7m to $7.8m) to the cost of each locomotive, and delay deliveries at least one year.[17]

[17] "Wisconsin Zapped by EECSSAP," *Railway Gazette International,* March 1996, 127.

CHAPTER

5

RISK MANAGEMENT

Risk management—and its fundamental ingredient, risk *reduction*—is what a disaster planning and recovery *strategy* is all about! Unfortunately, and much too frequently, disaster planning (is this "planning *for* a disaster"?) as well as disaster recovery sit in the limelight. In some connotations, the "disaster planning and recovery" concept takes the form of planning to compensate for the loss of computing capabilities or facilities during the interval of loss. This context might be excusable if one is promoting or marketing resources that aid in the recovery process. The focus of this guide is on *risk management* and *risk reduction*: reducing the level of risk that any out-of-course event will occur; reducing the level of risk that the event will impact your people, your place, or your processes; and reducing the level of risk that consequences and affects will ensue from the impact and impede, impair, interrupt, or halt the as-intending functioning of people, place, and processes. Inherent in each of the "reducing" processes is that the reduction be to a level as low as reasonably practicable (ALARP). Inherent in "management" is the provision for compensatory or countervailance or mitigation mechanisms that provide the means to reestablish as-intended functioning of the people, place, and (as they are the nuclei of the organization) the processes within a predetermined-to-be-acceptable lapse of time.

The less the chance that an event, impact, or consequences and affect will occur, the less will be your need for recovery, as such. And additionally, there will be fewer occasions wherein your recovery plans will have to be implemented.

Thus, the core and the foundation of any disaster planning and recovery strategy—any plan—is risk management. The guide might well have been published with the term "risk management" as its title, or as a part of the title. Through popularized usage, "risk management" has become the province of the insurance departments or the insurance underwriters. On their patch, "risk management" conveys a comparatively restricted, narrow meaning wherein the "if" in "What if . . . ?" becomes *may be* compensated with cash payments. To their credit, many insurance companies do provide counsel on risk reduction in the sense here under consideration. But such is intended to *reduce the likelihood of their having to pay a claim* rather than the vital objective of enabling continuity of functions in spite of adversity.

Your risk management undertakings—the *management* of risks is an indispensable module in creating an integrated, comprehensive disaster planning, and recovery strategy—entail a four-tined approach: (1) *identification of risks* of out-of-course events striking, having impact, or resulting in consequences and affects on your people, place, or processes; (2) *measurement* of the level of each risk; (3) *reduction* of the levels of risk as low as is reasonably practicable (ALARP) or to an "acceptable" level; and, (4) the establishment of means for the processes (as well as for the people and place) to continue on an as-intended, or near-as-intended, or-to-be-restored basis. The latter, fourth-tine component is the "recovery" or "recovery-from-the-out-of-course-event-strike" part of the strategy created. (An important aspect of the plan you will create emerges in the previous sentence: in risk management, "recovery" from the root-cause of the strike, impact, consequences, and their affects does not infer that "recovery" is from a "malady"—the organization will be positioned to "bounce back" from the out-of-course event or problem, without it having caused any "malady.") Tine number four might be termed *countervailance, mitigation*, or even "disaster recovery" or "disaster planning" (in their popular senses!).

The first step in your endeavors to *manage* risk, is to *identify* all the various out-of-course events that may occur in the totality of the environment in which your people, place, and processes are located. It would be impractical—if not impossible—to recite all the possible out-of-course events that could befall your people, place, and processes. In this guide, groupings—for convenience—of such events are listed in the "Disaster Defined" section. The groups of potential out-of-course events that you identify as having the potential to strike your people, place, and processes should be all-inclusive. At this point in the planning process, potentials should not be dismissed of the basis of relative unlikeness. Select for further consideration *all* potential out-of-course events that might strike! Your list should be quite extensive; if it is not, your selection process may well have been faulty!

In planning, the simple fact that an out-of-course event *may* occur does not mean that it will impede, impair, interrupt, or halt the as-intended functioning of any process. This is an important consideration in planning: money, time, and effort can be unnecessarily expended to counter the *expected* affects of an out-of-course event (that even might have a good likelihood of occurring) unless determination has been made that there *will actually be* <u>bad</u> affects. In terms of your people, place, and processes, you have to determine *if* the out-of-course events (identified as a potential problem or a potential strike-force) will in some manner have an *impact* on people, place, or processes. As an example, the higher-than-normal tides that invariably accompany a hurricane (the level of risk of the hurricane striking having been determined) will likely have a considerable *impact* on a place situated on low ground abutting the shoreline. Protection against the ingress of seawater is important. But the place will be less prone to the ingress of seawater if it is situated on high ground, or well inland. Rain ingress, and wind damage, however, must be anticipated in both situations.

It is, therefore, necessary not only to determine the level of risk of the out-of-course event occurring, but also the level of risk of that event impacting your people, place, and processes. Further consideration of the out-of-course event may not be necessary *if* it is determined that it will not produce any impact (or if the levels of risk of the out-of-course event occurring, or its having an impact, are significantly low). Having determined that an out-of-course event will impact your people, place, or processes, you have to determine what the *consequences* of such impact will be. *Consequences* may or not occur as the result of an *impact*. Whether consequences, as such, will ensue following an impact is often a factor of the time when the impact occurs and the duration of that impact. The occurrence of an out-of-course event (say, the hurricane) resulting in an impact (say, interruption in supply of 440 V ac electricity to your place) might not have any impact if it takes place during a weekend period when the building is completely closed, and the electric service is restored prior to Monday's opening.

Consequences, when occurring, may or may not have any *effect* on as-intended functioning of business processes (or on the people or the place). If the only impact of the above-mentioned hurricane were flooded elevator pits in your two-story building, the consequence of that impact would simply be no operable elevators! This consequence would not have any *effect* on your processes if all the organization's functions were situated on the first story. (There might be some affects on any second-story activities: the ability of mobility-impaired people to reach the second story could be limited, or requirement of the elevators to move matériel up or down.) Determining consequences and their affects is further examined anon.

Thus, you need only be concerned with the management of the level of risk of those out-of-course events which have impact, consequences and affects. Those out-of-course events which do not "reach down" and affect any business process do not, in reality, have to be "managed."

All the *impacts* that may result from each out-of-course event, and *all* the *consequences* that can ensue from each impact, and *all* the possible *affects* must be determined. (It is essential that the *all* be taken under consideration in each of these three determinations.) An out-of-course event becomes a "problem" when it strikes your people, place, or processes, and has an *impact* that results in one or more *consequences* which *affect* the as-intended status of people, place, or processes. The level of risk of a *problem* occurring is what is managed in risk management. You need be certain that each and every potential problem is identified, through consideration of each and every impact and consequence. As an example, flooding need be considered in terms of—among others— inaccessibility to the site, damage to the building and furnishings, damage to the electrical, communications, and other wired systems, damage to or destruction of paper records, damage to computers and other electronics, *and* being the carrier, into the building, of pollutants, hazardous, and noxious substances.

Next, you must *measure* (1) the likelihood of each one of the out-of-course events occurring; (2) the likelihood of it impacting your people, place, and processes, and the severity of the impact; and, (3) the likelihood of the impact causing consequences that effect the as-intended functioning—and the severity of these affects—on the organization's or facility's functioning. An out-of-course *event* can occur without causing any *impact*; an impact may or may not result in *consequences*; the consequences may or may not *affect* what the organization is doing.

The third step in risk management is reducing—to a level as low as reasonably practicable (ALARP) or to an "acceptable" level—the likelihood of the problem occurring, or if it does occur, the likelihood of it impacting as-intended functioning, and if it does so impact, the likelihood of damaging or injurious consequences and affects resulting. This done, the fourth step is the creation of the necessary means to continue—or to reestablish or recommence—operations deemed essential. Thus, the strategy is built upon determining what "bad things"—the problems—might occur; measuring what damaging affects these can cause; preventing or minimizing that damage; and, providing means for the organization to continue to function, or to resume functioning, despite the minimized or unpreventable damage that resulted.

When investigating any potential out-of-course event, it must be studied in terms of its possible impact, consequences and affects on the organization as an entity (e.g., electrical or communications or HVAC failure affecting the entire building) as well as on *any* of the BPCs (e.g., a computer network failure only affecting salaried payroll or all payroll preparation or all accounting functions). All potential impacts, and their consequences and affects, associated with specific BPCs, have to be identified, as do the likelihoods of occurrence. The potential severity of the consequence and its affects must be considered, and countervailance or contingency planning based on the severest of those possible occurring. (The computer or communications or HVAC failure may last only seconds or minutes with only little affect on as-intended functioning, but as the time line of failure increases, so does the severity of the consequence and affects.)

The tasks inherent in establishing and maintaining the mechanisms intended to provide the means for the organization to endure the impact, consequences and affects of an out-of-course event are complex and demanding. The resources required can be very great, and there are many niches where the opportunities for poor investment loom high. The process of risk management—as the basis of creating a comprehensive, integrated disaster planning and recovery strategy *that will work*—provides the planner with another very important benefit: the process itself identifies the most effective ways to allocate and use the undoubtedly scarce resources of money, time, and effort. The risk management process, by identifying what mechanisms provide the best reduction in risk, and where risk is best reduced, enables the planner—and his or her organization—to derive the best bang for each disaster planning and recovery buck.

The management of risk should be focused, initially and principally, on a consideration of the potential impact, consequences and affects of an out-of-course event (problem) rather than on the likelihood of the out-of-course event occurring. Determining the particular problems which potentially result in the greatest disruption of as-intended function enables the planner to focus, first, on the problems which create the greatest threat to the organization.

It should be obvious (yet it is not always considered) that measures taken for the management one type of incident may not be appropriate in a different eventuality. planning must be flexible because any incident has the potential to develop in a variety of ways.

In analysis of the potential impact, consequences and affects of an out-of-course event, it can be beneficial to conduct a failure-mode and effects analysis (FMEA).[1] The possibility of a fault or failure occurring in a device or system is considered in terms of what it means to higher levels—*failure effect*—and to lower levels—*failure mode*—in the hierarchy of BPCs. Starting from the lowest level—the component or the horseshoe nail—the cascading or domino effect is studied as it moves up through the organization. This process—"What happens if . . .?"—facilitates the vital consideration of both *time* and *duration* of impact, consequences and affects. It is vital to consider not only "the device" *and* "the system" as targets or impact zones of a fault or failure, but also the place and the people as well as the processes that can be the *affectors* of the *affected*. Various types of out-of-course events that might impact your organization are catalogued in disaster defined in Chapter 1; it would be foolhardy to consider only "devices" (e.g., computers or telecommunications switches) or "systems" (e.g., the local area network for desktop computers). Unfortunately, many organizations place all their planning strategy and recovery investment and resources in what might befall a "device" or a "system."

The fault-tree analysis (FTA) approach provides a graphic representation to aid in assessing impacts, consequences and affects. Perhaps better-named the "pine tree approach" because of the typical shape the analysis takes, the out-of-course event or problem "tops the tree," with the ensuing consequences—some of which may halt or impede as-intended functioning—as the widening array of branches.

Other planning tools include action-error analysis (AEA) in which the human element enters the equation. This technique considers, as the source of a out-of-course event, someone doing the right thing at the wrong time, or the wrong thing at the right time, or nothing at all being done.[2] The event tree analysis (ETA) is also based on the "What happens if . . .?" but focuses on the unwanted event, per se, rather than on the consequences and affects of the event.

---

[1] FMEA—failure-mode and effects analysis—should not be confused with FEMA, the Federal Emergency Management Act.

[2] Action-error analysis is especially critical in countervailance. Specific tasks and responsibilities for the contingency manager, for each member of the contingency management team, and for all the other people, should be iterated in the plan manual and the primer for survival. This iteration contributes to an assurance that all that *should be done* is done, and done at the proper time. It also contributes to precluding well-meaning people from engaging in activities that may be counterproductive.

After the levels of risks (of out-of-course events, of impacts, of consequences, and of affects) have been reduced to a ALARP level, or to an "acceptable" level, it is essential to ascertain whether any *new* or *different* risks were introduced in the course of the risk-reduction process, or as a result of the precautions taken.

This process of *risk management* (which some prefer to call *management of risk*) provides the foundation upon which your disaster planning and recovery strategy is assembled and erected. It follows that if an organization does not take opportunity to optimize the risk management process, whatever disaster planning and recovery strategy is established, *it will not be* the best possible strategy that is achievable. Put another way, if you have to scrimp anywhere in your planning, do not scrimp on risk management, because doing that will undermine the effectiveness of your overall planning! *Risk management*, as such, provides the best return-on-investment (ROI) on any utilization of money, time, or effort in creating a disaster planning and recovery strategy.

There are four steps in the process leading to "management" of each risk: awareness, measurement, reduction, and countervailance.

"Risk" in *risk management* should be thought of as the relative "measurement" or "amount" or a "quantity" that a possible event will occur or take place, rather than as a possible *event* or *occurrence*. *Risk* is the relative likelihood that a specific event might occur. Each and every risk of occurrence that the organization is susceptible to must be considered separately if it is to be considered optimally, and each of the four steps leading to "management" must be tread if a "plan" is to work. Most unfortunately, many planners are deluded—through the use of software "packages" or other "aids"—into believing that a workable disaster prevention and recovery strategy can be designed without taking *all* possible out-of-course events into account, or without analyzing *each* possible out-of-course event within the focus of awareness, measurement, reduction, and countervailance.

Risk awareness not only includes the recognition that your people, place, and processes are subject to particular out-of-course events, but also the recognition of *all* the potential impacts, consequences and affects that can ensue when the out-of-course event occurs. (As an example, the freezing rain, accompanied by high winds—a nature-based event—that usually severs power lines in your area, would also be likely create road and travel conditions that would prevent, or seriously delay, many staff members from reaching your suburban office facility, or possibly delay or prevent the opening of the facility. In consequence, the business processes that normally take place there would not be able to function, or to function only in a limited way even if you had an emergency generator to provide all the necessary power.) The facility professional, in creating a disaster planning and recovery strategy must become aware of *all* of the risks present, not just those which are "highly visible" or which have a "high potential" for impacting the facility.

Risk measurement is the determination of the likelihood that a particular out-of-course event will occur within a specific time frame. (Historical weather records might indicate that a storm of a particular sort will occur in your area every seven winters. Local weather forecasts would point up the fact that such a storm is likely to occur within a 36-hour period. Weather information transmitted via the Planetary Data Distributing System could contain an advisory at 11 P.M. that a severe storm bringing freezing rain and high winds would commence within an hour. Your power supply was lost at 4:32 A.M.—they were right!) In determining the level of a risk, it is insufficient to look at the out-of-course event ("the risk") as an entity. The potential out-of-course event must also be viewed in terms of severity and/or duration.

As an example, the risk of a power outage may be 1 in every 10 months, while the risk of a power outage lasting more than 5 minutes may be 1 in every 10 years. When considering the time-line tolerance of interruption of the most critical BPCs, an auxiliary power generator capable of running elevators and the HVAC may not be warranted. When planning a riverfront facility, considering flood levels for a 75-year history is undoubtedly wanting (especially in view of the ease of access to much earlier records); the "never-above-that-level-in-seventy-five-years" information can be awash tomorrow!

The expression of risk—or the expression and interpretation of statistical probability—can be misleading or, at best, confusing. Risk, as noted above, is usually expressed as "one in . . ." or "once every . . ." In planning, you might determine from local historical records that the nearby river will rise above flood stage (and flood the place!) once every 13 years. Or, your risk—as a rail commuter—of being killed is one in 194 million journeys.[3] In your planning it is vital to realize and recognize that *13 years will not necessarily lapse* before the next flood. The first consideration, here, is that the last previous flood might have been 8 years ago, or

[3] The American Public Transit Association's statement of risk level in response to the U.S. Federal Railroad Administration's ordering, in February 1996, as a safety measure, the slowing of certain commuter trains. The APTA suggested that the slowed trains would result in passengers reverting to automobiles, which have a higher level of risk of death.

12 years ago, or 17 years past. (If the latter be the case, keep a weather eye out for the rising waters!) The basis of the probabilities are founded on the number of the events that occurred under similar conditions divided into the total number of years in the period in which they occurred.

In the case of the rising waters, "similar conditions" would mean before changes occurred in the water course, such as the building of dams, landfills or excavations, or provision of flood control means. In the total period considered, it would be unlikely that the river exceeded flood stage in exactly even intervals: there may have been two floods between 1970 and 1996—one in 1970 and the next in 1972!

As to rail commuting, the "similar conditions" would reflect the type of equipment, trackwork changes, signaling systems, operating rules, the engine driver (and his work schedule), and the like. If you arrive safely today, the level of risk does not infer that you are safe for the next 193,999,999 journeys![4]

The identical rationale has to be applied to your planning: if a particular out-of-course event strikes once in 11 years, or once in 5000 whatevers, it does not mean that you have that "home-free" period without problems! *The level of risk that any specific event will occur today, or will occur tomorrow, is simply 1 in 2: it will occur, or it will not occur.* Your disaster planning and recovery strategy has to be built around that basis. The river might not rise tomorrow (it being the dry season) but disaster planning is not just for tomorrow; it is a long-range thing. The "dry season" has less of an effect on the day's commuter rail journey, keeping the actual level of risk at 1 in 2. If there are two deaths tomorrow, it does not mean that there will be 388 million "safe" journeys ahead!

Risk reduction considers all that can be done to reduce the likelihood of the out-of-course event taking place, the out-of-course event having impact(s), and the impact having consequence(s) and affect(s). Some risks cannot be reduced or cannot be reduced easily, or there may be opportunity only for relatively little reduction. Any particular reduction, additionally, might require greater investment or resources than are available. In establishing a plan, it is vital to capitalize on every opportunity to undertake *out-of-course-event risk reduction*, *impact risk reduction*, *consequence risk reduction*, and *affects risk reduction*. *Risk reduction* yields the best ROI on investment of money, time, or effort in risk management.

---

[4] In any event, the statistician will point-up the quantitative distinction between 194 million and 194,000,000!

As in the case of *risk awareness, risk reduction* should be undertaken for *all* risks, not just those which are "highly visible" or which have a "high potential" for impacting the people, the facility, or the functioning of the organization. The investment and resources necessary to reduce the risk of a "low visibility" or "low potential" out-of-course event ALARP might be relatively little in terms of the incremental benefit from the reduction in risk level. In many instances, the costs of reducing the "low visibility" or "low potential" events from an "acceptable level" to a level that is ALARP might be quite low.

It would be nice if we could reduce each level of risk to zero,[5] but such is impossible. In compromise—considering the resources necessary to incrementally reduce risk—each risk should be reduced *ALARP* or to an *"acceptable" level*. (In the example, there is little you can do to reduce the risk of the storm occurring, but you can do much to reduce the risks of impacts occurring, and to reduce the risks of consequences and affects occurring. An emergency generator can be installed to power specific business functions. Arrangements can be made to assure the roads, parking areas, and pathways on the site are cleared of snow and ice, and sanded. A determination can be made concerning certain departments that would be closed; employees could learn of this through access to a dial-in recorded announcement (if telephone service remained functional) or through a prearranged (and preferably, coded) message to be broadcast by a local radio station. Procedures can be in-hand to assure that slush does not accumulate on flat roofs, causing leakage or collapse. Other planning will, obviously, reduce other risks of impact or of consequences.)

Countervailance—the steps you take to compensate for the *residual* bad or harmful or nasty effects *after* you have prevented the occurrence of consequences and affects through risk reduction—are sometimes referred to as "contingency plans." (In the example, the standby generator provides power for essential functions only, limiting HVAC in the building; the dress code for employees working under these conditions is relaxed. Many staff members will not be able to reach the site on-time or at all; through prearrangement, calls to the sales department are routed to another facility. The in-house catering group will be short-staffed; arrangements are in-place for delivery of prepared foods and use of disposable tableware and cutlery. Mail pickup and distribution is limited to First Class only. The computer "hot site" is placed on "standby" alert.

---

[5] Every risk is *always* present; levels of risk are always greater than zero (albeit, some levels of risk can be quite close to zero).

Countervailance planning takes into account as many potential affects as can be predicted.)

Many opportunities for *risk reduction* in a facility are related to the fault or failure of mechanical equipment and systems. The failure or malfunctioning of a mechanical device or system can have considerable impact, and ensuing consequences, on as-intended functioning of the BPCs. The increasing use of, and dependence upon, on mechanical support systems (which themselves may be supported by electronic systems) in the place or in individual work envelopes, requires that the risk of failure of any such device or system be reduced and maintained at a level ALARP. In addition to these "primary" systems, the nature of "backup" systems is such as to require that their risk of availability—when required—is as *high* as reasonably practicable. As cited in examples elsewhere in the guide, a "backup" system will sometimes fail when called upon simply due to lack of proper maintenance, and thus nullify some or all of the planning strategy.[6]

To reduce the risk of fault or failure in mechanical equipment and systems to a level ALARP, the installation, testing and preventive maintenance, and operation of the particular device must be according to the manufacturer's instructions and recommendations. The periodic testing intervals should be according to manufacturer's instructions (not only after completion of the installation), and tests should be conducted under "real life" conditions. As an example, a standby power generator should be proofed under full load, not as a stand-alone, unconnected machine. Inspection, monitoring, and replacement of consumables and expendables used on or by the device should be according to manufacturer's recommendations. Spares and supplies, and applicable instruction manuals should be available on-site.

A wide range of other opportunities to reduce the level of risk of harm to people exist within the place. Extremely important—and frequently overlooked—considerations include the fire resistance of furnishings, the air quality as a factor of materials used in the manufacture of carpeting and furnishings, the toxic or noxious fumes that these may release under heat or fire conditions, and the overall air quality within the place.

Although the characteristics of carpeting and furnishings tend to focus more on design and aesthetics than on risk reduction, both the fire

---

[6] The concept of "maintenance" must shift from a focus on use-costs minimization and on the preservation of physical assets to a focus on the *as-intended functioning* of the maintained asset-item.

resistance and the gaseous emissions under heat or fire conditions should be carefully considered. There are a number of standards that have been promulgated[7] and these can be considered, with profit, in the choice of furnishing and carpeting. The fire-resistance and emission characteristics of furnishing used in subgrade offices—often records centers, mail rooms, and other offices are not the focus of design and aesthetic planning—are especially important in the consideration of ALARP levels of risk.

Overall air quality within the place—with increasingly high percentages of recirculated air intended to reduce heating and cooling requirements—can increase the level of risk of illnesses resultant from airborne diseases.[8] Germs and other causes of diseases and annoyances such as the so-called "Legionnaires Disease" find good homes in, and breed from, air ducts and air cooling drippans. All of these should be checked, cleaned, and disinfected on a regular, programmed basis.

Faults and failures of mechanicals will occur (in spite of your precautions to reduce the level of risk of such ALARP!) and facility staff should be prepared to take some corrective or remedial action "until the doctor arrives." It is prudent to train and familiarize staff members (note the plural; coverage during all working shifts and vacation periods is vital) and to provide "fault tree" analysis information (which often starts with the question, Is it turned on?) to guide in the assessment and correction of the problem.

In the process of risk management, each risk—likelihood of occurrence—(risk of out-of-course events occurring; risk of the event creating an impact; the risk of the impact causing consequences; and, the risk of the consequences affecting people, place, or processes) must be *identified and measured*. In instances where measurement is not possible, the level of risk must be estimated as accurately as practicable. The out-of-course event/impact/consequence succession can be demarcated into three groups: a sequence or chain of happenings that are "tolerable," those that are "untolerable," and those where the level of risk of an out-of-course event, impacts, and consequences are "ALARP."[9] Those "tolerable" have little

---

[7] These include BR 6853 in Britain, and ISO standards under formulation for the European Community. The facility professional, in reducing risks, need not be xenophobic!

[8] It is generally taken that the air *within* a building is 100 times more polluted and contains more carcinogenics than the air surrounding the building.

[9] Some literature uses the terms "acceptable" and "unacceptable." In this guide, "acceptable" is used to describe an adjudged level of risk, not an impact, its consequences or their affects.

risk of occurrence and little risk of consequences or affects. Those "intolerable" have high risk of occurrence and/or serious consequences and affects, and should be the first focus in the risk management and risk reduction processes. The ALARP group must be viewed in a temporal frame of reference: Each risk may be as low as reasonably practicable at a moment in time, but the ever-changing conditions of people, place, and processes—especially the changing utilization of "technology"—can impact what had once been deemed "low." As an example, the BPC responding to customer enquiries concerning order status would be little-affected by HVAC failure if production and shipping records were hardcopy, but if they were mini-computer-based, responses might be impeded or halted.

A related concern—often neglected—in the management of risk is your neighbors' levels of risk. In a practical sense, there might be little, or nothing, that you can do about managing such "adjacent risks" other than the often-mentioned palliative: *move.* You should be aware of the nature and level of risks that could impact the people, place, or processes of your organization. The relative closeness or nearness of the presence of other organization's risks increases the levels of risks to your people, place, or processes, especially in cases where the other organization occupies stories immediately above or below yours within a building. Ideally, you should coordinate planning and risk management with your neighbors so that one organization's people, place, or processes are not, or do not themselves become a root cause of any out-of-course event that could strike and impact its neighbors.

MEASURING RISK

To effectively *manage* risk, it is first necessary to *determine* the risks present. Second, and equally vital, is to *measure* the level of each risk present. In measuring the level of risk, *impressions about the quantifiable are no substitute for measurement.* Too many "disaster planning aids" classify (not "quantify" or "measure") the levels of risk as high, medium, or low. Wherever and whenever at all possible, your planning should encompass quantification or measurement rather than using broad-based groups. Any additional expenditures of money, time, and effort involved in quantification or measurement will be well repaid. The process of quantification or measurement enables you to evaluate the level of risk—a process termed quantified risk assessment (QRA)—and facilitates determination of both the costs of, and benefits from, incremental reductions in the levels of risk of any occurrence.

The goal and objective is to reduce each level of risk as low as reasonably practicable (ALARP).[10] When the level of risk *is* ALARP means that the risk of casualties (both deaths and injuries)—or the risk of harm or damage to the place, or the risk that a process will be impaired, impeded, interrupted or halted—*in any scenario* has been *measured* and *justified* by everyone concerned with the facility in terms of getting the best value for their investment.

Measuring *each* risk that your organization might face—the level of risk of an potential out-of-course event occurring; the level of risk that an impact will result from the out-of-course event; the level of risk that consequences will ensue as an aftermath of the impact; and the level of risk that the consequences will affect people, place, and as-intended functioning of the processes—is the most significant aspect of creating a comprehensive, integrated disaster planning and recovery strategy. Measuring the level of *each* risk is inevitably inherent in risk management. Each risk level should be measured to determine (1) if effort should be made to reduce it, and to what degree; (2) the amount of investment or commitment of resources that are warranted to *reduce the level*; and (3) the amount of investment or commitment of resources that are warranted to compensate for the residual potential occurrence of the out-of-course event after the level of risk has been reduced as low as reasonably practicable.

A distinction should be drawn to clarify the distinction between the sometimes-encountered concept of "potential risks," and the concept, used in this guide, of "level of risk of an out-of-course event." Those writing or speaking of "potential risks" refer, generally, to events or happenings—usually with "negative" or "bad" implications—that *might* or *can* occur. There is no quantification (stated or implied) of the likelihood ["level of risk"] that the event or happening will actually occur. This guide considers "potential" events in terms of the level of risk (which can not be zero, although it can be close to zero) of their occurrence. *All* events or happenings *can* or *might* occur, and the likelihood of their occurrence *is* probably quantifiable and—in creating a disaster planning and recovery strategy—*should be* quantified if at all possible.

---

[10] There might be instances, in creating a disaster planning and recovery strategy, where an *"acceptable" level* for a particular risk may be agreed upon. By implication, an "acceptable" level would be higher than the ALARP level, yet low enough in the practical sense to not warrant additional expenditures of money, time, and effort as well as the commitment of additional resources to further reduce that "acceptable" further to an ALARP level.

Much disaster planning advice, and many planning aids, focus solely on the risk of the "disaster occurring"—considered in this guide as the risk of the out-of-course event occurring—and fail to view the *risk of an impact* as well as the *risks of consequences and affects*. In that an out-of-course event might occur without any impact (the facility professional has done their sums, and planned accordingly!), or the impact can befall the organization without any consequences or affects (again, proper planning!), the significance of measuring the risk of the event, its possible impact, and the potential consequences and affects becomes quite obvious. The method in which the facility professional considers the entire potential chain of events becomes the basis of success—or failure—of the planning strategy.

The techniques and means which the facility professional utilizes to measure or determine the levels of risk, and the accuracy of the measurements, is a key to the success of the disaster and recovery plan. Failure to properly measure risk—when risk can be actually measured—can be the basal cause of the plan failing when an out-of-course event occurs: you didn't think the out-of-course event would occur, or that it would impact, or that there would be consequences that affect people, place, or processes.

In determining the level of any particular risk, reference should be made to historic records, information in the public domain, in-house data, engineering judgments, layout and construction drawings, materials of construction, fire (and like occurrences) detection, suppression and containment equipment, incident records, population distribution, and the extremely important human factors involved.[11] In terms of the use of historic records, it is with considerable profit that the entire historic span of information be used, rather than the often-used, more restrictive (and less indicative) 25-, 50-, or 75-year records.

The first measurement that must be undertaken is the risk (actually, the level or degree or amount of risk) of an out-of-course event occurring. *The level of risk of out-of-course events is time-based. The level of*

---

[11] There is a growing recognition—and appreciation—of circadian affects on people. Changes in shift assignments, hours of sleep, and other personal habits, can effect both the manner in which individuals function, and the manner in which they will react to out-of-course events. The facility professional must recognize that circadian affects can raise the level of risk that an individual will be the root cause of an out-of-course event, or that an individual will not counter the out-of-course event in the optimal, planned manner. The latter consideration is especially significant if the individual is the CM or a member of the CMT.

risk is ordinarily expressed as a "once in . . ." basis. Thus, the level of risk of any hurricane striking your place might be once in 3 years. (For plan design, the facility professional would view the risk of hurricanes of various intensities: The level of risk of a hurricane striking a particular area with winds of 75 to 79 mph might be *one such hurricane* in a 3-year period; with winds of 80 to 84 mph, *one such hurricane* in a 5-year period; with winds of 85 to 90 mph, *one such hurricane* in 9-year period; and so on. Thus, in a nine-year period, one could expect a total of five or six hurricanes.)

Measurements are, put another way, measurement or judgment of when the out-of-course event will occur. When will there be *a* hurricane? *A* power outage? *A* total HVAC failure in the building? *A* computer crash? An *anything* today? Will "it" be each day? Within a week? A month? Six months? A year? Ten years? A thousand or a million years? *When?*

The key concept in this measurement is (again!) that *impressions about the quantifiable are no substitute for measurement.* Unfortunately for the planner, not all risks levels can be easily or truly quantified, resulting in the need to devote a significant portion of strategy investment on the research of recorded historical records of specific out-of-course events, especially when the out-of-course event does not occur either frequently, or with regularity. We must look at historical records. Some of these records—and as many as practical, extending as far back as feasible should be consulted—will provide a "good basis for planning" while others will offer just sketchy information.[12]

Some "historical experience" is presented in a "three times *in the last* so-many years (or decades or months or days)" basis. There may be serious pitfalls in accepting such information without taking a good look into the basis of these "averages." As an example, consider electrical power supply records. You might find that, over a period of 15 years, there had been 270 power outages averaging 30-seconds duration (an *arithmetic* average of 18 outages each year, yet providing absolutely no insight into their individual durations). But does this mean, say, that each of the 15 years had between 17 and 19 such outages? Or, does the 270 represent 200 outages last year, and an average of 5 per year for each of the previous 14 years? Obviously, your contingency or countervailence planning must be different if there were 200 rather than 18 such power failures

---

[12] The search of historical records can present an intellectual challenge. The time and efforts spent in libraries and other information repositories can result in valuable direction for the investment and resource commitment in the creation of your plan strategy. Thus, your time and efforts—and the time and efforts of others—is well repaid.

last year and if some outages lasted many hours while others only seconds! The provision and selection alternative power-generation and supply-continuity equipment (both costly, and requiring expensive maintenance and testing) required to feed supply-sensitive computers and other vital electric devices must consider both duration of outage, and number of outages. (But before embarking on some statistical undertakings, and selecting your power devices based on the possibly more-reliable statistics (pun intended!), an interesting venture into reduction of risk—and an important message here—would be to enquire just what the electric utility has done! *Before you* plan to countervail the level of risk of impact, consequence and affects it is prudent to determine what *they* have done to reduce the level of risk of occurrence of an outage as well as the outage durations!)

Some out-of-course events occur with less regularity, and are thus more difficult to quantify. Others are quite rare, and impractical or even impossible to quantify. In spite of these hindrances, an attempt at measurement of out-of-course events must be made to determine whether investment is warranted to reduce the risk of such event, its impact, and the consequences. Obviously, greater effort need be made to measure the levels of risk of events that could result in the consequences that would have the greatest affects on your people, place, and processes.[13]

The determination of *impact* does not present the same difficulties of measurement: In most instances there is a direct relation between the event and the impact it will wrought. We know—or can ascertain—what a power outage will mean. We can pretty well guess what 2 feet of snow will do. The minimal impact of a bomb explosion in the building is more difficult to predict; there are many more variables, including the nature of the device, its strength, and where it is placed or where it explodes. *The level of risk of the impact of out-of-course events is event-based. The level of risk is—again—ordinarily expressed as a "one in . . ." or "once in . . ." basis, but it would be in terms of an impact occurring after every so-many out-of-course events of a specific type.* Thus, the risk of impact *of a specific kind* (say, interruption in the supply of electricity to the place) might be one in every three hurricanes with wind intensities of 75 to 80 mph. The facility professional would, additionally, have to consider the

---

[13] One should prudently make greater investment into determining the level of risk—and its ensuing affects—of a public transport work stoppage [both *grève légal* and *se mettre en grève*] on as-intended functioning of the BPCs in a Paris office than one in a Los Angeles office. On the other hand, the level of risk of an earthquake or seismic event in Los Angeles would be of greater concern than of one occurring in Paris.

level of risk of *all other potential impacts* (possibly flooding, facade damage, up-rooted trees) from 75 to 79 mph hurricanes, as well as the level of risk of *all* potential impacts—and now there will undoubtedly be *additional* impacts—from 80 to 84 mph hurricanes. The process of establishing and considering both additional impacts, and the risk level of each under differing out-of-course circumstances continues.

Once a level of risk is determined, the range of risk reduction and countervailance measures can be weighted and their implementation planned. Judgment can be made of the measures most effective in a cost:benefit analysis.

The quantification or measurement of risk—whether the risk is of the out-of-course event occurring, of there being impact, or of consequence and affect ensuing—is, in the real world, not always achievable. This fact, however, should not preclude the planner from *attempting* to quantify the level of "unquantifiable" risk present. In any event/impact/consequence/affect chain of reactions, you may be able only to measure one (if that) level of the four or more risks inherent. The number measurable reflects the nature of the out-of-course event, of the potential impacts, and of the consequences, and of the affects that may result. The effort expended "to measure" rather than to "gain impression" would logically be a factor of the nature of the consequences and their affects. If the ultimate effect would be an interruption of electronic vaulting of computer records, an accurate level of risk of this occurring would be important influence in the nature of the countervailance or contingency preparations to be provided in the plan. If the nature of the consequence and affect would only be a shutdown of the supply of water to fountains in the building atrium, little effort to measure the level of risk would be warranted; here, an "impression" would generally suffice. *But* if the supply of water to the fountains also nourished a collection of rare, irreplaceable plants that are part of lengthy scientific research, and are an especially important tourist attraction, the importance of "quantification" over "impression" becomes a contingency planning consideration. The planner would need to know, inter alia, how long the plants could survive without the water (as well as without other elements of normalcy in the atrium), so that the proper contingency strategy can be put into place.

The terms "measure" and "quantify" have an implicit connotation of accuracy, especially when considered in contrast to "impressions." In risk assessment, while accuracy and exactness are desirable, the measurement or quantification process itself might not be able to achieve these goals. This also does not mean that *absolute* measurement or quantification is necessary in every instance. It can suffice in planning to reduce the levels of risk to know that the original level is, say, 1 in 10, or 1 in 50, or 1 in 100. To refine these to 1 in 10.084 or 1 in 49.83 or 1 in 101.8 would be more of an exercise in mathematics than a valuable adjunct to the effectiveness of your planning.

Even though it might be *impossible to measure* the level of risk of an out-of-course event, or its impact, or the consequences and affect—or even to *form an impression* that you would be comfortable with, it does not mean that you should or would discount the event, impact, or consequence and affect in your disaster planning and recovery strategy. A case in point is seismic activity: earthquakes or earth movements. The extent of concern for, and planning in respect to such events is, primarily, a factor of where the place is. But even if the place is not located in an "earthquake belt" the planner must consider the likelihood of such an event, its impact, the consequences and their affects on the people, place, and processes, and incorporate these into the organization's disaster planning and recovery strategy.

In the engineering considerations for Eurotunnel—the railway tunnel under the English Channel—the level of risk of an earthquake was an important concern. Research was undertaken to determine when the last significant shock occurred in the area (1531), and considerable study and effort were expended to estimate its magnitude. This single date cannot in any way serve to either *measure* or to even create *impressions* about the level of risk of the next significant seismic event. However low that level of risk (an impression) might be, the level of risk of impact (again, an impression) to the tunnel structure, infrastructure, and to passengers on the several trains in the tunnel at any one time was taken to be relatively high. Further, the levels of risk of the consequences of the impact—casualties (most likely, deaths) to the hundreds of people who would be on the trains, and well as to the place, were unacceptably high. In view of these unacceptably high levels of risk (albeit, each level an impression rather than a measurement), the tunnel itself, its infrastructure, and equipment were all designed and built to be resistant to seismic events, and to their impacts. Given that the level of risk of a significant seismic event under the English Channel is acceptably low (otherwise, Eurotunnel would probably not have been built), the impressions about the (unmeasurable) levels of risk of consequences and affects were unacceptable, and as a result of this, complex, extensive, and very expensive countervailance steps were taken to reduce the level ALARP.

Measuring—or even gaining impressions—of the level of risk of earthquake away from the "belt" is, at best, quite unscientific. As with Eurotunnel, the facility professional should focus attention on reducing the risk of consequences and affects on the people *when* a seismic event occurs. The level of risk of the seismic event itself may be greater than the life span of the place or the organization. The Lamont-Doherty Earth Observatory of Columbia University indicates that an earthquake of a magnitude of 5 greater on the Richter scale could hit New York City within the next 50 years. The last such events were in 1737 and 1884.[14] (There might be some mathematical fallacy in "the next 50 years." This span is based on the approximately 150-year interval between the 1737 and 1884 events, and presupposes that the next event will occur 150 years after 1884—a date now "within the next 50 years." If we find records that indicate the 1531 event also impacted what is now New York City, simple math would caution us that the next earthquake of a magnitude of 5 or greater would strike New York City in 2002!)

Another important way in which planning will, with profit, gain from efforts toward measurement is that the process can identify other factors that have the potential for causing impacts, or consequences and affects. Here, the process of endeavoring to measure can reveal relationships in the chain that were not otherwise apparent.

The *consequences and their affects* of any impact on the as-intended functioning of BPCs are accurately predictable once the business processes have been identified. We can accurately foretell, as an example, what will happen (actually, what *won't* happen) in the order-processing department if their computers experience a major failure. The obvious affects include the inability to process orders, and—as time marches on—unhappy customers! The level of risk of inability-to-process would probably be near 100% (an alternative expression for stating the consequences and affects resulting just about every time there is an impact). *The level of risk consequences and affects is event-based. This level of risk is ordinarily expressed as a "one in . . ." basis.* Planning considerations would take into account that there would be—say—specifically cited consequences and affects resulting each time (or every third time, or whatever) an impact of a specific ilk occurs. Again, planning continues to take the shape of an event tree topped by a particular out-of-course event. *Each* likely consequence and affect (and there will be the potential—risk—of many!) resulting from *each* likely impact (again, there will be the possibility—risk—of many diverse impacts) that can ensue following *each* likely out-of-course event (of *each* specific intensity and/or duration) has

---

[14] Buffy Vouglas, "The Big Apple and the Big One," *Contingency Planning & Management,* March/April 1996, 11.

to be considered. This is, admittedly, a gargantuan undertaking, but keep in mind that your efforts can result in preventing deaths and injuries; avoiding damage or harm to the facility, its infrastructure, furnishings and equipment; and enabling the organization to continue its functioning. Elsewhere in this guide the question, "How much is a life worth" is asked but not precisely answered. As a facility planner, designer, administrator, or manager regard your efforts as not only "saving the business" but also as saving lives.

In the computer-failure example just above, substantial reduction in that risk level could be achieved through the utilization of alternate, in-place noncomputer-based, manual order processing procedure with at-the-ready forms and previous staff training. The level of risk of unhappy customers might be reduced or controlled through implementation of pre-arranged telephone calls, "We have some problems; do you really need it by . . .?" The understanding and cooperation on the part of customers responding to this type of prompt communication (see Communication, further on) will undoubtedly startle some people in your organization.

The tasks involved in measuring the wide variety of risks of events, the impacts, and their consequences and affects potentially present and facing your people, your place, and your processes is not an uncomplicated task, nor is it unimportant. The process is a tedious one! Although some planning advisors suggest that characterizing the level of risk as "low," "moderate," or "high" is adequate in the creation of a disaster planning and recovery strategy, these subjective ranks can fail to recognize *just how* serious the potential danger is. In creating a strategy that is both comprehensive and that will work when called upon, knowing the risks faced, and the perils that each presents are indispensable. Measurement, per se, provides you with the groundwork upon which your strategy is constructed. Without proper measurement of risk, you may expend and invest, unnecessarily, on extravagant resources for a bulwark against something relatively unlikely to occur, or when it does occur, have little if any consequences on people, place, or processes. Moreover, without proper measurement of risk, you may fail to properly fortify against risks that are more likely to occur than would be apparent from a "low," "moderate," or "high" categorization. To some using these three categories as the basis of planning, that a level of risk be "low," or possibly even "moderate," conveys the implication that nothing further need be done, in terms of creating countervailence or contingency plans procedures, or in terms of reducing those levels of risk, per se. (See discussions of ALARP, and "acceptable" levels of risk, elsewhere.)

The more exactingly you can quantify each of the levels of the risks, the better able you will be to reduce them, and to plan to compensate for them.

Measuring risk has a role equally significant as computer-based modeling and simulation in affirming that specific prescriptives are not worth the investment necessary to reduce the apparent risk present. Under the Americans With Disabilities Act, the Washington (D.C.) Metropolitan Area Transportation Authority was ordered to install brightly colored strips with tactile bumps at 45 of its 83 stations, to help the blind and partially sighted locate platform edges. The cost would have been $30 million. Research (by the Battelle Institute, 1995) revealed that the mandated "bumpy edges" did not reduce the level of risk of off-platform falls lower than the WMATA's standard edges, and, further, that none of the five types of surface was more easily detected by blind people than any other. In the 19 years of WMATA's operations, only two blind people have been killed falling off platform edges, and six others injured.[15] *If* the tactile platform edges would have prevented the deaths, it would represent a value of human life of $15 million.

London Underground Limited planned (1992) to fit equipment preventing drivers from opening doors on the wrong side of trains at stations, at a cost of £10 million ($15.5 million) (1991 prices). Wrong-side door openings, as reported by Her Majesty's Railway Inspectorate in 1990, occur approximately once every "few *million*" [HMRI's words and emphasis] station stops, with no passenger ever having been killed or injured as a result.[16] This is an example of the availability of extremely good statistical materials that demonstrate an extremely low—as well as both ALARP and "acceptably low"—level of risk of casualty. Yet, extremely scarce resources were invested in so-called safety problems which kill and injure nobody!

In another measurement of risk, for A/S Storebaeltforbindelsen, it was concluded that an accident involving dangerous materials in the Great Belt tunnel is likely to occur once in 8000 years. With that tunnel's life estimated at 100 years, Danish State Railways decided that the level of risk is low enough (at an "acceptable" level") to allow most categories of dangerous goods to travel through the tunnel.[17]

It has been observed that "An evolutionary safety culture is [being] replaced by a quantitative analytical culture" and "few of those involved

---

[15] "Cost of the Edge," *Railway Gazette International,* June 1995, 333.
[16] "Mind the Doors," *Railway Gazette International,* January 1992, 13.
[17] *Railway Gazette International,* June 1995, 333.

understand either the technical or the cultural implications of what is being attempted."[18] What this means to the facility profession in creating a disaster planning and recovery strategy is that, in the measurement and analysis of the levels of risk that are present, it is vital for to also *ask the right questions* about the quantitative analysis, not to just "accept the numbers," and to use them as the basis of the organization's strategy. In creating the plan strategy, it is incumbent upon the facility professional to know what the right questions are. In measuring risk, and in searching for vulnerabilities, as well as in examining the consequences and affects, seek the *truth*, not simply the numerical facts. These "facts" may tell only a part of the disaster story!

Measuring the risk of occurrence of an out-of-course event is not always a simple matter. The complexity and difficulty of the process increases in arduousness as the planner narrows the window of time of impact. The determined level of risk for some out-of-course events, impacts, consequences and affects is not "permanent" but may change from year to year, or from season to season. The level of risk of impact can vary as the result of some inherent change in the nature of the out-of-course event; the same is true with the level of risk of consequences, and of affects. Countervailence and contingency planning and preparation should change correspondingly. Take, again, as an example, hurricanes. Although you have determined that the level of risk of a hurricane impacting your place as once in every 4 years, the storm activity during the "hurricane season" (which lasts from June 1 to November 30) varies from year to year. Each year, prior to the beginning of "the season," meteorologists at the National Hurricane Center predict the number of storms and their expected intensities.

Based on these predictions (level of risk of out-of-course event occurring, and the levels risk of storms of various intensity impacting your place), it can prove prudent to review—and modify, if appropriate—"standing" countervailence and recovery planning. The facility professional—in preparing for these storms—should review the risk of occurrence, and the risks of impacts of various levels, the potential consequences, and the probable affects, each year. Contingency and recovery plans that were "acceptable" for the previous year's storms, or for the "typical" year's storms, may prove to be wanting when the current season's storms strike. Another approach would be to plan for the "worst case scenario." The latter, however, might prove to be an unwise (or wise!) allocation of assets

---

[18] Roger Kemp quoted in "Help Us Build Trains That Work," *Railway Gazette International,* June 1995, 391.

and resources. In addition to considering the level of risk of hurricane occurrence, and where the impact will take place, the levels of risks of various hurricane intensities has to be considered. These challenges might be well met by moving the facility inland!

MODELING AND SIMULATION

An Invaluable Tool for Risk Management

Computer-based modeling and simulation can be, when properly utilized, one of the most—if not *the*—most valuable tools and techniques the facility professional can turn to, and profit from, in creating a disaster planning and recovery strategy for any organization. The creation of such a strategy can really be defined as reducing as many risks as possible to levels as low as reasonably practicable. Recently developed modeling and simulation techniques, as well as the enhancements and more sophisticated processes being actively created in the latter part of the 1990s, increase the value of this methodology for the facility professional in determining the both the risk-level-reduction-effectiveness, as well as the cost-effectiveness, of alternative means of risk reduction. The facility professional can exploit the benefits of modeling and simulation to reduce the risk of casualty to people, or of damage or harm to the place, or of the processes being impaired, impeded, interrupted or halted—whichever of these is under his or her aegis. This risk-reduction goal or goals can be undertaken whether or not the facility professional is participating in any "formal" disaster planning and recovery efforts.

The facility professional engaged in the planning and design of a place can utilize modeling and simulation to determine which alternative of design provides the lowest levels of risks for each of the risk-reduction investments made. The simulation aspects of this planning tool enables variables of space, shape, materials, fitments, and large numbers of other variable factors, to be changed or modified or varied in determination of the alternative that provides the lowest levels of risks for the least investment. The best of the design alternatives, in terms of least risk to the people, place, and processes, can be determined *before* committing mortar to brick.

In management and operations of a facility, the professional can gain valuable insight and benefit from modeling and simulation used to provide the basis for analysis of whether the place is configured in a manner that reduces the level of risk of casualty or harm to the people and the processes. Simulation can also serve as the *only* practical determinant whether the stipulations of an in-place or proposed disaster plan are optimal in terms of reduction of risk and of value-for-money in risk reduction, or which potential alternative in a disaster planning and recovery strategy provides the greatest reduction in risk for the investment made.

Experienced facility professionals have plenty of ideas about what is needed to be done to enhance the working environments for an organization when creating, modifying, or operating the place. But how can those responsible for the safety and well-being of the people, the place, and the processes ensure that the designs and projects selected are the most effective and efficient in risk management terms? One historic approach has been to treat this as a complex optimization problem, but this kind of analysis is often hampered by the lack of relevant information about the infrastructure, operational processes and goals, and the personnel involved that the analyst was trying to model.

Today, modeling and simulation techniques and technologies are available which can, as an example, using animated simulators, allow a planner to observe directly on a computer screen—as though watching evacuees move in real time—the effects of each of the navigation path configuration alternatives, and of fitment alternatives, and of the consequences and affects of various impacts relating to the evacuation. Here, it is possible to follow the evacuees on the screen, seeing immediately the effect of each variation decision input ("taken") by the planner. This process leads to a much better understanding of potential problems, and immediately improves the knowledge and understanding of the planner who is using the simulator. The results are very worthwhile: A solid basis is provided for subsequent consideration of how the particular element of the place should be configured, and how the movement of people through it can be controlled and optimized. Examining the possible configurations or changes (here, in the evacuation paths) to achieve an optimum management of risk requires analysis of a great number of individual complex optimization processes; these are "taken into consideration" by the simulator. Other factors that are "taken into consideration" include costs, impacts and consequences of various out-out-course events on the evacuation process itself, the reduction in risk of casualties, and the "soft" benefit of people's peace-of-mind.[19]

Creating the Place

Computer-based modeling and simulation ("modeling and simulation") has proven to be an extremely valuable tool that can be utilized by

---

[19] Raymond Bergmark and Bo Östlund, "Comprehensive Modelling Produces Rational Investment," *Railway Gazette International,* March 1994, 171+.

the facility professional in a most important facet of creating a disaster planning and recovery strategy. Modeling and simulation can be beneficially used by those facility professionals who are counseling as planners, designers, architects, and engineers in the creation of a new place, or in an alteration, or modification of the place. The modeling and simulation technique provides guidance in the selection of the design and materials alternatives that will reduce the risk of casualties (both injuries and deaths) as low as reasonably practicable (ALARP) in the event of an evacuation. Modeling and simulation can also be utilized to determine design and material alternatives that reduce the risk of out-of-course events ("problems") impacting the place to a level ALARP. Modeling and simulation techniques can also be used to provide insight into specific design and materials alternatives that will provide the ALARP risk levels in terms of impact of the problems, and the consequences of those impacts. The determination and concept of *ALARP* is most important; budget constraints are omnipresent, but it is vital to achieve the lowest level of risk possible in terms of the investment made. Detailed studies at an early stage may influence the final design of the place, offering critical savings when the place is being designed, when it is being built, and in its ultimate operations. Simulations also give confidence that, when a plan is implemented, it will function satisfactorily.[20]

Put another way, for both the designer and the planner, the cost-saving, time-saving, effort-saving advantages of simulation and modeling in, for example, evacuation path and procedures design, stem from the ability to experiment with layouts before committing to mortar and brick. The modeling and simulation process provides a means to assess any combination of an extremely large number of factors related to the response of the people (who may have little or no knowledge of the place, and whose reactions will in any event undoubtedly be under stress) to the adequacy of detection, communication, protection, and emergency provisions within the place. Indispensably considered is a combination of factors including (1) geometry of the spaces within the place; (2) materials of construction; (3) facilities for the disabled and impaired; (4) communication systems and procedures, including public address systems, signage and the languages used, and other user aids incorporated in the place; (5) characteristics of the people, especially visitors and transients in the place; (6) time of day; (7) detection and protection systems in place,

---

[20] Nigel G. Harris and Simon J. Dean, "Simulation Pays off at the Planning Stage," *Developing Metros (Supplement to Railway Gazette International)*, 1995, 17–18.

and which of the potential out-of-course events they detect and protect against; (8) preparedness of the organization's people, their mobility, their familiarity with the facilities, and their ability to read and/or understand the signage and public address announcements; (9) the preparedness of the organization's emergency response staff, and whether each member understands his or her own duties, and those they owe to others in the chain; (10) familiarity of the civil emergency services with the people, place, and processes; (11) systems reliability; (12) ventilation systems; and, (13) standard of housekeeping. These factors are combined with well-established and recognized studies into the way people "flow" or navigate through various routes or passageways.[21]

Modeling and simulation can be an invaluable mechanism for the facility professional responsible for a tenanted place when modifications or changes are being considered, and when there is concern whether the risk of casualties (both injuries and deaths) that would occur in an evacuation has been reduced to a level that is ALARP. In terms of modifications, alterations, or changes to the place—as in the case of the design and engineering professionals—modeling and simulation provides insight into the alternatives that provide the greatest reduction in risk for the investments made.

In planning or managing a facility, modeling and simulation can be used to assess the adequacy of fire protection, detection and suppression systems; the provisions for meeting emergency services' requirements; as well as to assess the adequacy of any combination of factors including geometry of the space, including common and public areas, elevators, escalators, and stairs; passageways; materials of construction; profiles of the various people who might be present at different times of the day; facilities for the disabled; communications systems; time of day; preparedness of staff and emergency services; systems reliability; ventilation; and standards of housekeeping. As fire and smoke are probably the two greatest hazards to life in buildings, the probability of a fire occurring and the effects of it and the accompanying smoke hazards can be evaluated by investigating the quantities and types of materials likely to be present, the extent of reliability of the fire detection and protection equipment, and the provision for any other mitigating factors.

"Virtual reality" in modeling and simulation provides three-dimension simulation as a design and planning tool. This enables the designers

---

[21] Enr. Ing. W. M. Heath, Dr. P. Proctor, and P. Dray, *Evaluating Personal Risks Associated With Tunnels,* Tunnelling Symposium, Department of Trade and Industry, Overseas Trade Services, June 1995.

and planners to create spaces and evacuation navigation paths according to human behavior patterns. This is invaluable in exit analysis, provisions for fire and safety, and for the training of the facility's emergency or crisis management personnel. Modeling and simulation offers the means to analyze navigation—both normal and evacuation—paths (people or crowd routing), as well as congestion-point relief.[22] This is especially vital in large office buildings, sports venues, shopping malls, and transportation facilities.

The difficult realm of assessing human behavior under stress conditions can be assessed, and the existing empirically based guidelines can be verified for the movement of people. The individual factors affecting crowd safety and evacuation are complex, and their influence is often interrelated and interdependent. It is unlikely that there is any single people-factor that alone contributes to casualty risk level; thus, such risk management requires attention to each influencing factor—not only of the evacuees themselves, but also such factors as the impact of shift patterns on the evacuees, on facility personnel integral to implementing the evacuation and the emergency response procedures, and to those a part of recovery procedures—and how it influences people behavior in the place and while conducting the processes.

Modeling and simulation can pay off at the planning stage. Operational considerations for the place often come behind economic justification, and demand forecasting when any investment is being planned. Detailed studies at an earliest possible stage may influence the final design, offering opportunities for critical savings in construction and operating costs, as well as resulting in lower levels of risks.[23] Analysis made feasible through modeling and simulation also gives confidence that, when a plan—whether it is the *plan for the place,* or the *disaster and recovery plan*—is implemented, it will function satisfactorily.[24] Simulations can be carried out safely to determine the probability of risks, and give a better understanding of the key variables and design factors which affect those risks.[25]

The modeling and simulation process enables the planner to (1) establish the relationship between design of the place and the people's be-

[22] J.A. Leather and L.T. Buckman, "Simulation Offers Congestion Relief to Station Planners," *Railway Gazette International,* November 1994, 'Passenger Portfolio' supplement, page 8.

[23] Lower levels of risk should really be the primary consideration!

[24] J.A. Leather and L.T. Buckman, op. cit.

[25] E.W. Godward and M. J. Gorman, "V[irtual] R[eality] Offers 3-D Simulation in Design and Planning," *Railway Gazette International,* November 1994, 735–738.

havior; (2) identify the factors which could affect the people's behavior; (3) identify potential hazards and problem areas within the place; and (4) identify "good practice." The information derived from the analysis can be input, with profit, into a number of areas, including (1) place design modification; (2) evacuation management; (3) provision of communication and information; (4) selection and training of emergency response staff; and (5) structuring of emergency provisions.

The planning and design professional can demonstrate whether the applicable prescriptives serve to reduce the levels of risk as low as reasonably practicable (ALARP), as well as ascertain the potential for further reductions in levels of risk and the incremental costs that would be associated with them. Of extreme value (here, "value" means very substantial savings in money!) in planning and design, the simulation technique can be utilized to determine whether specific prescriptives *actually serve to reduce the level of risk in the manner intended or in the manner thought*. The modeling and simulation methodology has been successfully utilized to provide an acceptable basis for exemption from prescriptives because—in specific instances—it has revealed that the prescriptives do not work in the manner intended.

Managing and Operating the Place

Facility professionals within organizations can profit from modeling and simulation techniques in the same ways: determination whether evacuation navigation paths (in-place or planned) provide an ALARP risk of casualties, and whether the infrastructure, equipment, and furnishings reduce the risk of problems, impacts, and consequences ALARP. (Simulation and modeling can also be employed to determine whether the in-place structure and organization of processes affords the greatest resistance to suffering from interruption—the affects—in the event of a problem occurring. This determination of which organizational alternatives reduce the risk of impact and consequences ALARP would be based on techniques different than those used for physical building alternatives.)

The modeling and simulation technique can provide a comprehensive and detailed risk management of the problem, its impact, and the consequences and affects of (1) fire in or near the building, or elsewhere in the place; (2) power failures, both total and partial, and power shortages; (3) communications failures, both total and partial; (4) HVAC failures and shortages; (5) flooding, leakage, and other water damage; (6) presence of gas or other hazardous substances; (7) equipment or infrastructure failure; (8) explosions; (9) staff or transient accidents or injuries; and (10) evacuations, whether mandated, precautionary, or reactive.

Evacuations

An evacuation from a building or site can be *ordered* by a responsible person in the facility (this person should be the designated contingency manager)—whether it be in response to a problem or the impact or consequences of a problem, or as a *precaution* in view of a recognized unacceptably high risk that a potential problem or the impact or consequences of a potential problem will occur, or because *some people perceive* that a potential problem, impact, or consequence looms over the place and elect to leave without waiting for official notification to evacuate. That "some people" evacuate on their own initiative will sometimes occur when emergency officials, or the CM, deem that only segments of the building or site need be evacuated.

Those who plan evacuations, those who initiate the actual evacuation, and the evacuees themselves, face three considerations: when to go; which way to go; and which way not to go. Each of these considerations involves—consciously or not—the risk of injury or death.

Evacuations involve the movement of numbers of people through complex spaces, usually under perilous and stress-enhanced circumstances. Evacuation safety management is the planned and tested means of moving these people to a safe area with the least number of casualties. In any evacuation—for any reason—of the facility you are planning or administering, injuries and deaths may occur. Evacuation safety management has been—and remains—a neglected area in disaster planning because of the impossibility or impracticality of creating a testbed for plans and strategy. Because the facility professional cannot (or should not!) set fire to, or explode a bomb in, the place as a means to test an evacuation plan, reliance must be on prescriptives, such as NFPA 130. Consider the sometimes-mandated fire drills: Rarely do these achieve 100% participation, and rarely do drills use "alternate" egress to compensate for paths that may be blocked in a real evacuation. Rarely will the drill be held in cold or inclement weather. Modeling and simulation techniques now make it possible to estimate the number of casualties, and to compare casualty reduction strategies on the basis of effectiveness and cost.

Whenever any place is being evacuated—because of fire, explosion, storm, gas or water condition, or because of an alarm, alert, or other emergency—it immediately becomes a perilous arena in which a series of complex interactions involving the people, the place, and the processes occur. These interactions often result in injuries and deaths. Many, possibly all, of these casualties may be averted. Simulation and modeling techniques have been developed and can be applied to model these interactions, and to analyze the evacuation process.[26] This simulation and modeling covers the configuration of the space and means of egress, the source and the nature of the reasons for evacuation, the effect of detection devises in raising the alarm, and of protection equipment. In simulations, many parameters can be changed, including the configuration of the space itself and the means of egress, provision and nature of signage, age and mobility of evacuees, their familiarity with the space, provision of lighting, public address facilities and their use, presence of foreign language speakers, training of staff, and the guidance provided by the staff. Each time a scenario is run, the simulation estimates the number of casualties, calculated from probabilities of injuries and deaths during the evacuation, and from failure to evacuate quickly enough.

This modeling and simulation can enable the facility professional to establish the number of potential casualties (both deaths and injuries) that will occur in various evacuation scenarios and under different circumstances. Possible modifications to building and infrastructure, to procedures, and to staff training can be evaluated. These can be tested and compared on the basis of both cost and effectiveness. The importance or otherwise of the variety of factors in casualty reduction strategy can be tested, and selection made on the basis of benefit and relative cost. Improvements or modifications that will provide the best casualty reduction for the least expense can be identified. Provisions in present plans that are not shown to be "risk reducers" can also be identified, enabling these unnecessary expenditures to be avoided.

Computer simulation and modeling techniques have been successfully applied, and accepted by regulatory authorities. As an example, these techniques have been used to determine whether the plans and procedures for evacuation of passengers from Eurostar trains halted for any reason in the Eurotunnel would accomplish the evacuation within the parameters established by the regulatory Safety Authority. The Safety Authority required demonstratory evidence that the maximum number of passengers that a train might carry could be evacuated, carrying their luggage, to specified "safe havens," within the designated time interval. Successful demonstration of compliance with requirements was needed before authorizing actual train operation. In that it was obviously im-

---

[26] These techniques should not be confused with other computer-based tools available to the facility professional, such as computer-assisted design, computer-assisted drafting, engineering software, facility management software, and the like.

practical to set fire to a train load of over 800 travelers somewhere in the tunnel, a computer model was created. A number of simulations was required to determine the correct set of variable required to achieve the evacuation goal. This methodology can be an invaluable tool to measure the effectiveness of evacuation management plans in place in your facility, and to determine the correct set of variables (lighting, navigation path marking, alarm and announcement systems, aisle and door widths, provision of guidance, and other physical characteristics and "soft" procedures) needed to accomplish an evacuation within time targets and with risk-of-casualties levels ALARP.

A computer modeling and simulation technique has been developed and applied to represent these interactions, and to enable the evacuation process to be studied and analyzed. Named SPECS (Simulation of Personnel Evacuation from Complex Spaces)[27] the modeling and simulation covers the source and nature of the reason for evacuation, the configuration of the space and means of egress, and the effect of detection devices in raising the alarm, and of protection equipment. A large number of parameters can be varied or changed, including the age and mobility of evacuees, their familiarity with the space, provision of lighting, signage and public address systems, presence of foreign language speakers, training of staff, and the guidance provided by the staff.

Each time a scenario is run, the simulation estimates the number of casualties, calculated from probabilities of injuries and deaths during the evacuation, and from failure to evacuate quickly enough. This enables possible modifications to the place (building and infrastructure), to procedures, and to staff training, to be tested and compared on the basis of both *cost* and *effectiveness*. The importance or otherwise of the variety of factors in casualty reduction strategy can be measured, and improvements selected on the basis of benefit and relative cost.

Simply put, in any evacuation of the facility you design or manage or administer, (1) there is a risk that deaths and injuries may occur; (2) the number of such casualties can be estimated; and, (3) casualty reduction strategies can be simulated and compared for effectiveness and cost.

The simulations are performed in a spreadsheet environment using standard building blocks which are replicated, modified, developed and interconnected to describe the physical characteristics of the place being studied. In this context, physical characteristics include shape, materi-

---

[27] SPECS is a propriety product of Trident Consultants Limited, 84 Uxbridge Road, London W13 8RH, England. The writer is not aware of any other like modeling and simulation technique available to the facility professional.

als of construction, fire protection, suppression and containment, and other sources of hazard and their mitigation. The simulations also include probabilistic data which can be based on the facility's historic records, information in the public domain, in-house data, calculated data, and engineering judgment. Evaluation of the logic and data is controlled by a simulation management program.

Simulations start when the incident under consideration is initiated and finish when evacuation of the survivors is complete. The model can then be run with other initiating incidents or following modification to include possible improvements. This technique focuses on those improvements where the best cost:benefit ratio is achieved. Information for the modeling and simulation is normally derived from layout and construction drawings (including materials of construction, fire detection, suppression and containment devices), emergency plans, population distributions, and emergency incident records. Once the model is created, it can be used to evaluate the "what if" effects of changes to the design, layout, protection, operation, and emergency preparedness planning associated with the particular configuration of the place.

Exemption from Prescriptives

Computer-based modeling and simulation has also been applied to another realm of considerable significance to the facility professional, whether engaged in planning and design, or in the actual management of a facility: the testing—and proving—the *noneffectiveness* of prescriptions. This substantiation of noneffectiveness can result in exemption from investment-intensive compliance with prescriptives. An important illustration of this relates to the Fennell Report[28] on the disastrous fire at King's Cross Underground Station, London, in 1987, which killed 31 people and caused many horrific injuries. The report (perhaps as suggested in Chapter 4, "politically motivated" prescriptives) recommended a range of improvements be made to underground railway stations to minimize the chance of repeat incidents. These recommendations—which required extensive fire protection hardware improvements, including automatic fire detection and suppression equipment—became law in the United Kingdom. Unfortunately, the complete range of recommendations needed large capital investments and some investments did not produce a significant risk reduction. This meant that there was a potential for spending lim-

---

[28] D. Fennell, *Investigation into the King's Cross Underground Fire* (London: Her Majesty's Stationery Office, 1988).

ited funds for little or no benefit. The estimated cost of total compliance for the hardware improvements alone was in excess of £500 million (over $775 million). However, for some areas the requirements were considered to be impractical and of little safety benefit. To obtain exemption for the latter, a full quantified risk assessment (QRA) and cost:benefit analysis with and without the prescriptive improvements in place had to be made.

Models were created of the several places being considered, and simulations of a number of fire and evacuation scenarios were undertaken for each, using full compliance with prescriptives, total noncompliance with prescriptives, and partial compliance with prescriptives. Based on the resultant cost:benefit analysis, it was determined that all prescriptives were not always justifiable. The analysis was presented to the regulatory authorities who accepted the proprietary methodology used[29] and awarded extensive exemptions from the prescriptions which resulted in an immediate cost savings of £10 million (over $15.5 million) without compromising the effective risk reduction from fire and smoke.

Other Applications

Computer modeling and simulation has progressed far beyond theoretical considerations, and has been applied successfully in several areas closely related to the place as conceptualized in this guide. In addition to being used as a tool to enable comparative studies of design alternatives such as tunnel design to reduce the risk of casualties in any evacuation, modeling and simulation has been applied to evaluate the standards for optimal levels of evacuation path navigation lighting, to determine of pedestrian flows on stairways and escalators, both in service and out of service, and to evaluate effects of design alternatives on possible congestion in the flow of people through open and restricted passageways. The potential application of modeling and simulation in creating a disaster planning and recovery strategy holds considerable advantages in that the facility professional can be able to "test" available alternatives in space planning, utilization of infrastructure and equipment, and human behavior patterns to determine the best opportunities for risk reduction and risk management.

A message often iterated in this book is that impressions about the quantifiable are no substitute for measurement. Modeling and simulation can be an exceedingly valuable tool that enables you to measure

---

[29] SPECS—Simulation of Personnel Evacuation from Complex Spaces—was used for this purpose.

rather than simply report (and rely on!) impressions in the course of creating a plan.

In many off-the-shelf software packages, and in most self-help guides to disaster planning, quantifications of *low, moderate, or high* are deemed sufficient basis upon which to create a plan. These subjective categorizations are simply too general to be a valid basis upon which to create the foundation and means of survival of the organization. If for no other reason, that which might be "low" to one evaluator might be "medium" to another. Rarely will the planner have to resort to categories of this subjective nature.

Modeling and simulation techniques not only obviate the need for economy of fact in low/moderate/high classifications, but—and perhaps more vitally—also enable you to "create" situations impractical to replicate in "the real world." Further, modeling and simulation techniques enable you to vary parameters and conditions, thus determining what impact results from each variation.

The simulation technique can also be used to predict risk in terms of probable loss of life or injuries as the result of other potential incident scenarios in the place—such as gas leaks or flooding—and can assess and rank the relative importance of the factors being considered and the affect of changes made to them.

Modeling and simulation also aids the planner in identifying and evaluating other risks and costs that can arise from possible precautions or potential risk reductions. Modeling and simulation enables the planner to apply value-for-money criteria to a rigorous analysis of the possibility of faults, failures, or perturbed conditions, based on hard statistical evidence.

Another benefit from modeling and simulation is the ability to pretest whether, when putting the plan into action, the faults and failures will be dealt with in the correct sequence. The simulation can also verify whether the plan has the ability to deal with the totality of faults and failures with which it is likely to be presented under the most adverse conditions.

RISK REDUCTION

Risk reduction, as such, is one of the most important aspects in your creation of a disaster planning and recovery strategy. Every reduction in the level of risk that you accomplish is really equatable to an *increase* in the level of risk that your facility and organization will *survive* an out-of-course event, its impact, the consequences and their affects. Call this the "see-saw syndrome": As the level of risks of "bad things" go down, the levels of "good things" go up.

As there are actually three categories of "risks," there are three arenas wherein you can find opportunity for risk reduction. First, there is the level of risk of an out-of-course event *striking* your people, place, or processes. (It is important to remember that the "event" can be an "out-of-course event" of the ilk described in Disaster Defined, Chapter 1, or a fault, or a failure. Each of these categories of "out-of-course" events can strike your people, place, or processes. As discussed in Fault Management, elsewhere, a *fault* occurs when certain units of infrastructure, equipment, or furnishing *at or of the place*, or when some business process, does not function or work or perform in its as-intended manner. A *failure* occurs when the unit of infrastructure, equipment, or furnishing, or the business process, *stops* working or functioning in its as-intended manner.) Just because an out-of-course event occurs does not necessarily mean that it will strike your people, place, or processes.

Second, there is the level of risk that such a strike will *impact* the as-intended functioning of people, place, or processes. Here again, just because the out-of-course event strikes your people, place, or processes does not mean that there will be an impact. Third, there is the level of risk that there will be consequences and affects of the consequences, that will ensue from the impact. As in the case of the event and strike, an impact can ensue without producing any consequences and affects. (This is the goal and objective of the strategy you are creating: prevention or avoidance of any of the likely effects of the out-of-course event!)

It follows that each of these three levels of risk can be reduced. Not all of the risks in each of the categories can be reduced, nor can they be reduced to a level that is ALARP or to a level that is "acceptable." It is the nature of the particular event, impact, or consequence and affects that governs whether the level of risk of occurrence can be reduced; it is *not* the resources you are able to commit to risk reduction alone. (No matter what resources you commit, you are unlikely to affect weather-related out-of-course events, notwithstanding the fact that cloud-seeding can increase the likelihood of rain under certain given conditions.) It is the fact that there is a sequence of events—or chain reaction—of out-of-course-event-then-impact-then-consequences-and-affects that impedes, impairs, interrupts, or halts as-intended functioning that makes essential the creation of a proper strategy focusing on reducing each of the levels of risks of occurrence in each of the three categories.

By their very nature, individual out-of-course events (see Disaster Defined, Chapter 1) have different levels of risk of occurrence, and thus offer differing opportunities for reduction. You cannot reduce the risk of nature-based events occurring. As Mark Twain (almost) suggested, everyone complains about the weather but no one *can do* anything about it. Unless your role is that of a design or planning professional, you can do little to reduce the risk of occurrence of design-based, engineering, construction, and materials-based, or place-related events (especially after the bricks are in place and the mortar is dry; reduction in risk would require moving the bricks—or placing new ones—and mixing new mortar). There are but scant opportunities for risk-reduction for civil and governmental (except, perhaps, in the voting booth, but it would be hard to identify a vote-and-effect relation), human-intervention or people-rooted (although comprehensive testing and screening of your organization's people, and enhanced management of access to the place could help), or transport-related events. The balance—business-process, information, infrastructure, maintenance, and technology-based events—provide substantial scopes for risk-reduction opportunities.

To some degree, the opportunities to reduce the risk of *impacts* of out-of-course events are related to the opportunities in the events themselves: the risks of the waters of a flood, the winds and rain of a hurricane, or the induced electricity of a lightning bolt cannot be reduced directly. (You *can* reduce the risk of *impact* by high waters of a flood by siting on high ground, or of winds of a hurricane by siting the facility sufficiently inland or by choice of design and selection of materials; these are important considerations in the planning stages.)

The *impacts*—and, to a greater degree—*consequences and affects,* and those out-of-course events that are *faults* offer, generally, the greatest opportunities for reduction in levels of risk of occurrence. The return-on-investment, or cost:benefit ratio, for reduction achieved is also usually better.

The level of risk of occurrence of each possible out-of-course event should be reduced—ALARP or to an "acceptable" level—in all instances. It is not a case of "whenever and wherever possible"—this would not result in ALARP levels. When such a risk level is reduced, the planner cannot assume that all possible has been accomplished. Additionally, the levels of risk of each *impact* (of each out-of-course event) should be reduced to a level ALARP or alternatively, to an level that is "acceptable." The same applies to the *consequences* and to the *affects* of each potential impact: The levels of risk of occurrence should be reduced ALARP or to an "acceptable" level.

Any subtle distinction between "ALARP" and "acceptable level" rests upon the semantics of "reasonably," "practicable," and "acceptable." The process of creating a disaster planning and recovery strategy to reduce the likelihood of casualties, damage to the place, or interruption of business functions should not be an exercise in semantics; it must be a means to save the people, place, and process from harm. If you can save an additional life or prevent an additional injury or preclude a significant business loss or damage to the facility by an investment of $50,000, such investment is undoubtedly worthwhile. But if it requires an incremental investment of $25 million to prevent one additional injury or death, or to activate the "hot site" 15 minutes faster, the already-incurred expenditure could equate to ALARP although that injury or startup might not be "acceptable" from an ethical (moral or business!) point of view. The $25 million might not be defined "reasonably" or "practicable" for your organization.

The planner must examine what reduction in any level of risk could be accomplished by each incremental investment of money, time, and effort, and the commitment of resources. Then—the hard question—is the reduction in level of risk worth the additional investment. The answers in regard to levels of risk of to people—casualties—are more difficult to contemplate than those to place or processes. In practical strategy development, the planner will often find that the economics of the consideration may shunt aside some of the unavoidable emotions inherent in the consideration. Usually, the costs of reducing the risk of each incremental casualty will be several orders higher. As an example, the costs of reducing the risks of the first through tenth consequential casualties may be $50 thousand each, but reducing the risks of the eleventh through fifteenth casualties might cost $7.5 million each. Some elements of question are obviated by the costs; but no one said that being a facility professional was without emotional considerations.

Before you can undertake to reduce the level of any risk, you must be aware of the levels of risks of the out-of-course events, of the impacts, and of their consequences and affects that the people, place, and processes are exposed to. Given that *many* levels of risk can be reduced—although not to zero—you must determine which levels of risk you wish to reduce, how much you want to reduce them, and the investment of resources necessary to accomplish the reduction. The latter consideration inevitably evokes the question, Is it worth it? The answer is not always "yes." Enter the elsewhere-considered questions of reducing the level of risk ALARP and of "acceptable risk."

In considering *risk reduction,* you must first determine **what can occur**. This is the sum-total of all of the **out-of-course** events that can take place, all their **impacts** and all of the **consequences** and the **affects** that can ensue. These out-of-course events may be nature-based, technology-based, human-intervention or people-rooted, business process-rooted, civil or governmental-based, transportation-based, information-based, design-based, engineering, construction and materials-based, infrastructure-(both internal and external to the place) based, place-related, or maintenance-based. (A more detailed description of each of these out-of-course events appears in Disaster Defined, Chapter 1.)

The next planning step is to classify each out-of-course event, impact, and consequence into "**intensity**" categories. As an example, one of the technology-based out-of-course events can be an interruption in telephone service. The "intensity" would apply to the scope of interruption: service to a part of your facility; your facility's PBX, the exchange serving your site, all exchanges in your area, your long-distance carrier, several long-distance carriers, or a number of individual telephone instruments. In a nature-based event, abnormally strong winds can affect your place. The effect will undoubtedly increase with the intensity (both literally and figuratively) of the winds: 50 mph, 60 mph, 80 mph, or possibly greater.

Next to be considered is the "**duration**" of the out-of-course event, or how long it lasts. In terms of technology-based out-of-course events, a microsecond interruption in the power supply can be disastrous to certain power uses, such as computer-based processing. A computer crash could result, or an unintentional automatic transmission of an alarm of fire, or a flicker in corridor lights, or the loss of a significant amount of data. A split-second lightning strike might ignite a lot of electrical equipment or "fry" telephones "protected" by gas tubes rather than carbon arrestors. In terms of human-intervention events, or torrential rains, neither an "industrial action" nor a downpour lasting 45 minutes would probably have an impact in an office environment (although it might shorten lunch hours or dampen the annual picnic), but either could affect a manufacturing activity.

The **intensity** of an event determines whether or not that event *is* a "problem." The **duration** of an event determines whether or not that event *can become* a "problem." "Problems" are those out-of-course events for which the risk of occurrence (even after the level of risk has been reduced to a level ALARP or an "acceptable" level) is deemed sufficiently high so as to be an area for which there need be concern in formulating a disaster planning and recovery strategy. As facility professionals, primary concern (*after* concern for risk-level reductions) is with events that become problems. Facility professionals must be equally concerned with steps that can prevent events from being, or escalating into, problems. These are the integral elements in planning, and will be dealt with in due course.

Intensity and **duration** must be considered together: an event of substantial intensity lasting but a micromoment may or may not be of consequence, while that same event extending over time can have a substantial impact on the as-intended functioning of the organization. Conversely, an event of little or small intensity, such as a telephone installers strike, can have considerable consequence when it extends over a long period. A brief 60-mph gust of wind may do little damage to the site; but these same winds lasting for hours, or days, on end, might result in drastically different results.

The plan you create will, in actuality, have two separate, distinct parts: first, disaster planning, and second, the planning for recovery or reinstitution of as-intended functioning of the affected people, place, and processes when or after a disaster strikes.[30] The disaster planning segment is created to reduce the likelihood of something bad (a potential problem) occurring and impacting as-intended functioning of the organization. This planning is based on reduction of the risks themselves, of their impact, and of the consequences and affects of the impact, to a level as low as reasonably practicable (or to an "acceptable" level), in reflection of the nature of the risk, coupled with sound business judgments, mandated, or prescribed requirements, and the investment of probably scarce money, time, and people resources.

The recovery aspect takes into account two considerations: first, that *some* potential problems cannot be avoided, and the likelihood of *other* potential problems occurring cannot be reduced to an acceptable level; thus, problems of an intensity and duration sufficient to impact as-intended functioning will occur. Second, the investment necessary to reduce the likelihood of some potential problems occurring may not be an acceptable business expenditure. Recovery is the preplanning undertaken to assure that the functioning of the impaired, impeded, interrupted or halted BPCs is restored to the as-intended manner as quickly as is practical. Recovery also encompasses the preplanning that enables impacted BPCs to function in an alternative manner or through the use of alterna-

---

[30] There may also be need for planning for re-establishment of as-intended functioning in instances where the disaster did not strike. These would include "deactivation" of the "hot site," removal of protective hoardings, or proper shutdown of the emergency generator.

tive processes, in an alternative place, and possibly, with alternative people. Recovery planning considers the mitigation of damage that might occur to the site, building, infrastructure, equipment, facilities, and furnishings, as well as the repair, restoration, or replacement of these assets. "Insurance" is *not* equated to recovery, nor can it replace recovery planning. However, part of the recovery planning must take into account the activities and steps that will be necessary to assure that all insured values are recovered.

FAULT MANAGEMENT

A distinction has been made in this guide between *out-of-course events* and *faults*; it is important to recognize this distinction. The distinction—albeit somewhat artificial—is created because of the relatively greater "control" the facility professional has in the potential for reduction in level of risk of a *fault* occurring in comparison to what might be involved in reducing the level of risk of "non-fault" out-of-course events occurring. It follows that fault management—and the prevention of a fault from escalating into a failure—is a less-resource-consuming aspect of the disaster planning and recovery strategy. Fault management—the "for want of a nail . . ." considerations—are often, sadly, a neglected or totally overlooked aspect of disaster planning.

A *fault* occurs when some business process, or when certain units of infrastructure, equipment, or furnishing *at or of the place*, or one or more of the organization's people do not properly function or work or perform in the as-intended manner. A *failure* occurs when the business process, or the unit of infrastructure, equipment, or furnishing, or people *stop* working or functioning. There is an important distinction between a fault or failure and an out-of-course event: In the case of a fault or failure, it is the people, place, or process *itself* that is the anomaly. An out-of-course event would *impact* the people, place, or process, and—as the consequence and affects of that impact—the people, place, or process would not be able to continue to function or operate in its as-intended manner, or might stop.

This distinction is not an exercise in word-splitting: There is also an important distinction for the facility professional. Generally speaking, the facility professional has little or no control over many of the out-of-course events that can occur, or over the risk that they will impact the organization. In these instances, disaster planning can only effectuate means to reduce the risk of *consequences and affects*. You cannot reduce the level of risk that a hurricane will occur; you *can* reduce the risk that it will strike your organization by selection of place. You cannot reduce the risk of level that the hurricane will impact your place (unless it is sited underground), but you *can* reduce the level of risk of consequences by providing—as an example—an emergency generator (countering an interruption in electrical supply) and *can* reduce the level of risk of intrusion of water by selecting a site significantly higher and distant from tidal waters or by providing adequate (a relative term!) pumping capacity.

Business processes can be impaired, impeded, interrupted, or halted as the consequence of the impact of an out-of-course event, such as a nature-based or a human-intervention or a technology-based event. An interruption in the supply of electricity (resulting from any cause) can (unless you have alternate electric generating capability) result in the cessation of critical air cooling. A fault or failure, on the other hand, can occur to an item within your realm of control. As an example, you can reduce the level of risk of fault or failure of a critical air-cooling system by a proper inspection and maintenance protocol coupled with a performance-monitoring and alarm system.

The distinction is drawn here to emphasize the importance of the vulnerability search/vulnerability analysis/vulnerability rectification process—applied to items of infrastructure, equipment, or furnishing—as an vital tool in reducing the level of risk of the business processes being impaired, impeded, interrupted, or halted.

The *level of risk of a fault* occurring is determined and is categorized in the same manner as levels of risk of out-of-course events, of impacts of such events, and of the consequences and affects of these impacts. The occurrence frequency is stated in terms of time: *a . . . fault once in every so-many years (or months or days)*. It is important to differentiate between "faults" and "failures." In some usage, the "level of risk" of a particular fault occurring is expressed as "MTBF" (mean time between failures). The term MTBF, often used in association with the "reliability" of computers and computer-related equipment, is actually an expression of expected frequency of failures. The "*mean (or average) time between failures*" represents the average performance of two or more like units. If one unit failed after 100 hours' use, another after 300, and the third after 800, the MTBF of these would be 400 hours. In a practical application, the MTBF is based on the mean of *many* units (but were the worst performers included in the reportage?). In terms of level of risk for planning purposes, the planner would here prudently have to consider the level risk that a failure would occur once in every 100 hours.

There are many infrastructure or equipment systems within a place that can be ranked as "mission critical." Organizations depend on the reliable operation of extensive configurations of complex equipment to function. Put another way, if there is a fault in, or failure of, a particular system, the dependent processes, or business process cells (BPCs), cannot continue to function as intended, or to function at all. If you have a computer center, failure of the supplemental air-cooling systems within the computer room will result in either a shutdown in an preprogrammed orderly fashion, or cause the computer to "crash." If your office suites are located on the 86th story of a high-rise office tower, failure of the elevators can result in shutting down the offices because of the simple impracticality of people trekking up 86 stories to reach the workplace. If your fire detection system initiates and transmits a false alarm of fire, all processes may be interrupted during the evacuation, investigation, and return-to-work procedures.

Your disaster planning and its provision for alternative means that enable the BPCs to continue functioning must take into account the possibility of such out-of-course events occurring in the place, many of which can be categorized as technology-related. Reducing the risk of occurrence of particular technology-related faults and failures is usually directly related to the maintenance (or lack of it!)[31] afforded the particular item or system. It is vital to properly manage plant and equipment to improve service and reduce costs, and—here, especially—to reduce the risk of fault or failure. And, with the increased usage of technology-related systems and the redundancy provided to ensure failures are less frequent comes another penalty: there are more systems that *can* fail although the redundancy should ensure that failures are less frequent!

Up to the midpoint of this century, the usual approach to maintaining the continuity of performance of technology-related systems was simply to fix them when they broke. While there were some diagnostic aids and preventative maintenance techniques available, the fault or failure generally came as a surprise. This approach remains in use for many of today's mission-critical systems, and when they fail, the domino effect on business processes still comes as a surprise.

---

[31] The importance of a change in the approach to "maintenance"—from one that preserves physical assets to assurance that these assets function in the as-intended manner—is an area of increasing focus by facility professionals. Put another way, the new approach is not concerned with the failure of the particular item, as such, but with the consequences and affects that will ensue when the item fails.

In the 1960s, the concept of periodic inspections, with some reliance on statistical probability of faults and failures, came into vogue. While reducing unpredicted breakdowns, it did not eliminate them, and there were still many surprises. The costs inherent in this approach—unnecessary inspections and replacement of some parts and components still functioning to specification and that still had some life expectancy—were excessive. Two decades later, in the 1980s, focus switched to monitoring the state or condition of every component of the system. This approach revealed latent faults—faults that were about to occur could be revealed—but required constant monitoring to reduce the risk of deterioration and failure between samplings. This approach was good in principle, but was less-that-satisfactory in practice. None of the three traditional techniques eliminated an unacceptable risk of in-service failure; these in-service failures continued to cause interruptions and result in considerable otherwise avoidable costs.

A new approach to maintaining the performance of technology-related mission-critical systems has been developed. This approach virtually eliminates the surprise factor of faults and failures, and thus reduces the ultimate impacts and consequences on processes, as well as reducing the costs of maintenance when the systems are functioning in an as-intended mode. This approach combines aspects of fault diagnosis, manual, automatic and predictive fault detection into relational database and expert systems.

While a detailed consideration of this approach is outside the scope of this guide, a very important message for the facility professional prevails: multiple benefits that can be derived from disaster planning. A change in procedures to reduce the risk of a technology-based disaster, per se, can bring down direct costs of equipment maintenance while also minimizing faults and failures that might only cause some "inconvenience" to the BPCs. There are opportunities for the facility professional to pull benefits from more than one of his or her hats!

A good many of the potential faults and failures that will occur can impact business processes, and have disastrous consequences. One of the more frequently-occurring types of fault or failure is related to the supply of electric power to the place. As the use of electric power increases, utility companies have less and less control over the quality of power supplied to the place. That, coupled with increased usage and other circumstances *within* the place, results in even less quality-control of the power provided at the user's outlet. Exacerbating *this* very significant problem is the fact that the electronic equipment using the power is becoming more sensitive to the quality of that power! On the one hand, electronic equipment requires increasingly "better" power while on the other, the quality of the power is getting "worse." In data processing—both mainframe and personal computing—the "problem" power can be translated into incorrect data, lost memory, premature hardware failure, and mixed or garbled data. In a manufacturing environment, "problem" power can set a robot on an errant course resulting in irrecoverable damage to costly equipment, or result in an invalid code in a programmable controller resulting in lost production time. In a medical setting, "problem" power can mean incorrect data or inaccurate diagnosis.

"Problem" power includes voltage spikes, transients, under- and overvoltages, and outages. The technical characteristics of these are not overly important in fault and failure management; what is important is that they occur with frightening frequency. To counter this, *proper* power conditioning devices should be installed to reduce this risk of damage to your computing, communications, and other sensitive electric-powered devices, and to reduce the risk of damage to, or loss of, the data being processed or stored or transmitted by these devices.

To protect against the "ultimate" power problem—outage—battery-based backup power, to enable orderly shutdown of certain computing devices, and to energize emergency evacuation path lighting and communications devices, should be a part of contingency planning. Many buildings and organizations have installed generators to provide emergency, substitute electrical power over a longer duration, but fail to provide for the *proper conditioning* of such auxiliary power. It is important to consider that the capacity and rectification abilities of power conditioners to process utility-provided electricity may not be sufficient to correct the "quality" of the power being generated by the on-site generator.

Another important consideration in risk management of potential faults in the power system is the fact that the "management" you have in place today might not be suitable for changed conditions. This is especially important in the facility where ever-dynamic, ever-changing circumstances prevail.[32] Proper steps may have been undertaken to reduce the risk of power distribution or power "quality" problems within the place *at some point in time,* but the adequacy of these steps under the changed conditions, and circumstances must be taken into consideration. Equipment requiring "proper" power is frequently added, relocated, or moved. Importantly, other devices that may have been installed or changed—

---

[32] It is also important because the utility may "change" the power reaching your D-mark. The characteristics of the "power" which you recently analyzed may today be different; ongoing monitoring of power characteristics is essential.

copying machines are but one example—can impact the "quality" of the power supply delivered to other "sensitive" devices.

Because of the inherent nature of faults, with little consequence and affect on the people, place, or processes, the countervailance measures can be termed "incident management." The management of an incident—or remedial or corrective action or response—is very often neither time- nor resource-consuming when planned in advance. The on-site availability of proper measurement and diagnostic tools, spare parts, consumable supplies, as well as the instructions related to installation or use of these, and designated staff trained to use or install these, can provide adequate countervailence for faults that develop in infrastructure devices, and equipment. Monitoring of proper functioning, inspection, and proper maintenance are each important elements in preventing faults from occurring; detection and alarm systems are vital in both detecting symptoms of developing faults as well as annunciation of faults that have occurred or are imminent. Whether monitoring and inspection, or detection and alarm is the better method to recognize impending or occurring faults depends upon the complexity of the device sensitive to the fault, the risk of the fault elevating into a failure, as well as the possible consequences and affects of the fault or of the failure.

You would undoubtedly opt for detection and alarm of any certain conditions affecting the computer center, while "visual inspection" might suffice for copier-output quality. However, if the actual quality of copies was a vital part of a business function, and only one copier was available, automatic copy quality monitoring would prove prudent. Here, the fault—possibly insufficient toner or want of a proper adjustment—could be rectified by a staff member with knowledge of copier function and access to a maintained stock of toner.

CHAPTER

6

MANAGING RISKS: REDUCING THE PROBABILITY OF PROBLEMS, IMPACTS, AND CONSEQUENCES

Out-of-course events—the *problems* that are the focal points in a strategy for disaster planning and recovery—will invariably occur and create *impacts* on the people, place, or processes with which facility professionals are concerned. The variety of potential problems is vast (see Chapter 2); the level of risk or the likelihood that any one of them will occur at any time varies from "extremely high" to "relatively low." The *impacts* also take a wide variety of forms. The impacts themselves are not unique to the problems that create them; a variety of different problems can result in the same impact. As an example, a hurricane, sabotage, transformer failure, fire, or explosion are but a few of the problems that can interrupt the supply of electricity (the impact) for (or at) your place. Also to be considered is the fact that any one problem can create more than one impact. The heavy rains, high winds, and low barometric pressure that accompany a hurricane can each, for example, have its own, separate impact or array of impacts.

Each *impact* can cause one or more *consequence*. The actual consequence is a factor of what is struck when the impact occurs, how powerful or vehement the hit is, and the time span over which it lasts or extends. It is *if and when* the consequence and its affects prevent a business process cell from functioning as-intended, that the consequence is something to be dealt with in creating the plan.

Thus, there is an inseparable chain linking the problem, the impacts, and their consequences and affects. In that out-of-course events, or problems, *will* occur, and create impacts on people, place, and processes, and that these impacts have consequences and affects on the organization's ability to function in its as-intended manner, logic and common sense instruct us that the first priority in creating a strategy for preventing disasters should be to reduce the risk or likelihood that each of the potential problems will occur. There is very good reasoning here (although it is not manifest in every plan!), for whatever the amount the risk of a problem occurring is reduced, the planning necessary to deal with impacts and their consequences and affects is also reduced. If the risk of the problem is reduced to a level near zero, then there may need be relatively little concern about the impact and consequences and affects. If the risk is reduced to an ALARP or an "acceptable" level, then the planning (and here, its inherent investments of money, time, and effort, and the commitment of resources) for impact and consequences and affects can be less that would be necessary if the level of risk had not been reduced.

It is important, in planning, to consider that most occurrences that ultimately affect as-intended functioning of people, place, or processes can be the *out-of-course event*, as such, or its *impact*, or the *consequence*. As an example, you might try to turn on the lights, your computer, or the air conditioning; nothing happens. This condition could be the result of a *technology-based out-of-course event* (wherein there is no electric power "arriving" at your place because something has happened to the power generation utility, transformer or switching stations, transmission lines, or cabling), or it could be the result of the *impact* of a nature-based out-of-course event (wherein the power lack results from lightning striking the transformer station, causing all circuit breakers to fault and fail), or it could be the result of the *impact* of a human-intervention event (the backhoe operator did not correctly interpret underground cabling diagrams, severing—with a blinding blue flash—a feeder cable). In each of these three scenarios, the ultimate *consequence* is that everything electric-powered won't work! The *affects* would, obviously, depend on what the electric-powered devices are used for, and their function in terms of the people, place, or processes. The importance to the facility professional is that the reduction of risk and the countervailance measures must be separately considered and planned for event (here, no electric power) occurrence as (1) an out-of-course event, (2) an impact, and (3) the consequences and affects. Depending upon the nature of the event, risk reduction should be considered for each of the three types of occurrence. The risk-reduction strategy in each instance can be totally different, although the countervailance measures (here, an emergency power source such as an on-site generator, batteries, or access to an alternative power grid that might not countervail any of the three occurrences[1] that can enable the as-intended functioning to continue, for a finite period, at least) to counter the *affects* can be the same.

The level of risk of some problems cannot be reduced. The risk of others can be only slightly reduced. The price or costs of "risk reduction" is a factor of both the problem itself, and the "point of departure" from which the risk reduction is undertaken. There are some problems which can be identified, yet neither the impact of them, nor the consequences and affects, are certain. In terms of dealing with problems of this nature, the *potential* consequences and affects must be considered; these potential consequences and affects might not directly affect the business processes.

Inherent in the process of *managing* risks (of problems, their impacts, and the consequences and affects of them) is *reducing* the likelihood that they will occur. Given that no risk can be reduced to zero (although we can—and endeavor to—get as close to zero risk as we can) we face the very real prospect of dealing with risks that *cannot be reduced*. Earthquakes and other seismic events can be taken as examples: The only way in which disaster planning can be structured is (1) to reduce the risk or impact or impacts of the problems, and (2) to reduce the risk of consequence or consequences and affects of the impact(s). From this— risk management—perspective, reducing the risk of consequences and affects is equated to taking actions to lessen the number of consequences and affects that will occur. This can be done in several ways: foremost is the very nature of the design and construction of the building itself. Other "structural" characteristics include design or presence of exposed lighting fixtures, piping, and HVAC duct-work. Other like aspects include the nature of fastening (if any!) of otherwise movable objects, ranging from book shelves and file cabinets to desks, tables and partitions, and any equipment on them. There is no harm—as a means to reduce impact (here, the movement of objects that could result in injury to themselves or to people)—in fastening such items, and to fasten plants and other

---

[1] An important consideration lurks here: many "hot-site" or "alternate-site" providers base their "continuity" on electric supply from a grid different than yours, or on a two-grid supply to their site. The potential problems here are that (1) the separate grids may be supplied from the same generating facility or transmission lines, or (2) even when supplied from separate generating facilities, load-shedding can bring down both (as well as many other) grids. The latter effect has been at the root of regional blackouts.

nonstructural artifacts. Many of these items can—and do—act like missiles during an earthquake! By taking actions of this nature, you will be reducing the risk of *impact* (the objects will not fall or move), and because they will not fall or move, the risk of *consequences* (damage to the objects themselves, and to objects and people in their projectile path), and *affects* (inoperability halting the functioning of a BPC, replacement or repair costs, or deaths or injuries to people struck) will also be reduced.

It would be impractical, if not impossible, to list all the possible out-of-course events that might strike your people, place, or processes. Chapter 1—Disaster Defined—classifies the various types of events into 12 groups.[2] To provide the facility professional with insight into the actual process of managing risks—reducing the probability of out-of-course events occurring, along with the reducing the probability—if the out-of-course event does strike—that there will be resultant impacts, consequences, and affects on your people, place, and processes, some events within each group can stand as exemplars for your planning. These include obvious events and some with less-than-obvious opportunities for risk reduction. Some events, although they might be less apparent to the planner, may present a high level of risk of occurrence, with a high risk of consequences and affects on people, place, or processes. The diversity of risks to be managed might be equated to a dog's dinner! The planner must be aware of all of them. As examples, consider the following:

Managing Risks: Business Process-Rooted Out-of-Course Events

Among the frequently encountered high level of risks *within* a BPC is a lack of documentation of just *what is done* within the BPC, and *how to do it*. All remains love-and-roses within the process until key personnel or key processing equipment is not available, accessible, or usable. Technology-related and people-related out-of-course events here aside, the lack of documented or written instructions, or systems and procedures documentation or manuals, presents a level—perhaps unacceptable—of risk that the particular BPC will not be able to function in an as-intended manner simply become no available person knows what to do or how to do it. The consequences and affects of impairment or interruption of the particular BPC can impair, impede, or interrupt the related BPCs, and cascade into an adverse affect on the as-intended functioning of the organization.

---

[2] A lesser, or greater, number of groups may be cited in other guides.

Contingency planning or countervailance measures often provide for the continuity in the BPC's computing resources, but rarely is there documentation of *how* the BPC functions, or *what* to input or compute or output. The level of risk of impact and consequences resulting from a lack of detailed understanding of the BPC and its functioning by "external" management and staff[3] is often significant; it is as vital to provide systems and procedures documentation for use under contingency conditions as it is to provide—for example—a computer "hot site" or an emergency generator.

Managing Risks: Civic and Governmental-Based Out-of-Course Events

This category might well have the lowest levels of risk you will encounter in formulating your disaster planning and recovery strategy. However, this levels of risk in this group of events—as *all* levels of risk—are greater than zero, and planning consideration must be given to them. Typical civic and governmental-based out-of-course events can be exemplified by use of your office building or site as a fire fighting platform (fighting the 12th-floor fire in an across-the-street building from *your* 12th floor—something quite common in areas of narrow streets); the closure of your place because of civic infrastructure failure (a watermain break has undermined the street and sidewalks where your building fronts, or an steam main burst is thought to have released asbestos fibres into the air, and your building is among those cordoned off); or, riots or curfews restricting or prohibiting access to your place.

There is little that can be done, from a practical point of view, to reduce the level of risk of these out-of-course events (other than the pleonastic palliative, *move*). However, since losses from the consequences and affects of civic and governmental-based events *may be excluded* from your business interruption and other insurance, it is important to review your present coverage, and to consider additional protection.

Managing Risks: Design- and Engineering-Based Out-of-Course Events

Design- and engineering-based out-of-course events emanate from the design itself. Thus, the level of risk of various design- and engineering-based out-of-course events can only be reduced in the *design stage* or through a *redesign*. It is the facility professional (as a planner or designer) alone who is able to reduce the risk of design-based out-of-course events.

---

[3] And often by those "internal" too!

In that "design" might be considered as the encapsulation of form, function, and prescriptives, the risk management consideration in disaster planning and recovery strategy is, "Does the particular design result in levels of risk ALARP?" If it is determined—through modeling and simulation, or other convincing means—that the particular design element (as examples, the evacuation path, the provision for fire containment, the emergency lighting, the cabling ways, the roof structure) does not result in levels of risk that are ALARP, then the (proposed) design must be changed, or the (in-situ) design be changed or modified. The stage at which changes can be made most cost-effectively is during the *planning* or *design* processes, rather than when bricks and mortar are in place.

Design-based problems can strike the people and processes as well as the place, and the risks of impact and ensuring consequences and affects upon people, place, and processes can be unacceptably high.

Managing Risks: Construction- and Materials-Based Out-of-Course Events

These risks, distinct from design- and engineering-based out-of-course events, are frequently characterized as faults or failures. The impact, consequences, and affects on the people and processes—in addition to those on the particular place—range from inconvenience to significant numbers of casualties.

The risks associated with construction and materials, and the levels of these risks, can be brought to an ALARP or an acceptable level through quality control or quality assurance techniques, and through proper supervision. Whether quality control or quality assurance measures (or the specifications to which the measures are applied) undertaken by the material provider are adequate, or whether these should be supplemented, remains open to question.[4] The level of risk of impact from materials that may not have been properly or correctly tested, or not tested by the manufacturer or supplier, can be cost-effectively reduced by (additional) testing before use or installation.

[4] The severe flooding that ensued after a 60-inch 7-year-old watermain burst in New York City in 1995 was initially thought to be the consequence of an infrastructure-based out-of-course event. Subsequent investigation found the root cause to be in the improper or incorrect testing of the steel from which the main was formed. The question arose as to who should have been responsible for the testing: the contractor installing the main; the city purchasing department or water supply department; the company that fabricated the main; or the mill making the steel. One ultimate effect of this shortcoming in testing is the necessity to replace several miles of buried mains manufactured from like steel. (Was this actually a business-process rooted out-of-course event in that none of the BPCs were aware of their quality assurance and testing roles?)

Managing Risks: Human-Intervention Out-of-Course Events

There are two, broad categories of human-intervention out-of-course events: those which are rooted in, or caused by, people "anonymous" to your organization, and those which are the result of actions on the part of individuals a part of your organization or who were once connected with it.[5] The former are usually the "mad bombers" while the latter are usually the "saboteurs" or "assaulters" or "mischief-makers." First, some thoughts on the "anonymous" human-intervention.

The bombings of the World Trade Center, and the Federal Office Building in Oklahoma City are but two events that have served to remind the disaster planning and recovery strategist that the level of risk of such events might be considerably higher than generally perceived. Although precautionary measures that were in place in each of those venues did not prevent human intervention, there are several areas where the facility professional can lower the level of risk.

The need for what has been termed "defensible space design"—a term coined by the architect Oscar Newman in 1972—in both public and private places has been addressed in a number of manners. From the restriction of parking access (ranging from signage to hydraulic barriers), to the control of egress by a security force assisted by state-of-the-art surveillance technology, to the appropriate placement of barricades (often disguised as outsized pots of geraniums) and bollards around the venue, to the creation of a "buffer zone" surrounding the building, to use of a computer-assisted analysis to determine whether a building will collapse from a bomb, and the "risk" of death or injury, there are numerous means to reduce the risk of the human-intervention out-of-course event from occurring, or to reduce the risk of consequences and affects of the impact of the event, if it does occur.[6]

Appropriately placed barricades and bollards can prevent ingress by bomb-laden vehicles, or can serve to funnel all vehicles into a security and inspection area. Bollards and barricades can also reduce the risk of *any* errant vehicle from inadvertently—or advertently—smashing into a building. (The risk of a vehicle with failed brakes or steering would be a

---

[5] "Anonymous" in this context refers to "unknown" or "faceless" persons. Although the individual, or a group the individual holds allegiance to, may have some "connection" to your organization, he or she is a "random" person.

[6] Patricia Leigh Brown, "Designs for a Land Of Bombs and Guns," *New York Times,* 28 May 1995, sec. 5.

technology-based out-of-course event; advertent smashing, human-intervention!) The so-called "buffer zone" serves not only to facilitate checkpoints, but—importantly—to protect pedestrians from falling and flying glass, a primary source of injury in a bombing.

The level of risk of human-intervention out-of-course events that are caused by persons who are (or who once were) a part of your organization, or connected with it, offers opportunities for reduction through several approaches.[7]

One possible focus is to countervail the potentially causative individuals who might be violent (assaultive persons), or who might perpetrate acts that impact the as-intended functioning of the organization (disruptive persons). Although much of the literature on this subject is devoted to "crisis intervention" rather than to risk reduction, the focus on "intervention" might be a more practical (if not more effective) means of reducing the level of risk of impact and of consequences and affects.

In the perspective of this guide, there are two problems to be faced. First is the identification of persons who might be the potential root of assaultive or disruptive activities. Here, the level of risk and consequences and affects of *incorrectly* identifying such persons (beyond, of course, normal pre-employment screening) can be extremely costly. The level of risk of discrimination in hiring, or of wrongful discharge can be very high, and the damages assessed can be quite substantial, although in certain organizations (e.g., atomic power plants) where the impact and consequences and affects of disruptive activities can be extremely disastrous, routine screening for specific "profiles" is appropriate and is routinely done. The same screening may not be appropriate in your organization, and—perhaps—might not be sensible. The intervention—by staff members or by outsource service personnel—into a disruptive incident (whether a verbal dispute or apparent in-progress sabotage or the presence of a gun-wielding individual) can itself be a high-risk involvement. Professional training in this area is available, but may increase—rather than decrease—the risk to the person intervening. With regret, this guide can offer no advice in this area that *cries out for reduction in level of risk* other than, perhaps (facetiously!) purchasing the available manuals and videos, and when confronted with a disruptive individual, toss the manuals and videos at him or her, and duck!

---

[7] These might reside within the domain of human resources in the organization or within the scope of responsibility of the facility profession. Wherever the authority and responsibilities are placed, opportunities for risk reduction should be captured!

Managing Risks: Information-Based Out-of-Course Events

An area that presents of high level of risk of consequences and affects, both financial, legal, and operational—yet often not considered as a part of the organization's disaster planning and recovery strategy—is *records management*. Records management, in terms of your recovery strategy, requires that needed information (and data) will be available, accessible, and usable when and where required. The vital considerations of *specifically what information to save* as well as *how long to save it* are external to the considerations in this guide; the legal and business determinants must be evolved within the context of your own organization. There are, however, aspects of records management to be examined as a part of your plan.

All of the organization's information and data[8] (its memory, knowledge, and learning) must be saved and protected. The concept of *all* might be foreign to your records management practices; however, is it not a question of *what* must be saved (*all!*) but *how long*. The time interval consideration of *how long*, based on business and legal determinations, ranges from *zero* to *permanently*. That the information (either the "original," or "backup copy" in the event that the original is not available, not accessible, or not usable when and where needed) will be *available* is based on the requirements that (1) it be saved or recorded, and (2) that it be preserved and protected for the correct length of time.

Accessible means, simply, that you can get at the information when you need it. When your "original" information is not available, accessible, or usable (it may have been damaged or destroyed, or you cannot get into your building) you would ordinarily rely on "backup" information (which presumably has been routinely prepared!). But if the "backup" is stored in a bank vault, it would not be *accessible* outside of daily banking hours, or during weekends. If your off-site records storage was six blocks away from the place, it might be impacted by the same event that impacted the place. Your plan has to consider not only creating the backup information, but additionally, the ability to get at it when necessary.

Usability of backup information is a frequently overlooked consideration in the countervailance and recovery aspects of planning. Equip-

---

[8] "Information" being that which is eye-readable (generally paper-based, but inclusive of microfilm and microfiche) and "data" being that which is recorded on magnetic or optical media (tapes, disks, and the like). (Bubble-based data storage, thought promising in past decades, seems to have fizzled out.)

ment or hardware, software, and code structures necessary to retrieve, interpret, or image the information or data must be available if the information itself is to be made available. Too frequently, organizations might save computer tapes or disks, but not the programs or codes necessary to get at the information, or the equipment upon which to process or image it.

There exists a significant collection of (some, controversial) statistics describing the organizations that fail as a result of their records (read, information and data) not being available, accessible, or usable when and where needed. Any controversy aside, there is a high level of risk that when needed information (or data) is not available, accessible, or usable, the consequences and ensuing affects on one or more BPC will be devastating.

The "saving-everything-for-ever" syndrome is not the answer! There is as great a risk in preserving information and data for which there is no good legal or business basis for saving as there is for *not* saving that which should be retained. Again, statistics describe the litigation, penalties, and—at best or at worst—embarrassment that has befallen organizations that have retained files or excessive or "unknown" or "personal" copies of files that need not have been retained.

A properly structured records management program, as well as a forms management program, can do much to reduce the level of risk associated with information-based out-of-course events. The organization's records manager and forms manager should obviously be both a part of the team developing your disaster planning and recovery strategy, and a member of the CMT!

In another perspective—wherein an information-based out-of-course event is not the root cause of the impact, consequence and affect, but the consequence of an out-of-course event, such as water, smoke, fire, or other damage to the data storage medium is—the choice of data storage media is directly related to the level of risk that data will be lost and the quantity of data that will be lost. Paper, as the medium for storage of information, probably provides the lowest level of risk of loss of the information itself as well as the volume of information lost. A totally unrecoverable file drawer may contain three thousand documents (which may not have been lost if stored in a protective cabinet). As the data capacity (in terms of "document equivalents") of the medium increases, not only is there an increased level of risk that some or all data will not be recoverable, but also that the volume of unrecoverable data stored on the medium will be greater in order of many magnitudes. As an example, an optical disk might contain the data equivalent to 8 million 8½ × 11 inch pages; the level of risk that all of this can be lost (as a result of smoke, heat, fire, from being dropped) is very, very substantially higher than the level of risk of loss of 8 million 8½ × 11 inch pages, per se (which can withstand heat, smoke, falls, and many instances of fire). *The amount of data that will be lost* if there is a loss is a vital risk management consideration that must be taken into account in decisions concerning the choice of information technology.

In terms of information-based out-of-course events, the year 2000 (perhaps a or *the* "Millennium") is presenting unique disaster planning and recovery challenges: It is coming, and few are ready. It is also a sterling example of an out-of-course event that has a level of risk of occurrence that is 100%. (In that regard, it shares a rarefied atmosphere with death and taxes!) Yet so few are prepared.

When organizations consider establishing a disaster planning and recovery strategy, their well-intended desires are sometimes shunted into an eternal postponements based on a notion that "it won't happen to us; we've followed all the codes, and—if something *does* go wrong, we have insurance!" Rarely does the corporate clairvoyant encounter a out-of-course event that unquestionably has a risk level of 100% chance of occurrence, and an event that can be predicted to the precise split-second of occurrence. *And* an event that has been described, reliably, as having affects ranging from an estimated cost of $20 million for a major insurance company to rectify the consequences and affects, to "going out of business,"[9] to an estimated cost to a bank of at least $25 million,[10] to estimates that 20% of business applications will fail (in 1996) because of invalid date computations, and as many as 90% by 1999, if corrective measures are not taken. The "highly respected and conservative technology trend watcher estimates that the cost of solving the problem, worldwide, will be from $300 to $600 billion."[11]

What is the out-of-course event that may cause vastly greater damage than any previously occurring disaster? January 1, 2000. *January 1, 2000.* **January 1, 2000!** It should not came as a surprise! That this event—not really "out-of-course"—will strike, with 100% certainty, at precisely a moment after 12:59:59 P.M. on December 31, 1999, has been known for quite some time.

---

[9] Kevin Schick, research director of the Gartner Group, quoted by Joe Celko, "Start Fixing Year 2000 Problems Now!," *Datamation,* 1 January 1996, 36+.

[10] Elaine L. Appleton, "Call in the Cavalry Before 2000," *Datamation,* 1 January 1996, 42+.

[11] Peter de Jager, "Take a Reporter to Lunch," *Datamation,* 1 January 1996, 76.

The out-of-course event is the result of human intervention or is people-rooted (Hi/Pr)—although some *people* moot that it is a information-based event—simply because people invented the calendar! In another view, the Hi/Pr root cause still holds simply because it was the actions of computer programmers who typically and traditionally provided for the expression of "year" as two digits (YY) in legacy programs! For the computer attempting to distinguish between 1900 and 2000, or to calculate time spans bridging the millennium, the task is impossible,

Other problems arise because 2000 has a lot of zeros in it, and because it *is* an ("unexpected") leap year. But we knew all of this! As regards the zero-based problem, many computer system clocks will celebrate the beginning of the millennium by indicating the year as 1900 or something else other than 2000! Others will jump back to 1980 or 1984. (*Some* systems began to fail with the advent of 1996 and indicated the year as *1*.) As regards 2000 being a leap year, several extremely popular programs erred in not providing for this, resulting with February 28, 2000 as being followed by March 1, 2000. Interestingly, corrective reprogramming did properly provide for February 29, 2000 but in doing so, also erroneously created a February 29, 1900. (One Macintosh program cannot deal with the years 1900–1903.)

Arguably, the "millennium" may begin on January 1, 2000 or on January 1, 2001, but whatever the reckoning, legacy programs utilizing two digits for the year will fail with the advent of January 1, 2000! The impact and consequences and affects on business will probably exceed the total damages of *all* recorded disasters if the Gartner estimate of $300 to $600 billion is anywhere near correct. The great tragedy is that rarely did a programmer look far enough to the future to recognize that there was a 100% risk that the year 2000 would occur and that it and the years that follow it must be provided for. That great tragedy is magnified by the reality that—despite increased focus on this situation started appearing in the technical magazines and professional journals beginning in the late 1980s—even at this (mid-1996) writing—many small, medium-sized, and large organizations in both the public and private sectors have failed to initiate recovery or countervailance measures.

The problem—which will cost hundreds of millions or even billions of dollars to correct—simply should have never existed! There were, in the later 1940s, many involved in EDP (remember that precursor of computers, electronic data processing?) who realized that the MMDDYY configuration then used by IBM would not fit into many applications. Some employees were born in the 1800s; some might live into the 2000s. Some infrastructure, equipment, and other assets dated from the 1800s; some were planned for use into the 2000s. Leases covering periods of 500 or 999 years were not uncommon, and—like other dated materials—had to have their dates of validity recorded into 80-column tab cards! The "costly" investment in *two* "extra" columns to represent "year" was made recognizing the risks of year 2000 coming, having considered the risks of impact and consequences and affects if the information was not available.[12]

The Year 2000 Problem can not only impact an organization's computer-related BPCs, but may well, additionally impact other computer-based systems within the place, such as security systems, elevator management systems, energy management systems, copy machines, and other devices. The problems, here, will undoubtedly have to be solved by the individual manufacturers or service organizations.

At this writing, mid-1996, there are still opportunities to reduce the risk of consequences and affects of the problem, ranging from a wide variety of software packages that enable "problem detection" within an organization's programs, to, as an example, learning from a "Year 2000 Solutions Conference & Expo" presenting "resources & strategies for managing the year 2000 date conversion problem." The problem, which has acquired an identifier of "Y2K," could have been avoided, and probably at a cost less than the $1400 charge to attend the conference. But how many disaster planners will take advantage of any of the means of countervailance?

Managing Risks: Infrastructure-Based Out-of-Course Events

The levels of risk of fault or failure of the *systems* infrastructure of the place—including heating, ventilation and air conditioning systems, the elevator and escalator systems, fire detection, alarm and suppression systems, as well as the "specialty" systems intended to protect computer and telecommunications equipment, the cafeteria food storage refrigeration, and vaults—can effectively be managed, and kept at an

---

[12] The present writer—who discovered in 1953 that some Social Security numbers formatted XXX-XX-XXXX *plus an alpha suffix* existed—*had* sat smugly from 1949, when he made provision for YYYY to accommodate the 1800s and to be ready for Year 2000, until shortly before this writing. Then, in an attempt to enter a lease written on 24 January 156⅚ [a common style during the early Elizabethan era when the New Year was marked in some venues on 1 January and on 25 March after Christmas in others] covering land, tenements and appurtenances in Sussex, England for a period of *20,000 years* into a data base. . . .

ALARP level, through a proper inspection and maintenance protocol. Some items of inspection and maintenance are described in the *vulnerability search* and the *vulnerability search checklist*. The "don't fix it unless it's broken" syndrome serves only to increase (usually substantially) the level of risk that the particular item of infrastructure will not function in an as-intended manner, resulting in undesired impact, consequences and affects on one or more BPCs.

The risk that pipes or mains will burst or leak can be reduced, among other ways, by maintaining above-freezing temperatures in winter. The risk of fault or failure of other items of infrastructure—mains, sprinkler systems and standpipes, drains, elevators and escalators—can also be reduced through application of a proper inspection and maintenance protocol.

Managing Risks: Maintenance-Based Out-of-Course Events

The most important considerations, from the facility professional's point of view, in reducing—to levels ALARP—the risk of each potential maintenance-based out-of-course event occurring are, first, to assure that the manufacturer's maintenance requirements for the particular device or item of equipment or machinery are known, and are properly expressed (that is to say, that the persons responsible for carrying out the maintenance procedures are fully aware of what to check or measure and the measurement tolerances; what and how to lubricate and the lubricants to be used; and what to tighten or adjust and to what degree); and second—and of equal importance—to assure that the maintenance requirements for each device and item of equipment or machinery *are* carried-out according to the manufacturer's exacting standards in terms of both periodicity and fulfillment.

Many "disasters" have occurred simply because the planned and in-place countervailance measures failed to function in their as-intended manner. Emergency power generators have failed to start, or failed after only minutes of operation, simply because of lack of fuel or fuel-related problems. Neglect in checking fuel levels, failure to replenish fuel after generator test runs, faulty gauges, pumps connected to the prime power source, water accumulations in diesel fuel, and fuel supply temperatures have obviated the best-laid plans of facility professionals. Spare parts, replacements for expendables, and diagnostic and maintenance and repair manuals are vital to the readiness of an emergency generator. (See the vulnerability search checklist for a listing of generator-related items.)

Managing Risks: Nature-Based Out-of-Course Events

Whether or not you can reduce the level of risk of specific out-of-course events, and the degree of reduction that can be achieved, is a function of the event itself. You cannot reduce the level of risk of occurrence of an earthquake or seismic event.[13] But you can reduce the level of risk of impact on your people, place, and processes. You can achieve *some* reduction through the incorporation of certain design, materials, and construction techniques into the place.[14] Yet you can achieve *significant* reduction in the level of risk by locating the place away from areas of frequent seismic activity.[15]

Managing Risks: Place-Related Out-of-Course Events

Place-related events reflect out-of-course events that impact your place *just because of where it is.* Place-related is, perhaps, a residual grouping of out-of-course events simply because the impact or consequence cannot be directly attributable to any other category of event. Simply put, your facility happens to have be "in the wrong place at the wrong time." The level of risk associated with place-related events is usually quite low.

An example of a place-related event would be an aircraft—or falling piece of equipment from an aircraft—that crashes onto your place or a

---

[13] Some experimentation—the injection of fluids into the Earth—has been undertaken to reduce the risk of occurrence or risk of intensity of earthquakes. But don't sit waiting for the application of this experimental technique at your place, or bet on its effectiveness!

[14] Each subsequent earthquake of significant intensity demonstrates that the previously employed, frequently used impact-reduction approaches and techniques have been based on an other-than-complete understanding of seismic activity and its effects on different types of structures. Seismic activity usually sends the designer, trembling, back to the drawing board!

[15] You *can* also reduce the level of risk associated with earthquakes without siting the place away from the seismic activity area. Nippon Telegraph and Telephone Corporation chose to construct their Disaster Prevention Center in Kobe City despite the tremendous damage that occurred there during the 1995 Great Hanshin Earthquake. The Shin-Kobeko Building—presumably seismic-proof—will have 23 stories above ground, and 2 below, providing 35,000 square meters of floor space for overall network control, an earth station for NTT's communications satellite, and systems for assuming emergency control of any of nine other network control centers in the Osaka and other Kinki areas. A heliport, on the structure's roof, is designed to ensure physical access during emergencies. The decision to build in Kobe City was in addition to three other policy goals set by NTT's Large City Devastating Earthquake Planning Committee: (1) Install optical access networks for multimedia; (2) lay more lines underground, where they are sustainable to damage; and (3) decentralize communications centers.

highway accident that releases toxic gases that are wind-borne to your place. (Highway accidents that cause leakage of hazardous substances or that cause significant fires are becoming increasingly common and a growing concern of federal regulatory agencies. The increasing number of fires resulting from propane tanker-truck accidents—exemplified by a massive explosion and fire that resulted from a crash because the driver had fallen asleep at the wheel after working more hours without rest than permitted by law—has prompted the National Transportation Safety Board to recommend that the "Jersey wall" highway dividers be redesigned to resist the impact of trucks.) You can—through site selection—reduce the risk of such out-of-course events impacting *your* place.

A circumstance where the level of risk of place-related out-of-course events (the planner might, validly, categorize these as transport-related or technology-based events) becomes a very important consideration is when one or more BPCs operate on a "just-in-time" (JIT) basis. Whether the JIT is related to incoming or outgoing materials, goods, information or whatever, when production scheduling is based on JIT, the location, as such, of the place can result in high levels of risk that—for example—motor carriers or trains or aircraft will be delayed, or there will be intermittent interruptions in electrical supply, or communications links might be impeded. The impact, consequences and affects of the out-of-course event (e.g., the truck carrying the shipment of components vital for the JIT shipment of product cannot reach the place because of a coating of sleet and ice [a nature-based has entered the arena!] has made the up-hill roadway on the place impassable) could result in a halt in the business process, an early closure and dismissal of people, loss of business, loss of customers, litigation for failure to perform according to an agreement, and so on. The risk can be reduced by site selection (obviously!) or by providing plowing and sanding crews to clear that roadway. However, the latter risk reduction does nothing to reduce the impact and consequences of the sleet and ice adjacent to the place!

Managing Risks: Technology-Based Out-of-Course Events

Electromagnetic fields (EMFs)—sometimes referred to as electromagnetic forces—are among the numerous potential technology-based problems.[16] EMFs bestow on the facility professional unique challenges

---

[16] It has been determined that electromagnetic fields result in both thermal and nonthermal effects in the human body. The *thermal* effects are relatively straightforward, relating to the heating of the water in our bodies. The *nonthermal* effects have manifest in experiments as permeability of cell membranes and changes in the phagocytic activity of lymph nodes.

in the planning, the design, and in the administration of the place. No one doubts the existence of EMFs, but experts disagree as to their effect on the human organism.[17] Because the effects—and there is good evidence that the effects are very real—might be so catastrophic, consideration of EMFs should be integral in all phases of planning for the facility. In some environments—perhaps the place under your aegis—the people may be subjected to or exposed to relatively strong fields. The ultimate grave consequences and affects of such exposure on the people may not (or can not) be discernible while there are occurring. But because the *impact* is discernible and measurable, efforts should be made to detect and measure the presence of EMFs, in the workplace areas, and in any public areas of the place.[18]

EMFs can emanate from a variety of sources in communications (e.g., transmitters for AM and FM radio, television, cellular phones, wireless LANs, police and fire radio, microwave radio, radar, military communications); industry (e.g., high-voltage power generation and distribution, food processing, welding, railway overhead power supplies, microwave ovens, induction heaters, metal refining); and in science and medicine (e.g., plasma heating, diathermy, electosurgery).[19, 20]

The proximity of your people or your place to any of these *can* impact (here, contaminate or destroy) the integrity of data being processed on or transmitted by on certain types of digital equipment. The risk of this occurring as the result of high-voltage lines can be reduced to an acceptable level by containing the equipment within a Faraday cage

---

[17] Although debate continues on exactly what field intensities cause what degree of harm, the standards that have been developed address the dangers as we currently understand them.

[18] Legally binding limit values for electromagnetic radiation (thus, the EMFs to which one would be exposed) are currently being framed as a CENELEC (European Committee for Electrotechnical Standardization) standard. Recommendations for personal safety applications have been published by the IRPA (International Radiation Protection Association), WHO (World Health Organization), and in several countries, and in the United States, by the IEEE (Institute of Electrical and Electronic Engineers).

[19] A summary of studies of the effects of electric and magnetic fields emanating from *electric power* (only), an explanation of terms, typical levels encountered, helpful information, some things to worry about, and an extensive bibliography is published by the National Institute of Environmental Health Sciences and the U.S. Department of Energy in *Questions and Answers About Electric and Magnetic Fields Associated with the Use of Electric Power* (Washington, D.C.: Superintendent of Documents, U.S. Government Printing Office, 1995).

[20] A study, by the American Physical Society, cited in "Physicist Study Finds No Definite Connection Between EMF and Cancer," *CEE News,* August 1995, indicated ". . . the effects of electromagnetic fields (EMF) on health has found that there *appears to be* no causal relationship between EMF and cancer." The emphasis is added.

(a properly grounded copper wire mesh six-sided enclosure). The risk faced can change. In the up-grading retrofit of a federal government office building, the local area network computer cabling was run in the freight elevator shaftway; ever time that elevator was started, EMFs from the motor "leaked" into the LAN, and corrupted the data being processed. (Interestingly, the source of the interference was not discovered until someone correlated the impact with the weekly Friday afternoon arrival of supplies which were taken to an upper-floor storeroom.) The voltage level on power lines may be increased; the utility may erect new lines on their right-of-way; and—more commonly—the organization may change the equipment in use to something that is more susceptible to EMFs.

The facility professional should recognize the potential risk of EMF impact in site selection, site renovation, and in equipment location within the facility. The EMF potential from "external" and "internal" sources is measurable, albeit with highly specialized equipment. Determining the EMF tolerance levels—and emission levels—of specific computing equipment and related devices is (for reasons beyond logic) a tedious process, but the necessity of compliance with FCC regulations and European Community standards has motivated most manufacturers to ascertain this information.

Following the completion of the Channel Tunnel (Eurotunnel), a study of EMF emissions from the electric locomotives to be used for hauling the short-headway Tunnel trains was conducted by Newcastle University. It was determined that these EMFs may affect the compasses of ships passing in the vicinity of Goodwin Sands (in the English Channel), and may disrupt the annual migration of jellyfish to the Folkestone vicinity. Although the previously known requirement to immunize signaling and telecommunications systems against such EMFs was taken into consideration in the design of the Tunnel, consideration was not given to EMFs that might penetrate the concrete walls of the Tunnel, or "collect" in them. The presence of these EMFs might require modifications in the running patterns of the trains.

The question of whether there is an impact of EMFs on people's health remains unanswered in both the laboratories and in the courts. Some research has indicated a link between EMF (and microwave) exposure and in vitro biological effects such as cancer in children. Other research is examining the relationship of cellular telephone radio signal with brain cancer, and with pacemakers.[21] The possible effect of micro-

---

[21] *Compliance Engineering,* July/August 1995, 19 et seq. This publication has reportage on EMFs in most issues.

wave ovens on pacemakers is well-established. The health issues related to EMFs should prompt the facility professional to act as prudently as possible whenever possible. If the organization provides or uses microwave ovens, proper cautionary signage should be in-place. The message might go beyond a warning to pacemaker users. If the organization provides cellular telephones or two-way radios for staff members, it can be prudent to obtain a written acknowledgment, which incorporates a "health hazard" warning, for the use of these. Your legal counsel should provide the guidance on this issue.

Too often, in the course of a vulnerability search, the facility professional will fail to scrutinize for the presence of EMFs, or—if EMFs have been detected—underestimate their potential impact and consequences and affects on the organization. In effect, will the organization survive a slow, silent, invisible problem that can impact both people and processes, with consequences and affects that have high levels of both risk of death and of business processes faults and failures? EMFs can radiate from both natural and human-made sources; those flowing from the electrical wiring and from radio-like devices are very common in the business place. The risk that EMFs are present is very high. The VS—if conducted with *honesty* and *thoroughness*—must determine the presence of EMFs and measure the level of risks both of impact and of consequences and affects that exposure to them present to people and processes. A facility professional *might be able to*—scientific evidence does not yet permit us to aver *"can"*—save one or more of the people under their care and responsibility from falling victim to cancer. Wouldn't it be nice to think that *you* did!

Many studies have suggested, but none has yet proved, that there is a link between exposure to certain EMFs and various types of cancer. In addition to risks thought to be higher because of electrical wiring and load changes, studies have pointed to higher risk levels resulting from high-frequency transients generated by switching of electrical loads where wiring is according to very-high-current-configuration (VHCC), and to grounding connections to conductive plumbing. This guide does not suppose to be a forum for the methodology or validity of these studies; however, the *risks* are indisputable.[22] So-caused cancer can result in tragic and needless deaths to the organization's people, but also can result in litigation against the organization based on failure to "be prudent" and to have effectuated means to shield against the EMFs. There additionally exists the level of risk of litigation that can stem from an employee's

---

[22] For an entirely different perspective on these studies, see Jon Palfreman, "Apocalypse Not," *Technology Review,* April 1996, 24+.

or member of the public's *belief* that EMF radiation has caused a disease such as cancer. Whether such claim is valid or not can be less important than the fact that the alleged injured party thinks so and has filed suit for damages. The costs incurred by your organization to defend the suit (whether found guilty or not) can be extremely high.[23]

The affect of EMFs on various types of modems and on wireless communications devices is well-known: your modem-linked commuter output may be "garbled" or otherwise lose its integrity. The results can range from "vexation" to financial or other grave operating misfortunes.

The VS process *can* be used to detect and *measure* EMFs present. The "S" in VS should—not only on behalf of the people, but also on behalf of the processes and, ultimately, the organization—search for them. It can be the most worthwhile part of your planning.

Your duty and responsibility, as a facility professional, is to reduce the level of risks ALARP. To prevent or avoid exposing your people to EMFs *may* be a means to reduce the level of risk of cancer. No one is definitively sure at this writing, but the nature of the risk, the potential impact, and the consequences and affects unquestionably warrant seizing every opportunity to reduce the level of risk ALARP.[24]

Managing Risks: Transport-Related Out-of-Course Events

Transport-related out-of-course events, and the level of risks associated with them, are related to the arrival (of people and goods) and the departure or shipment (of people and goods) at and from your place. In addition to the arrangements for the timely delivery of information, ma-

---

[23] William E. Bean, "Digital and Hand-Held Instruments Enable Precision EM Field Measurements," *Electronic Component News,* March 1996, 13+.

[24] The facility professional should read, with profit, "Managing the Electromagnet Environment," ". . . in Massachusetts, for example, several hospitals have banned the use of cellular telephones on their premises to avoid interference with electronic critical-care systems" (Roland Gubisch, Ph.D., *Compliance Engineering,* July/August 1996, 23), and "Electromagnetic Fields: Power-Line Issues and Emerging Guidelines," wherein, inter alia, property devaluation is discussed (Ben Turner, *Compliance Engineering,* July/August 1996, 55+). Additional thought-provoking information can be found in *The Metatonin Hypothesis: Breast Cancer and Use of Electric Power* (Richard G. Stevens, Bary W. Wilson, and Larry E. Anderson, Eds., Columbus: Battelle, 1997).

The facility professional (especially architects, and designers, and installers of electrical writing systems) should note the IEC standard on architectural electromagnetic interference in IEC 364-4-444 (First Edition), "Electrical Installations of Buildings, Part 4: Protection for Safety, Chapter 44: Protection against Overvoltages, Section 444: Protection against Electromagnetic Interference (EMI) [EMF] in Installations of Buildings" prepared by IEC Technical Committee 64.

terials, equipment and supplies at the place—which is, in part, a factor of carrier selection—as well as for the dispatch of these, you need be concerned about the level of risk of the people being delayed, or unnecessarily fatigued, in arrival at the place in a consistent, timely basis.[25] If the people can't get to the place, they cannot function or perform in the BPCs.

Some organizations have failed to recognize this risk: A major insurance company relocated some functions to a suburban office center without regard for the lack of public transport for thousands of clerical workers, many of whom could not afford cars. (In the event, which was taken as a policy of covert discrimination, the company ultimately provided transport.) In recognizing the level of risk of several thousand workers driving to and from their place, causing road congestion, parking problems, and inconvenience to customers, an entertainment complex provides shuttle buses from outlying, secure, employee parking lots.

Other potential transport-related risks involve potential loss of valuable shipments, or the delay to time-sensitive shipments. The level of risk of such loss or delay can be reduced to a level ALARP or to an acceptable level by careful selection and performance-monitoring of carriers.

Site-selection considerations should take into account transport-related risks. In our practice, a priority in the selection of a imaging service center location was highway-access proximity (for incoming and outgoing shipments). However, the necessity of consistent journey times between the center and the postal facility (driven by output production schedules and precommitted arrival times at the postal facility to qualify for reduced postage rate entitlements) dictated site selection with access to a highway with a predictable, acceptably consistent, traffic pattern. Access to an alternate route (with similar characteristics) to an alternate postal facility was deemed vital. The potential impact and consequences of the level of transport-related risks to this organization would be—in summary—delays that cost tens of thousands of dollars in cash flow and postal fees, as well as the nonavailability of critical business information.

A Note on Some Risk-Management Tools

The risk of occurrence of some out-of-course events cannot be lowered; of others, not lowered to a point where impact and consequences

---

[25] In the context of manufacturing, especially in the context of "Just In Time," some transport-related events can might sit comfortably with consideration of place-related out-of-course events.

and affects are acceptably avoided. An important aspect of managing impacts and consequences and affects is to know *when* and *where* specific out-of-course events will strike. As most measurement of risk can only provide a "once in 10 years" or "once every 100 days" or the like, the disaster planner really does not know *when* in the time span the event will occur. Valuable information can now be obtained about tornadoes, thunderstorms, tsunamis, and earthquakes advisories from Federal Emergency Management Agency (FEMA) bulletins, Environmental Protection Agency (EPA) toxic spill warnings, and ultimately much more. As these conditions can severely impact an organization, and have considerable consequences and affects on as-intended functioning, accurate and timely information about these nature-based events should be obtained from sources more reliable than a local radio or television station, or before Emergency Broadcasting System announcements are initiated.

Information upon which to make important judgments concerning early closings, openings, board-ups, and other storm preparations will be available from the Planetary Data [sic] Distribution System. The PDDS will ultimately carry national weather information and images as well as every emergency bulletin, advisory, and rapidly changing piece of information federal and state governments have to offer.[26] The few hundred dollars that will be required to receive this nature-based event information will provide good return-on-investment.

DETERMINING THE CONSEQUENCES AND THEIR AFFECTS

The underlying reason for creating a disaster planning and recovery strategy is to protect the organization's people, place, and processes from harm. This reason is often expressed from a different perspective: to enable to organization to continue functioning (creating its products or delivering its services) in the face of adversity. The latter, as the emphasis, tends, first, to stress planning efforts to "save the computer" rather than to "save the business," and second, to grossly neglect efforts to "save the people" and to "save the place." The facility professional—as well as the organization—has the responsibility and obligation not only to save the organization, but to save its people and its place.

There are two reasons why it is necessary for the planner to determine the consequence (and its affects) of each impact of each out-of-course

---

[26] David A. Rosenthal, "Emergency Weather Information . . . from Satellite to Desktop," *Satellite Communications,* November 1995, 38+.

event. First, it is vital to ascertain the affect of the consequence on the people, on the place, and on the processes. Can—perhaps, will—the out-of-course event result in casualties? Will there be damage to the place? Either of these, alone or in concert, may or may not affect the capacity of one or more business processes to continue to function in its as-intended manner. Occurrence of casualties or damage to the place may also cause a business dysfunction related to profit making or delivery of services. Second, it is equally vital to ascertain the resources—money, time, and effort—that are necessary to enable the business processes to *continue* to function or, alternately, to enable the business processes to *resume* functioning after the lapse of a predetermined "tolerable" interval or put another way, determining the costs of overcoming or preventing a business or service dysfunction.

The concept frequently referred to as a "business impact analysis" does not always take into consideration the *profit* element, and rarely, if ever, the matter of casualties and damage to the place. There can be some function of the organization that would be severely impeded by the consequences of an impact of an out-of-course event. However, the particular *function* may have little or no actual value (either hard-dollar or strategic) to the organization; it may be slated or considered for discontinuance. In view of this, there would be little value investing in the means to enable it to continue or to resume after the impediment. (The maxim, "Why put good money after bad?" applies.) The particular impeded function may have an appreciable "out-of-service" tolerance interval that warrants little investment to ensure "continuity" or short-interval interruption. But needless to say, the planner *would* invest in order to reduce the level of risks of harm to the people and the place associated with this function!

The concepts for the creation of a disaster planning and recovery strategy in this guide place the greatest importance on the manner in which the consequences of an impact of the out-of-course event affect the people, the place, and the ability of a business process to function in its as-intended manner. The level of risk of occurrence of some out-of-course events can be reduced to an ALARP or to an "acceptable" level; there are other out-of-course events that manifest a level of risk of occurrence that the planner can not alter. For the latter—immutable—events, the planner can endeavor to reduce the level of risk—the likelihood—of undesirable impacts. Some undesirable impacts, understandably, cannot be evaded. The same characterizations apply to the consequences of impacts: the level of risk of some occurring can be reduced; others, not reduced.

It is important as well as beneficial for the facility professional to recognize that not all out-of-course events are detrimental. Not all impacts are harmful, and not all consequences result in the likelihood of resulting in damage or loss or injury. Likewise, not everything you do will result in lower levels of risk: Some actions or plans might actually increase the levels of particular risks.

In creating a disaster planning and recovery strategy, it is also necessary to keep in mind that a particular out-of-course event *will not always* strike with the same impact, nor or in or on the same place or thing. A specific impact *will not always* affect the same consequences, nor will a certain consequence or set of consequences *always have* identical affects on people, place, or processes. A civil or governmental-based out-of-course event—a work stoppage by municipal sanitation workers (something that, arguably, can be classified as human intervention!)—may not significantly impact your facility if the stoppage occurs *between* normally scheduled waste removals, but such would have greater impact if major construction or alterations in the place was creating a significant volume of waste. That significant volume would not create the same consequences in a rural or suburban setting—where the waste might be shunted to a remote corner—as it would in an urban office building. In an urban building, the construction might have to be halted (and possibly extending the period of inconvenience to the people) until the waste could be removed.

Not only will an out-of-course event have different impacts at different times, but also, as it might be difficult to predict the *time of impact*, the impact and its consequences can differ as a factor of the strike time. No only will the storm intensity and wind direction of a hurricane be a determinant of the extent of certain consequences (wind and rain damage), but additionally, the degree of flooding resultant from the hurricane will be a not only a factor of the intensity, wind direction, and the length of time these have prevailed, but also of the tidal conditions at the time of strike. The message here, obviously, is that countervailance planning must be broad based in consideration of a number of variables, and anticipate and prepare for the "worst case scenario."

Another reality of any out-of-course event is that—no matter what its impact, consequences and affects were in the *last* strike—the impact, consequences and affects may be somewhat or even entirely different at the next impact. Consider a computer system fault or failure that halts processing of telephone orders: a two-hour interruption (both the backup computer system and the manual system were to no avail because the order-taking area had to be evacuated because a sprinkler-system malfunction completely dampened the spirit of order takers!) that occurs during the "off season" has significantly less consequence and affect on operations than if a 5-minute interruption occurs during the busiest preholiday order-taking period. Countervailance planning must take into consideration the "worst scenario" conditions; in this example, when the order volume is at its greatest and when any interruption in the order-taking process has the greatest affects on other processes in the organization.

Out-of-course events ("problems") create or cause, when they occur, an *impact* or *impacts* on people, and/or place, and/or processes. The actual nature of the impacts, their individual intensities, and their durations are factors of the problem itself, and *what* is or are impacted. The intense winds associated with a hurricane (the problem) can have impact on the people be preventing them from reaching (or leaving) the place. The place can suffer damage from the impact created by the intense winds and rain, or from air-borne debris. These—and all other—*impacts* result in *consequences*. The *consequences* vary with the problem, and the impacts that the problem causes. *Consequences,* and their *affects* on people, place, and processes, are what your disaster planning and recovery strategy intends to prevent, or to counteract. The very nature of the *consequences* and their *affects* on *your organization* should be the premises upon which your plan and your investment in planning are based.

The reaction chain of event/impact/consequences/affects ultimately ends with the people, the place, and in one or more processes or business process cells (BPCs). In order to "protect" the people, place, and the functioning of a BPC, it is necessary to determine what affects any likely event/impact/consequences chain will have on each specific BPC. This undertaking should be a "consequence analysis" (an *analysis* of *consequences*—emphasis of each word much intended) rather than the usual questionnaires-and-interviews sometimes termed a "business impact analysis" (BIA).[27] It is undoubtedly preferable to use the term "consequence analysis"—rather than "business impact analysis"—to the describe methodology of "consequence analysis" described here.[28] The BIA approach

[27] The concept of "business impact analysis" is considered, by some, as a *sine qua non* step in disaster planning. The BIA is, however, frequently linked with attributes actually wanting, and with tasks that it does not accomplish. Some commonly held misconceptions of what the BIA is and what it is thought to accomplish are described in Steps in Planning, Chapter 2.

[28] A reason, inter alia, is that the planning may be for an organization other than a "business." The not-for-profit group, educational institution, civic or governmental body, charitable foundation, or the like—all of which require a disaster planning and recovery strategy—surely loathe the appellation "business."

or technique itself, and many of the "business impact analysis tools" that are available, do not provide as sufficient an "analysis" as is imperative to create a proper strategy. Further, the BIA fails to sufficiently consider the *vulnerabilities* that may be present in the people, place, and processes. Off-the-shelf BIA tools tend to overgeneralize, and, in presenting multiple choices as input for the computer-based "analysis" fail to take into account quite vital considerations. As an example, in a "BIA input" the consideration of fire extinguishers (as a part of fire suppression devices) might be restricted to a Yes or No regarding *presence* without further appraisal of placement, class, accessibility, identification, servicing, and other characteristics (explained in the Vulnerability Search, later) that might limit—or obviate—any value as a firefighting resource. Use of the descriptor "BIA" to identify a process that provides significantly greater planning foundation and substance is not only a disservice to your efforts, but additionally might diminish the credibility and justification of your undertaking.

Determining consequences and their affect—on people, place, and processes—is an examination of a wide range of What if? scenarios. What if 16 people (of the total staffing of 17) in accounts receivable are at home ill with the flu? What if the accounts payable department itself cannot be used because of smoke, fire, and water damage that occurred this morning? What if a computer failure prevents an accounts payable person from advising the now-ready-to-act debtor who has owed the most for the longest time? What opportunities will be lost in each scenario? What countervailance is warranted for each?

The determination process can be likened to the creation of a cause-and-affect tree for each out-of-course event for which there is a likelihood of an impact on the people, place, or processes. In such a diagram (of each event), each *impact* (after risk-level reduction, and after countervailance) is determined. Each event will, undoubtedly, have more than one impact; there can be multiple, identifiable, and discernible impacts on the people, on the place, and on the processes. Each such impact need be incorporated into the "tree." (If this appears to be a tedium, no one ever validly claimed that the creation of an integrated, comprehensive, workable strategy to prevent undesirable things occurring and befalling the people, place, and processes is a simple task!)

Further expanding, each probable *impact*—in addition to the possible "no impact" aftermath—will have one or more consequence which has to be identified and defined. Each individual *consequence* will have to be judged in terms of what (if any) affect it will have on as-intended functioning.

Take, as an example, an office situated within 80 meters of a high-voltage power transmission line. The electricity-generating company, because of changing demand patterns, increases the voltage and the line as well as the period during which the line is at maximum capacity. (Yes, this does happen.) In this technology-based out-of-course *event*, the EMF level within the place (which you have detected in your periodic vulnerability search reviews of such levels) has risen notably. There are several *impacts* immediately apparent: some computer operations have started to do increasingly strange things; there are new ambient noises in the telephone system; the wireless LAN seems to be out-of-sorts at times; and—not hierarchically of the least significance—the staff notice increasingly louder "60-cycle hums" in the vicinity of the transmission lines. Thus, the impacts incorporated into the "tree" include that (1) on computer operations, (2) on telephone service, (3) on the LAN, and (4) on the people.

The *consequences* of the impact on computer operations is readily observable: The imaged output of printing devices is often jumbled or scrambled; in a word, wrong! The *affects* of this are apparent: unusable output, dysfunctioning of departments that rely on the output, and various forms and fashions of customer "unhappiness." Importantly, the out-of-course event—as it occurs—is not a "disaster" yet it can easily and quickly escalate into one. Ongoing problems with the output can (in various ways you can well imagine) result in circumstances that impede, impair, interrupt or halt the as-intended functioning of one or more BPC, and hence, the accomplishment of one or more of the organization's missions, such as profit making. The effects on the telephone system—the background noise—can, in addition to being thoroughly annoying, create customer annoyance when it's *always* a case of "a bad connection" wherein calling back never helps! As to LAN dysfunction, iteration of affects on the staff and their relations with other staff, and with customers and suppliers is not necessary. As to rectification of the latter two circumstances, fitting of filters to the telephone systems might reduce the incidence of noise; if it doesn't, this can be a good example of an impact, consequence, and affect that could well escalate into a disaster.

That the people hear a "hum" or "frying" sound emanating from the power lines necessitates at least two "affect" branches on the "tree": There is the "branch of concern," and the "branch of harmful affects." If determination has been made that the now-ambient level of EMFs within the building is at a "safe level" (regrettably, this guide cannot present even the slightest hint of what a "safe level" might be), then the level of risk of harm from EMFs to the people's health remains unchanged (hopefully,

ALARP). If this "branch" indicates an affect of increased risk of harm to the people, then corrective undertakings are essential! As regards "concern," a focused, credible communication effort to mitigate the staff's anxiety should receive priority. This "concern" could escalate: If one or more staff "vital" members left the organization because of health concerns, or there is a higher level of absences because of perceived illnesses, then there is a potential for impaired or impeded functioning. Such termination could result in an adverse ruling in an unemployment compensation or in a workers' compensation case based on level of risk to the worker's health. The perceived illnesses could prompt individual or class-action litigation that—whether the organization is found to be at blame or not—could be quite costly in terms of legal fees, settlements, or judgments.

When viewing this abbreviated example of an event/impact/consequence/affect tree, an inevitable question may well arise: Why did we locate so close to an overhead transmission line?

Yes, the process of determining the consequences and their affects *is tedious*. The amount of ennui is not insignificant, and grows with the size and complexity of the people, place, and processes. Consider, when thinking of this, just what you can be preventing, and what you can be saving from harm.

COMPENSATING FOR CONSEQUENCES

There are two areas that need be considered when creating the strategy to compensate for the consequences (of an impact of an out-of-course event): First, there are the "contingency plans" or the means arranged to minimize the extent of casualties suffered; to minimize the amount of damage or harm to the place; and to enable the business processes to continue to function—or to resume functioning within a predetermined span of time—despite the impact. Second, there are the "mopup plans" or the means arranged to mitigate damage, to repair or restore the place, and to restore business process functioning in its as-intended manner. Sadly, little can be planned—or done—for the casualties.

Many "disaster plans" have failed simply because the "contingency plans" themselves fail when necessarily implemented. There is a frequent oversight or omission, on the part of planners, to investigate the integrity of the "contingency" provision with the same care as the need for it was investigated and considered. Put another way, the level of risk of the "alternative" succumbing to an out-of-course event, its impact, or its consequence has to be evaluated as precisely as the risks to the place itself.

Most frequently provided for in "contingency plans" are (1) the "hot-" (or "warm-" or "cold") sites intended to sustain or (after some—hopefully predetermined-to-be-acceptable—interval) restore data processing or computing activities; (2) the provision of "additional" hard-copy-based information and/or magnetic-media-based data intended to assure availability of the information or data if the normally used media are inaccessible or unusable; (3) telecommunication paths via alternate routings, carriers, or modes; and (4) standby sources of electric power to enable some continuity of operations, or to provide for emergency lighting, enable proper computer shutdown, sustain communications, and possibly provide emergency elevator and HVAC operation.

The importance of these provisions notwithstanding, organizations need to develop paper systems that will allow them to continue operating without the use of their computer systems. This is vital consideration in your disaster planning and recovery strategy, for the nonavailability or nonusability of computer systems, per se, might be the *only consequence* of an out-of-course event. The alternate, paper systems can enable the BPCs to continue functioning, albeit perhaps, at a lower level of efficiency.[29] While it may be difficult to revert to the use of pens or pencils and paper, it could mean the difference between survival and financial catastrophe. A key consideration is to *develop* paper systems; the prior-to-computerization paper systems might no longer be suitable to present processing requirements. Stocks of forms, stationery supplies, instructions, pens and pencils[!], and flowcharts and procedure manuals should be prepared, and available to—and in—the BPCs. The personnel in the BPCs should be familiar with the use of paper-based systems, and practices sessions using this alternative should be conducted.

The basic consideration in selecting a "hot (or of a different temperature) site" is whether that site will have the capacity to accommodate the business process needs of the organization when the impact and consequences of an out-of-course event occurs. Typically, "sites" commit their operational capacity to more than one customer, thus accepting the inherent risk that not all customers will be impacted by out-of-course events at the same time. Thus, each "seat" (the generally used measure of alternate-site capacity) is frequently committed to more than one potential bottom. When an out-of-course event impacts a wide area, and thus a number of organizations, the demand for "seats" can, and often does, exceed the number available. Providers can compensate for this by

---

[29] The reversion to paper-based systems almost invariably unveils some startling revelations.

linking any geographically separate sites, but there remains a risk that separate out-of-course events can strike the various site-areas simultaneously, or that it is impractical for your people to relocate at the more distant site!

Another vital consideration when selecting alternate sites is the capacity of a particular site to sustain itself during the impact and consequences of an out-of-course event. A major provider of "hot site" and electronic vaulting services was itself shut down when flooding knocked out its electric power supply. The site had not installed standby diesel-powered generators because it was connected to two separate power grids which, presumably, would not simultaneously fail. The *combination* of the level of risk of rain-caused flooding, with that of the level of risk of concurrent failure of both of the two separate power grids, (or possibly, the individual levels) had either not been measured or determined, or had been deemed to be "acceptable."[30] The facility professional should determine whether risk levels of this sort—apparently acceptable to the "hot site" provider—are acceptable for his or her organization's disaster planning and recovery strategy.

Given that *information* (and information stored on magnetic or optical media, *data*) is one of the organization's most valuable assets, provision must be made to assure that needed information and data will be available, accessible, and usable, when and where needed. This "assurance" process is often vested in a department or business process identified as "records management." The business and legal considerations that provide the foundation of the determination of what information is kept, in what format, and for what period, and what is destroyed, aside, records management has a vital role in disaster planning and recovery strategy. This is the realm of information-based potential problems, and encompasses the availability, accessibility, and usability of information and data necessary to conduct business functions. Has the requisite business information (business records) been gathered and saved where necessary, and stored and protected as appropriate? Will this information (perhaps created in a digital-based data format) be available when needed, accessible as required, and be in a (or be convertible into a) usable format?

In terms of the records management establishment (if there is one) in the organization, the facility professional, as well as the records manager, in planning recovery strategies, must assure that the risk that

---

[30] Barton Crockett, "Sea-Land Rethinks Recovery Plan After Comdisco Outage," *Network World,* 11 November 1991, 29+.

"backup" information or data will be available, accessible, and usable, when and where needed, will be as *high* as reasonably practicable. (An example of "good risk"!) In addition to the vulnerability search of on-site records management processes and places of storage, a vulnerability search should be conducted at every off-site storage facility to determine whether the risks there are ALARP. Additionally, the processes and procedures of transport of records to and from the records storage sites should be considered in a vulnerability search. Sadly, these off-site facilities are rarely visited by records professionals, and when a visit does occur, there is little, if any, consideration given to the full range of out-of-course events, and the levels of risk (including those related to the systems and procedures employed) that could impact the facility.

The increasing reliance of businesses on telecommunications increases the need for proper recovery strategy in the event of failure—from any cause—of as-intended paths and path availability. (Examples of some major telecommunications failures are described in Chapter 3, Problems . . . , Impacts . . . , Consequences. . . .) There are several important considerations concerning a recovery strategy for telecommunication services. It is frequently suggested—and something that should well be heeded—that one or more separate POT (plain ordinary telephone) lines be provided for emergency use in the facility in the event of failure of the PBX or other telephone system failure. At least one POT should be installed in your contingency management center. Ideally, the POT should be served through a telephone company *central office* (c.o.) other than the c.o. to which your PBX or other telecommunication equipment is linked, so that if an out-of-course event impacts your place and the c.o., or the c.o. alone, the level of risk of service interruption will be reduced.[31] Too often—and in error—it is suggested that the POT be served though a different *exchange* (as distinct from c.o.). However, in many cities, several *exchanges* are housed in one *central office* building; the risk of *all* exchanges in a c.o. building being impacted by an out-of-course event is much higher than the risk of different c.o. buildings being impacted.

Some organizations have thought that provision of a private microwave link between facilities is a viable alternative to interrupted common carrier or dedicated-line telephone and data transmission system links. An important consideration is frequently overlooked: determina-

---

[31] It cannot be assumed that cellular telephones nullify the need for separate c.o. service. The cellular exchange may be served by the same, failed, exchange or central office.

tion of the risk level—and its acceptability—of failure of the microwave system due to a nature-based problem, such a heavy rains associated with severe storms, hurricanes, and typhoons, or to sunspots and other electromagnetic storms.

A number of organizations in New York City—following the repeated failure of their long-distance carrier—subscribed for alternate services to be provided by different carriers. In this bustle, planners neglected to recognize that three separate carriers were located in the *same* building, which occupied a square block, and were served by the same underground cable vaults. Each carrier used a different street as its address, inferring a separately located c.o. Any out-of-course event that impacted the building or its vaults would probably impact all three carriers located there, negating any value in this recovery strategy! (The facility housing the three carriers' switches is well known, and a landmark building. A mild knowledge of the city's geography would have reduced the risk of this error to a truly acceptable level!)

There are three potential sources of alternate or standby electric power: First, the facility can be served by more than one electric grid. In addition to far-from-universal availability of multigrid service, consideration has to be given to (1) the level of risk that there will not be multigrid failure; and (2) the level of risk that failure will be in the feeder system, rather than on the facility's side of the D-mark (where the power supply enters the facility). When the risk levels associated with multigrid (if available) failure, or with point-of-failure, are not acceptable, the facility can install the second potential source of power: a standby generator.

Standby generators—a truly good alternate power source—are sometimes installed without full regard for all the inherent considerations involved. There is usually some time gap between power failure and the ability of the generator to come online: what befalls electrical-powered devices during this interval? (There are generator configurations available that provide a zero time gap, but these seem to be little-known, or little-utilized, perhaps because of the additional costs involved.) Generators have a limited output: Will the generator chosen be able to cover all that you expect it to? Will it shed excessive loads if overtaxed, or will it fail? (The facility might require a dual wiring provision to power "emergency" lighting and equipment.)

Generators are usually placed out-of-doors, adjacent to the facility if space permits, or on the roof of buildings in built-up areas. In the case of out-of-doors generators, provision may need to be made for crankcase heating, for fuel tank heating, and for regulation of the proper temperature of the starter batteries. In areas where weather *might get* cold, these are vital considerations! It's great to have a generator, but it must be able to start and run! Too frequently, attention is not focused on the ability of the generator to "turn over" and start, and to battery charge level and battery condition: very high risks of failure! Fuel tanks must be monitored to assure "topping-off." (When an earthquake interrupted the supply of power to a major bank's computing facility in California, the standby generators were started and switched online in an orderly, planned fashion. However, the thought-to-last 14 day supply of fuel was exhausted in 17 minutes. The vital, faithfully performed frequent generator testings had depleted the supply of fuel; there was nothing in the procedure manual to provide for periodic check of fuel level or for refueling!) Diesel fuel tanks need also be drained of water on a periodic basis.

In addition to instances of generator failures at data centers of major banks simply because of a lack of expendable spares or knowledge of where to obtain them and how to install them (!), one New York bank's generator was sited on the building's roof. The fuel storage tanks were located in the building's sub-basement. There was an electric pump intended to lift the fuel from storage to the roof; the pump, and the system, performed with complete satisfaction every time it was tested. When a explosion and fire at an electric substation resulted in a power loss in the entire area, there was no means to lift the fuel (since the pump was "plugged into" the power system); the generator could not be used!

The third source of standby power (for computer and connected devices) is the UPS (uninterruptible power supply). These devices are designed to intercept (and correct or compensate for) any power line glitches, sags, and surges that might damage hardware components, and, in addition, are intended to provide a backup battery-based power supply that enables orderly equipment shut-down without harm to hardware or software. (Glitches, sags, and surges are factors in the mains-supplied electric power to the facility, as well as where within the facility the equipment intended to be protected is located. Computer-related equipment located near, or sharing wiring with, copy machines, elevators, and other devices with intermittent large-load factors are especially susceptible to glitches, sags, and surges.) In considering the UPSes to be used in conjunction with the facility's recovery strategy, and to reduce the risk of loss of use of the equipment or of the equipment itself, it is vital to consider the UPS unit's power capacity, and the maximum backup time protection.

Some devices that protect *only* against glitches, sags, and surges are sometimes also—but incorrectly so—referred to as "UPSes." These should be used to reduce the risk of damage to equipment resultant from the impact and *certain* consequences of technology-based problems, but not mistaken as devices that provide a continuity of electric power, as such.

Standby power—for exit signage illumination, evacuation navigation path lighting, alarm systems, and public address systems—is frequently provided by batteries. The major focus for these devices is to assure that the correct batteries are installed in the unit, and that they are fresh, fully charged, and workable. Nonrechargeable batteries should by replaced on a time-cycle basis, rather than waiting until they are weak or flat.

An important consideration in your planning to compensate for consequences and affects is whether or not the "compensation"—be it a "hot site" or an emergency generator or archived information or data or whatever—will be available, accessible, and usable *in spite of* the impact, consequences, and affects of the out-of-course event that has struck your people, place, or processes. Put another way, what is the level of risk that your countervailance provisions will not work? As an example, when an a power outage—or major storm or telecommunications interruption—strikes your site, will it also strike your "hot site"? Or, what might be the level of risk that the storm that interrupted your supply of electricity also be the cause of flooding that renders your "hot site" inaccessible or inoperable (even though you chose—wisely—a site served by a different electricity grid)? Your contingency planning need consider that *the same* or *a different* consequence of the out-of-course event that impaired, impeded, interrupted, or halted your people, place, or processes might also effect your contingency or countervailance resources.

A vital aspect of compensating for consequences is the precontracting (an activity that is a part of the "before" phase of planning) for the services and resources that might (read, usually or probably) be needed to restore as-intended functioning following the impact and consequences of an out-of-course event. *Precontracting* is an extremely crucial consideration: When your organization suffers the consequences and affects of an impact of an out-of-course event, other organizations may likewise be suffering, and be vying for the same resources. Precontracting provides your organization with the advantages of having the provider as a partner in recovery. As a partner, consideration should be given to having key persons representing the various providers as members of your CMT. As such, they can often provide valuable information leading to reducing the level of risk of faults or failures to items or devices within their arena of expertise.

The precontracting process can provide your organization with the advantages of timely response, and availability of services. In addition, the *knowledge* advantage—floor layouts, knowing what to save, what to save first, where it is, and how to save it—is especially important for the protection of information and data, and of art, antiques, and other valuable properties.

The services and resources, and the circumstances under which they are brought into play, should be listed in the plan manual. The services and resources, here, again, in alphabetic order include (but are not limited to):

- Alternate sites from which continuity in computer operations can be provided. (These may be "hot" or "warm" or "cold" depending upon the nature of your computing operations and your needs for continuity.)
- Alternate sites that can be used as office space when the place is unusable or unaccessible. (Increasingly common cellular telephones and laptop computers enable a greater choice of potentially usable spaces, but you still will need light, ventilation, heating or cooling, and desks or tables upon which the staff will work, and chairs or crates for them to sit on, and some place for them to eat!)
- Board-up providers. (Boarding-up, prior to the strike of hurricanes and other high-wind storms, or riots, should be a routine procedure. Board-up is often necessary to provide protection following damage to glass windows, curtain walls, and other structural items following storms, earthquakes, fires, and malicious damage.)
- Catering services. (To be arranged for your site and for alternate sites in the event that restaurants are not proximate or will be unable to provide for your people.)
- Cleaning, deodorizing, drying, cleaning, debris removal, and salvage services. (One or more providers might be necessary to arrange for the total spectrum of these services.)
- Computer cleaning and repair. (Computer components and other related hardware, often totally lamed by smoke or water damage, can often be cleaned and restored to original condition. Here, one must be cautionary in not undertaking repairs or cleaning that might be more costly than replacement of the hurt item.)

- Computer (desktops, portables, printers, and other equipment) rentals and supplies.
- Document restoration. (Fire and water damage to paper-based documents, microfilm, and microfiche can be usually be mitigated, the documents restored, and the information recovered. An important factor in the ultimate restoration and recovery is the quick initiation of conservation processes, often beginning with freeze-drying of the documents under controlled conditions.)
- Data recovery from hurt hard drives, removable and optical cartridges, floppy disks, and magnetic tape. (Depending upon the nature and extent of the harm, data can be recovered from items that have been hurt by power problems, hardware malfunctions, fire, water, smoke, or by dropping. That data recovery is feasible—albeit often costly, incomplete, or impossible—should not preclude the selected archival retention of paper-based records.)
- Emergency (or temporary) air conditioning.
- Emergency (or temporary) electric generation.
- Emergency (or temporary) heating.
- Emergency (or temporary) lighting.
- Emergency (or temporary) telecommunications (including services to key-personnel residences, and to other sites.)
- FAX, copier, furniture, and other office mechanicals rentals.
- Lodging for staff. (Pre-reserved accommodations at hotels near the place for use in the event that staff may have to lodge overnight, and at or near alternate sites, for people who may have to remain there or nearby.)
- Security service. (To provide protection and security of and for the place.)
- Temporary personnel agencies.
- Transport services. (To provide a requisite transport service level for staff, mail, equipment, and other necessities between sites, and between sites and residences or lodging.)

An interesting example of planning to compensate for consequences of a major disaster in a large city, the Nippon Telegraph and Telephone Corporation (NTT)—following the earthquake that hit the Hanshin and Awaji area in January 1995—initiated a general review of their approach to disaster response, particularly to earthquakes directly striking an urban area that might be difficult to predict. Five specific policies, to be instituted at a cost of ¥75 billion, include the following:

1. Provision of voice mail services to allow the storage and retrieval of messages concerning the safety of people in the disaster area. This will relieve congestion of the network.

2. Use of a communications satellite that will enable the passage of vital communications and secure information hubs in the disaster area.

3. Installation of more communications cables underground.

4. Provision of free use of existing public telephones in the event of an electricity failure, and provision for free-of-charge services on temporary-erected public telephones.

5. NTT, as a communications carrier, will cooperate with local governments, with organizations providing assistance to victims, and with utility companies suppliers, to supply and distribute information throughout the disaster area.[32]

Planning of this scope may be outside the arena of concern of many facility professionals. It is, however, well-illustrative of countervailence measures that can be taken to reduce the risk of consequences of the impact of a nature-based out-of-course event. For the facility professional's domain are a range of devices, from fitments to prevent desktop equipment—such as desktop computers and printers, fax machines, telephones, and other office mechanicals—from shifting and falling during a seismic event, to seismic hardened enclosures for sensitive electronic devices.

---

[32] "NTT Enhances Disaster Sustainable Communications Services," *NTT Monitor,* September 1995, 3.

CHAPTER

7

THE VULNERABILITY SEARCH, VULNERABILITY ANALYSIS, AND VULNERABILITY RECTIFICATION

The most important phase in creating a disaster planning and recovery strategy is, arguably, the vulnerability search, vulnerability analysis, and vulnerability rectification process. It is an indispensable part of risk reduction (and therefore, of risk management). The VS/VA/VR is absolutely essential in planning! The rectification enabled *is* risk management and when properly accomplished can (1) reduce the level of risk that certain out-of-course events will occur and strike your people, place, or processes; (2) reduce the level of risk that an impact will result; and (3) reduce the level of risk that consequences and affects will ensue. The VS/VA/VR process will also provide you with guidance to enable the levels of risk, as such, to be reduced to a level as low as reasonably practicable (ALARP) or to a level that is "acceptable." In addition, the VS/VA/VR undertaking will undoubtedly also provide you with the opportunity for the greatest degree of reduction in levels of risk for the investment of money, time, and effort!

The vulnerability search, and the analysis and rectification processes for which it is a groundwork, is the quest for at-risk conditions. This analysis is the determination of the levels of risk inherent in each condition, and identifies opportunities for reduction in those levels of risk. The rectification undertakes reduction in the levels of risk to a point ALARP or to an "acceptable level," and indicates the necessary countervailance to enable continuity of as-intended functioning, the persisting affects, and residual risk and not withstanding.

The VS/VA/VR process—when properly done—encircles the totality of people, place, and processes. Risks, and levels of risk, not otherwise apparent can be revealed and dealt with (read, reduced and/or countervailed). The importance of the VS/VA/VR should motivate the facility professional to pursue the process with the doggedness of a truffle hound!

The facility professional—whether personally conducting or participating in the VS/VA/VR or just administering it—must, first and foremost, be *honest*, and second, but of no lesser import, be *thorough*. One cannot afford to be "a nice guy" or "a nice gal" and ultimately ignore or omit or overlook or passover some vulnerability simply because its presence might be an embarrassment or within a particular individual's bailiwick or within a friend's area of responsibility! One cannot afford to *not* consider a vulnerability because it might *seem* inconsequential or unimportant. One cannot skip searching a particular floor in the building, or a part of a floor simply by assuming "it's just like the rest." The search must extend everywhere!

An initial consideration in the conduct of the VS/VA/VR is whether or not the facility professional should undertake these processes *alone* (be the sole *searcher*[1]). With quite rare exceptions, it would be both prudent and judicious for the facility professional to enlist additional expertise and experience to assist and opine in technical matters, and to overcome the often-difficult requirement to distinguish the trees from or within the forest! As a participant in the search, the facility professional can guide, with profit, the experienced searcher through the site and building, and can "open" the necessary doors. Additionally—and of vital importance—the facility professional can usually provide the necessary implementation of corrective actions that warrant immediate rectification.

The vulnerability search and the vulnerability analysis is also the substance of the most vital implement in the facility professional's disaster planning and recovery tool kit: *awareness*. The facility professionals representing the owners developing or managing a site, building, or group of buildings need be aware of the out-of-course events that could strike the property (site-specific risks), as well as the impacts and consequences of such strikes. They must be aware of the levels of risk present, and take opportunity to reduce those risks to levels as low as reasonably practi-

---

[1] One need also be a *soul* searcher!

cable. Such risk reduction not only "protects" the property, but can reduce costs, and can be used as a marketing tool or "plus." Facility professionals employed by the occupants or tenants must not only manifest that same awareness, but also further extend their awareness to reach the impacts, consequences and affects on people, place, and processes, as well as rectification and recovery of the business processes (business process-specific risks). Architects, designers, planners, and engineers must be aware of the site- and building-specific risks, the people-specific risks, and—if planning for a specific occupants or tenants—the business process-specific risks. Facility professionals concerned with transportation properties and facilities need be aware of the site-specific risks; those concerned with hotels, casinos, resorts, convention properties, and the like, need be concerned with site-specific risks, and event-specific risks. *Awareness*—in the practical sense—will be a valuable reward for your own search for vulnerabilities, and your analysis of them. The vulnerability search, vulnerability analysis (which may be acceptably termed assessment), and vulnerability rectification processes, described in this chapter, plus the consideration of Problems . . . , Impacts . . . , Consequences . . . (Chapter 3) and the vulnerability search checklist (Appendix II) will serve well in heightening your awareness.

Once you are aware of what can happen and what it will do to the people, the place and the processes, your planning can focus on protecting the people and place, and on the means to assure a continuity—or restoration—of the processes. The vulnerability search, analysis, and rectification undertaking is a process that will enable you, the facility professional to: first and most importantly, avoid costly and irreversible errors that would otherwise become apparent only when the disaster plan and recovery strategy are implemented; second, to reduce the level of risk—as low as reasonably practicable, or to an "acceptable" level—of casualties (both deaths and injuries) that can befall staff, visitors, and others present at the place, and of harm or damage to the place and processes, when the out-of-course events occurs; third, but not of less importance, to enhance the staff's "confidence level" that all reasonable and practicable steps have been taken to assure their safety and well-being (and the continuance of the organization!) when an out-of-course event occurs.

The three-pronged process of vulnerability search, vulnerability analysis, and vulnerability rectification is a most important element in your disaster planning. You should apply the VS/VA/VR process not only in creating a disaster planning and recovery strategy for the place your organization currently occupies, but also in evaluating any contemplated move within that place, and in evaluating any place that you are considering relocating or expanding to. In terms of the place where you are, the process enables you to reduce—often significantly—three types of risk. First, you can reduce the level of risk that some out-of-course events will occur. Second, you can both reduce the level of risk that some unavoidable out-of-course events will impact the people, place, or processes when they do occur, and you can also reduce the magnitude as well as the consequences and affects of those impacts. Third, but of no lesser importance, you can both reduce the level of risk that the unavoidable impacts will wrought consequences and affects on people, place, and processes, and reduce the extent of the consequences and affects that do occur.

When considering a new or different place, the VS and VA can provide assistance in evaluating which of the alternatives is "best" through creation of an awareness of the level and number of risks present at each place being considered. Knowledge of risk level and presence can also motivate preclusion of a particular site or building. Vulnerability rectification prior to a move into a selected building or space can usually be accomplished at a lesser cost before move-in, and surely with less disruption. A VS and VA of plans during the design stages for new or remodeled places can be of considerable benefit by identifying levels of risk that present opportunities for reduction or rectification through plans modification. Changes or modifications made during the planning stages, rather than after the bricks are in place and the mortar has dried, are almost without exception less costly and less disruptive. Changes "after the fact" are often forsaken. The examination of the design plans (with the potential for considerable assistance and substantial benefit derived from computer-based modeling and simulation) can reveal significant opportunities for reduction in levels of risks at substantially lesser costs than would be likely after completion of the site or building or space. The vulnerability search is a step which requires relatively little investment of money, time, and effort, and can provide a good return for that investment. The VS may reveal circumstances or conditions that are high-risk sources of potential faults or failures. Many of the level of risks unearthed in a typical VS can be reduced or countervailed with little investment and with minor effort.

In looking at both a present place and a prospective or proposed place or space from the "positive" perspective, the VS/VA/VR process can considerably increase the probability that the organization will be out of harm's way whenever an undesirable event occurs. While we would like to achieve 100% risk or assurance or probability or confidence that the undesirable will not occur (conversely, zero risk that anything "bad" will occur), in the real world zero risk cannot be attained. The gap between the assurance we can achieve that the organization to remain out of harm's way, and the assurance that we would like to be able to provide is bridged by the countervailance and "recovery" aspects of planning strategy. Thus, the VS/VA/VR process also identifies the provisions necessary for countervailance of impacts, consequences and affects, and for recovery in the plan.

The vulnerability search (VS) process is concerned with out-of-course events: which of the latent out-of-course events will occur (potential problems that become manifest as a problem), and what is the level of risk that it will occur? The vulnerability analysis (VA) is concerned, first, with the level of risk that the problem will impact the organization, and the magnitude of the impact. The VA is concerned, second, with the level of risk that the impact will result in consequences as well as the nature and extent of those consequences, and their affects on the people, place, and processes. The vulnerability rectification (VR) deals with the actions and activities inherent in reducing the levels of risk, reducing the impacts, reducing the nature and extent of the consequences and affects, and providing the means to counterbalance and countervail the affects of the consequences, as well as the actions and activities of damage mitigation and restoration of as-intended functioning.

In the course of the VS/VA/VR process, there may be *levels of risk* of out-of-course events, or of impacts, or of consequences and affects, that are detected and determined to be *relatively low* or that may be considered *acceptably low*. The facility professional should not be satisfied with such levels, but should ascertain what resources (if any!) would be necessary to further reduce the levels of risk to a point where they are as *low as reasonably practicable* (ALARP). Whatever may be their spheres of their magnitude, or their nature, or their extent, *relatively low* or *acceptably low* should not be deemed acceptable as levels of risk without ascertaining what investment of money, time, or effort (if any!) would be necessary to reduce any or all of these levels of risk ALARP. In the course of the VS/VA/VR, many opportunities may be found wherein further reduction in risks, or impacts, or consequences and affects can be achieved without investment of resources, or with investment at incremental costs small in contrast to the benefits derived from the reductions themselves.

The VS/VA/VR undertaking enables you to: first, identify the risks present, and the level of those risks, that certain out-of-course *events* might occur, and to reduce the levels of such risks; second, identify risks present, and the level of those risks, of certain *impacts* resulting, and to reduce the levels of such risks; third, identify the risks present, and the level of those risks, of certain *consequences and affects* resulting, and to reduce the level of such risks; fourth, determine what resources will be necessary to enable the organization to continue functioning—or to resume functioning—on an as-intended or an as-desired basis, despite the events that have taken place. The VS/VA/VR process, in the end, eliminates or minimizes the consequences and affects of an out-of-course event by providing you with a systematic, orderly process for planning.

Conducting the vulnerability search, accomplishing the vulnerability analysis, and executing a vulnerability rectification are not one-time events! *Each* condition you evaluate as a potential vulnerability is liable to change: What is not a vulnerability today might become one tomorrow or sometime in the future. Some items in your search process are more likely to change than others. Aisle widths are *fairly* stable, but might change with modification to space layouts. What may be placed or stored in the aisles—blocking evacuation navigation paths—can and often does change. The entire search process must be conducted as a customary element in plan review. Additionally, *all* members of the staff should be alert for "transitory" conditions—such as aisle blockage, improper storage practices, presence of hazards, and the like—and bring these to the attention of those responsible for plan operation.

The search, analysis, and rectification is, typically a three-part process. There will undoubtedly be found, in the course of the search process, a significant number of vulnerabilities that should be rectified or corrected immediately; no "analysis" will be necessary here. This circumstance will occur as the result of a variety of factors. First, vulnerabilities that place the organization at an exceedingly or excessively high level of risk will be revealed. These, because of their (possibly) obvious potential impact, consequences and affects will warrant rectification without any delay; an "analysis," as such, will not be necessary. In such instances, you should at least reduce the level of risk to an immediate-term "acceptable level," and then at an appropriate time, establish an appropriate rectification process. An example of this—typically found in most vulnerability searches—is the improper storage of paints, inflammables, dangerous cleaning chemicals, or other substances or materials in closets and out-of-the way places. You would want to remove these to a proper storage site immediately, without delay and surely without "analysis" since the level of risk of potential fire, explosion, or health hazard is, quite obviously, unnecessary high. The rectification—in the form of education of the cleaning staff, provision of proper storage facilities, and establishment of a closet inspection protocol—can come later.

Second, vulnerabilities that unnecessarily place the organization at a level of risk higher than that ALARP, although the level of risk of impact, and the consequences and affect might not be very high, will be revealed. Many of these unnecessarily increased risk levels can be corrected "on the spot" and simply. As an example, you might encounter propped-open doors that should be shut, unlocked doors that should be locked, or locked doors that should be unlocked. You might find cartons of supplies "temporarily" placed in aisles or other improper places. These are, perhaps, a category of easy-to-rectify vulnerabilities, and because of that, it is obviously advantageous to rectify them without delay. An "analysis" is not needed to make one aware that the simple rectification can take place, "on the spot," and immediately. As in the previous example, a protocol can later be established to help avoid reoccurrences of such vulnerabilities.

There are, in addition, *apparent* vulnerabilities that will be discovered. These, when analyzed, can turn out to be at a level of risk so low that rectification is not deemed necessary, or that the cost of rectification to lower the level of risk is excessive in terms of the ultimately achieved risk level. An example of this might involve the body of water which the building faces. In-place hurricane barriers might protect the site against storm tides and reduce the risk level of tidal flooding to less than three times in 150 years. The cost of changing the flood barrier configuration—the rectification—would involve expenditures of tens of millions of dollars—an amount deemed not warranted in terms of possibly reducing the risk level to twice in 250 years![2]

Another example of *apparent* vulnerability is a circumstance that is perceived as having an unnecessarily high level of risk, but upon analysis it is determined that what was thought to be a vulnerability actually was not. You might have thought or been led to believe that there is an underground watercourse adjacent to the building foundation that is a potential source (put another way, having an unacceptable level of risk) of basement and sub-basement flooding, especially at times when other watercourses are at higher-than-normal levels.[3] (It is more often the case that an underground watercourse that no one remembers will suddenly be brought to mind when flooding occurs!)

---

[2] Importantly, such information does not signify that there will be a 50-year interval between tidal flooding with the present barriers, or that the additional protection will mean tidal flooding will occur only once in 125 years.

[3] You might wish to set your mind at ease—or otherwise—by consulting Egbert L. Viele's 1865 reference, *Topography and Hydrology of New York* [City]. This sixty-foot-long colored map shows original watercourses, landfill, and geological environs. It would be a vital reference if your facility is in New York City!

HOW IS A "VULNERABILITY" IDENTIFIED?

A "vulnerability" has several attributes: A "vulnerability" can be relatively easy to discern or readily detectable. Your "vulnerabilities" should be somewhat obvious, although they might be overlooked by someone who has difficulty in seeing the trees when in the thick of the wood. A "vulnerability" often embodies an unnecessarily high risk of susceptibility to impact and/or unnecessarily high risk of consequences and affects. The nature of *many* vulnerabilities is such that the level of risk of impact and/or consequence can be reduced as low as reasonably practicable (ALARP) with relatively small investment of money, time, and effort. Many vulnerabilities manifest a departure (either advertent or inadvertent) from an as-intended condition. Thus, it can be extremely beneficial to seek out "vulnerabilities" (sometimes referred to as "seeds of disaster"), to analyze and to rectify them, even if little else is done in the realm of establishing a disaster planning and recovery *strategy*.

Vulnerabilities can, for planning convenience, be placed into categories. Some vulnerabilities are subject to impacts resulting from out-of-course events "external" to the place. In the planning, you can not reduce the level of risk that the particular vulnerability will be impacted by an out-of-course event, but can only plan to compensate for the impact and its consequences and affects. Other vulnerabilities are "internal" in nature in that you *can* reduce the level of risk of impact, and thus, the levels of risk that the impacted vulnerability will result in consequences and affects. Some vulnerabilities are exposed to both "external" and "internal" out-of-course events.

As an example of something "external," if your building is heated (and possibly cooled) by piped-in steam from a central source, a shortage or interruption in that supply will impact your HVAC operations, and could cause shutdown of the building because of temperature levels. It would be unusual to have a central source supply of steam *and* in situ heating boilers. There is little—if anything—you can due to reduce the risk of steam supply failure, and little—if anything—you can do to compensate for the consequences of the supply failure. An "internal" out-of-course event, such as increased temperature levels resulting from failure in the building's air-cooling machinery could result in shutdown of computer operations because of too-high an ambient temperature level, but the risk of such shutdown can be reduced ALARP by the provision of localized, standby air-cooling equipment in the computer space. Telephone communications could fail "externally" (possibly as a result of a cable being inadvertent severed) or "internally" resulting from a fire in the cable D-mark room. The risk of impact and of consequences of either of these events can be reduced to an acceptable level by, as an example, the provision of alternative microwave or other radio-based communications.

Since "vulnerabilities" are usually aberrant conditions, the discovery of any vulnerability, as such, is not only important in and of itself as a matter for analysis and potential rectification, and thus, a risk-reduction opportunity, but also raises an additional, important issue of concern: How long has that condition existed, and why and how has it gone undetected? Consideration of this concern can provide the facility professional with insight into areas symptomatic of inspection or maintenance procedures and processes that are deficient, and can provide the basis and opportunity for remedial action to prevent the re-emergence of the vulnerability, or the development of other vulnerabilities.[4]

The VS and VA can, additionally, launch an review of the organization's insurance coverage. The VS/VA process can detect instances where insurance coverage is excessive or unnecessary. Conversely, the search and assessment can identify levels of risk where insurance coverage might be prudent but that is not in place. The quantification of specific levels of risk, when undertaken, can also detect consequences (which the insurance company will call "risks") that are excessively or unnecessarily covered (reduced premiums may result), or that are not provided for and should be. The VS/VA process can also (and very often does!) identify instances where compliance with the provisions of the insurance policy is deficient. These, when discovered, should prompt rectification of the circumstance or change in the policy itself. Inadequate coverage can be modified, and "thought-to-be-in-place" coverage can be written if determined to be warranted.

In the course of the vulnerability search—as well in the assessment and rectification, and in all phases of disaster planning—a unity of direction is vital. It is judicious to empower the facility professional with the authority and responsibility to effectuate this direction. With such structure, the need to overcome institutional habits (read, "bad habits") in creating a disaster planning and recovery strategy is more easily accomplished. The engineering, electrical, building and structural, and maintenance personnel of the organization, and perhaps those of outside contractors, may be called upon to participate with the facility professional in the VS and VA. These groups will, undoubtedly, be involved in the

---

[4] "Maintenance" should focus reducing the levels of risk of faults or failures, thus, reducing the levels of risk of consequences and affects of any faults or failures. This focus should replace the "traditional" roles of maintenance—minimizing costs and preserving physical assets. The latter do not reduce the levels of risk associated with potential problems.

rectification phase, and should cooperate under a unity of direction led by the facility professional.

THE VULNERABILITY SEARCH PROCESS

There is little in the way of a "learned" or "scholarly" approach to conducting a VS that can be encapsulated in this guide or in any tutorial. In addition to governing importance that the VS (as well as both the VA and VR!) be systematically planned and undertaken, thorough in its scrutiny, and that it should comprehensively encompass the people, the place, and the processes, it is of especial significance for the search and the assessment phases to be conducted by, or aided by, "outside specialists." The value of this is in their ability to discern "the trees from the forest"— perhaps through instinct, to recognize vulnerabilities of a "technical" nature that might escape the eyes of others, and that they lack any "vested interests" within the organization.

In the search process, there are two separate realms to investigate in relation to potential out-of-course events: First, there must be a search for, and identification of, domains that can be *impacted by* out-of-course events emanating from roots not a part of the place itself. Examples of these would be areas that can be targets of impacts from severe weather conditions, a communications interruption due to a fire in the central exchange building, or a power shortage caused by a grid switching failure. Second, there must be a search for, and identification of, the roots of potential out-of-course events that *are present* in the place. Examples of these include storage areas where inflammables could ignite and cause a fire, or a weak pipe support that could fail causing a pipe to fracture with flooding a result, or an electrical wiring pattern that could emit EMFs. In addition to the search for roots of potential out-of-course events, the domains that can be impacted by this latter group of out-of-course events must also be searched for, and identified. Thus, the search process seeks both "external" and "internal" possible out-of-course events, as well as what both groups of events can impact.

Granted that the "search" process is complex. However, as the benefits—achievable reductions in risk, impact, and consequences and affects—greatly outweigh the efforts, the entire risk-reduction, impact-reduction, and consequence-reduction processes should not be omitted or neglected in your plan strategy. Focus must be on the reduction processes and on the "recovery" procedures; unfortunately, too many, if not all, "prepackaged" plans concentrate only on the "recovery" aspects of disaster planning, omitting the vital "prevention" approach.

In searching for vulnerabilities, you must look at all the "conditions" (which will be exemplified below) in the environment that the organization provides and/or is responsible for. In addition, you must look at those "conditions" which the building owner and building management provide and/or are responsible for, and those which the utilities, suppliers and contractors, and service suppliers provide and/or are responsible for.

SEARCHING FOR THE "SEEDS OF DISASTER"

The vulnerability search is actually a search for conditions that are "seeds of disaster." Like many varieties of seeds, some may grow and blossom in a relative short time span; others may lay dormant for long periods and then burst into bloom. Some seeds may germinate in ways one might not expect. The vulnerability search *is not* intended to be an examination or evaluation of the organization's security policies and procedures (but should opine on the relative integrity of employee badging), or of a safety program (although the VS would evaluate navigation path lighting and evacuation management), or of computer and telecommunications security (but a disabled access control to "secure" areas would be observed).

In planning the VS, there are two considerations that warrant special focus: first, the planning of the physical search process itself, and, second, the selection of the people to conduct the VS (who can be referred to as "searchers").

The VS must be, if it is to be fully effective and to have maximum value in your plan strategy, both comprehensive and complete. To systematically accomplish this, the assessors should be provided with up-to-date plans and diagrams of the place: the site, building, infrastructure, and equipment, including the wiring, piping, and other conduits. (In the real world, many facility professionals do not have access to such plans and diagrams. This is not because the information is considered "privileged," but because the plans and diagrams simply either do not exist, or do not exist in an updated form. It is a critical element in your disaster planning and recovery strategy to assure that your plans and diagrams are created where necessary, and are updated on an ongoing basis. In a large facility, "ongoing" can mean "daily." It is equally critical for a copies of the updated plans and diagrams to be made at each update, and for a copy to be on file in the CMC, and for a copy to be stored at a secure, off-site location that is accessible whenever need occurs. In this same real world, millions—if not tens or hundreds of millions—of dollars go down the drain simply because there are not up-to-date or correct diagrams of what exists beneath any street in New York City, or because solitary copies of wiring diagrams of complex facilities go up in the same flames as the facility!)

Practical experience has shown that its most beneficial to start the VS from the outer-most reaches or extremities of the place, and to work inward. If the place is a suburban office park or campus or estate, the further out the VS can start, the better. The search, whenever feasible, should not be limited to the property line, but extend beyond. If your place is an urban building, you should commence at the curb line or the property line, whichever is the most distant from the building itself, or further out, if such is feasible. The actual starting point is a function of the nature of the place: The searcher of a suburban office estate might want to start at the property line, or at the town or county roads serving the site. At that point, the searcher should determine whether there is adequate signage (visible from all directions) indicating the site address, names of companies situated there, and—if there are subaddresses or building identifiers—whether the additional wayfinding signage is adequate. In an urban environment, the searcher could commence at the curb-line, and observe the potential results of an errant vehicle hitting the building.

Potential "vehicle intrusion" presents interesting design considerations and challenges. While the measured level of risk of a runaway motor vehicle crashing into the ground floor of a building is relatively low, there are circumstances where the provision of ample barriers should be considered. In one "real world" experience, the glass curtain-walled building housing a computer and telecommunications center of a major international financial organization, only a small patch of grass separated the paved parking area from the nearly-at-grade offices. A van, thought to be safely parked, lurched forward, crashed through the curtain wall, and came to rest inches from a major electrical service closet, after narrowly missing several workers. There was some damage to equipment, and some minor injuries. If the van had impacted the electrical closet, there would have undoubtedly been an interruption in computing and communications, and possibly a fire and explosion of the leaked fuel. After this incident, it was deemed prudent to place an architecturally acceptable vehicle barrier between the parking area and the building.

In a real-life VS it was observed that one of the organization's most critical and secretive work areas was located in a space with a glass window-wall that extended above and below the street level, itself a downgrade. Aside from the potential of "visual espionage," a motor vehicle could inadvertently—or advertently—crash through the window-wall. Potential staff casualties aside, the possible fire could destroy or damage the irreplaceable documents, or place documents in a position where they could be compromised. (A vehicle barrier, and a translucent surface applied to the glass, would reduce the level of risk of casualties and loss of information!)

It is important to "look around and about" the property to determine what potential problems may be present. Potential root causes of out-of-course events may exist in the design, in the engineering, construction and materials, and in the infrastructure of the place. Nature-based, place-related, technology-based, and transport-related potential problems can exist solely because of *where* the place is situated. At worst, you will be assured that there are no potential problems out there!

If your place is only part of an office building, your VS should start at the most distant exterior perimeter, and encompass all "public" and "common" areas. The "public" areas include lobbies, corridors, elevators, and any other space shared-in-use with others in the building. The "common" areas include those housing equipment, machinery, services, and storage provided for other tenants in the building, such as basement and sub-basement heating- and cooling machinery rooms, electrical vaults, HVAC equipment rooms, telecommunication cable rooms and closets, emergency generator rooms, and roof-mounted water towers and coolers.

On a multitenant site, and especially within a multitenant building, your VS should extend to the spaces that adjoin yours, on the sides, and on the floors above and below those which your organization occupies. The concept of a VS of adjacent-space tenants is a sensitive area. Building managements—and the adjacent tenants—should be, and most likely will be, cooperative and will give you access to their spaces. Your concern is with conditions that may be present in the spaces which surround you in terms of circumstances that could give rise to an out-of-course event that would impact the people and processes in *your* space, as well as that space itself. Your concern is also for impacts, and/or consequences, that could arise in *your space* resulting from an out-of-course event occurring in a neighbor's space.

Most importantly in the multitenant building, the VS of adjacent tenants can reveal conditions—such as potential water leakage into your computer rooms, or storage of flammables in closets or elevator corridors—of high risk to your people and processes as will as presenting high risk to your neighbors. On this premise—that *your* VS can be of important value to *them*—access to their spaces can be accomplished. Your lease

conditions—and those of your adjacent tenants—should (ideally!) provide for access for VS purposes.

The fundamental element in a VS is not to overlook anything. The
VS of *your* place must also include areas, such as records storage spaces,
food service areas, and storerooms, that might be separate from the "office proper." It is vital, additionally, to conduct a VS/VA/VR at sites—such
as record storage warehouses, computer operations alternate sites, and
satellite service locations—that are located away from your business place!

As to the second consideration—selection of people who will conduct the VS—practical experience has demonstrated that the VS is most
effective when the searchers are "outside" personnel, with the assistance,
aid, and involvement of facility staff professionals, technicians, and others, on an as-needed, as-requested basis. The VS searcher-specialist, in
the course of the assessment, seeks the facility management staff's assistance for answer to such questions as, "What's behind these locked
doors?," "Why is this alarm deactivated?," "Where does this cable lead?"
and other like-ilk questions that may lead to the discovery of "disaster
seeds." Many of the "seeds" may have been actually planted by facility
staff, but were not recognized as "seeds" per se. As an example, fire extinguishers are not incorrectly placed out of malice, but because of lack
of full consideration of the implications of the placement. Thus, the
"wrongness" may not be recognized. Alarm devices that have been "de-
feated" by a member of the organization's staff would not be considered
as a "seed" by him or her, or recognized as a "seed" by the facility's non-
technical staff. The VS should be undertaken by independent specialists
who both know where to probe for "seeds" that may be present, and can
distinguish any "seeds" that may be present. The nature of a facility, and
the use to which it is put, often points up inherent conditions where "seeds"
can be found. Law offices, with their characteristic desktop array of papers, kitchenettes, coffee and beverage facilities, desktop beverage warmers, and after-hours workers, can nurture "seeds" atypical of other
offices.

The actual search process planning, its detail, and its comprehen-
siveness is essential to the quality of the VS. The searchers, in the conduct of the VS, should utilize a "seed catalogue" or checklist approach to
minimize the risk(!) that anything may be overlooked. Experience has
shown that regardless of the efforts made to structure the checklist in a
comprehensive and all-inclusive form, the searcher will frequently find
unthought-of "seeds" in the VS! As a guide for the vulnerability search of
your place, a model or point-of-departure vulnerability search checklist
is a part of this guide [Appendix II]. It is most important to remember

that this checklist *is not* (emphasis intended) complete or all-inclusive, nor can any such checklist be complete and all-inclusive. The intention is to outfit the searcher with suggestions and outline guidance for the search for the "seeds" of a disaster. This checklist also provides the searcher with an inherent challenge: what can *you* find that is *not* on the list! No checklist cannot serve as a complete foreboding of all the "seeds" that may be encountered.

Some words of forethought: Do not adjudge any of these latent vulnerabilities as trivial. Each and every vulnerability should be considered; a possible vulnerability should only be dismissed when it is determined to be not present. Do not equate "trivial" with "technical." "Technical faults" (unlike *technology-based problems or out-of-course events)* are "oversights" or "omissions" and can be corrected or counterbalanced. Without correction or compensation, they can become the root of a fault or failure, increase the risk of fault or failure when a problem occurs, or broaden the scope for impact and consequences. Many of the "technical faults" you encounter can be corrected with relative ease, and with minimal cost.

THE BOTTOM LINE

The VS/VA process enables the facility professional to identify the key issues in preparing the organization's disaster planning and recovery strategy. Identifying the key issues is vital, for the key issues are pivotal considerations that are concerned with (1) the well-being of the people; (2) the physical condition of the place; (3) the functioning of business and other processes during normal or as-intended conditions; (4) the functioning of business and other processes when one or more out-of-course events impact as-intended functioning; and, (5) the continuation or restoration of business and other processes when the consequences and affects of an impact impede, impair, interrupt, or halt as-intended functioning.

Key issues are organization specific and time specific: What might be a key issue in one place at one time might not apply to another organization, or at another time. *Examples* of key issues found in organizations include:

- What vulnerabilities exist that could result in deaths or injuries to the people?
- What vulnerabilities exist within the organization's building, its infrastructure, and contents, and what is the risk of occurrence,

that could result in interruptions or slowdowns in the functioning of the organization, or in closure of the building?

■ To what extent is the organization's information and data at risk, and what is the nature of such risk?

■ How would the organization's computing or word-processing activities be able to continue (1) if the building is closed or not accessible, or (2) if the computer or word-processing hardware, software, or storage media are damaged or not available or accessible?

■ What conditions in the building are likely to cause accidents or injury? Are safety measures adequate? What additional safety-related measures should be considered?

■ What steps has the organization taken to assure business continuation when the consequences of the impact of out-of-course events occur?

In planning risk reduction, whether vulnerability rectification (VR), or formulating the *recovery* aspects of planning strategy, the realities of available resources, and of acceptable-levels-of-risk are the basic considerations.[5] The key findings, as well as all other findings, must be considered as an entity if the resultant strategy is to be comprehensive and all-inclusive. "Individual strategies"—such as a "disaster recovery plan" for the computer system—cannot be formulated and established in and of themselves. Consideration for the computer system must be an element in the organization's overall planning strategy.

Although it is possible to rectify some vulnerabilities "on-the-spot" when detected, or with little effort or expenditure thereafter, it is impractical or even impossible to do *everything* to reduce each and every risk ALARP. To aid in an evaluation of what will be done, it is beneficial to structure considerations—actually, the goals and objectives—on a comparative basis. In such a comparison, the vulnerabilities and associated levels of risk that have been found for each key issue, and for each other issue, can be listed with recommended risk-reduction potentials and the recommended precautions associated with each. These can be advantageously compared on an *action plan* (with its associated benefits)—*quasi-no-action plan* (with its associated benefits as well as its associated disadvantages)—*no-action plan* (with its associated disadvantages) basis.

---

[5] In this context, the phrase *acceptable-levels-of-risk* is hyphenated. The levels of risk under consideration might be ALARP or "acceptable" or neither, but the decision is made to "live with" them.

The benefits (including risk reductions, enhancements, and costs savings and avoidances), and the resources necessary to achieve them, can be compared with the disadvantages (usually *less* or *little* or *residuals*) of quasi-no-action or no-action plans.

SOME REAL-LIFE EXAMPLES

A most instructive manner in which to describe how to conduct a VS can be a description of vulnerabilities actually found in the course of real-world, real-life vulnerability searches. These examples indicate not only *where* to look, but—and of equal importance—the nature of vulnerabilities you have to search for. The ruling principle is to look *everywhere* and to suspect that *everything* and *anything* could be a potential vulnerability.

We shall conduct a vulnerability search. The examples of vulnerabilities cited are a composite drawn from several VS/VA/VR studies performed by the author and his firm. Some of the specific organizations studied, which must remain anonymous, include (1) a large-size law firm occupying urban buildings that the firm owns and manages; (2) a mid-sized law firm, occupying part of a suburban office building they own but do not manage; (3) a museum, occupying space over which they have only minimal facilities management control; (4) the U.S. headquarters of a major international financial institution, situated in New York City; (5) the primary data processing facility of a major U.S.-based international bank (whose risks differ from the aforementioned foreign-based financial organization), located in a New York City building which they own (but outsource facility management services); (6) a trading organization sited in a suburban office campus; (7) a multinational manufacturing company occupying three (of five) leased buildings in a campus-type setting; and (8) a large law firm that had offices in the World Trade Center tower. Examples of some other quite-apparent vulnerabilities observed at other properties are also included to highlight potential impacts and consequences to businesses that have remained outside the pale of disaster planning.

The search commences at the outward-most point feasible. The actual point varies with the facility under study. Where possible, potential causes of out-of-course events were pursued—and very frequently found—beyond the property line. The inward-quest ultimately brings the searcher inside the building itself, and into the business process cell operating offices and other areas. In this composite vulnerability search, the areas studied are grouped into those

> External to the site proper
> On the site
> A part of the building itself
> The building subgrade
> Lobby and ground-level areas
> Offices and special-use areas
> Corridors, passageways, stairwells.

The vulnerabilities found are not atypical; many prevailed on several of the sites. Of those found—and of the vulnerabilities that will be found in your search—a significant percentage are of a nature that requires but relatively simple assessment. The means for rectification of these vulnerabilities are usually readily apparent and often can be accomplished with little or no expenditure.

External to the Site

The external-to-the-site-itself segment of a vulnerability search for the proposed location of a major financial organization's computer imaging and operations site revealed (the quite obvious!) very high voltage (VHV) overhead power lines that crossed over the parking lot, about 100 meters from the building itself. Concern was expressed about the level of risk of EMFs radiating from the VHV lines impacting the functioning of the computer modems and the imaging equipment to be housed in the facility, as well as the people working there. The concern centered not only on the level of risk of EMF-impacted modems and imaging equipment not functioning as intended, but also on the level of risk of the EMFs having affects on the people. There was grave concern about the extent of the consequences of any impact on the facility's business processes, which included the production and mailing of the over one million pages of invoices, management reports, and operational information produced each 24-hour period, seven days a week. Any delay in the output would adversely affect cash flow on receivables, increase postage fees paid on the mailings, and create substantial (but difficult-to-quantify) operational problems. Logistic considerations favored that particular site.

The EMFs were measured (and found to vary with the power load—that, itself, a function of the time of day and the time of year—and with atmospheric conditions!), and their values submitted to the telephone company, and to the computer equipment manufacturers (all of which had difficulty in determining EMF tolerance levels for their equipment!). In that they could not provide assurance that the level of risk of EMF impact on their equipments was acceptably low in terms of the business process requirements, a Faraday cage (which reduced the risk of EMF interference to a ALARP level) was constructed to house modems and imaging equipment. The business processes have continued without interruption caused by the EMFs, although the effect of the EMFs on the people is not *proven*, there remains good research evidence that EMFs may be the root cause of cancer.

The external-to-the-site search also revealed other vulnerabilities: the consequences and affects of nature-based potential problems (especially snow!) and the consequences and affects of transport-related potential problems (especially public transport strikes) on the adjacent highway. Either of these would severely affect both the ability of people to reach the site, as well as the ability to timely dispatch and deliver shipments of the invoices and reports.

Viewing a site (in the suburban setting) from the perimeter, there was an obvious lack of signage identifying the either the name of the office park, or the several organizations—or their *business units*—that occupy the buildings. There is no indication of the official street name (which was created at the insistence of the Postal Service but unknown to most people). On the building exteriors, there are no identifying building numbers (although the companies speak of themselves as being in building One etc.), no identification of the tenant-organizations, nor any official street numbers. Police, fire, and medical services have found the site confusing; a private ambulance service (with whom the major tenant has a response agreement) serving the area has no concept of the building designations. Of importance (but less so, except if it is a visiting executive from a major customer!) is the confusion among visitors and those attempting to make deliveries. The risk of delay in response of emergency services is needlessly high. A delay in ambulance or emergency medical response could result in unnecessary complications, or death. A delay in the response of the fire department could result in avoidable damage. These risks can be reduced ALARP by the placement of proper signage providing wayfinding guidance to each individual buildings, whether identified by company name, building number, or street address. The building identifications themselves should be coordinated with the information for summonsing emergency aid provided in the manual and the primer.

Standing on the site of a major office building sited beside a tidal river, the searcher could not help but notice that the subgrade parts of the building—wherein vital business processes were conducted—were below the normal high-tide level of the river. An obvious question arises: What would be the consequences of a flood condition on the river? Apparently, no one had undertaken a study of flood levels on the river (although some were apparent on nearby bridge piers and pilings), and how such tides would impact the building. In a severe storm, the river level *did* appreciably rise above the high-tide levels and flood the building. The waters impacted electrical and communications cable vaults and flooded work and storage areas. The consequences and affects were quite indisputable: All business processes with in the building were suspended for several days while the water was pumped out and the infrastructure dried or replaced. In an assessment, it is obvious that the flooding cannot be prevented, but the *potential flood level* can be taken into account, with water ingress prevented by building design, or can be controlled by the provision of pumps with sufficient capacity. (Pumps must be provided with a reliable, alternate source of power!)

On the Site

Parking facilities can be the sites of various potential problems. A ground-level paved area was found to lack any means to prevent vehicles from impacting the building. (The risk, here, that a vehicle could crash, through glass windows, into the building was ultimately shown to be 100%. A courier van accelerated and *did* crash through the window, narrowly missing several staff members and stopped short of hitting a high-voltage electrical closet only by inches. Had the closet been impacted, there would, at the least, have been an electrical outage, and probably a fire igniting the vehicle's gas tank. This transpired in the interval between the VS and the VR; the latter recommended the placement of low-profile, unobtrusive vehicle barriers on the building side of the parking lot.) In an outdoor, multistory parking facility, the in-place barriers were sufficient to stop a slow-moving vehicle, but not sufficiently strong to halt a faster-moving or a skidding vehicle. The VR—reinforcement of barriers— was accomplished before the winter brought icy conditions in the facility.

In a vulnerability search of a potential relocation site, it appeared that while standing on the ground floor of the building, one could look into the harbor straight out at the top of the flood control gates built by the U. S. Army Corps of Engineers. That meant that the observer was standing perhaps 5 feet *below* what the CoE considered potential high water. The assessment phase would investigate what parameters the CoE used in their determination. A practical rectification of the risk was not to lease the site! The search of another potential relocation site revealed that the sub-basement level (where the records library and vital records storage were to be located) was directly over an underground river that was subject to flood flows. The recommended rectification—that those highly important functions (which could impact the as-intended functioning of the organization) be placed elsewhere in the building—was not adopted until after the records library itself and vital records were severely damaged by a flood that occurred shortly after move-in.

The Building Subgrade

The VS of one site identified significant, unnecessarily high levels of risks in a below-grade office that was used for highly confidential work. exterior windows extended above and below sidewalk level; the sidewalk was narrow, and the adjacent street a relatively steep downgrade. There was considerable—and unnecessarily high—risk that someone could stand at the window and observe or photograph the files in the office, thus compromising the information. There was unnecessarily high risk that someone intent on compromising or stealing the information could crash a vehicle (or with less technology, simply a rock) through the window. There was, additionally, an unnecessarily high risk that an out-of-control vehicle could crash through the window. The VA of the consequences of any of these events showed a very severe impact on business processes, including a potential liability for failure to prudently conduct the work in a proper environment. The immediate, short-term, rectification was to move the business process from the room! Other changes including installation of impact resistant, permanently opaque glass, and the erection of vehicle barriers. Although the costs were not insignificant, they were deemed valid in terms of the reduction in the risk of compromise of business information.

Lobby and Ground-Level Areas

In a large office building (that, in addition to the staff working there, had a large number of visitors) it was observed that the orientation of lobby revolving doors was not toward the street (parallel to the street—the almost universal orientation), but toward the right-angle intersection of a street corner. A number (albeit small) of people instinctively try to exit from the revolving doors toward the street (rather than toward the intersection), resulting in a banged brows, stopped doors, and embarrassed—if not angry—people. The orientation of the door resulted in an unnecessarily high level of risk of egress-rate reduction or stoppage, especially in the course of an emergency evacuation. Although a reconstruction of the door configuration was not practical, the provision of clear markings on the door surrounds or cylinders would reduce that risk—and the risk of other potential consequences and affects—at a very minimal expense.

The interrelations between vulnerabilities (as a part of disaster planning) and both site security and site safety are often overlooked. A VS confronted the "security" procedures in the entry lobby of building suite owned and managed by the principal tenant. The facility management staff judged the property to have the "quite secure" status that was desired and intended. The security officer or officers stationed in the lobby area were responsible for (among other activities) prescreening and channeling visitors to an out-of-view receptionist in an adjacent, large, reception area; control of service entry (viewed through a CCTV screen) and exiting; and the verification of parcel passes issued to professional and other staff members, and to visitors.

The organization was concerned about the risk levels of certain human-intervention and people-rooted events including theft, sabotage, espionage, rascality, and suicide. Assessment of the security procedures related to theft revealed that the risk level was not as ALARP. The parcel pass procedures were modified and rewritten in a manner that would reduce the risk level. The risks of sabotage, espionage, and rascality were reduced ALARP with the installation of "panic buttons" for both the receptionist and the security guards. These covert alarms—installed at little cost—enabled the receptionist to covertly signal the security guard, and enabled both the receptionist and the security guard to signal the telephone operator to telephone the police for assistance. Both the receptionist, the security guards, and the telephone operators were provided with "panic buttons" directly connected the private alarm service company. The risk level of potential suicide was not addressed for several reasons. However, it was deemed that presence of the security guards, or the police, summoned by the receptionist's signal might be a deterrent.

Corridors, Passageways, Stairwells

In one of a museum's two emergency exits, a stairwell landing was used for storage—on its side!—of a 55-gallon drum of highly inflammable paint thinner. The spigot on the drum leaked, so a 5-gallon pail was used to the capture the dribble. The stairwell was used as a "smoking room" by staff members. Not only was there an extremely high risk of a fire *starting* here and flowing *down* to the museum proper, but there was also the high risk of deaths and injuries to those who might use this emergency exit in attempt to escape. The rectification was simple: move the drum! (In instances like these where the risks were so great, the person conducting the VS often strongly recommends that the potential problem be removed in his or her presence!)

Such stories can continue . . .

CHAPTER

8

CONTINGENCY MANAGEMENT

"Contingency management"—as used in this guide—is what many others often refer to as "disaster management" or as "crisis management." The term "contingency" is specifically selected for two reasons. First, because a fundamental reason for creating and supporting a plan (your disaster planning and recovery strategy) is to prevent an out-of-course event, its impact, and the ensuing consequences and affects from "ending up as a disaster" or "escalating into a disaster"—that is, from impairing, impeding, interrupting, or halting one of more or the organization's business processes, or its as-intended functioning that enables product to be made or service to be delivered, for *longer than a predetermined time span*. Casualties (deaths or injuries to the people), or harm or damage to the place, are among the consequences that can affect both the as-intended functioning, and the time span. A *disaster occurs* or a *disaster arises* or *it is a disaster* when the organization is unable to recommence its as-intended functioning—the delivery of its products or services—prior to the lapse of a predetermined, tolerable, time span that is inherent in the disruptive consequences and affects of the impact of an out-of-course event. In the case of a business enterprise, the cash flow of the organization, and its intended profitability, are undoubtedly in some way affected by the disaster.

Second, the milieu associated with "crisis"—that word itself suggesting a lack of management or of control—is one of *lack* of planning or *want* of preparation for the eventualities. (As indicated in its title, a thesis of this guide is that proper planning *prevents* disasters from occurring.)

265

It is not a question of *if* an out-of-course event may occur and impact your people, place, and processes, but one of *when and where*. Contingency management is concerned not only with this *when and where*, but also with the *how* and for what *period*. Contingency management is the preplanned, tested, and practiced processes of countering the consequences and affects of the impact so that the number of casualties (both injuries and deaths) will be as few as possible, the harm or damage to the place kept at a minimal level, and any interruptions to business functioning will be as brief as possible. Put another way, contingency management is the process of controlling and minimizing damage.

In terms of the disaster planning and recovery strategy with which the facility professional is concerned, or is responsible for, an emergency *occurs* (or, in the operative sense, an emergency is *taking place* or a state-of-emergency exists) when (1) an out-of-course event is taking place or is immanent, (2) the out-of-course event is or is about to impact the people, place, or processes, or (3) the impact is resulting in or is about to result in consequences and affects on the people, place, or processes. Contingency management, then, prepares for an event that might actually take place (thus, preparation is prudent), or becomes functional when the event occurs.

Contingency management entails planning to *provide* the as-necessary people, place, or processes to cope with and to overcome the affects of an emergency. (The provided people, place, and processes in effect *protect* the people, place, and processes of the organization according to the established contingency management aspects of the disaster preparedness and recovery plan.) The operative word—"management"—imparts the concept that a designated person or persons is controlling the circumstances and conducting operations according to a preplanned schema, rather than "reacting" to individual events or conditions. "Contingency management" anticipates possible events and potential conditions; these are addressed in the manner previously determined as optimal, considering the circumstances.

The "people" of contingency management—actually, the organization's contingency manager (CM) and the contingency management team (CMT)—are those individuals designated and trained to deal with the out-of-course events, impacts, and consequences and affects, that might occur. Often, this team is headed by the organization's facility manager, and would include members of the facility's engineering staff, computer operations management and staff, telecommunications management and personnel, and other nominated persons (often mistitled "fire wardens") in the organization's several departments and in all physical spaces that the organization occupies or uses. Usually, a team is established and provided for the "normal business day." In addition to this "primary" team, it is absolutely vital to provide "alternates" for each individual so that there is coverage provided for absences, vacation periods, and for each other period or shift during which the organization may function. It is important to provide both for "prescheduled" or "normal" functioning times, as well as for other periods when staff or others may be present at the place. ("May" becomes an important word, even if the organization has only occasional after-hours or during-the-weekend activities. It is vital to provide for on-site CMT people for coverage during such periods.) "Good" CMT planning would have provision for routine notification (such as advice from a human resources function) to "alternates" when a "primary" CMT person will be on vacation or otherwise unavailable.

CMT structure varies with the size and nature of the organization. A CMT *sine qua non* is the team's top person—often, the contingency manager (CM)—who is vested with both the responsibility *and* authority to initiate any action necessary to prevent harm or damage to the people, place, or processes. The CM appointed should be a person whose usual responsibilities keep him or her present on or at the place; obviously, if an emergency is immanent or is occurring, the CM should not have to be sought out. The CM's vested responsibility and authority should be such that he or she can authorize an early closing, or nonopening, or suspension of operations, or order an evacuation or activate a "hot site" *without* further approvals or additional consultation. (We have seen some disaster plans that unwisely require a *committee* to be convened to vote on any evacuation, closings, or activation. Under such an ordering, it might be fitting for the chair to be named Nero, and a fiddle player! Some organizations require the concurrence of a management committee, or approval of the CEO, or the agreement of a group of managers, before *any* action can be undertaken to reduce potential casualties or protect property.) The CM should also be empowered to initiate use of "processes" such as emergency generators, pumping equipment, sand bags, and whatever else might be necessary to protect the people, place, or processes.

In addition to the authority to *do* things, the CM must also have the authority to spend prudent amounts of money during the crisis. The CM should have the authority to have access to, and to disburse funds deemed necessary to protect the people, place, and processes, and to do so without the usual purchasing process routines or petty cash processes. Expenditures that can be faced in the course of an emergency include damage mitigation and repair costs, catering and lodging charges, transport fees, charges for temporary staff, and whatever might be necessary to hasten the return to as-intended functioning. In organizations with many people, or a large place, or with numerous processes, it can be sensible to provide the CM (*and* his or her alternates) with check-signing authority (and the blank checks, preferably from a designated special account!) *and* ATM access cards (although the daily withdrawal limits are usually low, ATMs can provide *some* ready cash). These provisions may dismay your purchasing department or auditor, but you are not providing for normal times.

The CM should have designated CMT people (perhaps assistant contingency managers, if egos climb high) in each of the organization's major departments. These CMT members (or their alternates) would be responsible for "searches" (restrooms, lounges, records vaults, basement area, storerooms, and other "hidden" locations) and for rendering assistance to any mobility-impaired persons as well as for orderly shutdowns (computers, vault-closings, infrastructure machinery, and the like) *if there is time for "orderly."* Designated CMT members would have other specific responsibilities such as initiating alternative telephone carrier switching plans, alerting or activating the damage mitigation and recovery resources, as well as advising catering, lodging, and transport providers, and equipment, supplies, and temporary staffing resources.

The CMT should also include executive members of the organization's primary operating functions—possibly manufacturing, computer operations, and telecommunications—who would advise the CM of potential out-of-course events, impacts, or consequences that might effect their areas of responsibility and thus necessitate the declaration of an emergency.

There must be a *place*—a contingency management center (CMC) (or an "operations management center" (OMC) if prominence of computer operations seems to prevail!)—for the CM to function and from which to direct the CMT and other activities. A logical on-site place, most suitably located on the ground floor of a building, could be adjacent to the fire command center where the latter is required by local fire codes. (We have seen some CMCs located on a high story where the CM's office is located. The additional risk that comes with height, as well as the difficulty in communicating with emergency response personnel makes such a poor choice.) There must be provision of an off-site, alternate CMC or OMC for the CM to operate from if the site itself is inaccessible or unusable. If the organization has a "hot site" this place can also be utilized as the alternate CMC or OMC (if the CM and alternate CMs can reasonably be able to reach the "hot site" from the office or from home; otherwise, a more accessible alternate CMC or OMC should be chosen). The local emergency response services should be made aware of the exact location of the primary and alternate CMCs and OMCs.

It is vital to provide both the primary and alternate CMCs and OMCs with up-to-date copies of the organization's *plan manual*, *primer for survival*, site and floor plans, wiring diagrams, information related to computing, data storage, and retrieval, telecommunications, and whatever else might be needed for managing the incident. The CMCs and OMCs—both primary and alternate—should have battery-powered megaphones, powerful flashlights, building-system two-way radios, and (with benefit) cellular telephones (all batteries should be routinely checked!), hard hats and insulated gloves, for emergency use. The offices or workplaces of the CM, his or her alternates, the CMT personnel and their alternates should also have battery-powered megaphones, flashlights, building-system two-way radios, and (with benefit) cellular telephones (all batteries should be routinely checked!), hard hats, and insulated gloves, for emergency use. It is important to provide all two-way radios and all cellular telephones with prominent warnings reminding DO NOT USE IN EVENT OF A BOMB SCARE. (As elsewhere mentioned, public address announcements in the event of a bomb scare or alert should include stern warning not to use cellular telephones or two-way radios.[1])

RECOVERY AND RESTORATION STRATEGIES

Any out-of-course event *may* or *may not* impact your people, or place, or processes when it occurs. When an event impacts people or processes and the consequence and affects of the impact impedes, impairs, interrupts, or halts the as-intended functioning of one or more BPCs, the processes of business continuation and of reinstatement of as-intended functioning can be termed "recovery." When the place is impacted, the repair, mending, replacement, cleaning, or rebuilding of parts or the whole can be termed "restoration." When consequences affect people causing deaths or injuries, there is no "recovery" or "restoration" in the sense of either a return to as-intended functioning or a rectification of damage; in the case of people, the physically injured or mentally harmed may heal and re-

---

[1] Although the practices of some bomb squads discount the prospect of radio-activated bombs in the late 1990s, there remains an unacceptably high risk that a planted bomb *may be* radio-detonated. Human-intervention out-of-course events are difficult to predict! This risk of such detonation can be significantly reduced simply by not using radio devices.

turn to work, but the dead are lost to the organization. Some people, whether injured or not, may chose to leave the organization. In formulating a recovery and restoration strategy, the people should not be neglected. In addition to compassion and benefits provided for those who are casualties, the plan should provide for counseling services. Such professional counseling services—like all services to be called into use following the impact and consequences of an out-of-course event—should be preplanned and, as appropriate, precontracted. Your planning should include discussions with members of the clergy of various religious groups so that the names and telephone numbers of appropriate clerics can be listed in the *plan manual* so that aid might be promptly summoned in the event of need, and at a time when other organizations might also be seeking such help. Your planning might include providing this often-termed "crisis counseling" to members of your people's families.

"Recovery" includes such activities as relocation to a "hot site," power generator activation, and retrieval of off-site-stored records. "Recovery" *might* also include all the planned activities and actions of "restoration" (such as water removal, repairs to the building, moisture dry-out, de-sooting computers, etc.) that are required after the impact of an out-of-course event and its consequences to enable the re-establishment of as-intended functioning of the BPCs. "Recovery" includes the activities required to enable a BPC to continue functioning (at the place, or at an "alternate place") or to regain the ability to function, and to again function in its as-intended manner at its as-intended place.

There are two aspects of the recovery ("recovery" can be equated to both "keep going" or "get going again") strategy. First is the aspect of planning concerned with providing the resources for recovery. This encompasses the resources of a workplace, equipment, facilities, power, communication capabilities, information and data, forms and other supplies, people, food, lodging, transport, and all else that enables the business processes to continue or to be re-established—within the planned time-line basis—after being impeded, impaired, interrupted, or halted by the consequences and affects of an impact. All such resources must be readily available, accessible, and usable, when and where needed. The second aspect of the planning ("restoration") is concerned with impact, consequence and affect mitigation, and damage restoration requisite for the return to as-intended functioning. Inherent to "available" is the planning determination of what will be required in order to keep going or to get going again in any worst-case impact/consequence-and-affect scenario. The thoroughness of this determination will directly effect and facilitate recovery efforts.

"Accessible" means, simply, that you can get at or get to the resources when and where you need them. Archived computer tapes and disks kept in a bank vault will not be accessible evenings or during weekend periods. Even though you have need for such tapes and disks, say at 6:00 P.M on Friday, you will undoubtedly have to wait until Monday morning, or until Tuesday morning if Monday were a bank holiday even though you might be the bank's biggest and most important customer. "Accessible" also relates to storage within the place: If records are stored in your sub-basement, you probably could not get to them in the event of a flood, or of a building closure ordered by government authorities. In a practical sense, even though resources are "available," they do not "exist" if they are not "accessible." The same holds for "usable." The emergency power generator "does not exist" if it cannot be started or if it only runs three minutes or if it cannot generate the needed load. If the data you have archived *is* accessible on a timely basis, you must have the necessary equipment, computer hardware, programs, or codes available to interpret, process, or image the data (at *any* alternative site you have planned) if it is to "exist." In many recovery undertakings (as well as in many restoration efforts) it has been found that the necessary previous-generation computers or software or codes no longer exist, or the EAMs (remember, electronic accounting machines) needed to interpret or process vital records and archives preserved on punch cards or punched tapes have moved on to the scrap merchant perhaps even before the computer personnel attempting to make a recovery were born! You have the data available and accessible, but it's not usable!

Too often, the organization's information (the paper-based corporate memory) and data (the magnetic- and optical-based corporate memory) are not properly protected. Such lack of protection is manifest in the existence of "originals" only (no backup copy), lack of, or deficiency in the "protection" afforded to such "originals," and the lack of "protection" afforded to the backup copies. The organization's records management program should encompass *both* information and data, and should, in addition to specifying the retention periods for all records (which range in duration from zero to permanent), designate the creation and storage of duplicate and archival copies of records. The off-site storage facilities used for (both information and data) records should be subject to the vulnerability search/vulnerability assessment/vulnerability rectification processes appropriate for, and applicable to, the records stored within the organization's own place.

The selection of an off-site location for records storage (as well the selection of an off-site computing facility, and any other facilities) should consider the levels of risk of the same out-of-course event that strikes *your* place also striking that site.

The plural, in the title of this section, "strategies," is intended. There are two separate, distinct focuses in the recovery planning segment of your overall disaster planning and recovery strategy. First, there is the focus on facilities and procedures that are necessary to enable the business process cells to continue to function in their as-intended manners, or to be re-established within a predetermined time line, following an impact, consequences and affects of an out-of-course event that impairs, impedes, interrupts, or halts one or more BPC. These are the "substitute" sites, processes, procedures and equipment utilized. Second, there is the focus on the planning and procedures established to mitigate the affect of the impact, to restore damages, and to enable return to as-intended functioning. These are the "damage control" and restoration resources.

Time-line or time-scale considerations are vital in both. As a general rule, as the time period of tolerance *without* a business process functioning or operative increases, there will be less or fewer resources required to start up the "substitute" process, such as a "hot site." Put another way, the shorter the period that the business process impairment, impediment, interruption, or stoppage can be tolerated, the greater the investment required to assure timely restoration. This "phenomenon" underscores the necessity of determining accurately and realistically intervals that can be tolerated. There is a tendency, in any "business impact analysis," for the person responsible for a particular function or process to aver that only the minutest time interval is tolerable before the entire organization will crash. Determination of accurate and realistic time-interval-tolerance is vital, even thought such might tread upon the toes of some administrators or managers.

Restoration is the reconstruction, repair, cleaning, decontaminating, or replacement of the place, its buildings, infrastructure, equipment, furnishings, and equipment. ("Restoration" can be equated to "repair" of "fixing.") In terms of restoration, there is also a time:cost relation. The more time allowable for cleanup, rebuilding, procurement of new equipment and furnishings, and the like, the less the unit costs will probably be. However, there is an important consideration in scheduling the "damage control": In the course of the necessary activities, additional "problems" may emerge extending the rectification period. Thus, not only are accurate assessments of damages and rectification times extremely important, but additionally, there is value in awarding contracts for work on a completion-by-a-certain-time basis rather than on a time basis or task basis. The completion-by basis places the onus on the service provider and works to preclude any "surprises."

In examining out-of-course events, their impacts, and the consequences and affects, in the formulation of your recovery and restoration strategies, both *event tree analysis* and *fault tree analysis* techniques should be used to (1) determine alternate courses of action; (2) examine merits of competing courses; (3) weigh costs and cost-effectiveness of alternatives; (4) weigh costs and strategic benefits of alternative investment strategies; (5) create action-plan modules of building blocks, and their benefits; (6) consider quasi-action-plan benefits and disadvantages; and (7) consider no-action-plan disadvantages and penalties.

You must identify (1) the consequences and affects on the organization's overall operations if the affected BPCs are not restored within specific time lapses; (2) determine which, if any, non-impacted BPCs can absorb the aborted functions, and for what time span; and (3) the minimum BPC requirements to continue or restart a BPC after it has been impeded, impaired, interrupted, or halted. You must also provide alternate BPC facilities and means to overcome the impeded, impaired, interrupted or halted processes.

An Example of an Unusual Recovery and Restoration

To assure continuity of lighting service in Grand Central Terminal, New York City, in the event of failure of *both* the New York Central Railroad's own high-tension electric system *and* the New York Edison system, two standby batteries were provided which together would maintain all lights at full candle power for 25 minutes. The standby batteries consisted of 150 cells, each weighing 4550 pounds. Each cell consisted of a large wooden lead-lined tank, 7 feet long, 2 feet 9 inches deep. The entire mass was moved—without damage or interruption in backup continuity—from Fiftieth Street between Lexington and Park Avenues (where cells were lowered 55 feet by block and tackle), to Forty-third Street and Lexington Avenue (where the cells were raised by elevator), in January, 1930.[2]

---

[2] "Moving Terminal Power Plant Unique Engineering Feat," *New York Central Lines,* March 1930.

A Checklist of Recovery-Vital Information, Data, and Tools

- Copies of "working" information (files, vital records)
- Copies of "working" data (diskettes, tapes, disks)
- Copies of archival materials
- Copies of site plans and drawings
- Copies of building plans and drawings (floor plans, office layouts, wiring—electrical, communications—diagrams)
- Copies of fixed assets lists
- Copies of inventory records of equipment (including serial numbers) and furnishings
- Copies of insurance policies
- Supplier lists
- Vendor lists
- Service-provider lists for damage mitigation and damage restoration
- Priority listings: *what to save, what to save first, and where it is located*
- Photoluminescent marking tapes to identify evacuation paths, fire exits, areas of refuge for evacuation, areas of no exit, blockages
- Flashlights and lightsticks

CHAPTER

9

"... BUT THE PROCESS
IS TEDIOUS"

The very processes (note the use of the plural) of creating an integrated, comprehensive, suitable disaster planning and recovery strategy for your organization (or the organization to which you are providing counsel) *that will work* are tedious. Unlike other planning "techniques" or "tools" you might come upon, this guide does *not* suggest or infer that there is any effortless—or uncomplicated—path leading to establishing the basis of an appropriate plan.[1] Having selected your "approach" and "gear" (which can be a part of your "planning methodology"), but before embarking upon any actual action, you must consider the prime risk that you face in the planning process itself: The level of risk inherent in whether your ultimate plan will actually do what you think—and expect—it to do. Put another way, it is not a question of whether the plan will work, per se, but whether the plan will work in the way you are expecting it to, and whether the plan will achieve what you are depending upon it to accomplish, and whether the plan will work when you need it to.

You are facing a risk that your plan will not—simply put—work. You face this risk before embarking upon any planning, and will face this risk when any plan is implemented. Thus, you face levels of risk in regard to *the plan itself* as well as the levels of risk related to the occurrence of out-of-course events, of impacts, and of consequences and affects. The risks associated with planning and the plan are often overlooked. It is incumbent upon you, as a facility professional, to reduce

[1] See Myths and Some Precarious Perceptions, Chapter 11.

each of those risks as low as reasonably practicable (ALARP). Inherent in achieving ALARP risks, there are a number of pitfalls to avoid.

First, you must not assume that an off-the-shelf, prepackaged "disaster planning" software, or "suite" will reduce *all* these risks ALARP. Many of these "packages" do not characterize *all* of the potential problems that can impact your people, place, and processes. Many such "packages" focus only on saving the processes, and then, some only the computer-involved or computer-related processes. Often, there is no provision—or, at best, only minimal guidance—made for any of the three major considerations in creating a plan: reduce (ALARP or to an "acceptable" level) the risk of any out-of-course event occurring; reduce (ALARP or to an "acceptable" level) the risk of impact of the event when it does occur; and, reduce (ALARP or to an "acceptable" level) the risk of consequences and affects of the impact when it does occur. (That's what saving the business or saving the organization is all about! Here it might be better to remember that saving the business or saving the organization really means saving the people, the place, and the processes, for—as the facility professional—your concerns and efforts should be directed toward all three groups. The hierarchy for priority stated promulgated in this guide—first, the people, then, the place, and lastly, the processes—may form a different sequence in your own professional sector, but whether you are a planner, designer, steersperson, or administrator, your achievements in the reduction of levels of risk will result in reduction of likelihood of injury, death, harm, or damage.) The focus of planning strategy is to *minimize* risk of occurrence, and to *minimize* the risk of impact and to *minimize* the risk of its consequences and their affects.

There are "packages" that tend to mix oil-and-water types of out-of-course events,[2] or to measure impacts in terms of consequences (rather than affects),[3] or to create a direct bonded connection between the event and ultimate affects.[4] While there may be, in some instances, a link between these, it might be the weakest link in the chain you are striving to forge.

---

[2] An earthquake or other seismic event should not be considered in the same breath as a flood or tornado.

[3] As considered in this guide, a *consequence* of the impact of an out-of-course event —say, a power outage resulting from lightning striking high-voltage line that caused a short-circuit in a transformer—might not have any *affects* on the as-intended functioning of the BPCs simply because the facility's [properly maintained—see vulnerability search checklist!] emergency generator came on-line in a timely manner. Countervailance measures—here, the generator—preclude or negate any affects.

[4] As an example, damage to the place does not always result from winds and from rain associated with a hurricane.

Many "packages" cluster several potential level-of-risk-reduction-methods,[5] suggesting that the entire array can be addressed as a unit. As an example, in some "packages," the presence—or lack—of fire hydrants, sprinkler systems, and fire extinguishers is considered as an entity. Quite clearly, the lack of fire extinguishers *or* their placement and identification as well as the class of fire for which they are designed, and whether they are properly charged and serviced are factors that are not addressed in that "package," yet these factors can be readily remedied by the facility professional. Fire extinguishers may reduce the level of risk of consequences of a fire but surely they cannot reduce the level of risk as low as—or in the same manner as—as sprinkler systems or hydrants! But less can be done—if, in the real world, anything at all can be done—about the lack of fire hydrants or of sprinkler systems.

The purpose here is not to denigrate such "packages," for some do fulfill certain useful purposes. Consideration, when thinking of these as a tool in planning, should be focused on the following: (1) has the "package" been written to "*sell*" or to "*work*" (there is a very important distinction here!), and on (2) has the "package" been designed as a *planning tool or planning aid* or as the *plan* as such.

Second, your *principal* focus and effort should not be on recovery nor should it be on redundancy. "Recovery" is provided to compensate for the unavoidable. "Redundancy" is providing the organization with both a belt and braces; however, trousers can fall even when you are wearing both! Organizations, considering the consequences of an interruption in telephone services, often wisely provide for service through an alternate exchange if an impact and its consequence halts as-intended service. Yet, in such consideration planners fail to contemplate whether the alternate exchange is housed in the same telephone company central office building, whether the same cabling routes apply, and whether cables from the alternate exchange enter the place at the same point (the D-mark). In providing for alternate-carrier long-distance service (failure of long-distance carriers' switches are not rare), the fact that both switches are situated in the same building is often overlooked.[6] Provisions for a "hot site" and for "hot-site data vaulting" can be an extremely important element in your planning, but these should be viewed as components in *continu-*

---

[5] A caveat: Risk reduction is not accomplished by "methods" or "techniques" or "means." Risk reduction is a *process* starting with identification and measurement.

[6] Not all carriers have their own cables; some are simply resellers of purchased-at-wholesale blocks of usage-time. If—or when—the underlying carrier's switch or other infrastructure faults or fails, the reseller's ability to provide service can come to a halt.

ity rather than as factors in *recovery*. The role of recovery and redundancy elements in your plan are the "last resort" or countervailance: alternative or contingent systems, procedures, means or methods that have been planned and can be activated and called upon to counter *affects*. The level of risk of strikes, impacts, and consequences have been reduced but since risks cannot be reduced to zero, *things will still go wrong*!

A third pitfall to be avoided is the belief that "hardware"—not in the computer sense, but equipment and devices such as alarm systems, signage, security systems, emergency lighting, and the like—that is prescribed and/or has the endorsement of or recognition by Underwriters' Laboratories, the National Fire Protection Association, Factory Mutual Research Corporation, Underwriters' Laboratories of Canada, or any of the numerous local authorities, such as the California State Fire Marshal in and of itself equates to risks of out-of-course events occurring, or the risks of impact, or the risks of consequences being reduced ALARP. These items of prescribed or endorsed "hardware" *can* serve to reduce various levels of risk, but do not themselves inherently reduce such levels as low as reasonably practicable. As an example, in a specific situation within a certain environment, a particular fire extinguisher containing 5 pounds of fire suppressant can reduce the risk of a fire spreading, but one of 25 pounds capacity might lower that risk to a greater extent, while a 50 pound capacity device could actually lower the risk to a level ALARP.

Among the major objectives of the entire planning process is to ascertain the practical lowest level of risk that can be achieved (often determined through modeling and simulation, and undoubtedly a level ALARP) and then effectuating that level. Simply lowering the levels to *some degree*, while praiseworthy, will likely not serve to provide continuity or desired resumption or restoration of as-intended functioning of the organization's processes, nor do all possible to prevent deaths or injuries to its people, or harm or damage to its place. The investments of money, time, and efforts, and the resources committed, involved in lowering the levels of risk to *some degree* may actually be entirely wasted if the "partial planning endeavor" is unable—when called up—to protect the organization in the manner intended.

There is often a tendency, when tackling a major project—and the creation of the disaster planning and recovery strategy *is a major project*—to desire to complete it in the least possible time, and to budget the completion of phases, and of the entire project accordingly. This proclivity might be more manifest when considering the facility professional's plate ordinarily overflowing with a myriad of other duties, responsibilities, and "on-hold" projects, problems, and challenges. The facility professional would be ill-advised to shortcut or scrimp on the formulation of a disaster planning and recovery strategy. The stakes are high: people's lives, the functioning of the processes—actually, the possible future existence of the organization—and the preservation of the place. This is yet another reason why both the commitment, support, and endorsement of top management is vital. Planning, and the creation of the plan, should not be shunted aside as others' "disasters" quickly disappear from local headlines and fade from memories.

CHAPTER

10

COMMUNICATION

A disaster planning and recovery strategy must provide both for *communication* and for *communications*. "Communication" (without the final "s")—in the arena of disaster planning and recovery—entails the presentation ("delivery" or "dissemination," if you will) of information about the plan to the people in the place, and elsewhere. In addition, "communication" includes the creation, collection, and control of the information that provides guidance for the actions to take, or to be taken, when an out-of-course event occurs, or is about to occur. Communication is that vital element in a plan that informs people what to do and how to do it in the light of potential problems, and when these become problems, striking the people, place, or processes.

"Communications" is the term usually applied to the systems or networks—such as telephone, fax, E-mail, Teletype, and like devices, with their hardware, software, and other "technology equipment"—that are used to move or transport the information and the data that comprise the organization's "memory" and "knowledge" within a BPC, or between or among BPCs. This "communications stuff" should properly include the Postal Service, couriers, messengers, pneumatic tubes, and the like, for these are also used for *moving* information and data.

Many plans fail to give proper consideration to the importance of communication (although providing for their organization's *communications*), and to what elements it encompasses.

There are four domains of "communication." Each has its own vital importance in your plan strategy. Each is of vital importance in preventing an out-of-course event from developing into an "emergency," or that emergency from escalating into a "crisis" or a "disaster." Some of this information is collected, controlled, and delivered in the *planning stages* ("before"); other elements of information are dynamic, and are collected, controlled, and delivered as the out-of-course event emerges ("during"), and some in the course of return-to-as-intended-functioning ("after"). The first domain is that of the plan manual—the document which details what the plan is, how the plan works, and when and how the plan is implemented, from the declaration of an "emergency" until the return-to-normal-functioning and the necessary recovery and restoration activities. The plan manual also details the responsibilities of various individuals (the contingency manager and his or her contingency management team) who carry out the plan. The manual will be described in greater detail later.

The second domain is *communicating your plan*. This is the process of education and of providing information about your plan. Your people must be educated in terms of what the plan is, how it works, and their individual role in implementing the plan: what to do, when to do it, and how it should be done. People must recognize their individual roles in the before, during, and after phases of the problem, its impact, and the consequences. *Communicating your plan* also extends to persons who are in the place—visitors, staff members from other locations, service personnel, and other transients—as well as to emergency service personnel (fire, police, ambulance, and disaster groups) who will respond, or who are responding to some event there. In many circumstances, there is value in communicating your plan to stakeholders, to the local community, and to the financial community.

Additionally, the people's "education" must include training, practice sessions, and drills to assure that the "communication" is up-to-date and has been effective. *Communicating your plan* is described later in this chapter.

The third domain of "communication" is that of the *primer for survival*. (The primer is individual's guide to the disaster planning and recovery strategy, while the manual provides direction for the contingency manager and the contingency management team.) The primer serves several important functions: First, the primer provides information and guidance *to* and *for* the people, as individuals, concerning means they can take to reduce the level risk of casualties—injuries and deaths—both to themselves and to others whenever they, the place, or the processes are impacted by an out-of-course event; or whenever they, the place, or the processes are susceptible to the consequences of an impact. Second, the primer provides instructions concerning the processes and procedures to be initiated and implemented to reduce the risk of damage to property (site, buildings, infrastructure, equipment, facilities, and furnishings), and the risk of loss or damage to information and data, and to enable continuation of the organization's processes, whenever an out-of-course event occurs. Equally vital, the primer should be designed to create an *awareness* of risk, and of risk levels, so that individuals will be vigilant to non-ALARP risk conditions, and thus be able to advise the facility professional of such circumstances.

The forth domain is concerned with *warning and alarm*. The contingency manager must be aware of impending out-of-course events or problems, and must be able to track changing conditions. The CM must appropriately, on a timely basis—according to guidelines provided in the plan manual—sound or transmit the appropriate alarms that launch the planned actions and responses, such as early dismissal, closing the facility, evacuating the building or site, starting the emergency generator, or activating the "hot site." The decision to issue a warning advisory, or raising an alarm, should be made as soon a conditions warrant. There is no value derived from delaying the process; conversely, the levels of risk of casualties and damage may increase with the delay. Inherent in the warning advisory, or in raising an alarm, is the sine qua non that the people know what the warning or alarm means to them, how they should individually react or respond, and then, react or respond on a timely basis.[1]

COMMUNICATION OF THE PLAN

All management and staff personnel should be furnished with a primer for survival. If an individual has a role in plan implementation, he or she should also be provided with applicable and appropriate section(s) of the plan manual. Distribution of information in the plan manual should be on a "need to know" basis, thus facilitating the up-dating, and aiding in keeping plan information confidential. The primer should contain detailed information about how to raise an alarm if the person detects or suspects[2] an out-of-course event, and how to respond and act when an alarm is sounded. The who-to-and-how-to notify instructions should be compre-

---

[1] Depending on the nature of the advisory or alarm, and the individual's "what to do," the reaction or response might be immediate, or following a predetermined time interval.

[2] In some organizations, the raising of an alarm relating to a "suspected" event is discouraged. The downside of delays inherent in investigating "suspicions" is that the out-of-course event, or the fault or failure, might escalate and increase the level of risk of casualties, of harm or damage to the place, or of impairing, impeding, interrupting or halting one or more BPC. "Where there's smoke there's fire" or at least something that is amiss. The raising of any alarm should not be delayed until "there's no reasonable doubt that . . ." is taking place.

hensive and all-encompassing. Information, as an example, concerning raising of an alarm of fire should detail where internal fire alarm pull-boxes are located, whether or not it is necessary to notify of the fire department separately, and the applicable telephone number(s) for emergency services.

It is important that the primer iterate the best means of raising an alarm. The use of the quite-common but not universal "911" to summon fire, police, ambulance, or other emergency services can be confusing, especially when the caller is under stress. Proper instructions should be clearly iterated in the primer, on posters, and on stickers mounted on telephone sets. As the availability of "911" dialing is not universal, the person wishing to raise an alarm might reside in a 911-serviced area, but the workplace may not have that service. As mentioned in Myths and Some Precarious Perceptions (Chapter 11), dialing "911" in a nonservice area can result in nonconnected calls, operator or equipment intercept, or delays in connection. If the facility is served by 911 service, telephones should be labeled to indicate whether it is necessary to dial "9" prior to "911" (changes to your switching equipment could overcome this need, but this change should be carefully weighed, taking into consideration typical calling patterns). If some telephones are not provided with "dial 9" access, these should be clearly marked as nonavailable for summoning emergency services. (Here, again, modifications to some switching equipment can enable dialing "911" while restricting "dial 9" access.) Alternate telephone numbers for the emergency response services should also be provided. The primer should also provide instructions and guidance to enable the deaf, hard of hearing, and speech-disabled people to raise an alarm. These instructions should be developed in conjunction with the emergency services organizations serving your place.

The address or site identification should be iterated on the dialing instructions; the caller, under stress, might not be able to recall or provide the best possible information. Information concerning specific site identification is especially important in suburban and rural areas where "911" calls may be answered by a distant response center serving an entire county. If the organization is located within an office or industrial park or campus, information concerning specific building location should be provided. This important information should be conveyed to the widest possible audience. The use of posters and telephone-mounted stickers is especially important in conference and meeting rooms, training areas, and other spaces where "off-site" people may gather.

The primer, and posters, should also explain—using words and visual representations—the meanings conveyed by, and personal action that should follow, building alarm signals. Many "modern" alarms systems sound a variety of signals or sound patterns which may be difficult to distinguish or remember, and confusing to visitors to the building. Some might be different than those in use in visitor's own places.[3] Such posters are especially important in conference and meeting rooms, training areas, and other spaces where "off-site" visitors may gather. Postings in these spaces should also incorporate prominent indication of emergency evacuation paths.

The primer should also contain information about "shutdown" procedures in the event of an alarm, the evacuation navigation paths applicable to specific parts of the building and site, alternate paths, assembly areas, head counts, and information concerning "all-clear" or dismissals. There should be instructions concerning evacuation if the individual is not at their usual work site, and for "common areas" such as meeting, conference, and training rooms, cafeterias, exercise rooms, or company library. Too frequently—and often greatly increasing the levels of risk of personal injury or death—there is a tendency to first return to one's usual work site to gather personal belongings rather than to immediately evacuate.

For the facility professional who is responsible for the operations, or administration, or the management of a place (in contrast to those facility professionals who, as architects, designers, or planners, were responsible for creating the place), an extremely vital part of your disaster planning and recovery strategy is *communicating* the plan you create. The plan is not complete until it has been effectively communicated to all concerned.

There are several different audiences you should address. Each of these audiences has a different "need to know" and the message you communicate to each should be specifically tailored to that need, and should comprehensively address it. Broadly based, there are both "internal" audiences, and "external" audiences. Those "internal" include the management and staff of the organization, its board of directors, and its shareholders, in all, all the "stakeholders" of an organization. If you were a member of the organization itself, the "internal" audience would include

---

[3] The entire question of whether or not to use of event-specific tone- or sound patterns to signify different "conditions"—a fire but don't evacuate, a fire but do evacuate, evacuate for other reasons, and so forth—as well as any benefits and advantages derived, should be carefully mooted. If you are considering specifying or installing such a system, you should, with great profit, not only read the manufacturer-furnished information and the relevant published literature, but—even more importantly—personally experience what transpires in a building so-fitted when the cacophony commences.

the people of your organization. But if you, as a facility professional, were responsible for a place occupied by one or more tenants, your communication should be with the same peoples within tenant organizations, albeit probably through a tenant representative rather than with those peoples directly. "External" audiences include customers and suppliers; the emergency services—fire, police, medical, and "disaster"—that protect and serve your place; the news media; and the people who work and reside in the community where your place is situated.

Your plan to enable ongoing functioning when a disaster impacts the organization can be—and should serve as—a public relations tool (both for staff and for external audiences) as well a providing a marketing advantage. Your people, the organization's stakeholders, as well as its other external constituencies, can find positive value or benefit in the existence of a plan that will prove of benefit to them, directly or indirectly, when it is implemented.

Your "internal" audiences need know of your plan, how it works, and how it affects them individually: Your people should be well aware of what you do to reduce the likelihood of an out-of-course event from occurring, and what is done to reduce its impact and consequences. Your local emergency services should be advised of just what processes take place in your organization, the presence and location of any hazardous materials, and special response equipment or considerations that might be necessary. There are numerous recorded incidents where fire departments were not able to most effectively deal with a fire because they were not aware of poisonous gases or flammables present in a factory, or what was being manufactured there.[4]

The emergency services should be aware of building occupancy times, and that you have a plan in place, and what that plan includes that would impact their response to an emergency, such as the location of handicapped individuals within the place.[5] Other "external" audiences should be provided with abstracted parts of this information, as would be applicable to who they are, and what they do for or with the organization.

---

[4] The heat generated by a fire in a factory that manufactured aluminum baseball bats caused some bats to "self-launch" in the manner of a projectile. The fire department, not knowing what products were being manufactured, thought military missiles were being surreptitiously assembled, and initiated a major military alert and call-in of specialized military personnel.

[5] An after-normal-business-hours fire in a computer center located in high-rise building in New York City nearly resulted in the needless deaths of several firefighters. The firefighters conducted searches because there were no records kept by building management of the personnel present, and where they might be, in the building at the time of the fire.

Whenever an out-of-course event affects your organization, the attention focused on it by the media is usually close behind. Just *how close* is usually a factor of the importance of the organization in the community or in the overall economy, of its size, or of the products or services it creates. It is not hard to imagine that a very large, multinational company will *usually* receive greater attention than a small, local plant, except if that plant makes or stores dangerous substances! The plan's provision for communication must be prepared for, in addition to response to out-of-course events that cause interruptions in functioning-as-intended, the wide range of other out-of-course events encompassing life-threatening product failure, environmental violations, workplace violence, financial distress, downsizings, retrenchments, acquisitions or mergers, relocations, and other like potential causes of "upsetment." Proper relations with the media, whenever some out-of-course event strikes your organization, or is thought by the public to have struck your organization, can serve to preserve—and potentially benefit—its image and reputation. It seems that, within hours of an out-of-course event, the public—and especially your customers and potential customers—have begun to scrutinize not only the consequences and affects that have occurred, but also what the organization is doing about them and what it is saying about them.

Therefore, an important part of your communication concerns information available for, or furnished to, news media if an out-of-course event severely impacts—or is thought to have impacted—the organization. This realm might be described as "public relations," and how it is dealt with is an important part of your plan. The various news media—especially television—are often "disaster hungry" and their interests would have to be dealt with if your organization is severely impacted by an out-of-course event. While many "large," "sophisticated" organizations have specialized public relations (p.r.) functions that *should be* best prepared to deal with incidents of this nature, the number of times wherein the p.r. department has failed in an emergency are legion. If your organization does have a p.r. department, it should be well-aware of the special needs in handling media relations when an out-of-course event creates a severe impact. The p.r. should be preplanned (as a part of the overall strategy) and when implemented, be handled by, and be the responsibility of, a predesignated spokesperson. The p.r. spokesperson or persons should be members of your CMT. This segment of your plan or overall strategy is often referred to as a "crisis communication plan."

It is not an intended role of this guide to function as a *guidebook* in this specialized aspect of public relations. There are, however, some important concepts to recognize while formulating your strategy.[6] The media should be advised, as soon as practical after the event, just what happened, and how it impacted the place, people, and processes. The vital consideration in this communication with the media is *accuracy*. Accuracy should be inherent in information your provide to the news media. Speculation, inaccuracies, guessing, unconfirmed reports, rumors, and other foundationless information should be avoided, and if some of these have reached the media, they should be countered or corrected.

Obviously, cooperation with the media is vital. Access to the place should be given, if requested, and if possible without any risk of casualty to the media representative, under controlled circumstances. If the media is advised that the information is not available, you should be sure to provide it when it does become available, even if the event has "fallen out of the news."

The other vital communication tool for your "internal" communication is the plan manual. This manual should contain detailed information and specific instructions guiding individual actions and reactions whenever any problem has impacted, or is thought to be about to impact, your facility. The plan manual, its contents, and the necessity to maintain the currency of the manual, will be discussed in a separate section of this guide.

It is very important to keep in mind, when considering the contents of the primer and of the plan manual, and other the elements of communicating your plan, that both "actions" and "reactions" mandated, sanctioned, or suggested, for any stage of preparedness ("before"), implementation ("during"), or recovery ("after"), can be either "active" or "passive." Put another way, an instruction of the plan can specify that, in a specific circumstance, you *do a particular thing or take or initiate a particular action*, or that you *do nothing*. The plan contains the correct guidance: Act in a particular way, or do not act. There should not be any "unanswered questions."[7]

Of nearly equal import, you need to communicate what you have found, and what you have done in view of those findings, to the management and staff of your organization. The employees in the place should be furnished with information concerning their role in disaster planning and recovery, in reduction in the levels of risk, as well as the information

[6] Some hints, and a brief bibliography, can be found in Kathryn Milea, "Fear of Frying," *Profit,* March/April 1996, 32+.

[7] The level of risks of casualties, of harm or damage, or of impaired, impeded, interrupted or halted as-intended functioning can increase if "all eventualities" are not provided for. Put another way, if specific guidance is not provided, the individual might do something wrong. To counter this possibility, if there is nothing to be done, the primer should clearly indicate *don't do anything.*

they need to respond to, and deal with, any out-of-course or emergency situation.

Certain segments of what you have found, and done, should also be communicated to your shareholders,[8] and to other stakeholders, as appropriate, especially your customers and suppliers, to the community, and to the local emergency response services. You should inform, and/or encourage, and/or motivate specific audiences about your plan, and how it might affect the particular constituency.

A requirement to communicate your some of your findings, and thus, portions your plan, may be rooted in law, mandate, or other prescription. You may wish to communicate to your community (who might be wondering what transpires within your gates, and what potential problems could arise from the processes) because of a commitment or sense of responsibility you have as a "good corporate citizen" within the community. You may be required to communicate specific information in view of CERCLA, NEPA, OSHA, and SARA[9] requirements, or because of state, county, or local mandates. You may be required to communicate specific information to your own employees, and may wish to apprise other staff members (especially nonproduction employees in a production environment) because of their *impressions* about potential out-of-course events and the ultimate consequences. Often, it can be advantageous to go beyond the prescriptives, and to share information about the risk of problems occurring, and the planning to deal with the potential impact and consequences if a problem becomes manifest, with all staff and management, as well as with the community in which your place is located. This is especially important in a manufacturing environment dealing (or thought to be dealing) with dangerous materials or product.

Decisions about *what* to communicate about your plan and the planning that created it must take several factors into consideration. Although "well informed" people might be a goal, there *is* information that might prove advantageous if not disclosed. It is of benefit to inform all people in the organization that the disaster planning and recovery strategy has searched for all potential out-of-course events that might occur, and that effort was undertaken to reduce the risks of occurrence ALARP.[10] Staff members should also be informed of efforts to reduce the risk impact of

---

[8] Some planners aver that the capabilities and limitations of disaster recovery and business continuity plans and equipment *must* be communicated to all stockholders. In this writer's view, conveying "limitations" might not be a prudent move.

[9] The Comprehensive Environmental Response, Compensation, and Liability Act; National Environmental Policy Act; Occupational Safety and Health Administration Act; and, Superfund Amendment and Reauthorization Act, respectively.

[10] And, that these processes continue on an ongoing basis!

out-of-course events, and the risk of consequences. This information—the creation of a "safe working place aura"—is important for employees, although it might not be a conscious concern to them. Information about the organization's planned recovery strategy—the provision for ongoing operations—should also be presented to the staff. Knowledge of contingency planning (as distinct from "contingency plans" which should be disseminated on an "need to know" basis only) can contribute to a "peace of mind" if employees ponder, "What will happen to us?" or, "Will we be without jobs?" if a "disaster" strikes the organization.

Some information, especially concerning the presence of specific risks of out-of-course events that could lead to casualties, and certain unusually, or unavoidably, high risk levels, might best be restricted as "privileged information." The judgment should be based on consideration of whether "disclosure" will be of "positive value" to the employees, or will create an uneasiness, concern, or worry. Judgment should be carefully made: As an example, if there are dangerous substances present in the working place, what should be told to employees (in addition to prescriptive information)? A carefully crafted balance must be struck: Too much information might create unnecessary worry and concern, or deter performance; too little information can create an dangerous complacency.

Plan information that might compromise security—such as the placement of event-monitoring equipment installed to reduce the risk of human-intervention out-of-course events—should be disseminated on a need-to-know basis only. While employees can find "comfort" in the knowledge that this risk-reduction effort is in place, the negative-side considerations—such as perceived or actual invasion of privacy—undoubtedly should prevail.

The medium or media used for specific communication should be based on what the nature and purpose of the communication is. McLuhan was correct: The medium *is* an integral part of the message![11] In addition to print media (for the manual, the primer, postings, handouts, memos, and signage), you should utilize video, slides, and other projected media; and tutorials and discussions.[12] Whatever the medium used, *effective* communication is the keystone. Printed materials should be legible, read-

---

[11] Marshall McLuhan, *The Gutenberg Galaxy* (Toronto, Ontario, Canada: University of Toronto Press, 1962).

[12] Some planning guidelines suggest that the plan's equivalent of a "manual" or "primer" should be distributed on computer disks. Any merits inherent in this medium over hard-copy print medium are paled when an alarm is sounded, smoke fills the workspace, when power fails, and when any other of the vast array of out-of-course events, or consequences occur.

able, and understandable by the audience at whom they are directed. If necessary, presentations should be in languages in addition to English.[13] Placement of signage—especially navigation and way-finding signage— should enable visibility under the most adverse conditions (such as dense smoke), and should clearly indicate their intended meaning. Multilingual signage should be advantageously utilized where appropriate, and the so-called "international symbols" that might be unfamiliar, and therefore confusing, should be avoided if their message may not be clear to your people. The proper level of lighting, as such, is an important element of your message; it communicates a path for movement or way-finding. If lettering or icons on a sign cannot be discerned under adverse conditions, then the signage is useless or possibly contraproductive.

Specialized literature is emerging in the field of communications and its specialized area of interactive exchange of information and opinions concerning human health and environmental concerns and the consequences of out-of-course events, as required by the federal acts, agency regulations, and by state laws and mandates.[14] This "risk communication" (which actually takes the form of an encompassment of potential problems, the likelihood of their occurrence, the areas of impact, and resultant consequences, as well as steps undertaken both to reduce the likelihood of occurrence, and to mitigate the consequence) is intended to inform both the employees involved and the community-at-large of potential problems, to encourage a discourse between those constituencies and the planners, and to motivate the constituencies to respond and to follow the proper guidance in the event of a "disaster." In reviewing this literature, the facility professional must recognize that the terminology used—especially the concepts of "risk," "risk communication," "risk management," and "risk assessment"—is not always consistent, and is sometimes self-contradictory.

The communication you establish should serve to create a credibility, a fairness, and a trust concerning what you have found, and plans you have put into place to deal with any perturbances in as-intended functioning that might result in peril to health or safety. You should communicate the potential problems faced, the levels of risk that each might

---

[13] And that in non-English languages should likewise be legible, readable, and understandable by the audience at whom they are directed. Why is there a tendency to print "other languages" in relatively smaller type?

[14] Regina Lundgren, *Risk Communication: A Handbook for Communicating Environmental, Safety, and Health Risks* (Columbus, Ohio: Battelle Press, 1994) is one example, and it presents an extensive bibliography.

occur, the impact, consequences, and how your plan is designed to reduce the risk, and mitigate both the impact and its consequences and affects.

The messages to your people should be presented and delivered using four types of media: print, oral presentations, visual representations, and meetings and tutorials.

First, consider print media. Your plan and your planning should be documented in a plan manual, and in a primer for survival. Those people concerned with creating, implementing, and maintaining the plan should be provided with copies of the plan manual. The plan manual provides specific procedures and instructions for dealing with out-of-course events, their impact, and their consequences, and with recovery procedures involved in restoring as-intended functioning of processes.

A valuable function of the primer is to create an awareness for potential problems that may exist, or that might arise, and that may have not been considered in the plan. Often, in the course of creating a plan, some potential problems are not seen by the planners, but are—or become—apparent to those who work within a specific environment on a daily basis, or who deal with elements of technology daily. The means to "detect" such potentials should be outlined, and staff encouraged to present their discoveries, concerns, and observations to a specific person—ideally the facility professional—so that these can be properly and promptly dealt with. Staff members should be encouraged to so participate in planning, and not made to feel that they are "ratting" on some process, procedure, or persons when they are trying to contribute to the planning process.

In addition to training sessions for staff members who are involved with plan implementation and plan operation in the event of an out-of-course event, or during a recovery period, when a plan is first established, there should also be group meetings to explain to employees what has been done, and what the plan will do in the event of an out-of-course event. Of particular importance in these meetings is the presentation of materials covered in the primer, giving opportunity for questions and detailed explanation, where necessary. These meetings should be repeated, periodically, for new employees, and as "refresher" courses for on-board staff. These meetings or training sessions should also provide encouragement for feedback of ideas, impressions, and observations—as provided for in the primer—that participants might have.

Another important communication path is the use of visuals, such as posters, telephone stickers, and occasional and periodic handouts, as "reminders" or "reinforcements" of alarm signals, emergency telephone numbers, security procedures, and the like. These media should also be used to advise the staff of any *changes* or *modifications* that have been made. These can be used effectively in combination with "permanent" posters (describing, with visual representation, alarm signals), and "topical" reminders, such as seasonal, weather-based procedures for closings.[15]

Of equal import is communication with "outside" constituencies. The creation of a plan—in many respects, a means to preserve and protect the organization's assets and its income-producing ability—and the basic manner in which the plan functions—should ideally be communicated to all stakeholders. That a plan exists will indicate to shareholders that a "good" executive suite is in place, and to stakeholders that a "good" organization it is place!

Your customers, and your suppliers, should also be advised that a good disaster planning and recovery strategy is in place. Such knowledge can enable your customers to have a comforting assurance that plans exist to provide a continuity in delivery or product and/or services, and that these plans will be implemented whenever the need arises. It is quite important that certain of your customers' purchasing agents or buyers have the assurance that not only do you have such a plan in place, but that *they* would be, as a part of contingency operations, apprised of order and delivery status. Suppliers, too, would find this of value; understandably, each supplier considers your organization an important customer and would be comfortable with assurance that you would be able to continue as such.

Whomever the audience, the communication should ideally take form in more than one medium. The language used should be simple, appropriate to the audience, and should avoid the technical terminology necessarily inherent in formulating the plan and the plan manual. Objectivity should be the highest priority, and the communication should be made honestly and clearly. The same overall information should be conveyed to all audience segments. The organization should encourage feedback, and its "ears"—ideally those of the facility professional—should be prepared to listen to and to deal with any concerns or uncertainties perceived by the audiences.

You need to understand your audiences: Some have a need-to-know while others want to know what you have planned to reduce the risk of problems as low as reasonably practicable, or how you plan to reduce the impact and its consequences as low as reasonably practicable.

---

[15] "Permanent" should not be taken literally! Such postings should be revised when changes or modifications to their messages occur.

After your constituencies, both management and staff, and members of the community, are informed, they should be encouraged to engage in a rapport with you, the facility professional spearheading the plan, and with others—such as the CM—in the organization concerned with disaster planning and recovery. This creates a forum for exchange of ideas and suggestions that might be an added value in your planning, and can serve to allay false impressions and needless concerns. Well-informed, your own staff, as well as members of the community, would be better motivated to participate in any needed response—an evacuation of the area, as an example—if such was to be deemed necessary because of a problem within the place.

Communicating an Out-of-Course Event

Many places (especially public places) fail to take into account human reaction to fire (and other) alarms. People in public places who hear fire alarms typically assume that it is a fire drill. They don't begin to evacuate until they see other people moving first. There is also the unfortunate tendency of those in the higher echelons of an organization to completely ignore a raised alarm until someone "in authority" specifically and personally (and often, almost forcefully) prods them to evacuate. In general, people are almost desensitized to the threat of fire.

When the evacuation finally does commence, there is—especially in public spaces—confusion while people try to figure out what to do and where to go. The precious time lost in these processes unnecessarily raises the level of risk of casualties.

Participation in fire and other emergency drills should be mandatory. The plan should provide for evacuation guidance appropriate to the people in the place. The greater the numbers of transients or visitors that are usually present (either routinely or on an ad hoc basis), the greater should be the provision for guidance in the event of an evacuation, whether a drill or an actual emergency.

In some places, the raising of an alarm—both internal and to emergency response services—is delayed until the root of an "apparent" out-of-course event, or its impact has been determined. The cause or source of the smoke filling the lobby, or of the water cascading down the fire stairs, or of the unusual sounds in the computer room electric closet are investigated and determined *before* any alarm is raised. Although this sequence might reduce possible disruption to business processes, it can serve to greatly raise the level of risk of casualties (both deaths and injuries), harm, and damage.

Signage and Wayfinding

In the context of disaster planning, the primary objective of signage and wayfinding devices is the reduce the risk of casualties (injuries or deaths) whenever people evacuate the place. *Evacuate* means leaving the place for other-than-normal reasons, or under other-than-normal circumstances. The evacuation of the place—usually the building or part of it, but often the entire site—can take place either (1) in response to the raising of an alarm or public address announcement, or (2) because people sense that other-than-normal circumstances prevail or are about to occur, and they should remove themselves from harm's way. "Signage" includes eye-readable (both text and symbols) and Brailled-character information, as well the eye-readable arrows. "Wayfinding" fitments include navigation path striping (painted and luminous), lighting, light strips, flashing beacons, and sound-emitting devices used to augment or reinforce the signage.

The purpose of signage and wayfinding devices is to distribute and reinforce directional information to all constituencies that may be present in the place. In designing an emergency signage and wayfinding system, it is especially important to consider that the people's normal movement—especially through complex pathways—can be restricted by the stress and/or disorientation associated with an out-of-course event, decreased visibility that may be caused by smoke conditions or the disruption of normal lighting, or as a result of path blockage. (As discussed elsewhere in this guide, designers, in creating space utilization schema, should consider the relation of complex pathways, and the level of emergency lighting, to evacuation safety management.)

Signage and wayfinding devices must be planned with the needs of the distinct groups: the people who are usually in or at the place; the people who are there only occasionally or on a one-time basis; and the people who may be called upon to provide emergency response or services at the place. The organization's employees must be given signage and wayfinding "guidance" from their usual work areas, as well as from other offices or areas within the building or site where they venture. Directional information in in-building parking areas, cafeterias, and training, meeting, and conference rooms should be given special reinforcement because some of the people in those places some of the times are not necessarily familiar—or may be less familiar—with the place. Signage and wayfinding directional information is especially important outside of the building, and at the perimeter of the site, to guide emergency response personnel and services to the area of need. This should be specifically considered when dealing with office and manufacturing parks, campuses, and estates, where "external" signage might only display a corporate name or trademark not associated with the identification tag given by the individual who notified the emergency response service. (It is extremely prudent, in the instructions for raising an alarm or for summonsing aid provided in the primer for survival, to correlate what appears on the exterior signage with the scripted information that will be given to a dispatcher.)

Signage and wayfinding information design should *not be limited by prescription requirements*. As discussed in Chapter 4, prescriptives do not always assure that risks are reduced as low as is reasonably practicable (ALARP), or, reduced to an acceptable level. There is also a tendency to chose and use "designer signs" or "minimalist" signs which, while they may establish a desired graphic image, can fall short in their intended mission of distributing and reinforcing evacuation safety management path information. Size of signage, size and style of lettering, letter spacing, and sign placement should be carefully weighed, and weighed in terms of viewer stress, potential confusion, reduced visibility, and limited lighting. *Alternate path* information should be considered. The sole dependence on symbols or icons as the only source of directional information should be weight with great care: Many "international" symbols are confusing or may not be understood.[16] *Language* is an important consideration in signage (obviously, that's why "international" symbols are offered as a "solution") and signs should incorporate the language(s) of the vast majority of the people who come to the place. Very often, English—or English and Spanish—represent the languages of only a small proportion of the constituencies!

An important consideration in the vulnerability search and assessment of signage is whether EXIT advisory signs *in all instances* indicate the optimal path for *both* fire evacuation *and* evacuation for other causes. Circumstances can exist where the level of risk of casualties may be reduced by indicating both (1) the prescriptive paths for egress in the event of a fire, and (2) the other (additional) egress paths that are safe to use in nonfire evacuations. An indispensable precondition for dual paths or dual signage is an alarm system that clearly differentiates (a consideration discussed elsewhere) between the two reasons for evacuation, and that such alarms are unmistakably understood by the people.

---

[16] The symbol frequently associated with "fire exit" illustrates a *male* stick-figure running up (or down) stairs. *Under stress conditions* might a female wonder if she should use a different exit? Should people *run*? Is the *best* evacuation path always the *down* (or *up*) illustrated? Would a person following the illustrated direction move *into* harm's way?

THE PLAN AND ITS PLAN MANUAL AND PRIMER FOR SURVIVAL

After creation of your disaster preparedness and recovery strategy—the plan—there remain three separate, distinct steps in the "appraisement" process necessary before the plan can be considered "complete" and before it can be documented in the plan manual and the primer for survival.[17] The purpose of the appraisement is to determine whether or not the plan will work, and perform in the manner intended. Will the plan work, wherever and whenever an out-of-course event occurs, strikes the people, place, or processes, and results in impacts, consequences and affects that cause deaths or injuries to the people; or modifies the manner in which they are able to perform their responsibilities; or harms or damages the place; or impedes, impairs, interrupts or halts the processes? These are not easily answered questions. The underlying hope is that the plan *will work*, but steps must be taken before a problem occurs to test the mettle of your endeavors.

The "appraisement" process has three parts: first is the *commissioning*. In this, the individual systems within the plan are proven. This means determining that each of the individual "systems"—the emergency evacuation navigation path lighting, the emergency generator, the alarm system, the "hot site," the default telephone system, and so on—are in-place, and individually work or perform in their as-intended manner.

Second is the *testing*. This is the period of adjustment and tweaking. Necessary modifications or adjustments are made to rectify any shortcomings detected in the commission process. As an example, the emergency announcement system or the alarm system might not be clearly audible in several restrooms; the volume of these would be adjusted. The *testing* period serves also as a demonstration *to and by* the implementation team and by the installers or providers of the individual systems that all the systems can work together. As an example, does the internal fire alarm system transmit (using both the hard-wired and alternate paths) the alarm to the local fire department, recall the elevators, and shut down certain ventilation systems? Or, will the caterer be set up at the "hot site" on a timely basis?

Third is the *trial period* in which the ability of the plan to deal with *normal* as well as with emergency conditions is proven. This is a very important consideration; often, elements of a plan can be so constricting

---

[17] The latter title is not intended to be a play on words! *PRIM-er* is defined as a book of instructions or a text book. British pronunciation holds this word as *PRI-mer*, which, to Americans, is a device that initiates a specific reaction.

or restricting that they themselves will impair, impede, or interrupt as-intended functioning. Examples of such would be smoke detectors that create an alarm condition although all might be normal in the smoking lounge, or heat detectors that create an alarm condition in the computer room even though temperatures remain within ambient limits. The *trial period* assures that—on the one hand—"false alarms" are not transmitted, or that "false conditions" are not detected, while—on the other hand—"indicative conditions" are not overlooked, or that "symptomatic conditions" are not ignored.

The plan, as ultimately created, should be in place, demonstrated as workable, commissioned, tested, given a trial period, and proven before being documented in the *final* plan manual and in the primer for survival.

The plan manual is *The Plan*. (The significance of this concept warrants a separate paragraph!)

The primer for survival—equal in import as the manual—serves to bring the disaster planning and recovery strategy to a "personal" level, creating both the ambiance of a safety culture for each individual "people" as well as an awareness that things *can* go wrong. The primer for survival provides guidance for individual actions and reactions whenever an out-of-course events strikes, or is about to strike. Additionally, the primer for survival contains the "what," "when," and "how" information and guidance that will assist individuals is detecting vulnerabilities that may be present, or become present, in the place, and the means to have any such vulnerabilities assessed and rectified.

It is probably most efficient to publish the manual as an overall volume applicable to the entire place and all the people and processes there. In terms of organization of the manual, certain specifics of the plan are applicable only to discrete business processes, or to BPCs, such as computing. For reference purposes, the manual can be set up along departmental or functional lines, although provision for certain out-of-course events—such as fires or explosions or flooding—should be on a place-wide basis.

In larger organizations, the manual might be established, with greatest benefit, on a BPC- or departmental basis. This structure can minimize the per-volume contents, thus simplifying the search for information, especially under stress conditions. The ruling factor is the ability to find (and understand!)—quickly and with ease—the necessary information and guidance without delay, page fumbling, or confusion. For clarity, certain elements of information are better iterated in more than one *applicable* section than cross-referenced with a "see page . . ." while other elements (such as citations applicable to prescriptives) are best omitted.

The specifics of the organization of both the manual and the primer are a factor of the size and nature of the organization, the size of the place, the number of people, and the character of the processes. The form and format for *your* manual and primer (*if* they should be separately published) reflects both your plan and the culture of your organization. Whatever the form in which they are published, they should be (1) simple and concise; (2) clearly written, without possible confusion to *any* reader; and (3) kept up-to-date and correct.

Before either the manual and the primer can be written, your plan itself should be—better, *must be*—created and had its "appraisement" process completed. It is impractical and surely inefficient to write a plan manual and then establish a plan based on what was written. A cart placed before the horse doesn't seem to work too well, and has great difficulty carrying its load!

The Plan

The shaping and implementation of *The Plan* consists of six stages. Stage 1 is the system design, in which the facility professional—as the disaster planning and recovery strategist and coordinator—and the organization's management must agree on the goals and objectives of the plan, on a time-line basis, and on the investments of resources of money, time, and effort that will be committed to the plan. Here, the costs and benefits of the plan must be considered on a whole-life basis, not solely upon the initial costs and benefits. The facility professional properly should have a real understanding of the basics of disaster planning and recovery *culture* to be able to optimize the value of the plan, and to enable the best return on the investments.

In Stage 2, the plan itself is structured and designed. That the plan is workable and reliable demands that the techniques involved be simple. Prevention and protection systems that are multi-level constrain the ability of the plan to adapt to change.[18] Complex plan structures reduce reliability, and can increase other risks during contingency operations. Then, the "appraisement" process begins: Stage 3 is the demonstration that both the ideas and the equipment do work in practice. Stage 4 serves as the validation that the plan functions as intended in real-life business condi-

---

[18] The ability to adapt, and the ease in so adapting the plan to changed conditions—such as changes in technology, numbers of staff, outsourced functions, and space occupied—are increasingly important considerations in today's organizational environments.

tions. Stage 5 provides the opportunity for any adjustments or corrections in the plan strategy. Stage 6—which is ongoing—serves as the test-bed for periodic reviews, updatings, and drills.

The plan should manifest the following characteristics:

- Simplicity in the design and structure of the strategy and the plan.
- Flexibility in scale and scope.
- Reliability assurance through integration of "departmental plan strategies."
- Limited duplication.
- Adaptive contingency and recovery strategies depending on the situation.
- Carefully pre-planned and structured communications to receive and disseminate information.
- Capability to readily recognize ability to return to as-intended functioning (recovery from impact and consequences).
- Scope for incorporating intelligent functions for the detection and management of out-of-course events.

In deciding upon a disaster planning and recovery strategy, there are four key issues that must to be considered. First, what continuity (without interruption) for the performance of the organization's processes is necessary, and what continuity is desired. There may be the need for a trade-off based on the realities of money, time, and effort to determine the width and the breath of the gap between "necessary" and "desired" that will be acceptable, or at least practical.

The second key issue concerns the vulnerability search and the vulnerability assessment: Which vulnerabilities impact the acceptable gap in continuity of processes, and how can the risk of their creating consequences that interrupt, impair, impede, or halt processes be reduced ALARP. Third, in that it is impossible to reduce the risk of any out-of-course event occurring, impacting a vulnerability, and resulting in consequences that affect people, place, and processes, to zero—or even to reduce many of the levels of risk to an acceptable level—what contingency strategy (ability to continue or to resume business processes following the "gap") and what recovery strategy (damage mitigation and restoration) investments are desired in view of the level of risk of the out-of-course occurrence.

Last, the fourth key issue must address whether the organization's in-place plans for contingency operations, and for recovery (if any!) should be scrapped or modified.

Consideration must be given to the chasm between theoretical procedures and practical steps which can be taken to reduce risks, and to assure the well-being of the people, the place, and the processes. In this process, it is vital to identify and evaluate *other* risks—and costs—that might arise from the precautions taken (that is, the reduction in risks achieved) themselves. The latter is especially important with the use of increasingly complex "technology" to monitor or rectify any situation. (As a simplistic example, a solid-state device employed to monitor electrical power, to activate a standby generator when power transients occur, and to switch to the standby power, might be damaged by the power transient itself, rending it unable to control the generator or to switch the power source.)

It is important that the sequence in which any consequence or any faults or failures is addressed and corrected be predetermined so that not only will the remediation process be in the most efficient and effective manner practicable, but additionally, additional faults or failures will not be initiated.

The strategy must have the ability to provide the types of responses that the planned contingency and recovery procedures can require under the most adverse conditions. (As an example, in addition to providing a standby generator, there must also be provision for storing a supply of fuel that will last a predetermined interval, as well as a procedure for measurement of stored fuel, and a means of lifting the fuel from storage to the generator itself.)

The disaster planning and recovery strategy must meet the needs for current conditions without limiting options for changed or future conditions, whether these encompass place, people, processes, the use of technology, on the size or structure of the organization.

In creating and documenting your plan, there must be an unambiguous definition of the business process cells or centers (BPCs), and a complete description of what each does and its characteristics.

All of this must be viewed in terms of value-for-money criteria.

The Plan Manual and The Primer for Survival

Your plan "documentation"—the plan manual and the primer for survival—are vital elements in your disaster planning and recovery strategy. The manual and primer should be more than (the usually) thick (and almost invariably) red binders to be placed, out-of-reach, on a shelf. The manual and primer are more than a set of dividers, yellowing with age, waiting to separate never-forthcoming, yet-to-be-written pages that should describe the means to achieve survival of the organization whenever a potential problem becomes manifest or other out-of-course event strikes. They are more than just landing strips for dust.

The manual and primer are more than a demonstration for senior management that the investment of money, time, and effort in creating the plan have been well-spent. The role of the manual and primer is not so much to *show* as it is to *tell*. The volumes should *tell* your people how to manage risk, how to properly countervail the impact, consequences and affects of a problem or out-of-course event, and how to recover and restore as-intended functioning of the business processes.

A significant problem with many contingency plan documents is, simply, that they are *not* contingency plan documents, but rather an assemblage of statements or accounts by others bearing only the slightest significance in—or total irrelevance to—the organization's plan strategy. Some organizations let it suffice that their manual be a collection of fire department practices, codes, boilerplate statements gathered at a conference, or claims or statements of service providers, or abstracts from magazine articles. The manual is a document for survival, not a scrapbook!

The plan documents are *action* guides, and should not be papered with fancy title pages, policy statements, letters from management, convoluted cross-references, or cutesy cartoons. The primer and manual should present, in a logical, clear-cut, unmistakable manner, the action steps the reader should take when a problem occurs or is imminent. Inclusion of the landscaping guidelines for the "hot site" are irrelevant!

Some writers suggest that you examine (hopefully, *prior to* a problem) the plan documents with an eye toward questions such as, "Does the contingency plan make sense?" and "Does the plan relate to the business?" and "Are the various premises upon which the plan is based correct?" and "Is the contingency plan realistic?" and other questions of like ilk. If you are asking those questions of your plan documents, then you have failed to create a workable, integrated plan! Disaster planning entails, first, creating the plan, and then, second, describing—and updating the descriptions—the plan and the steps of plan implementation in a manual and primer.

A good amount of the published material describing how to write a "great disaster recovery plan"[19] (something often indistinguishable from a plan document) is itself a disaster! With respect, an "executive sum-

---

[19] One might ponder whether the intent is to provide for a *great disaster* or for a *great plan?*

mary" or "administrative statement" provides little but fuel for a fire when it appears in a plan manual.

The plan that you create for disaster preparedness and recovery must be "formalized" for reference and review purposes. This formalization should be on two distinct levels, each level serving a specific purpose. First, there must be created a plan manual detailing all aspects of your plan and its implementation when necessary. The plan manual, or specific parts of it, should be distributed to all members of a designated cadre of staff members and others (the CMT) who have specific duties and responsibilities: (1) in the creation of the plan itself; (2) in implementing the plan whenever a problem occurs; (3) when a drill or practice is conducted; (4) when an audit of the plan is undertaken; and (5) in reviewing, updating, and otherwise maintaining the plan.

The second category of written communication, which can be called a primer for survival, presents the organization's disaster planning and recovery strategy to all other employees for their guidance as well as for their information. The purpose of this type of communication, in the establishment of the organization's strategy, is, primarily, to inform the people of the various potential problems that could impact them, the place, and the processes in which they participate. Of equal import in this communication—or set of communications—is to inform the people of what the organization has undertaken to reduce the risks of any of the potential problems occurring, to reduce the impact of the problem if and when it does strike, and what plans and procedures are in place to mitigate the consequences and affects of the impact.

In addition, the communication provides guidance to the people concerning the disciplined reactions or procedures they should follow when specific impacts occur. These "reactions" cover situations wherein individuals must participate in, or take specific actions in plan implementation—such as relocating activities to the "hot site"—and situations where in the individual response is only evacuation or preparation for evacuation from their own work sites within the building or place.

Your plan, and the plan manual describing the plan and its implementation and operation, will—for the typical organization—be an *integration* of planning not only for the organization as an entity, but also an incorporation of "specialized" plans and "specialized" needs that have emerged for activities such as data processing, data security, telecommunications, computer networks, records management, security, and safety. Frequently, an organization will establish a "disaster plan" or a "recovery plan" covering, each individually and independently, one of more of these activities without consideration of the needs for a comprehensive disaster planning and recovery strategy for the *entire* organization. A multiplicity of plans not only constrains the flexibility of the organization to adapt to change, but also the inherently (and unnecessarily) complex plan structures that result also reduce reliability, posing a greater threat to overall functional continuity and recovery during and after impacted operations. In creating an integrated strategy and plan for the entire organization it is unquestionably best to start with a fresh sheet of paper rather than to attempt to improve and joint together several disassociated, separately designed plans. A "multitude" of "plans" reduces reliability because of their complexity, and at the same time increases operating costs, but without offering any increased risk management. Any increase in complexity, inherent in segmented plans, results in a reduction in reliability. This factor is frequently ignored by planners concerned only with their own patch of responsibility.

Your plan—thus, your plan manual and your primer for survival— should contain detailed explanation of your organization's pre-planned approach to, and provisions for, the following elements essential in an effective, efficient, workable approach to a disaster planning and recovery strategy. Information in the manual should be department- or BPC-specific, and detail-specific, indicating responsibilities for searches of both the "general" department or BPC areas, as well as specific areas (e.g., lavatories and other spaces not usually considered a part of the department or BPC), for closing of vaults and safes, and for assisting the mobility-impaired. The responsibilities for CMT members should be specified for each working shift, and for "other times." The CMT members—who should have a shift-specific or time- or day-specific reporting/completing hierarchy—should also be furnished with responsibility checklists that are shift- or time- or day-specific to ensure that all variables in space utilization, equipment, and facilities in use, and the presence of people are accounted for.

Your plan manual should be structured to reflect the "severity" of event so that, for specific categories of events, the CM or CMT member will know what actions to take and to initiate, who to notify, and just what information or notification should be given.

Some of the elements in a typical plan (if there indeed be one that is *typical*), and the considerations inherent in planning, are listed below. It is important to remember, when you create the manual and primer for your organization's own unique custom-created plan, that this list represents only the possible groundwork upon which your plan documents can be constructed. Your manual and your primer must comprehensively and fully echo both all the goals and objectives that your plan endeavors to accomplish, as well as the means within the plan to achieve these accomplishments. The goals and objectives here considered are arranged in alphabetic order rather than in a hierarchy of importance. Your plan manual, and your primer for survival are your plan. Your plan *is* the manual and the primer.

Assure Faults and Failures Are Addressed and Corrected in Proper Sequence The stress associated with the requirement, or with the desire, to restore the as-intended functioning of one or more affected BPCs often results in "wheel spinning" or counterproductive actions. The stress that occurs when there are casualties—injuries or deaths—or when there is harm or damage to the place, will, more often than not, result in greater "wheel spinning" or in actions that have greater counterproductivity. Such "wheel-spinning" and counterproductive actions can increase the level of risks of *additional consequences and affects* on people; increase the levels of risk of *additional damage or harm* to the place; increase the level of risk of *additional affects* on the BPCs; as well as resulting in *unnecessary or avoidable delays* in the restoration process. The manual should contain—for each out-of-course event, or its impact, consequences and affects—a "fault and failure tree" analysis and appropriate remediation steps.

Although the preparation of such remediation processes can be involved and time consuming, the potential ultimate value is great. As an (obvious!) example, if there is a failure in the supply of electricity to the computer center or to a group of desktop computers (which should be, with benefit, wired into a dedicated circuit with *proper* UPS power protection, rather than being individually plugged into a "power protection devices" priced in penny numbers), it would be imprudent to immediately start the emergency generator. The most appropriate initial step would be to switch all affected devices "off." The next steps would entail a check of the switches, fuses, and circuit breakers associated with the dedicated circuit. If these were determined to be without fault, the search would continue in a hierarchical pattern. When the fault or failure is identified, it should not be corrected (say, the circuit breaker reset) until the *cause of the fault* is determined.

The "fault and failure tree" associated with a flooded basement would not only exhort one to switch off electrical mains before wading into the area in search of blocked drains, but would also indicate what equipment and devices should be shut down—and what, such as sump pumps, should be activated—because of the incursion of water.[20]

Guidance in the search for, and rectification of, faults and failures not only reduces the risk of improper procedures, but can also be used with advantage by "nonspecialized" personnel.

Authentication Procedures for Contingency Operations Declaration   The circumstances under which the contingency manager or contingency management team members (see below) should take or initiate specific actions—and *which* specific actions—should be established, and iterated in the manual. This, in a general way, prevents both over-reaction and under-reaction that is likely to occur under stress or unfamiliar (the previously conducted drills, tests, and practices notwithstanding) situations. In addition, this also provides the basic parameters for certain "routine" actions—such as early closure when a blizzard is imminent—without time-consuming and delaying discussions often inherent in such decisions which are, in the event, ultimately made. (How often has a meeting called to discuss early closing extended—without resolution—beyond normal closing time?)

Procedures for authentication of certain ordering of actions or events—such as startup of "hot-site" computing or early dismissal—should be established between the contingency manager and those who will take or initiate the action. The authentication procedures should be privileged information, and should be changed on a routine and periodic basis. This means of muzzling the "cries of wolf" will help prevent "malicious false alarms" and needless expense.

Communicating the Alarm: Alerting Your People and Notifying Emergency Services   When an emergency is about to take place, or when a problem occurs—be it an *immanent* out-of-course event, or impact, that might have consequences and affects on your people, place, or processes, or an in-process out-of-course event that is impacting or about to impact (and thus, possibly have consequences and affects on your people, place, or processes)—the first priority is to *notify those who must respond.*

Those who must respond include—dependent upon the circumstances—your contingency manager, the contingency management team, your people (both those at the place, and those away from the place),

---

[20] The drains should have been checked for obstructions, and the automatic sump pumps tested, in the vulnerability search! But things can go wrong between the V/Ss.

public safety emergency response dispatchers or liaisons, precontracted vendors (including alternate site providers, and damage mitigation and restoration services), the news media (press, radio, and television), customers, suppliers, and other people and organizations that might also be affected by the consequences of the event.

The word "respond" means to act or to take some action. *Who is to respond* is a function of the nature of the out-of-course event and the impact, consequences and affects it is having or might have. Thus, you might have to notify your people to evacuate the building or the place. You might have to notify second-shift personnel not to report to work this evening, or all personnel not to report tomorrow. You might have to notify your customers that the widgets they are expecting next week will not be shipped or will be delayed (their "response" might be a rescheduling or canceling the order), or notify your damage prevention and mitigation services provider to commence a "boarding up."

The manual should contain listings of all "alternative" communications availabilities at the place, including CMT members' cellular telephone, and pager or beeper numbers. In addition to their home telephones, home-based fax numbers and e-mail addresses should be included to facilitate notification in the event of a telecommunications outage at either the place or the individual's residence. The place listing should include all direct (non-PBX) telephone and fax numbers, and the location of the devices. The location of in-place and of nearby coin telephones should be included (as well as information concerning whether the coin telephone takes in-coming calls, and whether you can use a calling card). A supply of quarters—if that be the local fee, otherwise a supply of small change—and telephone calling cards usable *on the specific phones* for local as well as long-distance calls should be a part of the CMT's supplies.

The primer should contain (in addition to that in the manual) detailed instructions on how to raise an alarm if the person detects an out-of-course event, and how to respond and act when an alarm is sounded. The who-to and how-to notify instructions should be comprehensive and all-encompassing. Information, as an example, concerning raising of an alarm of fire should detail where internal fire alarm pull-boxes are located, whether or not it is necessary to additionally and separately notify the fire department, and the applicable telephone number(s) for the telephone central office serving your facility to use for summoning fire or emergency services.

The use of the quite-common but not universal "911" to summon fire, police, ambulance, or other emergency services can be confusing, especially when the caller is under stress. Proper instructions should be clearly iterated in the primer, on posters, and on stickers mounted on telephone sets. As the availability of "911" dialing is not universal, the person wishing to raise an alarm might reside in a 911-serviced area, but the workplace may not have that service. Dialing "911" in a nonservice area can result in nonconnected calls, operator or equipment intercept, or delays in connection. Any of these can increase the level of risk of life-threatening or property-threatening consequences. If the facility is served by 911 service, telephones should be labeled to indicate if it is necessary to dial "9" prior to "911" (changes to your switching equipment might overcome this need). If some telephones are not provided with "dial 9" access, these should be clearly marked as nonavailable for summoning emergency services. (Here, again, modifications to some switching equipment can enable dialing "911" while restricting "dial 9" access).[21]

Both the manual and the primer should contain alternate telephone numbers for use in the event that "911" is unaccessible or jammed or unanswered within a reasonable time. Included should be alternate telephone numbers for the fire department (emergency alternate telephone number, numbers of nearby fire stations, and nonemergency numbers); for the local police department (emergency alternate number, numbers of nearby police precincts or stations, and nonemergency numbers); for the state police or highway patrol (emergency alternate number, numbers of nearby local *and* nearby stations, and nonemergency numbers); and for ambulance and other emergency response services. These telephone numbers are especially useful in instances—such as when a nature-based out-of-course has struck—when vast numbers of people are attempting to call emergency services, and when the telephone infrastructure may be damaged or fail.

Some organizations have plans to use a "private" ambulance service in the time of need (which, obviously, is reflected in their manual). The service's telephone number(s) and alternate number(s)—and any use-authorization information—should be included in the primer. Other emergency telephone numbers that should be included, as appropriate, in the primer are the State Police or Highway Patrol, the F.B.I., the U.S. Coast Guard, the U.S. Secret Service, HazMat services, and the U.S. Bureau of Alcohol, Tobacco and Firearms.

If any staff are users of TDD (Telephone Device for the Deaf) or TTY (Teletypewriter) services, the TDD or TTY numbers for *all* emergency

---

[21] See Chapter 11 for a bit more about "911."

services should be included in the manual and primer. In instances where the telephone numbers for TDD or TTY *and* non-TDD or non-TTY (voice) are the same (sometimes "911"), *both* the TDD or TTY *and* non-TDD or non-TTY telephone numbers should be listed under applicable captions to avoid any possible confusion or potential delay.[22]

When publishing *any* telephone number in the manual or the primer, or on informational signage, the appropriate area codes should be included in a "1+. . ." format. Where "1+800" or "1+888" telephone numbers are normally used for access, the alternate, non-toll-free telephone numbers should also be given. *Prior to publishing the manual or primer, each telephone number that appears should be actually dialed to determine if it correct. All numbers should be actually dialed to reverify correctness prior to reissuing or updating any pages.*[23]

The address or site identification should be iterated where the telephone numbers or dialing instructions appear; the caller, under stress, might not be able to recall or provide the best possible information or site identification. Information concerning specific site identification is especially important in suburban and rural areas where "911" calls may be answered by a distant response center serving a wide area or an entire county. If the organization is located within an office or industrial park or campus, information concerning specific building location should be provided. This important information should be conveyed to all members of the staff in the primer, on posters, and on telephone set-mounted stickers. The use of broadsides, posters, and stickers is especially important in conference rooms, training rooms, and other spaces where "off-site" people may gather.

It is prudent, in the instructions for raising an alarm or for summoning aid provided in the manual and in the primer for survival, to correlate what appears on the exterior signage with the scripted information that will be given to a dispatcher. The "real" address should be used—such as "950 River Road, near Third Street" rather than a "vanity address" such as One Ego Drive. (Although the Postal Service may recog-

---

[22] "TDD" and "TTY" are used interchangeably to identify the telephone numbers. This can only serve to increase the level of risk of confusion or delay in initiating a call—especially in stress situations—and thus increases the level risk of casualties or damage. Telephone companies should opt for only one designator, and urge their customers to use that "standard."

[23] An earthquake emergency manual published by the fire department of a major northern California city neglected this step. The unnecessarily high level of risk created by an incorrect area code can be quickly, simply, and cheaply lowered to an ALARP level!

nize such an address, they do not provide emergency services other than "Express Mail"!)

If the place is located in an urban environment, employees should be aware of the location of nearby outside fire alarm pull boxes, in the event that the cause for raising the alarm has interrupted telephone communications.[24]

Alarm information provided for visitors at the site should be meaningful. Fire alarm pull-boxes in public spaces in New York City (and probably elsewhere) present the prescriptive admonition (which one probably could not, or at least have the tendency not to read, in a fire or smoke condition) that after pulling the alarm, the person should notify the Fire Department "using the Bell telephone." Many people would undoubtedly wonder what a "Bell telephone" is, and where the nearest one might be located.

Competent Stewardship during Contingency Operations Your plan should designate a contingency manager (and alternates) who are vested with appropriate authority and responsibility for the declaration of an "emergency" (as well as the communication of "warnings," "alerts," and the raising of alarms), and to begin plan steps to prevent an escalation into a "crisis" or "disaster." The contingency manager (or his or her alternate at any particular time) is responsible for the management of all activities—ranging from alerting emergency response services to evacuation to place-closure to a "hot-site" startup—during the "emergency" period, including the "during" and "after" phases of the out-of-course event, its impact, and the consequences and affects.

The contingency manager (and alternates) are assisted by the contingency management team. This CMT are the designated people who have been assigned specific responsibilities in the event of an "emergency" to prevent—or to help prevent—the event escalating into a "crisis" or "disaster." The team includes evacuation guides and aids, searchers, the place's fire brigade, the organization's medical staff, and all others who have been assigned a role—such as helping a mobility impaired person or assisting with the emergency medical kit or directing the fire department to the fire location—in implementing the organization's plan. The actual "team" can, with benefit, also include any contracted impact and

---

[24] New York City, in 1996, has begun to remove fire alarm pull-boxes in an experiment to reduce malicious false alarm. About 25% of street alarm boxes have been removed. This (highly controversial) action may have serious impact on the ability to raise an alarm of fire. The facility professional in New York must be aware of the status of alarm boxes proximate to his or her place.

damage mitigation services that provide assistance "before" an imminent out-of-course event or emergency (such as "broad-up" and other protective and damage-minimizing activities, property and records removal), as well as during the "emergency" and afterward.

The contingency management team membership, contingency operations chain-of-command, and defined staff duties in the contingency operating environment, including vested authority for expenditures, should be defined.

The plan manual should contain the names, the current and correct addresses and telephone numbers of the CM, CMT and other staff members, and of resource and service providers involved with plan operation and implementation.[25] It is vital that this information be kept up-to-date. This "notification list" (which can include provision for each person notified to notify other designated persons) should include the individual's home telephone number(s), mobile or cell telephone number(s), and any pager or beeper number, fax number, e-mail address, or amateur radio operator's call sign and frequency. Notification logs (see below) should record the time individuals are called and by whom, and the nature of the message left (message content and whether given in-person, to another person, or left on an answering machine). Changes to team members' and other staff's addresses, area codes, telephone numbers, and other data should be coordinated by human resources or personnel, rather than being made on an individual basis.

Evacuation Management   There are circumstances wherein it is prudent to evacuate the building or the entire place, and there are circumstances wherein part of the building or place, or the entire building or place *must* be evacuated so that the risk of deaths or injuries will be reduced ALARP.[26] The manual (as guidance for the CM and CMT) should iterate the circumstances when an evacuation—as well as the nature and extent of that evacuation—should be ordered by the CM. Both the manual

---

[25] There is an interesting issue of privacy here. Some people may not wish such information to be made generally available. One way in which to deal with this situation is to have the information in a "sealed" format in each copy of the manual. This "sealing" serves similarly to the protective covers fitted to alarm pull-boxes.

[26] In some circumstances—such as a fire in a high-rise office building—the fire department may require only a partial evacuation, perhaps the two floors above and the two floors below the fire location. This partial evacuation may be only of limited comfort to others in the building, especially when viewing massed fire apparatus at the site. The CM need weigh—considering the guidance in the manual—whether the fire department's ordered evacuation plus any "self-undertaken" evacuation *or* a complete evacuation will effect the lowest level of risk of casualties.

and the primer should identify both the most efficient evacuation path to be followed by the people located in each BPC as well as alternate path(s) to be utilized if the primary path is unaccessible or unusable.

Evacuation management should be based on the "worst case scenario" and evacuations made using designated passageways, aisles, corridors, and stairwells only. The manual and primer should also indicate the circumstances wherein the use of elevators and "nonevacuation" stairwells does not increase the level of risk of casualties (e.g., in the event of an early closing in the face of an impending storm). Announcement made on the public address system should clearly indicate when and if the use of elevators and the additional stairwells is a safe course.

The question whether an early closing (in circumstances such as an impending storm) is an *evacuation* is an important consideration for the CM. It becomes a question of whether the people *may* leave or *should* or *must* leave. The CM must judge whether those who remain for a time will increase their level of risk of consequences and affects by delaying their departure, or if by remaining in the "safe haven" of place, they will reduce their level of risk of consequences and affects from the impact of the out-of-course event. This can be an example of "get out while the getting is good, or remain here until everything blows over"!

Instructions and Procedures for Initiation or Activation of Preplanned Impact and Consequence Mitigation Services and Activities The manual should describe, for the guidance of the CM and CMT, the *circumstances* when, or under which, the preplanned impact and consequence mitigation services and activities should commence, the *timing* of the commencement, and *which* services or activities should commence. These prestatements ease the under-stress decision-making considerations for the CM and CMT, and, further, help assure that all the appropriate planned services and activities are brought into use. These statements also serve to preclude both too-early or unnecessary initiation or activation, as well as delayed or too-late initiation or activation. In addition, the manual should include *instructions and procedures for initiation or activation of preplanned restoration and recovery services and activities* for the same purposes and benefits.

Instructions, Forms, and Supplies for Use of Paper Systems in the Event of a Computer System Failure In organizations where a continuity in the provision of services in or of a BPC is deemed important or critical (or is it the *provision for the continuity of services*?) the risk of computer failure can be countervailed by providing the appropriate people with the forms, supplies, instructions, and training that will enable them to "revert" to paper-based systems to enable continuity of BPC functioning during the interval between the computer failure and the restoration of computer processing.

That "the computer is down, please call back later" is an increasing source of irritation to customers and other callers. The level of tolerance to this decreases, especially in competitive environments. By the simply providing your staff with the *readily available* and *practical* means to transparently "carry on" without the usual computer support will reduce the level of risks of lost business and of customer dissatisfaction. Most often, the paper-and-pen-or-pencil fall-back contingency can be totally transparent to the caller!

(*Readily available* and *practical* are important considerations. Airline check-in counters provide a good case-in-point. Airlines must account for seat assignments/occupancy for all departing flights. When computer-based records are not available, preprinted diagrams—appropriate to the particular aircraft—are manually filled in. Staff training is provided, and forms are provided for each check-in point. When it is necessary to revert to the paper-based system, the diagram for the particular aircraft is almost invariably the only configuration that is not readily at-hand. Additional departure delays also result from the fact that the diagrams are usually printed on 11 x 8½-inch sheets, making the forms time-consumingly difficult to complete.)

Notification Logs   Preprinted notification log forms should be provided in the manual. The log should record the date, time, and the *message presented*, of all notifications *to and from* (1) emergency services, (2) the CM and to CMT members, (3) alternate site providers, (4) damage mitigation and restoration service providers, and (5) any others who have, or should have, knowledge of the event, such as customers, suppliers, the press or other tenants at the site or in the building. The log should indicate whether the notifications were given in-person, to another person, or left on an answering machine. Individual responses, or acknowledgments to the notification, should be recorded. Logs of in-coming messages should include the name and organization of the caller, a synopsis of the message, for whom the message is intended, the time the message was received, and the time it was delivered to the intended recipient. The on-site arrival times of services, equipment, staff, and of other personnel or individuals, should be recorded.

Notifications and Public Relations   Whenever an out-of-course event impacts the organization's as-intended functioning, the organization's several constituencies should be notified or advised. The message, as such, and to whom it should be delivered, is a factor of the event itself, the anticipated duration, and how it will affect the particular constituency. Just *what* should be said—and just as important, what *should not* be said—has been described at great length by public relations experts and by media practitioners, and is outside the scope of this guide. It is, however, important to mention here that information content should be *honest, truthful, and an accurate representation* of the event, its impact, as well as its consequences and affects. (The consequences and affects may not be known at the time of initial or early notifications. Here, a prudent statement should advise "more information as soon as it becomes available" rather than later-to-be-eaten-and-difficult-to-digest-words suggesting that all will be "love and roses.") As elementary as this might seem, some organizations fail to heed this common-sense imperative.

Whenever any out-of-course event impacts as-intended functioning, it is important to first notify your people, and to advise them how the event will impact them. This information should include closures, relocation of BPC operations, the existence of possible health issues resultant from the event, and—if the closure is anticipated to be relatively long-lasting—provisions for continuance of salary or wages or for unemployment compensation.

Others that should be notified or advised, depending upon the circumstances of the event, and its impact, consequences and affects, include the following groups:

1.   The press and other news media which should be presented with accurate information concerning the event and its affects, remembering that often the media's thirst for "disasters" sometimes outpaces its appetite for accuracy.

2.   Your customers, who can become concerned about a continuity in delivery of services and products.

3.   Vendors and suppliers (including the Postal Service, courier services, your local and long-distance telephone service providers) concerned about their delivery of products, materials, and services to your organization.

4.   Your shareholders and other stakeholders concerned about the affect of the event on their equity values.

5.   The community in which you are located, especially if health or environmental concerns might emerge—or are suspected—as a result of the event.

6. Governmental agencies that regulate your organization, if the event affects the delivery of services or products.
7. Your insurance carrier!

Periodic Reviews and Updating of the Plan Manual and Primer Provisions for, and schedules of, reviews and updating of materials in the manual and primer are an inherent part of the plan, and should be specified in the manual. In addition to provision for periodic reviews, changes, or revisions to the manual and primer that become evident as a result of practices and drills, the updating of *all* information relating to CMT membership and members, emergency response services, and impact mitigation and damage restoration service providers should be routinely made. There should also be provision for routine, periodic vulnerability searches, assessments, and rectifications; for review of prescripted announcements and tapes; for review of changes to BPCs and the technology they employ; and, for review of information and data retention schedules, archiving, and protection.

Periodic Vulnerability Searches, Vulnerability Assessments, and Vulnerability Rectifications As the VS/VA/VR processes are among the most important and most effective tools of risk management, your plan (and thus, your manual) should include provision for all-inclusive, comprehensive searches, assessments, and rectifications of the totality of people, place, and processes. These should be undertaken at least yearly, or—with additional benefits—twice yearly. It is beneficial for different teams or different people to conduct the processes (or to search different parts of the place or different processes) so that the investigations are accomplished by different "new" eyes, ears, noses, and minds each time.

VS/VA/VRs of less-than-total-dimension but appropriate to the circumstance should be conducted when (1) staff members so-suggest, as prompted by the primer; (2) when there changes to the place; and, (3) when there are changes to the processes and the technology inherent to them.

Both periodic and ad-hoc vulnerability searches should be conducted without prior announcement so that "usual" conditions can be noted.

Prevent Other Risks and Costs Arising from the Precautions (the Reduction in Risks Achieved) Themselves In the planning process, as well as in the plan itself, care must be taken both to not create new risks, and not to increase the levels of existing risks. Care must also be taken not to accrue unnecessary costs that *might* arise from a reduction in the level of risks but that are not inherent in the reduction, as such.

As an example, a fire (which might have been prevented by the en-forcement of established safety practices and procedures) in the Düsseldorf airport on April 11, 1996 killed 16 people and caused at least DM100m ($67m) worth of damage. In addition to delays in summoning the city fire department and lack of a sprinkler system in the building, *the wrong recorded evacuation announcement message was broadcast* to the people in the building. The instructions in the incorrect announcement brought the people *into* the arena of risk (the blazing fire) rather than guiding them away from it, and without doubt increased the number of casual-ties.[27] As described elsewhere in this guide, the use of prescripted or pre-recorded announcements is an extremely good practice, and should be incorporated into your plan. However, such scripts or recordings *must* be clearly identified as to both use and applicability so the proper and cor-rect announcement will be broadcast, and to prevent any risk-increasing information from being announced. Provision must also be made to pre-clude any "automatic" announcements being broadcast which might be incorrect or risk-increasing. (The activation and "automatic" broadcast of the incorrect announcement at Düsseldorf was attributed to cables damaged by the fire itself!)

Akin to this realm of precautions taken are a wide range of consid-erations such as whether or not the off-site records storage sites (for pa-per-based and for magnetic or optical media) used to store the corporate memory have levels of risk or harm or damage to such records that are ALARP. The vulnerability search and vulnerability assessment should be conducted at each off-site storage location. The VS and VA should also be conducted at each "hot site" and other alternate sites. It might not be at all surprising if you find vulnerabilities with unacceptably high levels of risks existing in your records storage facility (whether it is your own, or outsourced), data warehouse, or alternate computer operations site.

Procedures for Periodic Drills and Practice Sessions, Including Activation of, and Operations at, Alternate Site(s)   To assure that the plan will work as-intended, and continue to work with the passage of time (and with changes to people, place, and processes), it must be subjected to test and evaluation. The tests range from proof of the alarm and announce-ment systems to fire drills and evacuation drills to switching or convert-

---

[27] Andrew Fisher and Peter Norman, "Düsseldorf Airport Fire Blunders," *Financial Times*, 15 April 1996, 3.

ing to a contingency operations environment ("hot" or other alternate sites).

The frequency of testing is based on the complexity of your plan (which itself reflects the complexity of your people, place, processes), *what elements* are being proved at a particular test, changes or modifications incorporated into your plan (and its manual and primer) since the last test, and—especially—changes that have been made to people (e.g., staffing), place (e.g., space occupied and changes to space), and processes (e.g., the organization of BPCs, what they do, and the technology used). Frequency of testing of specific plan elements (e.g., fire precautions, fire drills, fire-extinguishing practices, and evacuations) may be prescribed by state or local regulations but such prescriptives may not reduce the levels of risk ALARP.

The manual—in addition to specifying *test elements* and their *frequency*—should specify what should be observed and evaluated in the course of the test. This would encompass such factors as alarm recognition and audibility; evacuation timing; shutdown interval timing; startup of contingency operations timing; loss of data and information; and other factors related to the nature of the test. Whatever the nature of the test, full participation by all people is vital. Planned tests should not be announced, but known—preferably—only to the CM.

The obvious purpose of the testing is to assure that the plan will work in the as-intended manner. Thus, all aspects of the test should be evaluated following return to normal functioning, and any changes or modifications to the plan deemed warranted and appropriate should be made.

Procedures for Switching or Converting to a Contingency Operations Environment in an Orderly, Efficient, and Cost-Effective Manner   These procedures deal, for the most part, with the switch from normal or as-intended functioning to a "countervailance operating" mode. This latter mode, sometimes referred to as the "contingency plan" or "recovery plan" or "disaster plan," represents what has been put into place to enable specific BPCs to continue to function on or at a predetermined level of continuity in the provision of services or products (both to customers and those external to the organization, and to BPCs within the organization). This "continuity" may be nonstop, or with a predetermined, acceptable interval of interruption. In many organizations, the "switching" represents activation of the "hot-site," "warm-site," or "cold-site" and working from there.

The contingency manager should be provided with exacting guidelines regarding both when to "alert" the alternate site, and then when to change from the "standby" status to actual initiation of the site use. The timing of these decisions are important: First, many alternate-site providers "sell" a significantly greater number of "seats" than they physically have (on the premise that the level of risk—to them—of "seat demand" greater than what they actually have available is acceptably low). An out-of-course event impacting several organizations within an area can result in a greater demand for "seats" than the number available. In such instances, the seat allotments are usually made to the organizations that first notify a "standby" or site-initiation condition. Thus, if the CM does not act quickly enough, there may not be any (or enough) "seats" available, or "seats" that are available at the desired (relatively nearby) site. On the other side of the coin—the second necessity for good guidelines—is the fact that an unnecessary or premature "standby" or initiation can be very costly because the "meter" starts to tick from that point.

The guidelines, and actual procedures, should be determined in conjunction with information managers, information technology managers, and those responsible for overall BPC functioning and ability to deliver their services and products.

Provide the Steps—Including Both the Procedures and the CMT Members Designated to Carry Them Out—to Enable Orderly Shutdowns to Be Carried Out in the Proper Sequence

These steps are necessary (1) to reduce the level of risk that avoidable consequences and affects—including casualties, loss or damage to the place, its infrastructure, equipment and furnishings, and loss or damage to information and data—will occur, and (2) to assure that the necessary steps are undertaken in the most efficient and effective manner, and in a manner that will avoid other risks and costs arising.

It is most important to emphasize to your CMT members, and to other staff members who might attempt to carry out the shutdown steps, that in so-doing they should not undertake any action that might increase the level of risk of injury or death to themselves or to others.

The procedures should designate the proper sequence of steps to "shut down" computer operations (both centralized and desktop) to eliminate or minimize data loss and hardware damage; to initiate alternate routing schemes in telecommunications switching centers; to place designated documents and other materials in predetermined safes or cabinets, and to close and secure these—and all other lockable safes and cabinets; to protect in-process paperwork, disks, and tapes; to cover furnishings and library shelving where possible; and to secure or cover or otherwise protect valuable property, including paintings, antiques, and other collections.

As a part of the "shutdown" processes, the proper functioning or closure of fire doors and curtains, and the intended automatic starting or stopping of equipment should be verified and recorded on CMT checklists.

The manual and primer should also contain information about "shutdown" procedures in the event of an alarm, the evacuation navigation paths applicable to specific parts of the building and site, alternate paths, assembly areas, head counts, and information concerning "all-clear" or dismissals. There should be instructions concerning evacuation if individuals are not at their usual work-site, and for "common areas" such as a cafeteria, exercise room, or company library. Too frequently—and at great personal danger—there is a tendency to first return to one's usual work site to gather personal belongings rather than to immediately evacuate. The staff should be given information concerning call-in procedures in the event of potential building closures.

Provide Systems and Procedures That Have the Ability to Handle That Which They Are Likely to Be Presented under the Most Adverse Conditions   Put another way, this means that you should *really* prepare for not only the "worst case scenario" but for that scenario having an extensive duration!

If your planning deems it vital to provide continuity in the computer processing usually undertaken by 200 people on every shift, the contracted availability of (say) ten "chairs" or "seats" at an alternate "hot-site" for a three-day period will quickly prove not be sufficient when none of the 200 are able to work in the fire-damaged office for a week or more. If you provide 50 essential "customer care" telephone answering positions, determine the level of risk that *all 50* will fail at the same time, rather than plan that only 10 or 12 might fail.

These provisions are associated with, and need reflect, not only the level of risk of particular out-of-course events, impacts, or consequences and affects occurring, but also the level of risk of the *intensity* of each as well as the *duration* of each. In planning the systems and procedures to countervail the consequences and affects of a hurricane, the systems and procedures must have foundations not only on the level of risk that a hurricane will occur, but also on the levels of risk associated with various hurricane intensities—which span a considerable range—and durations of strike and of impact.

Provision for Updating   A prime consideration is that the listings in the plan manual should be both complete and up-to-date. The organization's personnel listing should be routinely updated, preferably as a by-product of human resources change notices. Supplier and provider information should be provided and updated, routinely, by the purchasing department or other similar function. It is especially important to verify *all* listed telephone numbers and telephone area codes, and to incorporate the changes—which are increasing in number and frequency—made. Some area code changes are now being based on *specific exchanges* (rather than on geographic areas alone, as was once the case) and have to be checked accordingly.[28]

Remedial Activities to be Undertaken After the Impact, Consequences and Affects Have Subsided   The manual should specify—in addition to the (obvious!) damage mitigation activities, and the mop-up, cleaning, repair, and restoration tasks to be undertaken—the other activities necessary to minimize losses. Also specified—to eliminate or minimize costly and time-consuming delays, duplication of efforts, gaps, overlaps, and unnecessary expenses—should be the members of the CMT responsible. (These people may not have had a role during the dynamic phase of the out-of-course event but should be, with advantage, considered CMT members for control and coordinative purposes.) Among the activities might be professional counseling for people affected by the event. Losses that may be offset by insurance coverage must be documented.

A most important activity is the comprehensive review—a postevent debriefing—of how the plan was able to deal with the out-of-course event, its impact, and consequences and affects. Judgment must be made concerning any changes deemed or thought necessary to the plan and how it was implemented: Decisions concerning possible changes or modifications to the place, its buildings and infrastructure, and the equipment and furnishings must be weighed. The processes must be considered, and the functionings of BPCs—in terms of both how they *should have* functioned and how they *actually* functioned—have to be examined. Put another way, did the plan work in its intended manner, or what changes are required so that it *will work* the next time it is called upon?

---

[28] A January 1995 crash, in Scotland, of two trains, that resulted in the death of one railwayman, would have been averted if the control staff had been familiar with their radio contact procedures and had there not been a delay in "finding" the required "code" (similar to our area code) to warn the train driver of a disabled train in his path. ("S[ettle] & C[arlisle] Crash Caused By a 'Mix-up'," *Railway Magazine,* August 1996, 65.)

Roster of Impact Mitigation and Damage Restoration Services As discussed in Chapters 2 and 6, the contracting for impact mitigation and damage restoration services during the Before Phase can prove to be of immense—possibly indispensable—value. This arrangement is especially valuable when the out-of-course event strikes several organizations in your area. Information concerning these services, and the means to activate them, should be a part of the manual. (A copy of the applicable information in purchasing's files is of no value if that department is not accessible!)

Staff Training and Refresher Courses for Plan Activation and Implementation, and Training for Use of Alternate Facilities and Alternate Systems In addition to the training and refresher tutorials for your CM and CMT members, a vital aspect of your planning should include training *of the other people* for, and the practice of, fire drills and evacuation drills, shutdown procedure drills, the extinguishing of fires (as distinct from firefighting), first-aid and CPR, and other procedures and processes that involve the organization's people when an out-of-course event occurs.

Your contingency manager, and the contingency management team members, should be given comprehensive, special training covering the various aspects of their responsibilities. State and local police, fire, emergency services departments, and insurance companies often offer specialized training (and refresher courses) in their respective areas; your CM and CMT should attend these. In some jurisdictions, "disaster" training (earthquake preparedness, in San Francisco, is but one example) is available for an organization's entire staff and can well reduce the level of risk of casualties. The manual should specify the timing and content of both training and refresher sessions, and of drills.

The Primer for Survival

The primer for survival is the basic tool through which the plan is communicated to all members of the organization's staff. How the staff will use this tool, however, must be viewed realistically, keeping in mind that—often—instructional manuals are sometimes used only when "all else fails." The other communication media should *additionally* be used to convey, and re-enforce, information concerning raising an alarm, the meaning of alarm signals, evacuation procedures, paths and marshalling areas, "shutdown" procedures, "call-in" procedures, and other plan elements, especially those related to the reduction of risk of casualties and of loss of property.

All management and staff personnel should be furnished with a primer for survival. It may be important, in particular environments, to publish the primer in more than one language. If this is deemed prudent, accuracy in translations are especially important: The use of idioms and technical terms varies with geographic dialects. "Spanish" spoken in Mexico differs from that spoken in Spain, Puerto Rico, Cuba, or Catalan. "Chinese" of one province can be completely "foreign" to those from another province. This, as the potential confusion inherent in "international symbols," is actually a factor that can *increase* the risk of casualties when an out-of-course event strikes.

The primer (and posters, and other "visuals") should also explain—using words and visual representations—the meanings conveyed by, and personal action that should follow, building alarm signals. Many "modern" alarms systems sound a variety of signals which may be difficult to distinguish or remember, and surely are confusing to visitors to the building. Such posters are especially important in conference, and training rooms, and other areas where "off-site" visitors may gather. Postings in these spaces should also incorporate prominent indication of emergency evacuation paths.

The primer for survival should be structured to encourage and enhance staff involvement ("buy-in") in the plan through (1) increasing individual awareness of the plan, what it does, and why it exists; (2) individual participation in identifying and eliminating vulnerabilities; (3) participation in reducing the level of risks present; (4) participation in helping prevent the recurrence of incidents, faults, and failures; (4) creating an environment that supports active staff participation in the plan by making peer correction easy and acceptable; and (5) establishing standards and encouraging staff members to accept responsibility for self-correction.

The primer should also include information to provide the individual with (1) procedures for evacuation of the workplace; (2) guidance on how to recognize, reduce, or minimize risks; (3) action steps to be taken when undesired events occur; (4) guidelines to assure staff safety; (5) procedures to assure the security of the corporate memory; and (6) call-in procedures when individuals wonder about what has occurred at the place, or whether it will be open.

The primer should also establish an "awareness" among the people as to the potential existence of risks, and the manner in which they should bring newly detected risks, potential vulnerabilities, and increased levels of risk to the attention of specifically designed individuals.

The primer also importantly serves to inform your *people of what the organization has done in the interests of their safety and well-being.* An interesting example of a failure in that realm was on the part of the various planners who neglected to communicate to their constituencies—especially in view of the latter's very grave concerns—the steps taken to assure that proper consideration was given to all the levels of risk associated with travel via the Channel Tunnel between England and France. Although the safety case in planning the tunnel itself, for the trains and for the railway infrastructure in the tunnel, and for the operation of the railway through the tunnel, was undoubtedly the most comprehensive, profound, and far-reaching safety planning ever undertaken (and in the opinions of many, overly excessive), the levels of safety achieved were not successfully communicated to the potential travelers through the Tunnel. Forty-one percent of people surveyed are either very worried or fairly worried about traveling in the new Channel Tunnel between the UK and France,[29] a factor surely affecting the patronage of the services! (The navigators and jellyfish mentioned elsewhere were not included in the survey!)

Keeping It All Current

It is important that your plan, and thus both your primer and manual be kept up-to-date. Your plan is not "done" when your strategy is complete, tested, and proven, and after all has been documented. Your people change, your place changes, and your processes change, and any such changes must be incorporated into the primer and the manual. Too often the value of preparedness is greatly diluted because the necessarily referred-to plan documents are simply not up-to-date.

It is vital not only to keep your plan current and up-to-date, reflecting *changes of every sort*, but also to keep your "plan support" current and up-to-date. The process of "keeping current" has two separate bases: a periodic review process, and an input process when changes occur. Both of these are essential simply because changes might be made within the organization without the realization that the change itself can affect the levels of risk of impact and of consequences. Changes, too, can affect the needs for, and levels of, countervailence and recovery plans. Changes in personnel—or *to* personnel—can affect their participation on contingency management teams.

The plan, including its documents, should be revised every time there is a change to people, place, or procedures. What this really means is that when any change occurs, the plan and its documents should be reviewed to determine any need for revision, modification, or change.

---

[29] Kathryn Wilson, Editorial Advisor, *Marketing Without Frontiers: International Version* (Basildon, England: Royal Mail International, 1994), 30.

"Change" can emanate from a variety of causes: discontinuation of BPCs, a change in their mission, or the establishment of new BPCs; a move of BPCs within the place, or to a different place; changes to the place or its infrastructure or equipment; changes to people, including changes in staffing, where the staff resides, and changes to the membership of the contingency management team; changes in the utilization of technology, the application of technology, and the type of technology; and changes in countervailence support and recovery service contracts and contacts. A woeful number of plans encounter problems when the contingency manager or management team attempts to contact staff members or services providers: People have moved, and their new area codes or telephone numbers are unknown or unlisted; the recovery service provider's organization may have a new name or have moved, and cannot be located, or has gone out of business; a listed member of the contingency management team may have retired, or been transferred and a replacement not named or not included in the manual; the list of potential problems is seemingly endless.

The typical frequent moves within the place, and changes in technology used by the BPCs and the people, often create increased power demands and telecommunications needs. In addition to wiring modifications made when the change occurs, the facility professional must consider these demands and needs in terms of auxiliary power supply and contingency plan communications. Circuit loads (both electrical power and communications capacity) should be tested periodically to assure that emergency capacities are sufficient.

Whatever changes do occur, and whatever their effect on the plan manual and primer for survival, these documents should also be reviewed on event-based and periodic basis. The plan, and its manual and primer should be reviewed each time there is a drill or practice or alert, when the plan is put into action, and on a periodic basis, probably at least every six months.

One good, potential source for input into staff listings is from the organization's human resources or personnel department, as a by-product of any change notice.

Both the primer and the manual should be published in loose-leaf format to facilitate updating of information in individual copies. Updated sheets should be prepared and distributed to all personnel who have been issued copies of the primer or manual whenever change occurs. Updated information for other personnel should be published whenever any significant change to the plan occurs. It is well to task internal auditors with the responsibility for assuring that individual copies of the primer and manual are properly at-hand and correctly maintained and updated.

At the end of the day, you will have completed your plan, and will have embodied it in the plan manual and in the primer for survival. You will have tested the plan, and made refinements or modifications, as necessary. You are ready! But do not assume that when an *actual* out-of-course event strikes, or its impact occurs, or the consequences and affects ensue, it—or they—will exactly mimic the precise scenarios you anticipated and planned for. While your plan should envision and address every conceivable situation, you must assume—and your plan be able to deal with—any situation not specifically provided for.

CHAPTER

11

MYTHS AND SOME PRECARIOUS PERCEPTIONS

There is a surprisingly great risk—a level of risk that, without question, should be unacceptably high to all stakeholders—that an organization has yet to create its strategy for disaster planning and recovery. The statistical evidence (cited elsewhere in this guide) that demonstrates the percentage of organizations that lack any disaster planning and recovery strategy might cause many sleepless nights for the facility professional: What will happen to *my* organization? What will happen to *other* organizations I so resolutely depend on? What will happen to my *job*? Among the organizations that lack a disaster planning and recovery strategy, there is a great risk that their belief (better, excuse) that nothing will happen to them *is wrong*. The time period or duration of their "being correct" is continually lessening.

There is also a great risk among those who are creating a disaster planning and recovery strategy, or who have such, that they—simply put—have not or will not go far enough and will fail to take into account all the potential out-of-course events, all their possible impacts, and, all the likely consequences and affects on people, place, and processes. That an organization is not sufficiently prepared can be as harmful as not being prepared at all: The ultimate affects in terms of continuity of operations, casualties, and damage are a factor of *what* is planned for, not whether there is *some* planning. This circumstance—planning for the risks that the computer or the telecommunications network faces—can be attributed, for the most part, to what we read in the various publications that alight on our desks (but not necessarily *illuminate*), to some advertisements we read, and seminars and tutorials we are invoked to harken. Although the authors, copywriters, and presenters probably do not intentionally try to mislead, each usually has a row to hoe or a product to sell. Let the buyer (read, the facility professional focusing on disaster planning and recovery) beware! The incorrect perceptions, and the myths, that encircle what a "disaster" is, and what a planner might do in view of this, abound.

Too many planners—or their organizations—consider themselves to be "safe and secure" and properly protected against out-of-course events of all types. This perception results, usually, because the planner *believes* that all necessary steps of preparation and prevention have been taken. Often, too, planners think—and think quite logically—about the likely impacts and probable consequences of out-of-course events or "disasters." They decide that the consequences *should be* minimal, and therefore *will be* minimal. Planners must recognize that logic might have but very little to do with the extent of the consequences and the affects on the people, the place, and on the ability of the organization to continue to function, uninterrupted, in the as-intended fashion.

Tragically, it is not until after an out-of-course event occurs, bringing impact, consequences and their affects, that the planners realize their perceptions were wrong, that their complacency was misguided, and that the organization is in a potentially irreparable mess!

"Preparation and prevention" is frequently undertaken, and is sometimes assumed to be complete and comprehensive, in assuring that people and property are "safe and secure." While some disaster planning is sometimes better than none at all, complacency can result in high risk of potential disaster. There is always an inherent danger that for want of a small incremental investment in disaster planning the "shoe may be lost" and ultimate price paid, in terms of money, time, and effort—and possibly in terms of injuries or deaths—far greater than prudent investment that was forsaken. It is incumbent upon the facility professional to replace lingering complacence with complaisance. Some actual "preparation and prevention" endeavors exemplify how small bits of preparedness could significantly lower the risks that were present.

Often, too, planners incorrectly perceive that a disaster and recovery plan can be assembled from an assortment of different elements. While this might be *possible*, it is a vital necessity that the plan be both integrated and comprehensive. A plan can be assembled from diverse building blocks but the building blocks or elements must properly fit together, leaving no gaps between them (into which the entire organization might stumble!). By like token, any assemblage of building blocks should judiciously avoid overlaps, for these can be wasteful and costly while not affording the slightest reduction in the level of risk. The totality of the plan should be determined at the outset to assure that it will be both comprehensive and its parts integrated. Each and every aspect of the plan might not be implemented at the outset because of budgetary constraints or other reasons, but whenever additional implementation can be accomplished, that which can then be undertaken will be both a "known" and a "given."

THE MYTHS

There are many, many myths surrounding the vast domain of what one can do and what one should do in the realm of disaster planning and recovery. Perhaps the most significant three myths that the facility professional may face and should recognize—in response to in *any* planning or strategy formation—are

1. We've followed all the codes and other prescriptives, *therefore*
2. It won't happen to us, *but*
3. If it does, we have insurance.

The most dangerous assumption a facility professional can make—whatever his or her area of specialization or practice encompasses—is the belief that by following all the prescriptives applicable, the level of risk that any out-of-course event will occur, impact, and create consequences and affects, has been reduced to an absolute minimum. *This oft-held belief is simply not true.*[1] The risks, and the levels of those residual risks, present when in compliance with all prescriptives must be determined and compared with the levels of risks that would result after precautions *in addition to the prescriptives* have been taken. It then becomes incumbent upon the facility professional to determine the incremental costs:benefit value of the additional precautions in terms of casualties (both deaths and injuries) to people avoided; of damage or harm to the

---

[1] A tragic example of this occurred in a December 1995 fire at the Philadelphia Zoo. Twenty-three rare primates were killed, and ten others seriously injured. In addition to the loss of the animals—which cannot be replaced "from the wild"—there was much bereavement among the Philadelphia Zoo staff as well as in zoo communities throughout the world. It was reported that "the building, opened in 1985, had smoke detectors but not an automatic sprinkler system. The law does not require one." A question that cannot be avoided is, What steps were taken to determine the incremental reduction in risk of death or injury to these rare animals if sprinklers were installed, and at what cost?

place prevented or minimized; and of interruptions to the business processes precluded, reduced, or compensated for. You cannot assume that following all the prescriptives will result in risk levels as low as reasonably practicable.

The facility professional *may think* (or wish to believe!) that an out-of-course event will not occur or impact the patch they plan, manage, or administer. The truth is that it is not a question of *if* an out-of-course event will strike and impact their patch, wroughting consequences and other bad stuff, but a question of *when and where* the impact and consequences will occur.

That *we have insurance* may be true, but whether there is *coverage* in an inescapable consideration in disaster planning and recovery. There are several vital questions for the facility professional to deal with concerning the insurance: Of primary importance is the question whether or not the policy covers *all* the potential out-of-course events, impacts, consequences and affects for which there is a risk of occurrence present. Next, the facility professional must determine whether or not the organization or business or *modus operandi* is in compliance with *all* the provisions and requirements of the insurance policy. (This necessitates the dreadful undertakings of *reading and understanding* the policy, and determining compliance.) *Then*, if there is both adequate coverage *and* complete compliance, will the policy value (if collected!) cover the loss? Just what is the value of what might be lost? What is the value of a day's business? Of a week's business? *Of the business*? The stark reality may be that one cannot place a value on the potential loss; if the loss does occur, it may not be compensated for!

It is important to remember, when considering insurance coverage, that many of the out-of-course events that may strike your facility *may not be covered* under a "stock" or "off-the-shelf" policy. Some out-of-course events—potential problems—may warrant coverage and it may be necessary for you to purchase additional or extended protection. You, when planning insurance coverage, must keep in mind that insurance companies are not in business to pay you when you suffer a loss. Insurance companies are in business to make a profit, and that profit is based on paying the least possible in claims. Obviously, insurance companies *do* pay claims when warranted under the policy coverage, but it would be rare indeed for any insurance company to reimburse for a loss that is outside of the coverage simply because of their sympathy toward you or your organization.

Coverage, exclusions, and compliance with policy provisions should be reviewed when the insurance is first written, and reviewed, periodically thereafter, especially coincident with changes in space utilization and computerization. Additions of equipment and changes in types of technology utilized can result in incomplete coverage, underinsurance, a greater burden in coinsurance, or exclusions from coverage.

A sometimes-neglected consideration is the actual insurance agent who provides insurance counsel, and from whom the coverage is purchased. Using a relative or friend (or some executive's relative or friend) as the insurance resource can prove a grave dis-service. Simply put, some of these people, otherwise quite competent, may not be as familiar with the intricacies of the coverage required, and the nature of the policies as other specialists in the field. Favors and friendships can prove extremely costly if a loss is incurred and the thought-to-be coverage is not in-place, or compliance was not in keeping with requirements.

In some instances, insurance coverage is purchased but not needed. This can occur—in a "micro" sense—when the level of risk of a particular loss is ALARP or acceptably low, and the replacement represents a lesser potential cost than the cost of the premium. In these instances, the insurance carrier is placing the same bets on the same horse as you are, and it is a track where you need tread carefully. In a "macro" sense, an organization may reduce the amount of space it occupies but neglect to have the change incorporated into insurance coverage, and thus pay for coverage that is not necessary. Conversely, there may be an increase in the amount of space occupied, or a change of where within the building a particular square footage is situated. You should notify your insurance carrier (in writing, of course, to reduce the risk of such notification being lost or neglected!) when instances of this ilk are about to occur.

Whether or not there is compliance with the provisions of an insurance policy will undoubtedly be a determinant in whether or not a claim is paid. Provisions of compliance vary greatly: Valuable document coverage will doubtlessly specify that the documents are protected in a specific manner when not in use. Coverage for fire damage may be negated if certain doors are propped open, or if automatic closure devices are faulty, or if fire extinguishers are not properly placed or fit for their intended purpose. The vulnerability search can reveal deficiencies of this nature.

Another often-encountered myth (actually, also a *belief* held by many planners) is that the level of risk of occurrence of many (if not all) "disasters" can be reduced to zero. This belief—often held integral in planning strategies—is simply not true. *Every risk*, by its very nature, *is >0*. As a facility professional, you would love risk levels to be zero, and you try everything possible to achieve them. But the real world provides you with risks—risks that out-of-course events will occur, risks that these events will impact people, place, or processes, and risks that such impacts will have consequences and affects that prevent the organization from functioning in its as-intended manner or from functioning at all. Each and every one of these risks is inescapable but not irreducible. You have to determine *how much* risk (how high a level of risk) you can tolerate in the myriad of unique situations that comprise the organization you are a part of, or deal with, and create the disaster planning and recovery strategy on that groundwork.

Many of the other myths surround what you might do to reduce risks, and how simple it is to accomplish the reductions. Were that these myths be true, disaster planning would be a simple task, and all organizations would have a workable, reliable, inexpensive strategy in place.

There is another myth surrounding the creation of a disaster planning and recovery strategy that perils some (actually, *very, very many*) planners who recognize that the codes and prescriptives alone *might not* afford sufficient protection, and that something *may* happen to their organization, and that if it does, insurance alone *will not be able to save the business*. This myth is that the organization's computing resources as an entity is all that the strategy must encompass. Some "far-thinking" individuals also include telecommunications resources.

The PC-Based Planning Software Myths

Too many planners have been duped into believing that a comprehensive, integrated, *workable* disaster planning and recovery strategy can be achieved—and thus, the organization "saved"—by (1) purchasing a PC-based "disaster planning" software package; (2) inputting into the database all the called-for information; and, (3) simply "running" the program when the out-of-course event strikes. *Voilà*: The information that will appear on the screen gives you all the guidance and information you require to save your organization!

Over 26 different companies (in the U.S., 1995) provided some type of PC software packages, offered at a extremely wide range of base prices from $259.95 to over $90,000, strongly suggesting that there well may be some differences in what a particular program can do for you. In another survey (U.S., 1996) 23 companies were identified as offering "disaster-recovery-planning software packages."[2] Twenty-one of these were priced between $495 and $89,990; two indicated "contact vendor." Forty-six "features" were compared, although the *concepts of "risk management," "modeling and simulation," and "ALARP" were conspicuous by their*

---

[2] Sarah L. Cain, "The Planning Game," *Infosecurity News,* May/June 1996, 36+.

absence, making a sensible choice based on the information provided impossible.

Of the many packages on the market, each has its own strengths and its own weaknesses, making comparisons far from absolute. The suitability, and the applicability, of any package to your organization's needs is a factor of the type and nature of the plan to be developed, the planners' levels of expertise, the nature of the organization's business, as well as—very importantly—the amount of specific factors or elements you wish the plan to encompass. In selecting the package to aid you in implementing your strategy, you should—to paraphrase the late President John F. Kennedy—ask not what the package can do for you, but ask if it can do what you require to be done! Do not fool yourself into thinking that any software package will do everything necessary to create a plan based on a fill-in-the-blanks exercise. It is altogether possible that there will not be any suitable package found to accomplish what (or all of what!) your organization needs.

Incredibly, the very survival of organizations worth millions or even billions of dollars is often entrusted to a data base costing just a few thousand dollars (or even much less!) that will do little more than a pencil and a piece of paper, or to a routine that might only revive the computer system. The chasm between the information that such data bases typically provide for and what *should be recorded* is usually very wide. This chasm can usually be bridged with little incremental expenditures of money, time, and effort, but this need is seldom recognized, and rarely taken into account. Packages tend to provide "Yes" or "No" answers in instances where exact, quantitative information is necessary to create a (1) workable, and (2) cost-effective plan. Packages tend to provide for "events outside of your control" without consideration of events for which the *risk of occurrence* can be reduced. And in any event, the computer- or PC-based plan might not be accessible due to conditions of the out-of-course event itself!

The marketplace does not want for other products—both publications and seminars—that, for a token price, will be able to solve all your disaster planning and recovery strategy requirements. It would seem that by either purchasing (and reading!) one of these guides, or attending one of these presentations (and listening!), all your problems will be solved. Representative of these, with their sponsorship omitted, are a

- Business Recovery Planning Guide ($259.95).
- Disaster Recovery Planning Seminar ($1260). "You can't always prevent disaster, but you *can* recover quickly. Whether you are just beginning the disaster planning process or wish to validate

or upgrade your existing recovery plan, this seminar should be at the top of your agenda." Stated benefits include, "Negotiate/ obtain recovery support to minimize damage," "Address backup alternatives to ensure business continuity," "Take advantage of the latest developments by updating your plan on a regular basis," and "Ensure business survival through resumption of critical business activity and primary mission."

■ Disaster Recovery Planning ($350). Student will learn the skills necessary for designing a working disaster recovery plan to offset the effects of catastrophes. Students will learn: Disaster Survival Procedures, Organizational Charts and Facility Plans, How to Organize a Backup Facility, Critical Applications, Data Protection, Backing Up File Procedures, and Maintaining MIS Contingency Plans.

■ Better Facility Safety and Security ($159). Gain the skills you need to maintain facility user safety. Learn how much illumination your emergency lighting systems should provide.

■ When disaster strikes locate the crucial, hard-to-find services you need to get your operations back to normal ($98). A publication listing over 2300 vendors in over 300 categories including consulting services, drying and dehumidification, smoke odor counteraction, alternate sites, emergency equipment sources, software, training, publications, and associations.[3]

Aside, if "software" is *the* answer, then surely a two-day seminary and exhibition on "how to make the best business continuity and disaster recovery software purchase decisions"—wherein over half of the dozen speakers were representatives of packaged software providers—will prove to be invaluable!

The Data Recovery Myth

There are some who believe that the organization's data (its computer-based memory) (and even possibly its information—the paper-based memory!) need not be archived or protected, or that "data warehousing" will provide sufficient "backup" if original data is not at-hand. In addition to the problematic *unavailable*—was the data or information saved in the first instance—and *unaccessible*—can you get at it or to it—it is

---

[3] Any value of the listings notwithstanding, prudent planning demands that the facility professional locate, investigate, and establish a working relation—preferably a contract—with *each* organization that *might* be needed *before the problem occurs*.

assumed that magic wand of data recovery will breathe new life into the seemingly demised disks and tapes and paper. While much *might* be recovered and usable, the planner must consider that the process is (1) time consuming; (2) not always complete; (3) sometimes impossible; (4) not always feasible on a timely basis; and (5) very frequently, quite expensive. Reliance should be on data (and information!) protection, rather than on possible recovery.

The "911" Myth

That "911" (which some telephone companies and emergency services present as "9-1-1") is a universally available, universally usable service is, simply, *not true!* Whether one can dial "911" and reach an emergency services dispatcher is a factor of (1) the telephone exchange through which your call is placed, and (2) where you located geographically. Some telephones served by a PBX—although clearly labeled IN EMERGENCY DIAL 911—actually require that "9" or "8" or other access number be dialed first. In vulnerability searches, so-labeled telephones are often found, yet are "restricted" so that a caller cannot access "911."

NYNEX advised their deaf, hard of hearing, and speech-disabled customers "you can dial a special 3-1-1 number to report an emergency." What is *not* clear is that a Teletypewriter is required. The announcement also noted, "People [deaf, hard of hearing and speech-disabled?] who live in areas [served by NYNEX or anywhere?] where 9-1-1 is not available or cannot be reached can dial 3-1-1 [is a Teletypewriter connection necessary?]."

The UPS Myth

A "powerful" myth surrounds what is—and what is not—a UPS. Many believe that plug-in devices that provide some elements of power conditioning (but rarely, in fact, little more than basic surge protection) provide—somehow—uninterrupted power to the plugged-in computer or other device if the usual source of power is interrupted. This is probably more than a myth: It is outrightly incorrect!

Other "power-full" myths emerge from semantics: an advertisement for one power-protection device observes that an uninterruptable power supply (UPS) device is thought unnecessary because "over 90% of common power interruptions (surges, sages, spikes, and failures) last less than ½-second . . . [and] a standby UPS will miss most interruptions. . . ." *If* this truly characterizes the power supplied to your facility, determine (1) the level of risk that the characterization might eventually be wrong; and (2) what are impacts on, and consequences to and affects on, the as-intended functioning of BPCs when the other 10% of "common power interruptions" occur. What would be the incremental cost for reducing the risk of power interruption ALARP?

The Myth of What Disaster Planning and Recovery *Is*

Disaster planning and recovery *is neither* accident prevention *nor* safety (although accident prevention and safety are elements therein); it is not insurance to provide business interruption loss reimbursement or lost profits reimbursement; it is not fire protection; and, it is not safety engineering (although these are potential risk-reduction techniques).

The Myth of Certification

Another "myth" is that of *certification*. It is increasingly popular (and, presumably, for the individual concerned, important) to be able to place some initials after one's name. "Ph.D." or "C.P.A." or "M.D." or "A.I.A." need little explanation, and convey accreditation and infer competency. In British (or formerly British) countries, awards and certain memberships (Bart., KG, VC, FCIT) convey heritage, stature, or accomplishment. In the disaster planning / contingency planning / recovery planning fields, many practitioners have become "professionals" and identify themselves as "CDRP" [Certified Disaster Recovery Planner] or "CMDRP" or "CPP" [sorry! unable to find meanings] or receive entitlement to use "Fellow" or "Member" (of a certain organization) "in formal correspondence."[4]

Without casting aspersions on any individual using such identification, it is important for the facility professional planning to gain counsel from such persons to investigate the basis of the designation. Is it "awarded" by an independent accreditation body, or by what amounts to a business organization? Can some requirements for the "award" be accrued by simply attending a (costly) conference sponsored by the organization? What cross-pricing arrangements exist between the conference sponsor and the and the organization?

It is important that you, as a facility professional, or as a planner in any other role, recognize that any individuals selected to provide planning assistance and counsel (not in the legal sense alone) must be judged

---

[4] If a consideration in your choice of someone to assist in creating a disaster planning and recovery strategy is their "certification," you might wish to reduce the risk of a "wrong" choice by requesting to review the underlying "certification standards" and "units of competence." The element of surprise can be very real indeed.

and evaluated as to their individual proven competencies and experience as such, without placing undue—or any—reliance on a certification that *might not* give proof to that individual's ability to contribute to *increasing the level of risk of survival* of your organization.

A cautionary bit of advice: Any treatise (or computer disk!) on this subject or on a topic of this nature cannot be within the framework of a "kit" or a "fill-in-the-blanks" outline that will be, when completed, a plan workable for all organizations under any circumstances. At the end of any attempt to shortcut the planning process lies a vast abyss, filled with a highly probable inherent danger and potential pitfall: The plan is likely not to function at the time and in the manner for which it is intended. In another age, in other terms, it was said that, "A machine, called an *automaton* [which] was, not long since, constructed. This was designed to transport from place to place, by land, any load without the aid of horses, oxen, or any other animal. The master was to sit at helm, and guide it up hill and down, and over every kind of road. This machine was completed, and proved demonstrably capable of performing the duties assigned to it, and the only difficulty which attended it, and which hath hitherto prevented its universal use, was, *that it would not go*."[5] In *your* planning, you must take all steps necessary to assure that your plan will *go*, and will be able to carry its load!

Beware of the myths, and away with the fairies . . .

---

[5] David Daggett, *An Oration Pronounced On the Fourth of July, 1799, At the Request of the Citizens of New-Haven* (New-Haven: Thomas Green and Son, 1799).

APPENDIX

I

THE *BEFORE, DURING, AND AFTER* CHECKLIST

The disaster planning and recovery strategy you create—your plan—
should be molded to consider every potential problem, each of its potential impacts, and each potential consequence and affect that can ensue.
These must be viewed in terms of the three perspectives of time: *Before*
an out-of-course event or impact or consequence and affect takeplace;
During the incident; and *After* it has transpired. These *Before, During,
and After* considerations are related to the out-of-course events themselves as well as to the organization's overall planning strategy.

    This checklist includes illustrative items or areas that should be
considered in the course of a comprehensive and full exploration of what
might occur—and the means to deal with such occurrences—in each of
the three temporal aspects of a problem or out-of-course event. A list of
this sort, by its nature, cannot be all-inclusive or complete; it is presented
as a sort of "road map" describing a course to be followed. It does not
display all the turns and curves, stop signs and yield signs, limits and
restrictions, rest areas, nor any one-way cautions. These each—and all—
emerge from the nature of your planning and of your organization, and
what have been established as your goals and objectives.

    This list, like others in the guide, is presented in alphabetic order
rather than arranged in hierarchical importance, or in the sequence in
which the items might be approached. The crucial point is that they *all*
be considered.

BEFORE

■ Conduct the three-part vulnerability search, vulnerability analysis, and vulnerability rectification. (See Chapter 7 and Appendix II.) This process includes:

The search: (1) Determine what—in terms of people, place, and processes—is vulnerable to the impact of each potential out-of-course event that might possibly occur. (2) Determine the consequences of each such impact that might possibly occur. The search process identifies the risks present.

The analysis: Continuing into the analysis: (3) Determine *if* and *how* each consequence following any impact of an out-of-course event will *affect* the people, the place, or the processes. (4) Decide which affects are acceptable, and the time spans for acceptability, and which affects are not acceptable. (5) Measure or formulate the level of risk inherent in the occurrence of each out-of-course event that would impact people, place, or processes. (6) Measure or formulate the level of risk associated with each possible consequence that might occur. (7) Measure or formulate the level of risk associated with each possible affect that might occur. (8) Judge which of the levels of risk are as low as reasonably practicable (ALARP). (9) Judge which of the levels of risk are "acceptable." (10) Judge which of the levels of risk are neither ALARP nor "acceptable." The assessment process determines what is at-risk, measures the levels of the risks that are present, and judges the acceptability of such levels.

The rectification: Continuing into the rectification phase: (11) Reduce, to a level as low as reasonably practicable (ALARP)—or to an acceptable level—each possible consequence and each possible affect not previously judged ALARP or "acceptable." (12) Establish steps and procedures to countervail each consequence and each affect that might occur even thought the level of risk of such occurrence is ALARP or is "acceptable."

In addition, conduct vulnerability "re-searches," vulnerability "re-analyses," and vulnerability "re-rectifications" on periodic basis, and when there are changes to the place (including the allocation of space, the infrastructure, equipment, and furnishings); to the people (including changes to staff, and changes in responsibilities); to the processes; or to the technology, equipment, or facilities used by or for the people, place, or processes. The VS/

VA/VR process should also be undertaken when any members of the staff suggest or report the presence or existence of "vulnerabilities."

■ Conduct an audit of insurance coverage (an exclusions), and of compliance with policy provisions.

■ Conduct, on a established periodic basis, tests and drills of all aspects of the plan. Revise or modify the plan (and its plan manual and the primer for survival) based on test and drill experience.

■ Create, publish, and distribute plan documents (the plan manual and the primer for survival). Revise these plan documents whenever changes to the plan occur, or when there are changes to CMT or other information. Distribution should be on a "need to know" basis; the CM and CMT members should be provided with copies for homes and for their automobiles. Provision should be made for recipient's acknowledgment of receipt of revisions. Create, publish, and distribute other plan "communication tools" such as wayfinding signage, alarm identification, and emergency telephone numbers.

■ Establish contracts (1) for damage mitigation services; (2) for alternate ("hot-" or other) sites to enable continuity of services and products to be provided; and (3) for recovery and cleanup services. The key to effective contracting and planning is the determination of what to save, what to save first, and where it located within the place, and furnishing the service providers with current information concerning this.

■ Establish contracts for catering and lodging when staff are unable to leave the place or its vicinity.

■ Establish contracts for transport of staff to and from the alternate sites, and for catering and lodging for staff working there. Store stocks of current supplies and stationery at the site.

■ Establish data base to assure directed, coordinated responses to emergencies and out-of-course events.

■ Furnish the contingency manager and the contingency management team members with hard hats, insulated gloves, flashlights, "bull horns," gas masks, and smoke masks.

■ Investigate faults, failures, and other incidents. Whenever any fault or failure of infrastructure or equipment is reported or noted or detected, the cause should be investigated and remedial action taken.

■ Maintain—or *create and maintain*—a comprehensive index of the organization's memory (its information and data). A copy of this index, indicating file locations, storage box numbers and locations, and other storage information, should be maintained both on-site and off-site in a secure location.

- Monitor, on a ongoing basis, the quality of air both within and outside the building.
- Protect the organization's building, infrastructure equipment, furnishings, and other assets.
- Protect the organization's information and data to assure availability, accessibility, and usability when and where needed through retention and archiving of records, and use of alternate storage sites.
- Provide first-aid equipment. Maintain (and replenish or re-fresh on a timely basis) supplies of food, water, and medicines.
- Provide for personal security, especially for high-profile personnel. Establish CPR and first-aid training programs. Provide for on-call nurses and doctors, ambulance and EMT services, and hospital-of-choice. Establish policies for travel to "unsafe" cities and countries, and for air travel.
- Provide training, especially for the CMT, to help in their performance of duties and responsibilities under stress conditions.
- Provide for the coverage of contingency manager and contingency management team responsibilities in the event of absences, shifts, days off, off-site activities, and vacations.
- Record all the organization's fixed and other assets, including equipment, furnishings, and other property. Update with regularity (including additions and deletions) and provide *a copy* for the CMC. Maintain *a copy* a part of vital records (presumably stored off-site).

DURING

- Document, using (preferably color) video- or photographic media, damage or harm to people, place, and processes during the course of impact and after the impact has occurred. Automatic imposition, by the recording device, of time and date should be used (ascertain that the date and time—Daylight Savings or Standard) are correct. The documentation process itself—in part or in toto—must not increase the level of risk of injury or death to CMT members doing the recording. The videos or photos should record the removal of any items—and the damage sustained by them—from the building or site for damage mitigation, restoration, repair, safe-keeping, or for other reasons. Video or photo records should also be made of any people being treated for injuries or removed to hospital, and of any corpses being removed from the site.[1] The documentation process should preferably "over-record" rather than "under-record"—editing or selection can be done afterward; omissions judged in retrospect cannot be restaged.

■ Record, utilizing preprinted logs provided in the manual, the date, time, and the *message presented*, all notifications (1) to emergency services, (2) to the CM and to CMT members, (3) to alternate sites, (4) to damage mitigation and restoration services, and (5) as well as to any others notified of the event, such as customers, suppliers, the press or other tenants at the site or in the building. The log should indicate whether the message was given in person, to another person, or left on an answering machine. Individual responses, or acknowledgments to the notification, should be recorded. The on-site arrival times of services, equipment, staff, and of other personnel or individuals, should be recorded. The recording process should preferably "over-record" rather than "under-record"—editing or selection can be done afterward; omissions judged in retrospect cannot be easily or accurately reconstructed.

AFTER

■ Document, using (preferably color) video- or photographic media, all damaged assets (infrastructure, equipment, furnishing, and other property) before being cleaned, repaired, or restored on-site, or before removal from the site. Document, before their disposal, all assets damaged beyond restoration or repair. The documentation process should preferably "over-record" rather than "under-record"—editing or selection can be done afterward; omissions judged in retrospect cannot be re-staged

■ Evaluate the plan, the plan manual, and the CMT-member performances during and after the impact of the out-of-course event to determine if possible change or modification to the Plan is warranted.

---

[1] The CMT members engaged in the documentation (as well as the CM and other members of the CMT) should be on the alert for increasing-common instances where "outsiders" "jump into" or enter the impact zone or areas and assert that they were present when the out-of-course event took place. These individuals claim that they sustained injuries or other harm, and will undoubtedly initiate litigation.

APPENDIX

II

THE VULNERABILITY SEARCH: A MODEL VULNERABILITY SEARCH CHECKLIST

THE VULNERABILITY SEARCH

Your quest for vulnerabilities must be as broad in scope as is possible to assure that the ultimate level of an risk of out-of-course event (potential problem) occurring (becoming a problem), and that the level of risk that a problem will impact people, place, or processes, and that the level of risk that any impact will result in consequence(s) and ensuing affect(s) upon the people, place, or processes *each be made as low as reasonably practicable* (ALARP). That the *ultimate* risk be ALARP is not only the purpose of a disaster planning and recovery strategy, but is also an inescapable factor in your creation of a plan.

Some of the vulnerabilities—conditions—that you will encounter can be the potential *source* of an out-of-course event. Some, the possible *target* or potential *impact object* of an out-of-course event. Certain vulnerabilities, in fact, can be either the source of the out-of-course event (creating the impact) *or* the target of the impact (creating the consequences), depending upon the circumstances present. In your search, such items should be analyzed both *as a source* and/or *as a target*. In your analysis, you must consider the *consequences and affects* of the *impact* on its *target* and/or ultimately, on the people, place, and processes. You also must consider, too, how the *impact* will effect the recovery process—the restoration to as-intended functioning. It is necessary to identify each vulnerability so that you can (1) determine the risk associated with it, and (2) reduce the level of risk ALARP or to an acceptable level.

The checklist is not confined to "disasters" exclusively. Your search, analysis, and rectification processes should not only stalk conditions directly related to "disasters" but also should pursue items of "safety" and of "security" that are relevant to the well-being of people, fitness of the place, and continuity of the processes conducted.

Some conditions are site-related; some building-related; some, associated with the space within a building that the organization occupies, or is considering occupying; other conditions are associated with the business processes themselves. It is especially important to conduct a VS/VA/VR prior to committing to occupy a space. Some conditions listed are site-related (remember, the "site" can be extensive or just the plot on which the building is situate); these are especially important considerations when contemplating a move. Generally, there is limited opportunity for reduction in risk level for conditions associated with a site. If any risk level is unacceptable, you have two alternatives: First, you can either not move to the site, or, if you occupy the site, you can move. The second alternative is to remain, focusing on reducing the level of risks of out-of-course events occurring, of an out-of-course event creating an impact, reducing the level of risks that consequences and affects will ensue, as well as increasing the level of risk of survival of the people, place, and processes through providing proper recovery strategy and resources.

Building-related, and space-related conditions apply to the building and the space your organization occupies, to space any other tenants may occupy, and to common-use or common-purpose spaces such as building infrastructure, equipment, facilities, lobbies, corridors, stairwells, and machinery rooms. Although you probably have greater opportunity for risk-reduction for the conditions in the space your organization leases or occupies, some risks elsewhere in the building may be unacceptably high and offer no opportunity for reduction. Your alternatives to unacceptable levels of risk are the same as for site-related conditions.

Business-related conditions apply to the procedures that have been established to conduct business processes, and the environments in which they are conducted, including equipment and furnishings, systems and procedures, and administrative and operational practices. These conditions, characterized by the fact that the organization can exert full control, can be subject to frequent change (and resultant change in risk level) because of new or changed business processes, technology utilization, space allocation and furnishings, or staffing.

In some ways, this checklist is a Baedeker or travel guide. While it points up, highlights, and summarizes numerous essential conditions to be checked in the course of a vulnerability search, no suggested list can be absolute in its coverage. In the course of the vulnerability search, one must be alert for *les curiosités les plus marquentes*[1] wherein vulnerabilities—real and potential—might lurk.

There are some items on the vulnerability search checklist describing "permanent" or "semipermanent" conditions, such as the width of aisles or the provision of emergency lighting devices. Other items cover "transitory" conditions, such as storage of materials in the aisles, or whether the emergency lighting devices function as-intended. The vulnerability search should be conducted not only in the course of establishing your plan, but also periodically once the plan has been formalized in the plan manual and the primer for survival. Special emphasis should be focused on the "transitory" conditions, not only in the periodic, repeat vulnerability searches, but also in the course of day-to-day management of the place.

As no two places, or their people, or their processes are alike, it is most important to recognize that this is *not an exhaustive list*, but a memory-jogger suggesting not only some of the specific vulnerabilities you should search for, but also the range and variety of circumstances for which you must be vigilant, and incorporate in your own VS/VA/VR catalogue. The sharp-eyed vulnerability searcher or search teams will undoubtedly be able to annex a substantial number of other conditions to this checklist!

PREPARING YOUR OWN VULNERABILITY SEARCH CHECKLIST

The most important consideration in preparing a checklist for your own use is that it fully covers not only the *space* your rent or lease, but also the *site and building* you occupy or tenant. The *site and building* includes—in addition to your organization's spaces—everyone else's space, common-use spaces, support systems and infrastructure space, as well as any "open" space. You must search not only in your tenanted or rentable space, but also the roof, the basements (importantly, "basements" is plural), the corridors and lobbies, parking garages, and spaces occupied by contiguous tenants; all of these need provision in your checklist.

---

[1] *Pardon!* Unusual things that are quite hidden.

In selecting items from this model for incorporation into your own, formalized checklist, you should not create clutter (and its inherently resultant less-than-careful reportage). If you are in a one-story building without elevators, do not include items related to elevators. If your place does not have an emergency electric generator, do not include items relevant to such equipment. (But save the latter pages; the vulnerability rectification might prompt installation of an emergency power generator, and the pages will be indispensable in future VS/VA/VR undertakings!)

For each of the items on the checklist the searcher should indicate (by tick-mark) what he or she has discovered. There are four useful categories: (1) **Immediate attention required**. (2) **Potential problem**. (3) **Acceptable**. (4) **Not applicable**. Space should be provided for entry of cross-references [discussed below] and for comments or remarks, especially for both the first and second categories. An example would be *fire extinguishers* in the outdoor parking lot. *If* there were none—and the searcher did not perceive the need for any—then **not applicable** would be checked. If there were fire extinguishers provided, these would be cross-referenced and checked (for correct type, proper charge, accessibility, etc.) on the fire extinguisher portion of the checklist (where, obviously, *each* extinguisher would be categorized for **immediate attention required** [if, for example, an extinguisher was missing, damaged, discharged, or of the incorrect type], as **acceptable** [everything fit, correct and as-intended], or as a **potential problem** [nearing re-charge level or date, or mounted too high]).

An example—perhaps, an ultimate example—of an **immediate attention required** condition was encountered in a VS of a museum. There were *extreme* concerns about emergency egress if evacuation was necessary. Of the three "emergency" exits (in additional to the single normal entry- and exit-way), one was gated, chained, and locked (with the key located in an office some distance from that exit); another was "permanently blocked"; and the stairway landing of third was used to store a 55-gallon drum, on its side, of a highly inflammable paint solvent. The spigot fitted to the drum did not close properly, and a 5-gallon container used to catch the drippage was partially filled with the dangerous liquid. The drum would be a potential bomb in the event of a fire; a fire could easily ignite because of the inflammable and explosive fumes confined in the stairwell; and, the fumes themselves—even if not inflammable or explosive—were surely harmful to breathe! Indeed, a situation where there was **immediate attention required!**

A **potential problem** exists when (1) the item or condition being considered could (a) cause or result in injuries to people, or deaths; (b) cause or result in harm or damage to the place; or (c) interrupt, impede, impair, or halt process(es) when that item or condition is impacted by a problem or out-of-course event, or by the consequences of that impact; or, when (2) the item or condition being considered is itself at-risk, and could be the cause of an out-of-course event that could cause or result in injuries or deaths, or could cause or result in harm or damage to the place, or could interrupt, impede, impair, or bring process(es) to a halt. Potential problems warrant prompt, if not immediate, consideration: the analysis process must address what is at risk, the level of that risk, the impact, and the consequences and affects, as well as what can be done to reduce the risks to a level ALARP.

Mention was made of cross-referencing. There are several items on the "primary" checklist (e.g., alarms, emergency lighting, fire extinguishers) which warrant consideration beyond a simple "present" or "not present." These are identified with an "†". Model item-specific checklists are provided for these. The item-specific checklists you derive should be consecutively numbered before commencing the search. The searcher should enter the cross-reference consecutive number on the "primary" list, and enter the additional information on the item-specific list.

A SEARCH METHODOLOGY

Your search should commence at the outer-most limits of the site or place, and progress inward to the building itself. The building's exterior should be considered first, followed by "entering" and consideration of lobby, reception, or common areas located on the ground floor. The building search should commence *on* the roof with observation of the structures there such as cooling towers, water storage tanks, helicopter landing pads, and the roof surface itself. That completed, or at the same time, the individual *storys* should be individually checked, starting at the highest and working downward.

The search should extend to the below-grade levels including basements and sub-basements, boiler rooms, hoistways, machinery rooms, storage areas, below-sidewalk vaults, passageways, pipe chambers, electric and telephone cable vaults, as well as *everything else* that might be down there (although some of such spaces might not be too pleasant to inspect!). Bridgeways between or connecting buildings should also be searched for vulnerabilities.

On all levels, it is important—nay, *vital*—to open and inspect what is behind those "mysterious" doors which no one seems to know about, and for which no one has the keys. Rather than bypassing such locked doors, have them forced open!

It is important to search for *both the conditions that appear on this model checklist* as well as *like or similar conditions that might be present at or in your facility, but are not on this list.*

Site-Associated Conditions

■ Is site address and identification clearly visible from *all* adjacent public roads and highways?

■ Is there a directory of the site near the site entry?

■ Are individual building addresses and identifications clearly visible from on-site roads?

■ Are company names clearly visible from adjacent public roads and highways? (This is something you may *not* want if organization or its people are some way "sensitive.")

■ Can *all* on-site roads and bridges support the weights of fire and other emergency vehicles?

■ Is there sufficient clearance on *all* on-site underpasses for fire and other emergency vehicles?[2]

■ Is there sufficient clearance in parking garages to permit entry of fire and other emergency vehicles?

■ Is there sufficient clearance under "truck exclusion arches" to permit entry of fire and other emergency vehicles?

■ Can parking areas support the weight of fire and other emergency vehicles?

■ Are there any high voltage, or very high voltage power lines (overhead or underground) on the site or nearby? (These can be a source of EMFs or may attract lightning.)

■ Are there any electric railways or trams nearby (possible source of EMFs)?

---

[2] On November 6, 1995, a fire struck—and almost completely destroyed—the Rova, the Queen's Palace in Antananarivo, Madagascar. The catastrophic fire was likened to "Westminster Abbey, the Tower of London, and Buckingham Palace being destroyed at once." The Rova wasn't just the country's only significant monument; it was also the tomb of seven kings and queens. The estimated costs for restoring the Rova were $20 million, an impossible sum for one of the poorest countries on earth. "The first task," said Nalisoa Ravalitera, director of the Madagascar Culture Ministry's Department of National Patrimony, "is to build a ramp around the entrance arch so that the next time fire engines can get in." ("A Palace Inferno Sears Madagascar's Very Soul," Donald G. McNeil, Jr., *New York Times*, 22 June 1996, 2.)

■ Are there any radio, television, radar, microwave transmitters, relays on site or nearby (possible source of EMFs)?

■ Are there any water courses—rivers or streams—on site or nearby?

■ Is there any tidal water near site?

■ Are there any underground water courses beneath building or site?

■ Are there any changing water tables beneath building or site?

■ Are there any buried high-pressure gas mains beneath building or site or nearby?

■ Are there any buried petroleum pipelines beneath building or site or nearby?

■ Do freight railways pass near building or site (possible leakage of hazardous substances)?

■ Do trucks carrying hazardous substances routinely pass near building or site?

■ Are locations of siamese connections clearly indicated and visible from roadways?

■ Are *standpipe* and *sprinkler* siamese connections clearly distinguished, and correctly color-coded?

■ Are the connections free of foreign matter, and properly protected?

■ Are sprinkler system shutoffs clearly and correctly indicated?

■ Are hydrants correctly placed and oriented to enable prompt hookup with fire apparatus?

■ Are electricity supply shutoffs clearly marked?

■ Are gas (mains- or tank-supplied) shutoff valves clearly and correctly marked?

■ Are proper wrenches provided, and securely attached, where needed, for water and gas shutoffs?

■ Are vegetation growth and snow accumulations routinely removed from fire hydrants, siamese connections, and shutoff valves?

■ Are the courses of buried electrical cables clearly and correctly marked?

■ Are the courses of buried pipelines clearly and correctly marked?

■ Are the courses of buried telecommunications cables clearly and correctly marked?

Building-Associated Conditions

The Building: General

■ Is there clear identification of the address from exterior sidewalks and roadways?

- Are company names clearly visible from sidewalks and roadways? (This is something you may *not* want if organization or its people are some way "sensitive".)
- Are the locations of fire department standpipe and sprinkler siamese connections clearly marked? Are they readily accessible?
- Are exterior standpipe and sprinkler shutoff valves clearly marked? Are they readily accessible?
- Are *interior* sprinkler system shutoffs secured in the *open* position? Are they clearly and correctly indicated? Are the security chains, locks, or other devices provided with "break-away" links or locks?
- Are standpipe connections and hoses in good order?

The Building: Management

- How often are *building* fire drills conducted? Is there 100% participation? Are some drills conducted during lunch hours? During second and third shifts? During weekends?
- How often are *building* evacuation drills conducted? Is there 100% participation? Are some evacuation drills conducted during lunch hours? During second and third shifts? During weekends?
- Does *building management* have a "contingency management team" designated for all shifts? During weekends? Does the CMT have portable, emergency lights? "Bull horns?" Are CMT members trained in first aid? In CPR?

The Building: Access Control

- Is there a readily available building directory at main entry? (If this is computer-based, is there an up-to-date "hard copy" for use of emergency service personnel when there is a power failure?)
- Do the evacuation paths and placement of doors in lobby or ground-floor common areas assure the risk of casualties in any evacuation is ALARP? Are the navigation paths and doors properly marked†?
- Are any evacuation path egress doors normally locked or secured during normal business hours?
- Are any evacuation path egress doors normally locked or secured during second and third shifts? During weekends? Who has the keys to locked egress doors?
- If access control is computer-based, what "control" remains active if the computers are "down"?

- Are there, in addition to the evacuation path egress through "front doors," any alternate paths and exits? Are directions to these properly indicated *in the lobby or common area*? Are the "alternate doors"† properly marked?
- Is there sufficient access control and management *through lobby area*? (Checking and verification of employees, guests, visitors, messengers, delivery personnel? Are in-coming parcels checked? Are in-coming packages checked?)
- Are employees required to wear identification badges? Are the badges "secure" (not subject to counterfeiting or alteration)? Are badges periodically reissued? Are badges collected when employees terminate or are transferred to another site? Are badges "coded" to indicate areas of authorized access?
- Are visitors and transients required to wear identification badges? Is there a sufficient sign-in, sign-out procedure? Are ID badges collected upon exit?
- Is there a procedure to determine who is *still* in the building, remaining before off-hours sign-in, sign-out procedures commence?
- Is a log maintained of employees who might require assistance—and the nature of the assistance—in an evacuation? (Does the log indicate normal working hours, and where individuals work?)
- Is a log maintained of visitors who might require assistance—and the nature of the assistance—in an evacuation? (Does the log indicate whom and where they are visiting? Does the log clearly indicate that these visitors have left?)
- Is there a workable (and *working*!) parcel exit-checking system?
- Do lobby receptionists or guards have access to silent alarms? Is a direct-out-side-line telephone available?

The Building: Roof

- Is there lightning protection?
- Is there fire protection, such as standpipe connections and hoses† or fire extinguishers†?
- What is the apparent condition of the roof surface? Are there any apparent ruptures, cracks, or wear in the membrane? Vegetation growing? Trash present? Are *all* roof-top drains (including water tank drains) clear and unobstructed? Is the roof being used for any type of storage?

- What is the apparent condition of roof-mounted water tanks? (It is prudent to have roof-mounted water tanks periodically inspected by a water tank expert.)
- Is there—or has there been—any noticeable leakage from any roof-mounted water tank? Is there a leakage alarm system? Is it remotely monitored?
- Is there—or has there been—any noticeable overflow? Do roof-mounted water tanks have working over-flow controls? Is there low-temperature or freezing detection? Water heating devices? Is the water temperature detection and water heating monitored remotely?
- Are overflow and leakage drains clear and unobstructed?
- What is the apparent condition of roof-mounted cooling towers? (It is prudent to have roof-mounted cooling towers periodically inspected by a cooling expert.) Are gauges and condition-monitors remotely monitored? Are gauges and condition-monitors "fail-safe"?
- Are the building alarm systems audible above any constant (e.g., cooling tower fans) and transient (e.g., passing aircraft) ambient noise levels in *all* roof areas? Is the public address system likewise audible in *all* roof areas? If not, are workers provided with vibrating alphanumeric pagers that display text fire- and other-alarm-condition messages (in English and other appropriate languages)? Are these devices activated by the alarm system?

The Building: Elevators

- Do the elevators have automatic lobby recall when the fire alarm is sounded or transmitted?
- Is there provision for evacuation of disabled staff and visitors?
- Is an elevator and operator (for both manually operated, and automatic elevators that revert to manual operation under alarm conditions) designated to evacuate the medical and nursing staff, their emergency equipment, and any under-care persons? To aid in the evacuation of staff and visitors who might need assistance?
- Is there provision for rescuing trapped passengers in the event of elevator failure or misfunction?

The Building: Evacuation Stairwells

- Are evacuation paths stairwells clearly designated and marked?

- Is there sufficient lighting? Emergency lighting? Battery-powered emergency lighting? Are emergency "lightsticks" provided?
- Are there navigation path lighting strips?
- Is the public address clearly audible in all evacuation stairwells?
- Is there wayfinding signage in the evacuation stairwells?
- Are there navigation path sight bands for visually impaired persons?
- Is there re-entry from stairwells to the building proper? Are the doors unlocked or unsecured to enable opening from the *stairwell*? If locked or secured, are there emergency opening devices?
- Are the *floor numbers* indicated at each level in the stairwells?
- Are there any items stored in the stairwells?
- Are there obstructions in the stairwells?

The Building: Basement and Sub-surface Spaces (Be It the Building's or Yours)

- Are alarms audible in *all* areas?
- Is the public address system audible in *all* areas?
- Are aisles and passageways† properly fitted and maintained?
- Are detection and alarms systems† properly fitted and maintained?
- Are evacuation and emergency egress paths† properly designated and maintained?
- Is there proper housekeeping in machinery rooms?
- Are fire extinguishers† provided? Emergency tools?
- Is there any storage of hazardous materials (paints, solvents, oily rags, flammables)?
- What is apparent condition of piping systems, water and wastewater mains, cabling, and other conduits?
- Are drains clear and unobstructed?
- Are drains fitted with backflow protection?
- Are there sump pumps in subsurface areas? Are these monitored by the detection and alarm system? Are the sump pumps connected to the emergency electric power system?
- Are gas-powered portable pumps available? Are electric-powered portable pumps available? Are these pumps routinely maintained and tested (actually used to remove water!)?
- Are any subsurface spaces used for records storage free from moisture and water ingress? Are records stored off floor levels? Is

there any apparent danger of shelving collapse? Of piled cartons falling? Is there emergency communication facility in the records room?

■ Is there evidence of smoking in nonsmoking areas?

The Building: Electrical Service

■ Is there proper service capacity? Is there adequate distribution capacity?

■ Is in-coming power *continuously* (or, at least *periodically*) monitored for quality (sags, swells, impulses, voltage losses, and "noise")?

■ If all in-coming power is not monitored, is the power furnished to the computer room or computer center monitored for quality?

■ Do electrical risers pass through other organization's electric lockers and closets?

■ Are wiring and cabling diagrams routinely updated, archived, and included in contingency manager's files?

The Emergency Generator, Be It the Building's or Yours   The VS related to emergency generators should start with a consideration of the reasons why *such equipment is installed in your facility. There can be, generally, five reasons.*[3] *(1) To provide emergency lighting for safe egress, such as exit lights, stairwell, and corridors. (2) To provide power for fire-control and safety equipment, such as fire pumps, communications systems, fire detection and alarms systems, and security systems. (3) To provide power for critical equipment, such as sump pumps and elevators. (4) To provide power to permit operation of at least a portion of the facility during the power outage, such as communication centers, and public safety centers. (5) To provide power for lengthy outages beyond UPS capacity. The vulnerability search, and the vulnerability analysis must take into account that (1) the emergency generator might be damaged in the out-of-course event, as occurred in the World Trade Center bombing; (2) the generator might not start, or might soon fail, as occurred in several significant instances during power failures in New York City; or, (3) the fire department may order the generator shutdown, as is the New York City Fire Department protocol in high-rise building fires.*

---

[3] James E. Piper, *Handbook of Facility Management* (Englewood Cliffs, N.J.: Prentice-Hall, 1995), 382.

The generator may be in-place, yet it may not be able to provide power in circumstances where you expect it to. It is essential to probe potential vulnerabilities (1) in terms of the generator functioning in its as-intended manner; (2) in terms of the generator failing during the course of its use; and (3) in terms of it not being able to function.

- Is there periodic review and assessment of the load connected to the generator?
- Is the generator tested, routinely, according to manufacturer's protocols, under no-load conditions (to verify AC voltage production, and frequency)?
- Is the generator tested, routinely, according to manufacturer's protocols, under partial load, *and* under full load?
- Do control panel instruments and gauges function correctly?
- Do the controls provide both capacity/load-shedding, and load-shedding priorities?
- If the generator is located out-of-doors, are there crank-case and block heaters? Cranking battery heaters?
- Does the generator start automatically? Are the conditions that initiate starting routinely tested?
- What is the running duration of the stored-fuel capacity? Is the fuel tank contents monitored? (There is increasing use of control software to indicate tank status, fuel temperature, and fill ratio. This provides useful information during "as-intended" functioning, but raises the vulnerability issues of computer operability during emergency generator operation, measurement continuity during the power gap, and system-suffered consequences resulting from the outage.)
- What is the fuel availability? Is the stored fuel routinely checked for water or contaminants? Are fuel filters and air filters checked and changed? Are fuel injectors and spark plugs cleaned?
- Is the fuel-flow from the storage tank to generator gravity-based, or pumped? If a power-pumped supply, is there a hand-pump—permanently connected to the fuel-supply piping—for use in the event of power-pump failure?
- Is there a generator parts list available, and kept proximate to the generator? Are spare parts—especially expendables such as belts, hoses and clamps—available, and kept proximate to the generator along with service manuals and maintenance diagrams? Is a preventive maintenance manual or trouble diagnostics manual available? Is the generator manufacturer's service

representative name and (correct!) phone number posted on the generator control panel?

■ Is there are good preventive maintenance program in place, which provides regularly scheduled checking of engine performance, lubrication, cooling, air intake, and exhaust, the generator set, and the transfer switch?[4]

■ Is the cabling grease- and oil free? Are connections tight? Are batteries (and the terminals) clean? Is the specific gravity of each battery cell checked, and distilled water added if necessary? Are batteries replaced on a programmed basis as recommended in manufacturer's protocols?

■ Are belts, hoses, and clamps checked and tight?

■ Is there a periodic fuel level check? A periodic dip-stick verification of fuel level gauge? A periodic purge of water from storage tank?

■ Is there a backup or alternate (manual?) method for tank-to-generator fuel transfer?

■ Are generators sited so as to be immune from flooding, from watermain breaks, leaks in internal or external piping, sprinkler activation or leakage?

Your Facility or Your Organization's Part-of-the-Building-Associated Conditions

Your Facility: Management

■ How often are *building* fire drills conducted? Is there 100% participation? Are some drills conducted during lunch hours? During second and third shifts? During weekends?

■ How often are *building* evacuation drills conducted? Is there 100% participation? Are some evacuation drills conducted during lunch hours? During second and third shifts? During weekends?

■ Have specific places been provided and demarcated as AREA OF RESCUE ASSISTANCE, and fitted with emergency lighting, smoke masks, breathing-aid devices, appropriate signage, and known to all staff (especially those who may benefit from such

---

[4] "Maintenance" *should* focus reducing the levels of risk of faults or failures—in other words, the as-intended functioning of the item—thus, reducing the levels of risk of consequences and affects of faults or failures. The "traditional" roles of maintenance—minimizing costs and preserving physical assets—do not serve to reduce the levels of risk associated with potential problems.

assistance), to the CM, and the CMT, and to building personnel, to emergency response personnel?

- Does *building management* have "contingency management staff" designated for all shifts? During weekends?
- How often does *your organization* conduct fire drills? Do you insist on 100% participation? Are some conducted during lunch hours? During second and third shifts? During weekends?
- How often does *your organization* conduct evacuation drills? Do your insist on 100% participation? Are some drills conducted during lunch hours? During second and third shifts? During weekends?
- Do you have "alternate" or "substitute" contingency management team members appointed for second and third shifts? For weekends? For days off, absences, and vacation coverage?
- Are *all* CMT members trained in first aid? In CPR?
- Do the "alternate" and "substitute" CMT members have their own, properly maintained, copies of the plan manual?
- Are engineering and facility records and drawings up-to-date? Complete? Identified? Secure? Access-controlled? Archived and stored off-site?
- Are engineering and facility records and drawings copies provided for the CMT and kept in the CMC?
- Are fixed-assets and equipment records maintained? Are these up-to-date? Complete? Identified? Secure? Access-controlled? Archived and stored off-site? Copies provided to the CMT and kept in the CMC?
- Are all members of the contingency management team properly trained? Are they provided with duty checklists? Hard-hats? Insulated gloves? Flashlights†?
- Are floor plans up-to-date? Complete? Identified? Secure? Access-controlled? Archived and stored off-site?
- Are wiring diagrams (including power, telephone, computer network) up-to-date? Complete? Identified? Secure? Access-controlled? Archived and stored off-site?
- Are there *current and valid* backup computer and office forms, checks, stationery and supplies kept off-site for ready use if on-site supplies cannot be used?
- Is a bomb-detecting device for letters and parcels available? Is it routinely used? Do mailroom (or other) personnel know how to use it?

- Is a metal-detecting device available for use by building's or your organization's security staff?
- Are any EMF-emitting devices (such as diathermy and hyperthermia treatment devices, or manufacturing processes) used by other tenants, or by tenants in nearby facilities?
- Are tests made to detect and measure EMF levels *in all parts of your facility*? Do the measurements represent a valid sampling over a reasonable period of time?[5]
- Are access passes and keys collected from terminated employees?
- Is there a protocol in-place for changing combination locks? Keys (including tumbler, magnetic, bar-code, transponder, push-button, etc.)? Passwords? (E.g., every six months or whenever there is suspected compromise or when a combination, key, or card is lost or stolen or when there is a change in personnel)
- Are duplicate keys to *all* locks available, controlled, and labeled?
- Are "master," "grand master," and like keying sufficiently *controlled*? Can you account for all such keys that have been cut?
- Is there an overall access procedure (e.g., receptionists, card-entry or key-code entry access devices)?
- Are access cards and codes changed periodically?
- Do receptionists have "panic buttons"? Where are these annunicated?
- Are card-key and key-code entry devices monitored?
- Are employees required to wear identification badges? Are the badges "secure"? Are badges periodically reissued? Are badges collected when employees terminate or are transferred to another site? Are badges "coded" to indicate areas of authorized access?
- Are entry points alarmed? Where does the alarm sound?
- Is a record maintained of nonauthorized entry attempts using access-control-entry devices?
- Is there a periodic insurance coverage review? Exclusions review? Deductibles review?

---

[5] Although studies of the link between EMFs and certain diseases (mentioned elsewhere) have found only a undetermined relationship, there is reason to believe that changes in body functions occur with exposure to radiation. The question that remains is whether or not these changes are illness-causing. Conspicuously absent from ANSI/IEEE C95.X-1992, "The IEEE Standard for Safety Levels With Respect to Human Exposure to Radio Frequency Electromagnetic Fields . . ." [C-95.1-1992 describes exposure limits; C95.3-1992 covers measurement procedures] are values related to the frequencies now thought to be the source of the diseases only because at the time the standards were adopted there was no solid indication that a causal relation existed between exposure to the particular frequencies and disease.

■ Are storage, equipment usage, and other like practices and pro-cedures in compliance with insurance policy provisions?

■ Does the organization have business interruption insurance? Valuable documents insurance? Accounts receivable insurance? Extra-expense insurance?

■ Are emergency supplies of water and food stocked and main-tained? Are they routinely checked and supplies rotated to as-sure freshness?

■ Are emergency medical and first-aid supplies stocked and main-tained? Are they routinely checked and supplies rotated to as-sure freshness?

■ Are emergency lodging supplies (cots, bedding, linens, etc.) stocked and maintained?

Your Facility: Each Floor or Part-Floor

■ Is there air quality monitoring? What is apparent air quality?
■ Is there sufficient circulation of air?
■ Is there proper air circulation in computer rooms and other ar-eas with laser printers?
■ Are air filters changed routinely?
■ Where are fresh-air intakes? Can they be shut-off?

Aisles, Passageways, and Evacuation Paths (Each Aisle, Passageway, and Evacuation Path Should Be Individually Considered)

■ Does the (specific) evacuation aisle or evacuation pathways have wayfinding signage?
■ Does the aisle or passageway have sufficient width for emergency evacuation?
■ Does the aisle or passageway have navigation path sight bands and low-level lighting strips?
■ Is there emergency battery-powered lighting†?
■ Are flashlights† and "lightsticks" readily available and accessible?
■ Are there any obstructions ("Coke" machines, storage of sup-plies—temporary or ongoing) in the aisle or the evacuation path?

Battery Rooms

■ Do entry doors indicate presence of corrosives or acid within? What is condition of batteries? Is there leakage of acid? Is there temperature control? Is there a fire extinguisher†? Is there proper security (door locked, door alarmed)? Is housekeeping acceptable? Is there any improper storage in the battery room?

Cafeteria/Food Service and Preparation Areas

■ Are the alarms audible and/or visible? Is the public address system audible above the usual ambient noise levels at meal-times? Are detection and alarm systems† in-place? Are evacuation and emergency egress paths† properly designated? Are there fire suppression devices and fire extinguishers† in the food preparation areas? Are there fire extinguishers† in the eating areas?

■ Is the food preparation ductwork routinely cleaned? Are refrigerators fitted with temperature alarms? Are sink and washer areas fitted with water detectors?

Closets—Coat and Storage

■ Are any hazardous or inflammable items stored (e.g., cleaning chemicals and compounds, or solvents, adhesives or paints)?

■ Is there any clutter or improper storage (e.g., storage of files or waste paper, or tools or other equipment)?

Communications

■ Is the wiring for all communications media (including computer LANs) immune from EMFs?

■ Are wireless telephones and LANs immune from EMFs?

Computer Rooms

■ Are smoke *and* fire *and* heat *and* moisture *and* water detection and alarm systems† fitted? Are there underfloor sensors for the detection of smoke *and* fire *and* heat *and* moisture *and* water? Are fire suppression systems and fire extinguishers† inplace? Can alarms conditions be manually transmitted?

■ Is there any improper storage of materials or supplies, or blockage of aisles? Is underfloor house-keeping proper?

■ Are waterproof covers *readily* available to protect equipment from overhead leakage?

■ Are plants placed on or near any computer or other equipment?

■ Is there alternate HVAC available?

■ Have EMFs (from within *and* from without) been monitored?

■ In places subject to seismic activity, are all devices secured to prevent shifting or movement?

Doors

■ Are *all* doors (ingress, egress, closet, storage area, etc.) labeled to indicate where they lead or what is behind them?

- Do ingress and egress doors have sight bands (for normal-sighted and visually-impaired persons)?
- Do doors open in the direction of evacuation path movement?
- Are evacuation-path doors sufficiently wide for wheelchair passage?
- Have *all* locked doors been opened to determine what is behind them?
- Have locks or other securing devices been improperly applied to any doors?
- Are *any* doors propped open, preventing automatic closure?
- Are door-checks and door closing devices operating properly?
- Do "panic bars" work properly?
- Do revolving door "wings" fold back properly?

Electric Lockers and Closets

- Are electric lockers and closets locked and accessible only to authorized personnel?
- Are doors fitted with signs indicating presence of danger?
- Are doors, and smoke, heat, water, and moisture conditions monitored by the detection and alarm system†?
- Is there water above electric lockers or closets (in kitchens, kitchenettes, lavatories, storage tanks, etc.)?
- Are fire extinguishers or fire suppression equipment available outside, or near, electric lockers and closets†? Is the equipment *type* suitable for electrical fires?
- Is there *automatic* fire suppression equipment†?
- Are lockers free of improper storage? Is housekeeping good?
- Do evils lurk inside your building's walls? (Do you suspect old, or slipshod, or dubious wiring that might be the source of unseen electrical shorts or faults? A thermographic infrared scanning might be advisable.)

File Cabinets

- Is there anything other than files stored in file cabinets and file drawers?
- Is stored magnetic media (disks, tapes, and other like media) properly shielded from EMFs?
- Are file cabinets and file drawers that should be locked *actually locked*?

Halls and Corridors; Elevator Lobbies

- Are halls and corridors free of obstructions?
- Are evacuation navigation paths† designated?
- Are freight elevator lobbies free of trash (awaiting pickup) and stored items?

Housekeeping and Closets

- Are *all* closets and storage areas free of inflammables?
- Are areas free of clutter and improperly or incorrectly stored items?

Information Management and Data Management: Files and Records Policy and Practices

- Are policies and practices (a "records management program") in place to assure that paper-based information, and magnetic-based and optical-based data will be available, accessible, and usable when and where needed?
- Are records management policies and practices applicable to *all* desktop and portable computers (including those *in-office, at-home, and "on the road"*)? To *all* the disks created? Are there compliance reviews *of all three categories*?
- Is information and data routinely archived?
- Are there practices and procedures in-place for file tracking? Is there a file signout system?
- Are *all* practices and procedures both documented and satisfactory for *both on-site* and *off-site* storage/handling of papers? Archiving of disks? Storage of disks? File cabinet security? File cabinets fire resistance? Safes security? Rating? Combination-changing policy? Vault security? Combination-changing policy? Off-site dispatch and receiving areas? Destruction authorization? Destruction areas? Type of destruction? Off-site transfer pickup security?
- Are insurance coverage provisions applicable to "valuable documents" complied with?
- Is there a periodic VS/VA/VR conducted at off-site information and data storage areas, including "data warehouses" and "hot sites"?
- Are hard-copy and magnetic media restoration services under contract?

Nurse or Medical Facilities

- Does the nurse or medical staff have a standby emergency kit for use in fires, emergencies, and evacuations? Are flashlights†, hard-hats, and two-way facility or building radios a part of the kit? Is the kit routinely checked? In the event of an evacuation, is there a member of the CMT designated to assist in taking the emergency/evacuation kit to the ground level, to the CMC, or to where it may be needed?
- Is there a private ambulance service contracted by, or available to, the facility?

Offices and Workspaces

- Is housekeeping satisfactory?
- Are any hotplates, coffee warmers, or space heaters in use?
- Are there any excessive electric cords or extension cords or "loose wires" present?
- Is storage of paperwork and magnetic media in compliance with provisions of insurance policy?
- Are empty offices or workspaces improperly used for storage?
- Are halls, corridors, and passageways free of stored materials, vending machines, and other obstructions?
- Are discarded waste paper and disks shredded?
- If containers are provided for waste paper to be recycled, is there a container provided for "sensitive" papers (so that these can be shredded)?
- Is waste paper properly labeled and separated from records awaiting transfer or storage?
- In places subject to seismic activity, are all desktop computers, printers, fax machines, copiers, and other office mechanicals and devices secured to prevent shifting or movement?

Piping Systems

- Is there any apparent leakage from water, wastewater, steam, gas, sprinkler systems, or standpipe systems?
- Are caps, drains, plugs, and other fitments properly secured?
- Are air-conditioning unit drains and drip pans functioning correctly?

Power Conditioning and Battery Backup Equipment

■ Is *each* device in use provide *power conditioning* only, or does it provide *battery backup*, or does it also function as an *uninterruptable power supply*? Will the as-thought and as-intended protection be provided?

■ Is the power conditioning capacity, battery backup capacity, and/ or uninterruptable power-supply capacity *of each device* routinely reviewed in view of changes in the demand of what is connected to it? In terms of changes in lay-out, or moves affecting connected devices? In terms of changes to other power conditioning, battery backup, or uninterruptable power supply devices?

■ Does each device have rated capacity, based on protocols established by the manufacturer, for tasks assigned to it?

■ Is each device tested and maintained according to the protocols established by the manufacturer?

■ Is each device monitored by the detection and alarm system†?

■ Are power conditioning, battery backup devices, and uninterruptable power supply equipment areas properly cooled?

■ Will battery backup devices, or uninterruptable power supply equipment provide power for a sufficient interval (until generators come on-line, or there is an orderly shutdown of equipment)?

■ Are the equipment areas free of improper storage, and have proper housekeeping?

Protection of Equipment

■ Are waterproof covers available for the computer room, personal computers, the library, and the records center, telecommunications switches, power conditioning, battery backup devices, and uninterruptable power supply equipment, as well as for any other equipment or devices that might fault or fail—or be harmed or damaged—as the result of water or moisture ingress?

The Public Address System

■ Can announcements be initiated by the contingency manager? By members of the contingency management team? From the CMC? From remote locations in the building and on the site?

■ Is there battery backup† for the system?

■ Can the system be clearly heard and understood throughout the facility (including restrooms, lounges, conference rooms, theaters, food service areas, etc.)?

- Are hearing-impaired staff and visitors (and workers assigned to alarm "blind spots") provided with vibrating alphanumeric pagers that display English-text (or other appropriate languages) alarm-condition messages?
- Are there recorded messages? Are these clearly marked and color-coded to indicate the precise circumstances for use?
- Are there prescripted messages? Are these clearly marked to indicate precise circumstances for use?
- Are the public address system controls configured in a "fail-safe" mode to prevent incorrect recorded messages from being broadcast "automatically"?

Restrooms and Lounges

- Are audible and visual alarms fitted†?
- Is there emergency lighting†? "Lightsticks"?
- Is there wayfinding and evacuation path signage†? Identification of nonexit doors?
- Do navigation path sight bands or lighting strips extend into restrooms and lounges?

Telephone Equipment and Service

- Are telephone lockers and closets locked and accessible only to authorized personnel?
- Are doors fitted with signs indicating presence of danger?
- Are doors, and smoke, heat, water, and moisture conditions monitored by the detection and alarm system†?
- Is there water above the lockers or closets (in kitchens, kitchenettes, lavatories, storage tanks, etc.)?
- Are fire extinguishers or fire suppression equipment available outside, or near, electric lockers and closets†? Is the equipment *type* suitable for electrical fires?
- Is there *automatic* fire suppression equipment?
- Is the housekeeping satisfactory?
- Do cable risers pass through other organization's telephone closets or electric closets?

Telephone PBX or Switch Room

- Is the PBX or switch room locked and accessible only to authorized personnel?

- Are doors fitted with signs indicating presence of danger?
- Are doors, and smoke, heat, water, and moisture conditions monitored by the detection and alarm system†?
- Is there water above the PBX or switch room (in kitchens, kitchenettes, lavatories, storage tanks, etc.)?
- Are fire extinguishers or fire suppression equipment available outside, or near, the PBX or switch room†? Is the equipment *type* suitable for electrical fires?
- Is there *automatic* fire suppression equipment?
- Is the housekeeping satisfactory?

Telephone Service

- Is your organization served only by one local telephone company central office? (It is important to distinguish between service provided by *more than one exchange housed in a particular central office (CO) building,* and *exchanges housed in different CO buildings.* Ideally, you should have some telephone service provided by an exchange housed in a CO building other than the one providing your "primary" telecommunications service.) (It is also important to consider using more than one long-distance carrier. If this precaution is taken, you should ascertain whether the switches of both carriers are located in the same building, and whether their cabling shares the same vaults.)
- Are changes to phone-switching assignments recorded on an as-made, ongoing basis?
- Are backup copies of PBX software and phone-switching assignments made on ongoing basis, properly archived, and included in contingency manager's files in the CMC?
- Have telephone switching systems received the same kind of power protection and backup generation as computer equipment?

Security Management

- Are watch-clock stations properly maintained?
- Is a program for employee incident and exception reporting in-place and encouraged?

Staff Relations

- Is there an air travel restriction policy concerning key personnel on same airplane?

Surveillance System

- Is the system monitored at all times?
- Are there any obstructed views or nondetection areas?

Signage and Wayfinding

- Are *all* signs and wayfinding aids designed and placed for maximum legibility and readability?
- Is emphasis on *information and wayfinding* rather than on design? Has *true* legibility or readability been given precedence over any "identity program" design elements?
- Will the signs and wayfinding aids be readily discernible and understandable under all lighting (including nonlit) conditions? When smoke clouds the area?
- Is the information presented *both unambiguous and understandable*?
- Is utilization of available space for signage and wayfinding aids maximized?
- Is there low-level (close-to-the-floor) signage, as well as prescribed signage, provided for wayfinding and on exit doors?
- Are there navigation path sight bands?
- Are *arrows* distinct?
- Are any "confusing" or "mystery" symbols or icons used?
- Are signs normally illuminated as intended?
- Is the backup illumination functioning as intended?
- Is signage provided in languages other-than English?
- Does the in-place signage and wayfinding aids *actually indicate the correct directions*?
- Do EXIT signs actually indicate exits? Are fire extinguishers found proximate to FIRE EXTINGUISHER signs? Are emergency telephones, alarm pull-boxes, and other emergency equipment located where signage indicates?

Stairs and Stairwells

- Are evacuation paths† clearly marked?
- Is there battery-powered† lighting?
- Is the public address system audible?
- Is there evidence of use as a smoking area?
- Are there any items stored in stairwells?

ITEM-SPECIFIC CHECKLISTS
(ITEMS MARKED "†" ON PRIMARY CHECKLIST)

I. Aisles and Passageways Checklist

- Do evacuation aisles and pathways have wayfinding signage?
- Are aisles and passageways of sufficient width for emergency evacuation?
- Do aisles and passageways have navigation path sight bands, low-level signage, and low-level lighting strips?
- Is there emergency battery-powered† lighting?
- Are flashlights† and "lightsticks" readily available and accessible?
- Are there any obstructions (vending machines, storage of supplies—temporary or on-going) in the evacuation paths?

2. Detection and Alarm Systems Checklist

Detection and Alarm systems are used with advantage on the site, in the building(s) your organization occupies, or in the space within the building that your organization occupies. You may well find it prudent—put another way, *risk-reducing*—to provide more extensive detection and alarm capability than either prescriptives require or building owners or management provides.

The vulnerability search *is concerned with three distinct aspects of detection and alarm systems that are installed in the place: First, are the systems functioning as-intended? Second, do the systems provide the protection you <u>believe</u> they do? Third, what can be done to modify the systems to enhance their role in risk reduction? The search can also function to create an <u>awareness of need</u> for detection and alarm systems, but it is not intended to substitute for counseling by an alarm expert. Your vulnerability search of detection and alarm systems must focus both on <u>specific areas</u> in the place, as well as on <u>specific fitments and items of equipment</u>. Are the fitments and equipment appropriate for the tasks for which they are being used?*

Within <u>each area</u> the search must focus on what is there, or what is lacking, in terms of the detection and alarm system fitments and equipment needed to reduce risks. In considering detection and alarm system fitments and equipment, their as-intended functionality and effectiveness in the transmission and the broadcast (both aural and visual) of alarms that will be recognized and understood by all the people must be evaluated in terms of risk reduction.

Facility-Monitoring Alarms, Applicable to the Following Types of Risk-Conditions

Fire

Heat

Smoke

Flame

High-heat

Incipient fire

Intrusion

Sprinkler system pressure

Sprinkler system activation

Sprinkler shutoff valve positions

Fire-suppressant (e.g., CO_2 or Halon) release

Access

Temperature

HVAC malfunction

Elevator malfunction

Water and moisture

Gas presence

- Does the monitoring detect *all* of the potential at-risk conditions that might occur?
- Is the annunciator system or systems (where the detected anomaly condition is indicated by sound, visual signal, video screen, or a written record, or by a combination of these) installed where the condition *is detected* only, or, is it additionally transmitted to fire, police, or emergency response services dispatchers; to a central monitoring station within the building or site, or to an alarm company central station, or to company personnel (or a combination of these)? Are certain alarm conditions transmitted to appropriate personnel via pagers?
- Are the monitoring and detection sensors installed according to the protocols of applicable prescriptives, and those of their respective manufacturer?
- Are the monitoring and detection sensors inspected and maintained according to the protocols established by their respective manufacturers?

■ Are the monitoring and detection sensors tested according to the protocols established by their respective manufacturers?

■ Are the annunciator and transmission systems inspected according to the protocols established by their respective manufacturers?

■ Are the annunciator and transmission systems maintained according to the protocols established by their respective manufacturers?

■ Are the annunciator and transmission systems tested according to the protocols established by their respective manufacturers?

■ When changes or modifications are made to the software of a software-based alarm systems (because of changes to the alarm system), are the *software changes* affected by the change subject to a 100% "reacceptance" test? Are the initiating devices not directly affected by the change subject to a "reacceptance" test? Is the testing basis the prescriptive 10% of the initiating devices,[6] or are 100% of the initiating devices given a "reacceptance" test?

■ Are fire alarms transmitted *directly* to the fire department (in addition to any other alarm recipient)?

■ Do specific alarm conditions trigger elevator functions, release fire screens and doors, or shutdown specific air-circulation and ventilation equipment?

■ Are alarm transmissions are hard-wired, or radio-transmitted? Is *each* hard-wire alarm transmission system automatically backed up by microwave, radio-frequency or cellular paths, so if the hard-wire system does not receive "an answer" the system transmits via another medium? Do radio-transmission alarms systems have battery-power† backup?

"Fire" Alarms within the Building and Your Facility or Your Organization's Part of the Building

■ Are alarms audible only, or audible supplemented by visual strobe or flashing lights?

---

[6] The 1993 NFPA 72, *The National Fire Alarm Code*, Section 7-1.6, which deals with system reacceptance testing, requires that reacceptance tests be performed after any software change, and proper systems operations verified. All software functions affected by a change are to be 100% tested, and that 10% of initiating devices not directly affected by the change be tested. The code does not prescribe either *which* "10%," or the statistical methodology to be used in selecting a *representative* 10%. The level of risk of alarm system failure—resultant from compromise in the integrity of the system caused by nonapparent software flaws—can be (and should be!) reduced ALARP by testing 100% of the devices.

- Are hearing-impaired staff and visitors (and workers assigned to alarm "blind spots") provided with vibrating alphanumeric pagers that display English-text (or other appropriate language) fire- and other-alarm-condition messages? Are these devices activated by the alarm system?
- Are audible alarms sufficiently loud to be heard above the ambient noise level in each specific area?
- Is this [specific area being searched] an alarm "blind spot"? (Can audible alarms be heard here? Can visual alarms be seen here?) (This is an especial concern in lavatories, conference rooms, theaters, and food preparation and service areas.)
- Is the alarm *sound* distinct? Are several different *sounds* utilized to designated various conditions? If different sound patterns are in use, are people aware of the meanings, and what actions they should take? If visual and audible alarms with different sound patterns are used, how is the difference in alarm conditions conveyed to people who rely on the visual alarms? If different alarm sound patterns are used, is there information signage in areas used by outsiders and visitors, such as meeting and conference rooms, indicating the meanings of the different alarm sound patterns?
- Are there a sufficient number of alarm pull-boxes (for alarms of *all types*)? Are they strategically placed?
- Are the *fire* (and other) alarms pull-boxes properly identified and marked? Is there proper *signage* indicating location of individual pull-boxes?
- Are the other-than-fire alarm pull-boxes (e.g., intrusion, "panic buttons,") properly identified and marked? Is there proper *signage* indicating location of such individual pull-boxes? (Are specific "panic buttons"—such as those at a guard station or receptionist's desk—unobtrusive and unmarked?)
- Are fire and other alarm pull-boxes fitted with "protective covers"? Can these covers be easily and quickly be broken or penetrated, and the alarm activator accessed? Are the "protective covers" clearly marked to indicate they are *covers* and that, in addition to breaking the cover, the alarm must be activated?
- Does the power supply for the audible and visual alarms have battery backup†?
- How is evacuation and other "life-threatening" information disseminated? Is there a public address system? Are prescripted announcements used? Are prescripted announcements (both "hard-copy scripts" and recordings) clearly marked as to circum-

stances for use? Can improper use of a prescripted announcement bring people into a dangerous arena?

■ Is there provision for non-English speakers?
■ Is there a battery backup† for the public address system?
■ Are there any "blind" or "deaf" spots where public address cannot be heard (e.g., lavatories, conference rooms, theaters, and high ambient noise areas)?

3. Evacuation and Emergency Egress Paths Checklist

■ Are exit doors clearly marked?
■ Is there a clear sight-line to EXIT signs from all locations?
■ Where EXIT signage incorporates directional arrows, are the arrowed directions clear?
■ Are EXIT signs the prescriptive size, or are larger signs provided where there are long sight-lines?
■ Are low-level EXIT signs provided?
■ Do the EXIT signs have auxiliary lighting in the event of a power failure? Are these standby generator powered? (What would illuminate the signs if the generator failed, or if the fire department ordered generator shutdown?) Do the EXIT signs have self-contained batteries? Are such batteries tested and maintained†? Are the EXIT signs photoluminescent? Have you looked at them in an all-lights-out condition?
■ Do all doors opening in evacuation paths open in the direction of the evacuation?
■ Do all doors opening into evacuation stairwells open outward?
■ Are the evacuation and emergency egress navigation paths marked? Do they have navigation path sight bands or lighting strips?
■ Is there low-level evacuation and emergency egress navigation path markings? Do they have navigation path sight bands or lighting strips?
■ Is there evacuation and emergency egress navigation path lighting? Is the lighting independent of mains and auxiliary generator supply?
■ Are there any obstructions (e.g., placed or stored items or vending machines) encroaching into the pathway?

4. Fires Extinguishers, Standpipes, Hoses and Sprinklers, and Emergency Tools Checklist

■ Is the (individual) fire extinguisher properly maintained and serviced? Has it been recharged within specified period? Is the current charge within the recommended range? Is the seal and inspection tag intact? Is there a location index of all fire extinguishers?

■ Is the fire extinguisher the correct type for fires likely to be encountered in the area?

■ Is the fire extinguisher located at the *entry* to the area rather than at the opposite side?

■ If the fire extinguisher is located *within* an area, is it accessible from all parts of that area?

■ If wall-hung, can the fire extinguisher be easily reached and removed by *any* staff member?

■ Is there a fire extinguisher located proximate to where signage indicates an extinguisher location?

■ Are the locations of fire extinguishers clearly marked? Is the class of fire extinguisher indicated? Is the placement of fire extinguishers accessible to everyone?

■ Are there a sufficient number of fire extinguishers for the area?

■ Does the class of each fire extinguishers cover all types of fires that may occur within the area?

■ Are employees aware of the location of *all* nearby fire extinguishers? Are they trained in their use?

■ Are fire extinguishers kept in locked or secure cabinets? Can the "protection" be easily breached or broken, giving easy access to the extinguisher? Are the cabinets free of "foreign objects?" Are cabinets provided with rechargeable flashlights? Are cabinets provided with some form of cellular communications?

■ Are sprinkler shutoff valves properly secured in the *open* position? Do the securing chains or locks have a "break-away" link? Are the shutoff valve positions monitored by the detection and alarm system?

■ Are standpipe shutoff valves properly secured?

■ Is the standpipe hose properly secured? Have the hoses been inspected and tested in keeping with the recommended protocols?

■ Are standpipe hose areas accessible and uncluttered?

■ Is there correct clearance beneath *each* sprinkler head?

- Is sprinkler system activation monitored by the detection and alarm system?
- Are site- and building fire carts accessible and in an uncluttered area? Are specific members of the CMT *trained* to use them? *Assigned* to use them?
- Do *all* firefighting appliances have labels reminding users to activate the fire alarm *in every instance?*
- Are emergency egress tools and equipment (such as fire axes, hammers to break glass, fire blankets) easily accessible? If stored in "protected" cabinets, is access simple? Are tools and equipment sufficiently sturdy to accomplish their intended purpose (e.g., break windows)?

5. Flashlights and Other Battery-Powered Devices Checklist

- Is a log of battery-powered devices (e.g., flashlights, radios, two-way radios, cellular telephones, EXIT signs, emergency lights, public address system, auxiliary generator starting system, detection and alarm system monitors, bull horns), their location or placement, and to whom they are assigned, maintained?
- Is each device tested according to manufacturers' protocols?
- Are battery *chargers* tested according to manufacturers' protocols?
- Are dry-cells replaced periodically, based on manufacturers' recommendations, rather than when "weak" or "dead?"
- Are wet-cell batteries checked for proper charge, and for acid level and specific gravity?
- Are wet-cell batteries replaced periodically, based on manufacturers' recommendations, rather than when "weak" or difficult to recharge?

GLOSSARY

The keywords and the key concepts: a lexicon of disaster planning and recovery terminology. This glossary contains definitions of the disaster planning and recovery terminology that appears in this guide.

Several of the "technical terms" used in the guide carry meanings that may be more precise or that might otherwise differ from the facility professional's daily vocabulary.

Some disaster planning literature ascribes, to certain terms, meanings that are different than the definitions that are used in this guide (and that are defined in this glossary). In some literature, a reader can find, on different pages, more than one—often plainly contradictory—attribute given to the same term. Terms and concepts that are intrinsic to disaster planning—such as "risk" and "ALARP"—can be found carrying diverse (and sometimes, incorrect) connotations. "Risk" is a measurement, not an event. The "P" in "ALARP" represents practicable, not possible. The facility professional, in harvesting diverse sources, must be wary of such variances. Disaster planning and recovery is an emerging science and art (arguably, and art and a science); it cries for a standardized vocabulary. All concerned with the survival of people, place, and processes would profit from such a standardization.

This glossary, in addition to providing a more detailed explanation of the language of disaster planning and recovery used in this guide, can also provide the reader with a "frame of reference" for a plan when read as an additional—perhaps preferably the opening—chapter of the text. Perhaps this glossary should be read first.

A

Acceptable level of risk—A level of risk that the organization has determined that they "can live with." As an example, it may be considered "acceptable" that food services can "tolerate" the risk that there will be a 5-minute power outage once every 22 months. (Such an outage would have little, if any, affect on cooking and food preparation, or on serving and dish-washing. The cash register might be inoperative, but such might be deemed no more than an inconvenience. The costs of reducing the level of such risk—perhaps through installation of a dedicated emergency generator—would be considered an unwarranted expense in terms of gain.) Computer services might consider the risk of a 1-second outage every 12 hours as "acceptable" because the installed UPS can compensate for that period; the risk of a 10-second outage every 2 hours might *not* be "acceptable" as the UPS could not compensate for those intervals. (*See* ALARP)

Affect—The end-result of the cascading effect of an out-of-course event (q.v.) that occurs, and which strikes or has impact (q.v.) on the organization's people, place, or processes, that results in one or more consequences (q.v.)—such as an interruption, impediment, interference, halting, or other anomaly condition—that counters the as-intended status or functioning of people, place, or processes. It is the *affects* of the out-of-course event for which countervailance and recovery measures are established.

ALARP—As low as reasonably practicable. A level to which risk can be reduced without disproportionate expenditure of money, time, or effort. Further reduction in the level of risk *may be possible* but not deemed necessary, or the incremental costs inherent may be considered excessive for the additional reduction in level of risk attained. A risk level that is ALARP *may* be regarded as an "acceptable level of risk." "ALARP" is the most indispensable consideration in creating a disaster planning and recovery strategy.

Alternate site—A preplanned location, usually some distance from the organization's usual place for which it will serve as surrogate. The "some distance" considerations reflect power grid and telecommunications services, susceptibility to faults and failures in civic infrastructure, and other potential out-of-course events that might strike the place yet spare the alternate site. Alternate sites are utilized to provide (following a predetermined, acceptable interruption interval)—and, hopefully, assure—continuity in providing vital processes—often data processing, but frequently, for other business process cells—when an out-of-course event, impact, and the ensuing consequences and affects render the normal business or work place unusable, inaccessible, or unavailable. Frequently, such sites are referred to as a "hot site" or "warm site" or "cold site" in reflection of the site's state-of-readiness to take over the providing of nominated processes. "Readiness" is measured in terms of activation interval, equipment and furnishings, software and hardware availability, currency of files, provision of supplies, catering, lodging, and transport, and accessibility of the site by staff. The organization may provide its own alternate site, or may contract for the use of one from a specialized provider.

Apparent cause—The direct reason, or the reason-of-origin, of an *impact* on people, place, or processes. The *consequences and affects* of that impact may cause casualties to the people, harm or damage to the place, or may interrupt, impair, impede, or halt the processes. As an example, a shortage or interruption in the supply of electricity from the utility can impact one or more processes: there is no electric power coming into the computer room, and computer processing is halted. Your planning strategy may need to provide for means to restore or continue the supply of electricity through use of your own alternative emergency generating capacity. In many instances, you have no control of, or over, the *root cause* of the apparent cause (here, the utility's difficulty), and need not be concerned with it unless it is a frequent occurrence. The utility's difficulty—possibly a faulty transformer—is beyond the pale of your planning. A contractor's inadvertent severing an underground electric cable would be an *apparent cause* of an interruption, and planning can take this potential event into account. That the backhoe operator neglects to refer to the cabling diagrams furnished to him (or her) is the *root cause* of the outage, and something you have little control over.

As-intended (functioning)—The normal or usual methods, systems, and procedures through which the organization functions: the day-to-day interactions of people, place, and processes that occur in "getting the job done" in the "normal" or "usual" manner. "As-intended"—in the realm of disaster planning and recovery—is more *quantitative* than *qualitative*.

As Low As Reasonably Practicable—*See* ALARP

Assessors—Those experts, specialists and technicians, preferably people not a part of the organization's staff, who are selected to conduct the vulnerability search and assessment, and to recommend the required rectification.

At risk (often styled as at-risk)—A term used in some literature to describe the state of being susceptible (or, susceptibility) to "risks" (out-of-course events, their impact, and the consequences). The business is thought to be "at risk" when something could result in injuries or deaths, in harm or damage to the building, or interrupt, impair, impede, or halt business (most often, the computer) functions. ("At risk" is not a good disaster planning and recovery term! "Risk" is a *measurement* rather than a state or condition, and is always greater than zero. In reality, everything is actually "at risk" in some way and at all times.)

B

BIA—*See* Business impact analysis.

BPC—*See* Business process cell and Business process center.

Break point—The point at which the risks of out-of-course events, or impacts, or consequences and affects are unacceptable but their elimination or further reduction cannot be economically justified.[1] "Break point" stands in contrast to ALARP wherein attaining a level of risk of out-of-course events, or impacts, or consequences and affects is deemed economically acceptable.

Business impact analysis (BIA)—The term, in some literature, used to describe the process of determining—and quantifying—the relative vital-ness of some, but often not all, of the organization's functions and activities, and the affects that a "disaster" would have on these functions and activities, and thus, on the organization. These "affects" include inability to operate normally or to operate at all, financial losses and penalties, service characteristics, legal liabilities, and the organization's public image. Such "affects" are "analyzed" on a time-line basis in that they might not occur immediately after the impact, or accrue on a straight-line basis until as-intended functioning is restored. Thus, the BIA is the determination (better, an attempt to determine) of the ultimate results of a "disaster" on the organization—the "impact"—and the determination (again, an attempt) to assign a monetary value to those outcomes. In this guide, the concept of "consequence and affect" is used is describe what may ultimately ensue after an out-of-course event. Thus, the ensuing *consequence(s)* and *affect(s)* of an out-of-course event must be recognized and analyzed. (*See* Consequence *and* Consequence analysis.) (*Impact,* in this guide, is used as a noun (rather than as a verb) to describe the affect of an out-of-course event. An *impact* may or may not result in any *consequences.* The *consequences* may or may not have any *affects* on the as-intended functioning of the BPC, and thus, on the organization.)

Business process—An activity which the business or organization performs or conducts.

Business process cell or Business process center (BPC)—An arena of activity that is, or is within, a department or other unit of the organization. It is responsible for the performance of a specific task, such as payroll preparation, or payroll check preparation, or widget painting, or advertising fulfillment, or several tasks, such as accounting. Each BPC is, by implication, a fundamental and necessary activity in the organization (although an undertaking in business re-engineering might deem otherwise). Whenever a BPC is unable to function as intended, the func-

[1] For further discussion in the context of risk management, see "Three Year Research Programme Tightens The Grip on UK Leakage," *Financial Times Newletters: Water Briefing,* 2nd November 1994, 5.

tioning of the *entire* organization will be able to continue unaffected only for a predetermined period. This time span reflects the functions or activities the particular BPC performs. The period can range from the quite short-term—seconds or minutes—for computing operations supporting a financial organization, to a relatively long period—weeks or months—for, as an example, long-range planning to change the corporate identity.

There are, within any organization, one or more activities or functions that *support* one or more of the business process cells (BPCs). These functions provide a diverse range of support services; when these are impeded, impaired, interrupted, or halted, the BPC might not able to function as intended, or to function at all. Whether the function performs a "quartermaster" role (stocking and disbursing office equipment, supplies, forms and stationary), a "pacquet" role (collecting, delivering and distributing mails and parcels), a "facilities" service (providing printing and duplication, maintenance, security, cleaning, and other site-support activities), "communications" (telephone, facsimile, radio, Telex, Teletype, and computer networking), or "computing" (accounting, word processing, desktop publishing, design assistance, process control, and the like), each of these are also subject to out-of-course events, their impacts, and the consequences.

If the stockroom personnel are unable to provide a supply of a particular form, or of diskettes, or copier toner (because someone failed to reorder, a human-intervention caused event!) BPC activities can be impeded as severely as when the computer "is down." The guide will not consider means to reduce the risk of out-of-stock situations, or of computer network penetration, or of messengers delaying, misdelivering or losing their charge, or the like. It is, however, most important that the facility professional—especially those who are directly concerned with the day-to-day operations of an organization—recognize that there exist risks of such character, that their consequences and affects can be as interruptive as a computer failure or a hurricane, and that these risks have to be considered in the same light as any other out-of-course event. The techniques, practices, and principles applicable to these risks should also be applied.

Business resumption; business resumption planning—The process leading up to, or enabling, the return to normal or as-intended functioning. *Planning* to facilitate this process (which takes place in the "after" phase of an out-of-course event) should include arrangements (preferably, contracts) covering drying or dehumidification of paper and micromedia records, all aspects of cleanup, deodorization, repairs and restoration, or replacement, of equipment and facilities, and repairs and testing of infrastructure. The importance of in-place contracts is enhanced when an out-of-course event impacts other organizations (in addition to yours), and the several organizations are competing for services and products.

C

CA—*See* Consequence analysis.

Casualty—An injury to, or death of, one or more people.

Casualty, value of a—*See* Value of a human injury *and* Value of a human life.

Catastrophic failure—A failure of some unit of infrastructure, equipment, or furnishing, or of one or more people *at or of the place*, the consequence of which impairs, impeded, interrupts, or halts that as-intended functioning of one or more BPC. There are two distinguishing characteristics of the catastrophic failure: first, that the failure *could have been prevented*; second, that the failure impaired, impeded, interrupted, or halted the as-intended functioning of one or more BPC. What actually failed, or the reason for its failure, could—and should—have been recognized, and was within the aegis of those responsible for the planning or administration of the facility. What actually failed had presented disaster planning opportunities to (1) reduce the level of risk of failure; (2) reduce the level of risk of impact; and (3) reduce the level of risk of consequences and affects. That such opportunities were not taken, and that the failure occurred, resulted in the "catastrophic" consequences. (*See* Fault.)

"Cold site"—An alternate site without any resources or equipment, except (usually) HVAC and infrastructure that facilitates installation of computing and telecommunications equipment.

Command Center—*See* Contingency management center.

Computer modeling and simulation—A computer-based means enabling experimentation and investigation of the various parameters that could affect the levels of risk present. It is the process of creating a computer-based "model" of the place that enables the spaces, materials, and procedures to be changed so that the advantages, benefits, desirability and worth (if any) of the changes can be determined without or before undertaking any physical or procedural changes. As an example, the advantages (or disadvantages) in terms of numbers of people able to move, the times for their passage, and the decrease (or increase) in the number of casualties that would result from incrementally widening (or narrowing) the width of an evacuation path corridor can be determined, and the optimal passage dimensions decided, by simulating people-flow through various corridor widths that could be incorporated into the particular space. In this example, variations in levels of lighting, navigation signage, public address announcements, drills and practices, staff guidance, relative affects of smoke and fire stemming for various materials that might be used in construction are a few of the other elements that can be introduced into the simulation equations. Computer modeling and simulation, in applying a nearly infinite number of variables—rather than a few mathematical formulae—is also valuable in determining the cost:benefit ratios of potential changes. (See Chapter 5 for a discussion of the role of computer modeling and simulation in creating a disaster planning and recovery strategy.)

Consequence—That which may occur following an impact of an out-of-course event. An out-of-course event (e.g., a water main bursts) *occurs*; the event has an *impact* (flooding the streets and subsurface levels of the building, and halting the supply of water to the building); and creates the potential of a wide range of *consequences*. These *consequences* might include no electrical power, no water for drinking, sanitary, or heating or cooling, loss of vital records stored in the basement, no external telephone service, and—the list can continue. *As a result of these consequences of the impact of the out-of-course event*, the BPCs cannot operate: there is no electricity for lighting or power; the computers are [really!] down; and—because of the gaping hole in the street—staff are not allowed to enter the building. The ultimate "result" or "results" of a "consequence" or "consequences" is the "**affect**" (q.v.) on as-intended functioning of the BPC.

It is important to consider that the impact of an out-of-course event may not have any consequence on the organization. As an example, the river upon which the place fronts may rise to 10 feet above flood stage (surely an out-of-course event, or the result of one—although it might be a common one), but because the place has a 12-foot flood barrier to counter the perhaps otherwise devastating waters there would not be any direct consequence, and thus, no affects. (But as those waters rise to 143 inches above flood stage, so would rise concerns!) (*See* Consequence analysis.)

Consequence analysis (CA)—In some planning approaches, the identification (and possibly, also the measurement and assessment) of the outcome of a *particular* event that follows *a specific* impact, and what business functions may be effected by it. In a disaster planning and recovery strategy, it is the possible *affects*, as such, of the consequence that should serve as the basis for, and justification of the disaster planning and recovery strategy. The CA considers the What if . . .? scenarios wherein the "ifs" represents each of the potential out-of-course events. As an example, in terms of a nature-based out-of-course event—a hurricane, for example—the CA would identify as the "consequence" high winds and considerable rain. In this guide, the high winds and considerable rain are considered the *impact* of that out-of-course event. But there may or may not be any *consequences* of the impact. If there is a consequence, it may have no *affect* on the as-intended functioning of *all* BPCs, or it may totally halt the as-intended functioning of some, or its impede, impair, interrupt, or halt *some of* the functioning in *some* way. The determination, measurement, and assessment must be made on a time-line basis. A consequence may have little or no affect on a BPC when it occurs, but the affect can emerge or increase as time progresses, or the affect can occur at a specific time.

Although the CA can be an element in disaster planning and recovery strategies, it is far from an exacting art or science (some software providers suggest that the process *is* both simple *and* exacting—when utilizing their software!). The CA can suggest the foundation upon which to create a disaster planning and recovery strategy, and can indicate the basis upon which countervailence or contingency and recovery plans are formulated. The CA *should* consider all potential consequences and all the potential affects of each consequence that an out-of-course event may have on each of the BPCs—thus, on the organization's ability to deliver or perform its obligations to its constituencies and stakeholders.

Some elements in the CA might be quite subjective. A significant executive might deem that—no matter what happens—all incoming telephone calls must be answered by the fifth ring. Thus, it would behoove the facility professional planning an alternate site to provide sufficient "seats" and sufficient operators and sufficient in-coming telephone lines. The SE might deem that, in the event of an emergency, it wouldn't matter if payables were not made for 60 days; this, too, would govern planning.

Whatever means are used in the CA, consideration must be given— in addition to the affects on the as-intended functioning of the BPC—for revenue lost during the interval; additional costs to recover, including repairs, replacements, and restoration; fines and penalties that might accrue; lost good will; and lost competitive advantage. (An interesting variation can evolve where the organization might be operating at a loss; the interruption to business processes can result in a *gain* rather than in a loss.)

The concepts of "consequence" and "impact" may be difficult to visualize. "Consequence" is *not* an interruption, impeding, impairment, or halting of the as-intended functioning of the business or one or more of its processes—the *affect* of that consequence is. A process *may* be halted or interrupted as a *result* of the consequences of the impact (its "affect"). An *impact can occur and the consequences ensue*, but with proper countervailence planning, the process can be able to continue to function, albeit, at times in a somewhat different manner (no "affect"—the ultimate, perhaps unattainable, goal and objective of the disaster planning and recovery strategy).

The consequence analysis process, including the fiscal and operational ramifications, is referred to, in some literature, as the business impact analysis (BIA). The "I" in BIA gives an additional—and different, thus confusing—meaning to *impact*. If utilizing the so-termed "BIA" approach, it is important *not to* (as some suggest) reflect "threats" (out-of-course events), but only the *consequences* of the impacts created by the out-of-course event. In this guide, CA is preferred to BIA.

Contingency—An inevitable or inescapable or unpreventable out-of-the-ordinary occurrence.

Contingency management—Contingency management is concerned with the *when and where* (rather than the *if*) of an out-of-course event occurrence, and is the preplanned, tested, and practiced processes of countering the consequences and affects of the impact so that there will not be any casualties (either injuries or deaths) or the number will be as few as possible, that harm or damage to the place will not occur, or will be kept at a minimal level, and that there will not be any impediment, impairment, interruption, or halting of the as-intended business functioning, or that such will be as brief as possible. Put another way, contingency management is the process of controlling and minimizing consequences, and their affects; the efforts to prevent a "disaster" from occurring.

Contingency management center (CMC)—The designated place(s) where activities related to a declared (or about-to-be-declared) "emergency" are directed and managed in order to prevent the occurrence from escalating into a "crisis" or "disaster"; the "war room." Sensible disaster planning provides for a CMC on-site (advantageously on the main floor of the building, providing ready access to emergency response services, not on the upper story where the contingency manager's office might be), and a CMC off-site for use in the event that the on-site CMC is not accessible, usable, or available.

Contingency management team (CMT)—Those designated people who have been assigned responsibilities in the event of an "emergency" so that the event will not escalate into a "crisis" or "disaster." The team includes the contingency manager, evacuation aids, searchers, the place's fire brigade, the organization's medical staff, and all others who have been assigned a role in the plan manual or primer for survival. The CMT also might include representatives of contracted services that provide assistance "before" an imminent out-of-course event or emergency (such as "board-up" and other protective and damage-minimizing activities, property and records removal), as well as in the "emergency" or During Phase (damage and impact mitigation services), and in the After Phase (repair and restoration services).

Contingency manager—The organization's designated person (and designated alternates) vested with the appropriate authority and responsibility for the declaration of an "emergency" (including announcements of "warnings," "alerts," and the raising of alarms), and to initiate the plan to prevent a "crisis" or "disaster" from occurring. The contingency manager is responsible for the management of all activities during the "emergency" period.

Cost of casualties—The monetary amount or dollar value assigned to the value of human lives lost, plus the value of human injuries incurred, as the result of an out-of-course event. In planning, the cost of casualties is weighed against the costs for reducing the risks that the casualties will occur. (*See* Value of a human life *and* Value of a human injury.)

Countervailence—The steps taken to compensate for the *residual* bad or harmful or nasty affects *after* you have prevented the occurrence of consequences through risk reduction. These are sometimes referred to as "contingency plans" and include diverse readiness items such as electric generators, emergency lighting for evacuation path navigation, alternate sites, bottled water, and cellular telephones.

Credible fault—The behavior of a specific piece of equipment wherein any single, specified fault can be "tolerated" if the consequence of that fault falls within predefined limits. To deal with credible faults—and those which are not "credible"—the potential consequences and affects of each possible single point fault must be identified. (*See* Fault *and* Failure.)

Crisis—*See* Emergency.

Crisis management center—*See* Contingency management center. (The term "contingency" is preferred to "crisis" in that a disaster planning and recovery strategy is created to *avoid* a "crisis" from occurring through the establishment of contingency plans, and a center from where the implementation of such plans are managed.)

Crisis management team—*See* Contingency management team. (As explained above, the term "contingency" is preferred.)

Crisis manager—*See* Contingency manager. ("Contingency" is the term of preference.)

Critical needs—The essential requirements, in terms of people, place, information, data and equipment required by a BPC to function during an interruption in as-intended functioning.

D

Data-related events—*See* Information-related and data-related events.

Demarcation point (D-mark)—The point at which a public utility's service lines (electricity, gas, telecommunications, steam, water, or waste water) connect with those of the facility, and whereat the utility's responsibility terminates (or, in the case of waste water, begins) and the facility's responsibility commences. (This D-mark should not be mistaken for the "D-mark" that is the Deutsche Mark, Germany's unit of currency!)

Disaster—A *disaster occurs* or *it is a disaster* when the organization is unable to recommence its as-intended functioning after the lapse of a predetermined, tolerable, time span following the consequences and affects of the impact of an out-of-course event. As a result, the cash flow of the organization, and its profitability, or the delivery of its services, are undoubtedly in some way affected. Put another way, it is a *disaster* when the organization is unable to function because one or more of its BPCs cannot function. (Some writers[2] consider a disaster as "A sudden, unplanned calamitous event that causes great damage or loss. Any event that creates an inability on the company's part to provide critical business functions for some predetermined period of time.")

Disaster avoidance—A term sometimes used in the literature to describe (1) the activities undertaken to prevent or avoid a "disaster," or (2) the activities undertaken to control the affects of an out-of-course event, its impact, and the consequences. In this guide, the concept of "risk management"—and its elements—is used: reduce the level of risk (if possible) that an out-of-course event will occur; reduce the level of risk (where possible) that the out-of-course event will impact the as-intended functioning of the organization; and reduce the level of risk (where practicable) that consequences and affects of the impact will ensue.

Disaster avoidance audit—A variously used (perhaps, misused) phrase used to describe the process of searching for conditions presenting unnecessarily high levels of risk. Like "Disaster avoidance," the term is usually associated with data centers on the presumption that the needs of data centers are distinct from those of the rest of the organization, and are understood only by MIS staffs. There is—often—also an implication that the data center (or computing resources) is the only function in the organization that is at-risk to out-of-course events. In this guide, the con-

---

[2] "Disaster Recovery Glossary," *Disaster Recovery Journal,* January/February/March 1993, 66+.

cept of vulnerability search is used; the vulnerability search is applicable to the entire organization.

Disaster prevention—Reducing the likelihood—the level of risks present—of events, impacts, or their consequences and affects, that could cause a "disaster." Disasters cannot be "prevented"—the level of risk that they occur can be reduced to an acceptable level, or to a level that is minimized. *Disaster prevention* can also be defined as planning steps taken, individually or in concert, to prevent an out-of-course event escalating *into* a disaster.

Disaster recovery programs—A term sometimes used to describe the prestructured procedures and arrangements (1) to enable a continuity of activities *during* the period in which "consequences and affects" are operative, (2) to mitigate the impact, consequences and affects of the out-of-course event, and/or (3) to restore as-intended functioning, including the restoration and repair of the place, its infrastructure, equipment, and facilities.

Disaster recovery planning—A concept, or approach, considered by some writers[3] as "The advance planning and preparations which are necessary to minimize loss and ensure continuity of critical business functions of an organization in the event of a disaster." Conspicuously absent, here, is the necessity to reduce the *level of risk of the disaster occurring*. The "disaster recovery planning" approach can be equated to "locking the barn after the horse runs away."

E

Emergency—The period following the consequences and affects of the impact of an out-of-course event. The *emergency* might develop into a *disaster* if proper *contingency* and *countervailance* plans are wanting, or it may escalate into a *crisis* if the organization has failed to provide for contingencies.

EMF—Electromagnetic field (sometimes referred to as "force"). A technology-based potential problem. EMFs emanate from the sun, and from all devices using electricity, but EMFs emitted by power lines, building wiring, grounding systems, electric motors, VDTs (video display terminals), CRTs (cathode ray tubes), fluorescent lighting fixtures, and radio-transmitting devices—including "walkie-talkies," two-way radios, cellular telephones, wireless networks, radio- and television broadcasting

[3] "Disaster Recovery Glossary," *Disaster Recovery Journal*, January/February/March 1993, 66+.

transmitters, microwave and cellular telephone relays, and radar transmitters—present the highest levels of risk to both people and magnetic-based data processing devices and storage media.

Equipment—All those things in the place that operate to make or help it tick. An inclusive term, "equipment" is used to refer to the "more serious" machinery and devices (that are usually capitalized in the assets-accounting process) in contrast to "supplies" which are expendable. In disaster planning, the important characteristic of "equipment" is that it is usually expensive to replace or repair, or can entail a very time-consuming process to either repair or replace. Often, a piece of equipment that may be damaged beyond repair, or destroyed, cannot be replaced. In considering insurance coverage for "equipment," *replacement* costs (in today's marketplace, not last year's!) should be the basis, not depreciated original cost.

Evacuate (v.); evacuation (n.)—*Evacuate* means leaving the place for other-than-normal reasons, or under other-than-normal circumstances. The evacuation of the place—usually the building or part of it, but often the entire site—can take place either in response to the raising of an alarm or public address announcement, or because people sense that an other-than-normal circumstance prevails or is about to occur, and perceive they should remove themselves from harm's way.

Event—*See* Out-of-course event.

F

Facility search—A term used in some literature to describe what *should be* (and in this guide, *is*) conceptualized and conducted as a comprehensive vulnerability search, vulnerability analysis, and vulnerability rectification process. The "facility search," typically and shortsightedly, includes only a limited number of the potential "exposures." Rarely, if ever, does the "facility search" provide for either a broad-based probe into the place, people, or processes, or for *everything and anything* for which there is a risk of being the root cause of an out-of-course event. The "facility search" usually fails to, additionally, examine, in detail or at all, what might be the impact, consequences and affects of out-of-course events. The vulnerability analysis that follows the vulnerability search (1) measures that particular levels of risk present; (2) determines whether or not those particular levels of risk warrant efforts to reduce those levels—thus be levels that are ALARP, or "acceptable;" (3) identifies the processes for such risk reduction; and (4) determines whether or not to establish countervailance measures.

Facility professional—A person concerned with the planning, design, creation, operation, or management of the place, and—often—some of the processes therein. (*See* Chapter 1—The Facility Professional—for a detailed description.)

Failure—When some unit of infrastructure, equipment, or furnishing *at or of the place*, or one or more people, *stops functioning* or working or performing in its as-intended manner. As examples, when the air-conditioning system stops, or when the elevators will not run, or when the telephone switchboard ceases to switch calls, or when an insufficiently attentive or inadequately trained person causes a process "to crash." (*See* Catastrophic failure.)

Failure probability—The level of risk that a unit of infrastructure, equipment, or furnishing, or people will *totally or completely* stop functioning or working or performing.

Fault—When some unit of infrastructure, equipment, or furnishing *at or of the place*, or one or more people, does not function or work or perform in its as-intended manner. As examples, when the air-conditioning system only provides a little cool air, or when the automatic elevators will only operate on a manual basis, or when the switchboard only processes in-coming calls, or when an individual—for whatever the reason—does not accomplish what should be accomplished under the circumstances. (*See* Credible fault *and* Failure.)

Fault probability—The level of risk that a unit of infrastructure, equipment, or furnishing, or one or more people, will cease to function in its as-intended manner. In considering faults, levels of risk for the *degree* or *amount* of nonfunctioning must be taken into account. As an example, the levels of risk that the air-conditioning system will not be able to lower the temperature below 65° F (necessitating shutdown of computer operations) or below 80° F (warranting closing the facility) must be considered. Or, because of inadequate training, the productivity of some people may limit the output of a process.

Furnishings—Like "equipment," furnishings are inherent in enabling the place to operate. "Furnishings" is often used as the descriptor of rugs, drapes, desks, tables, cabinets, and the like. Often capitalized, they can be easier to replace than equipment, and if destroyed or badly damaged, "temporary substitutes" can be utilized until those of the desired design or configuration can be obtained. In disaster planning, an important consideration is the flammability of the furnishings, and whether (when new or afire) noxious gases will emanate.

G

Guide (n.)—A person who leads; one who shows others the best path (usually in an evacuation), or the means to reach a goal by providing advice and counsel.

Guide (v.)—To lead the way or to show the way (usually during and evacuation); to conduct, to instruct, by giving directions; guide implies intimate knowledge of the way, and all of its difficulties or dangers.

H

Harm—Injury to people and/or damage to property. In this guide, "harm to people" is described as *casualties* (death or injury) in reference to people, with *harm* or *damage* used in reference to the place. (Processes are *impeded* or *impaired* or *interrupted* or *halted*.)

Hazard—A potential source of harm. In this guide, use of the term *impact* or *consequence*—depending on the circumstance—is preferred.

"Hot site"—An alternate site that has the equipment and resources (including data processing and communications equipment, necessary software and programs, data, information, files and records, supplies, provision for transport, catering and lodging) necessary to provide continuity in operations of specific BPCs.

Human-intervention events—Theft, arson, malicious mischief, rascality, work stoppages or delays, shortages of staff, inattentiveness, lapse of concentration, workplace violence, and other acts *of* the organization's people, or *of* persons outside the organization. Human-intervention events also include sickness and illness, as it may impact either or both groups.

HVAC—Heating, ventilation, and air-conditioning—and its source of supply and delivery—in the place. Proper heating, ventilation, or air-conditioning is often inherent in computer, telecommunications, and other electronic devices inherent in BPCs. ("HVAC" can also be taken to represent high-voltage alternating current, a potential source of EMFs.)

I

Impact—The description—as a noun, rather than as a verb—of the effect of an out-of-course event. The impact of an information-based out-of-course event can be the lack of availability, accessibility, or usability of required information or data: The information or data was—simply put—not saved. A nature-based out-of-course event can deposit 2 feet of snow, with the impact that no one can get to the place. A technology-based out-of-course event, such as a fire in the telephone central office, can cause an impact of no telephone exchange service. An impact may—or may not—result in *consequence* (q.v.).

Impact analysis (IA)—The determination, measurement, and assessment of the manner in which an *affect* of a particular *consequence* of a specific *impact* of an out-of-course event will influence the ability of one or more BPCs to function in their as-intended fashion. (The CA considers the What if . . .? scenarios where in the "ifs" represents each of the potential impacts of an out-of-course event.) An impact may or may not result in any consequences. A particular consequence (if there is any consequence) may have no affect on the as-intended functioning of *any* BPC, or it may totally halt the as-intended functioning of some, or its impede, impair, or interrupt *some of* the functioning in *some* way, or there may be affects on *all* BPCs. The determination, measurement, and assessment must be made on a time-line basis. A consequence, as an example, may have little affect on a BPC when it occurs, but the affect can change as time progresses, or the affect can occur at a specific time.

The IA (like a properly structured CA) is a vital element in disaster planning and recovery strategies, and is far from an exacting art or science. It provides a foundation upon which countervailence or contingency and recovery plans are formulated. The IA *should* consider all potential impacts that an out-of-course event may have, all the potential consequences of the impacts, and all the possible affects of the consequences.

The Impact analysis process is considered, in some literature, as a part the business impact analysis (BIA). In this guide, consideration of the *out-of-course events*, their *impacts*, and the *consequences and affects* of the impacts are separately examined.

Infrastructure—Generally, the "permanent" installations in a place—such as piping, HVAC ductwork, elevators, escalators, boilers, and compressors—all of which are at risk of fault or failure.

Infrastructure-related events—Burst or leaking or blocked mains or pipes; HVAC undersupply or failure; sprinkler system failure, leakage or accidental discharge; road and pathway collapses or blockages or subsidence; building collapses and troubles concerning structural integrity, and the like.

Information-related and data-related events—Deficiencies in information (eye-readable files and records) or data (usually magnetic-media—disks and tapes—files and records) required for current or future functioning of the organization. Information-related and data-related events stem from failure to create or save files or records; failure to record information or data; unauthorized access; accidental loss or destruction; inability to locate, access, retrieve, image or understand the information or data; and errors or omissions in the files or records. The inability to locate, access, retrieve, or image data can be the result of the nonavailability of essential hardware, software, and programming codes. Information-related and data-related events can also stem from possessing files and records for which there was no legal or sound business reason, or archival value, for retaining.

M

Management of risk—*See* Risk management.
Mandates—The required actions, practices, or provisions—prescriptives—that exist as the result of the actions of a federal, state, or local governmental body, bureau, or agency, an executive order, or an official decree. Failure to comply with a mandate can result in civil or criminal penalties, or other types of censure. (*See* Prescriptives.)
Modeling—*See* Computer modeling and simulation.

N

Nature-based events—Events of nature or acts of God, such as lightning strikes or electrical interference, storms, earthquakes or earth movements.

O

Operations management center—*See* Contingency management center.
Out-of-course event—Any event that is not part of the normal circumstances under which the organization functions, or does not usually occur when the organization is functioning. Out-of-course events may be rooted in business processes; civil and governmental actions; in design; in the engineering and construction materials and techniques used; the availability, accessibility, and usability of the organization's information and data; the infrastructure; maintenance procedures and techniques; nature; technology; transport; or can be the result of human intervention, or be rooted in the actions or inaction's of people. (These categories are further explained in Chapter 1.) A potential out-of-course event for which the risk of occurrence is deemed sufficiently high so as to be a concern in formulating the organization's disaster planning and recovery

strategy is considered a potential problem. An out-of-course event may—or may not—have an *impact* (q.v.).

P

PBX—Private branch (telephone) exchange or in-facility company switchboard. "PBX" is also applied to other communications "switches" or "routes" such as Centrex, automatic dial, and cord-less equipment.

People—All the individuals who are present, or who may be present, at the place at any moment in time. "People" include the organization's staff, visitors, delivery people, outside service personnel, the place's staff if it is a tenanted space, and any transients. The disaster planning and recovery strategy must provide for *all* who may be, or who can be, present at the place.

Place—The site and building which accommodates part or all of the organization, and where some or all of the processes are conducted by the people. The disaster planning and recovery strategy must consider the *entire* place, not only the building, or the parts of the building used by the organization.

Planners—The facility professionals—including architects, designers, engineers (embracing the architectural, civil, construction, mechanical, structural, and electrical engineering disciplines)—who usually (but not exclusively) provide their services to an organization, but are (usually) not employees of the organization. Some large organizations have one or more of these planners on their staffs.

POT—A plain, ordinary telephone, devoid of "features" and one that *is not* connected through the PBX, and ideally served by a different telephone company exchange *and* central office. The POT is a valuable communications tool when service to the PBX, or the PBX itself, fails.

Prescriptives—The sum total of laws, rules, regulations, codes, standards, and accepted practices that apply to and govern the design, building, operation, and management of the place; the organization's relationships with its people, and the conduct of its processes. Prescriptives resulting from government actions can be designated as "mandates." (*See* Mandates.)

Processes—Simply, the activities of the organization—both those generic to the organization, and those which support them—and the systems, methods, and procedures used to accomplish these activities. "Activities" might include sales, manufacturing, distribution, accounting, payroll, human resources, premises security, and food services. Each of the processes is comprised of one or more business process cells.

Problems—"Potential problems" are those out-of-course events for which the risk of occurrence (even after the level of risk has been reduced to a level ALARP or an "acceptable" level) is deemed sufficiently high so as to be a concern in formulating a disaster planning and recovery strategy. The "potential problem" becomes a "problem" when it occurs. The problem may or may not escalate—depending upon your disaster planning and recovery strategy and the effectiveness of it—into a disaster.

Prudent person's rule—A legal concept (sometimes outdatedly referred to as the prudent man's rule) holding that grounds for liability exist if expert judgment could foresee the possibility of people and their interests being injured as being more than theoretical. The "prudent person," as an intelligent, circumspect, careful and conscientious expert, must take measures he or she considers sufficient, and which are reasonable according to the circumstances, and to the current state of technology, to prevent persons and property from being harmed. Put another way, where expert judgment could have determined the level of risk of an event occurring or could have foreseen the possibility of loss, but did not, or did not take countervailance actions in view of that level or possibility, there are grounds for legal liability.

Q

Quantified Risk Assessment (QRA)—A determination of level-of-risk based on statistical history and experience ("hard data") in contrast to levels based on impressions, or broad-based groups of "level" (e.g., high, medium, or low). QRA is the "measurement" in "impressions about the quantifiable are no substitute for measurement."

R

Reasonably Practicable—A planning goal or objective based on both accomplishments and benefits, and the costs inherent in achieving the accomplishments and benefits. In this guide, "reasonably practicable" relates to the *level of risk*. In the management of risk, determination of "reasonably practicable" takes into account the nature of possible out-of-course events, their impacts, and the consequences and affects, *and* the costs of any remedial work that reduces the levels of risks of the events, the impacts, and the consequences and affects on people, place, and processes. What is "reasonably practicable" is, in part, determined by the ratio of costs to benefits (benefits being reduced levels of risks), and the incremental costs for additional benefit. (*See* ALARP.)

Recovery—All the planned activities and actions (including—as examples—the when-necessary evacuation, firefighting, power generator activation, retrieval of off-site records, water removal, etc.) that take place after the impact of an out-of-course event and its consequences, and that enable the re-establishment of as-intended functioning. "Recovery" includes the activities required to enable a BPC to continue functioning or to regain the ability to function, and to again function in its as-intended manner.

There are two aspects of the recovery strategy: planning concerned with enabling the business processes to continue or to be re-established—within the planned time-line basis—after being impaired, impeded, interrupted, or halted by an impact; and, planning concerned with impact mitigation, damage restoration, and the return to as-intended functioning. ("Recovery" can be equated to "keep going" or "get going again.")

Rectification—The process of correcting an anomaly—or reducing it to a level as low as reasonably practicable (ALARP), or to an acceptable level. (*See* Vulnerability rectification.)

Restoration—The reconstruction, repair, or replacement of the place—the site, its buildings, infrastructure, equipment, furnishings, and equipment. ("Restoration" can be equated to "repair" or "fixing.")

Risk—The relative likelihood that an event will occur; a statement of the relative probability of occurrence. "Risk" is usually associated (incorrectly!) with "bad" or "undesired" events. "Risk" is also defined as the probable rate of occurrence of a hazard causing harm and the severity of that harm.

Risk analysis—The process of determining—measuring wherever possible—the *relative* risk present . . . the chances that something specific will occur. The *risk* considered can be of an *event*, of the *impact* of that event, or of the *consequences and affects* of the impact. It is important to recognize that "risk analysis" (as used in this guide) *does not* identify the "risks" that are present, and that the process of "risk analysis" (1) *does not* identify and/or assess the critical functions necessary for an organization to continue to operate; (2) *does not* define means to reduce "risk"; and (3) *does not* determine or evaluate the costs associated with these. "Risk analysis" is also sometimes described in disaster planning literature as the investigation of available information to identify hazards present and to estimate their probable rate of occurrence.

Risk assessment—The analysis and evaluation of identified risks.

Risk management—The process of (1) determining which of the potential out-of-course events can occur; (2) identifying what impacts of such events on people, place, and processes could result; (3) establishing what the ensuing consequences and affects would be; (4) measuring the level of the risks associated with each of these events, impacts, and consequences and affects; (5) reducing those levels of risk ALARP or to an "acceptable" level; and (6) providing the necessary countervailence measures for the residual impacts, consequences and affects.

Put another way, risk management (also termed management of risk) is the efforts to control what ever might erode an organization's bottom line, or whatever might straddle the organization with unacceptable costs. Management of risk is the most vital aspect in the creation of a disaster planning and recovery strategy.

Risk reduction—The processes of reducing the level of risk that any particular out-of-course event, or impact, or consequences and affects will occur. Although desirable, risk cannot be reduced to zero; the level of risk of *any* event is always greater than zero. In creating a disaster planning and recovery strategy, the risk reduction goals and objects are to achieve levels as low as reasonably practicable (ALARP), or at "acceptable" levels.

Root cause—The initial, or basic, source or basis of an event. An interruption in the supply of electricity to your place (a technology-based event) may result in interruption of processes, but the *root cause* of that interruption may be a drought (insufficient water for a hydroelectric plant), generating equipment failure, power-line fault, poor quality control by the manufacturer of the generator or the switch gear or the transformers, or some other, like event beyond the scope of your planning strategy. A *fire* (the *apparent cause*) may interrupt one or more of your processes, but its *root cause*—spontaneous combustion—can be with in the realm of your control through proper maintenance and housekeeping disciplines. In planning, you should *first* focus your attention on the *apparent cause*.

S

Safety—The condition of reduced risk of death or injury *in* the workplace—very often a manufacturing or other industrial environment—or *from* workplace activities. Safety—as the quality of being devoid of whatever exposes one to danger or harm or antisocial actions—extends to include all people working on the site and in the buildings, as well as to any others who may be visiting the venue. The latter-described "safety" characterizes the "disaster planning" in venues such as sports arenas, meeting places, hotels, and convention centers. "Safety" ranges from the avoidance of slippery floors and pathways, protection from movable parts of machinery and equipment (as may be prescribed by an insurance carrier or mandated by OSHA), to the placement of video surveillance cameras or "help" telephones in a parking area. Safety can also be described as lack of unacceptable of risk of harm. Most frequently, the risk reduction achieved in "safety" *is not* a level of risk ALARP, but only the reflection of applicable prescriptives. "Safety" deals only with the risks of casualties (deaths or injuries to *people*); not with the risks of harm or damage to the place or the processes of an organization.

Safety Case—A concept of risk management based on the creation of *an environment* wherein the risks—even if the calculated probabilities of occurrence are extremely low—of any out-of-course event, its impact and consequences (or combination of out-of-course events, impacts and consequences) to people, place, or processes are *further reduced* to an acceptable level. (In the "safety case" concept, *the organization*—be it an office building or complex, an industrial park, sports venue, hotel, airport, or railway—itself establishes the risk level for each of the various risks inherent in its operations, and submits these levels to a governmental or other regulatory body for the approvals necessary to operate or conduct that organization. This concept is opposite to that wherein the organization is subject to statutory prescriptives or "recommended practices." The safety case approach was conceived as a means through which significantly lower levels of risk could be achieved by recognizing the uniqueness of specific situations, while reducing the involvement of government in the risk management process. In that the "safety" in "safety case" does not relate solely to the condition of reduced risk of death or injury in the workplace, "safetycase" or "safety-case" might have been a better-chosen nomenclature!) (*See* Chapter 2.)

Safety-of-life concerns—Those out-of-course events, their impacts, or their ensuing consequences which—when occurring—can result in loss of life or injuries.

Seats—A term used in alternate site planning to describe the number of staff that can be accommodated at one time at a "hot site," "warm site," or "cold site."

Security—"Security" encompasses the physical means, and the systems and procedures related to them, employed to reduce the levels of risk associated with certain human-intervention out-of-course events, and to reduce the risk of impact from fire (whatever its root-cause out-of-course event may be). "Security" includes access and intrusion control; detection of bombs explosives, guns, and metal devices; theft prevention and detection; and the alarm and event-recording systems associated with these.

Significant executive—An individual in the organization who can, because of his or her position in the organizational hierarchy, determine or nominate which BPCs are important, and which are not, on a time-line basis, when as-intended functioning has been interrupted, impaired, impeded, or halted. The opinions of the SE can be as vital in formulating countervailence provisions of the disaster planning and recovery strategy as the IA.

Simulation—*See* Computer modeling and simulation.

Signage—Displays intended to clearly convey information of importance or peril—using words, pictures, symbols and Brailled characters—to the beholder. In disaster planning, aural (voice announcements, tones and bells) and visual (flashing lights and photoluminescents) systems, and tactile surfaces are used to supplement signage.

Stakeholders—The people and organizations—individually or collectively—who have some interest that the organization be successful. "Stakeholders" include the board of directors; all employees, including executives, management, and staff; investors; customers, suppliers, service providers, and contractors, and their staffs; members of the community; and other groups that have some link with the organization, such as landlords or tenants, banks and bankers, insurance companies, and utilities. "Stakeholders" gain some advantage when the organization functions and flourishes, and will suffer in some way if the organization cannot or does not function as intended.

T

Technology-related events—Events related to the use or employment of technology, or its products or services, in any form: failure or shortages in the supply of electrical or steam power; failure or shortages of communication systems or paths; computer failures or crashes; software failures or viruses; interception of radio-based transmissions.

Threat—A term used in some literature to conceptualize "out-of-course event." In this guide, "out-of-course event" is preferred since the level of risk of some "threats" may be low enough ("acceptably low") to rule out the necessity for consideration.

U

Uninterruptable power supply (UPS)—A device, often battery-powered, but sometimes a combination of battery power and alternate generation, or an alternate mains system, or other similar configurations, that assures a continuity in the provision of electricity in the required quantity and quality for a predetermined time span. (Surge protectors, power conditioners, and like devices *alone* do not a UPS make.)

V

Value of a human injury—A monetary value ascribed to an injury to "*one people*" so that the benefits of reducing the level of risk that an injury will occur can be compared with the investment necessary to prevent that injury. Because of the vast range of possible injuries—and their permanent effects—it is difficult to determine the value of an injury.[4] In planning, the values of a human injury and of a human life are often combined into a "value of a casualty" in determining cost:benefit ratios.

Value of a human life—The monetary amount ascribed to a human life ("*one people*") so that the benefits of reducing the risk that the life will be lost can be compared with investment costs necessary to prevent that life from being lost. This widely ranging value is often applied or recommended by a governmental agency: Britain's Department of Transport values a highway fatality averted at £665,000 (approximately $1.06 million). In practice, £100 million to £120 million was invested by British Rail in 1991–1992 per fatality averted. The U.S. Federal Railroad Administration limits safety spending to $2.6 million per fatality averted. In Canada, C$1.5 million (approximately $1.1 million) is the investment level for aviation and highway projects.[5, 6, 7] In planning, the values of a human injury and of a human life are often combined into a "value of a casualty" in determining cost:benefit ratios. In a sampling of U.S. Government regulations,[8] the "estimates of the minimum value of a life . . . [taking] into

---

[4] A major law firm, weighing the potential benefits of an $80,000 vulnerability search, analysis, and rectification, recognized that the price-tag was lower than the cost for one sprained ankle the VS/VA/VR could surely prevent.

[5] Ian Savage, "The Price of Saving Lives," *Developing Railways 1993*, 1993, 23–24.

[6] The "value of life" has been considerably inflated in recent years as a result of pioneering work conducted by Professor Michael Jones-Lee and his colleagues at the University of Newcastle-upon-Tyne. Jones-Lee used "stated preference" techniques to ascertain what people would be willing to pay in order to reduce the probability of their own death. This should be considered when assigning a "value of life" in cost-benefit analysis.

[7] "Spate of Accidents Triggers Over-Reaction," *Railway Gazette International*, April 1996, 177.

[8] Peter Passel, "How Much for a Life? Try $3 Million to $5 Million," *New York Times*, 29 January 1995, sec. 3, 3. Source cited is the Harvard Center for Risk Analysis.

account the medical and hospital costs avoided because the lives were saved, but they ignore other benefits like prevention of property damage and injuries that do not result in death," range from $400,000 (safety standards for X-ray equipment) to $1.2 billion (for asbestos banned in automatic transmission parts).

(Under the Americans With Disabilities Act, the Washington (D.C.) Metropolitan Area Transportation Authority was ordered to install brightly colored strips with tactile bumps at 45 of its 83 stations, to help the blind and partially sighted locate platform edges. The cost would have been $30 million. In the 19 years of WMATA's operations, only two blind people have been killed falling off platform edges, and six others injured. *If* the tactile platform edges would surely have prevented the deaths, it would represent a value of human life of $15 million. However, research by the Battelle Institute showed that the mandated edging did not reduce the risk of off-platform falls any lower than the WMATA's standard edges![9])

Vulnerability—A condition or situation in the place, or of the people, or related to the processes that creates a target for an anomaly—be it an out-of-course event, the impact from the event, or the consequences and affects that ensue as a result of that impact.

Vulnerability analysis (VA)—A systematic undertaking—most vital in the creation and maintenance of a disaster planning and recovery strategy— that examines each vulnerability found to determine (1) its relation to as-intended functioning, and (2) the most advantageous manner in which the correct the anomaly. (*See* Chapter 7.)

Vulnerability rectification (VR)—The process of correcting or removing the anomaly, or providing countervailence for it, or reducing the level of risk that it will affect people, place, or processes to a level ALARP or to an acceptable level. (*See* Chapter 7.)

Vulnerability search (VS)—A systematic undertaking—most vital in the creation and maintenance of a disaster planning and recovery strategy— that reveals conditions and situations present in the place that may be at greater-than-acceptable levels of risk (or at levels of risk *not* ALARP) to out-of-course events, their impacts, or to the consequences and affects of the impacts. (*See* Chapter 7, and the vulnerability search checklist, Appendix II.)

[9] "Cost of the edge," *Railway Gazette International,* June 1995, 333.

W

"Warm site"—An alternate site with more than the "bare walls" of a "cold site", but lacking all the provisions in a "hot site". A "warm site"—because of that lack—cannot immediately assume the functioning of a BPC.

Wayfinding—The ability to navigate one's way—especially during an evacuation—through unfavorable conditions such as smoke, fire, limited ambient lighting, or crowd conditions, to a predetermined assemblage area. Wayfinding fitments or aids include navigation path signage and lighting (including emergency lighting, luminous strips, light strips, flashing beacons, flashlights and light sticks), and sound-emitting devices used to augment or reinforce the signage.

Workplace violence—Any antisocial—or socially unacceptable—action involving two or more employees, or a former employee(s) or outsider(s) and staff member(s). Workplace violence encompasses sexual harassment (although actual "violence" might not occur), fights, shootings, and other types of aggression occurring between people, or at the place.

Worst-case scenario—A consideration in planning that when *something* goes wrong (an out-of-course event occurring, an impact resulting, or consequences and affects ensuing) it *can* or *will* take place in the extreme degree. As an example, if there is a relatively high risk that the place can encounter winds as high as 100 mph, disaster planning would provide countervailence for winds *at least* that velocity. Or, if the river adjacent to the site has risen—at flood—in a range from 6 inches to 12 feet, "worst-case scenario" planning would reflect the 12-foot rise, even though the level of risk of flood height declines with the amount of rise.

INDEX